Combating Security Breaches and Criminal Activity in the Digital Sphere

S. Geetha
VIT University, Chennai, India

Asnath Victy Phamila
VIT University, Chennai, India

A volume in the Advances in Digital Crime,
Forensics, and Cyber Terrorism (ADCFCT) Book
Series

Published in the United States of America by
Information Science Reference (an imprint of IGI Global)
701 E. Chocolate Avenue
Hershey PA, USA 17033
Tel: 717-533-8845
Fax: 717-533-8661
E-mail: cust@igi-global.com
Web site: http://www.igi-global.com

Library of Congress Cataloging-in-Publication Data
Names: Geetha, S., 1979- editor. | Phamila, Asnath Victy, 1978- editor.
Title: Combating security breaches and criminal activity in the digital
  sphere / S. Geetha and Asnath Victy Phamila, editors.
Description: Hershey, PA : Information Science Reference, [2016] | Includes
  bibliographical references and index.
Identifiers: LCCN 2016003151| ISBN 9781522501930 (hardcover) | ISBN
  9781522501947 (ebook)
Subjects: LCSH: Computer crimes--Prevention. | Computer security.
Classification: LCC HV6773 .C6495 2016 | DDC 363.25/968--dc23 LC record available at http://lccn.loc.gov/2016003151

This book is published in the IGI Global book series Advances in Digital Crime, Forensics, and Cyber Terrorism (ADCF-CT) (ISSN: 2327-0381; eISSN: 2327-0373)

British Cataloguing in Publication Data
A Cataloguing in Publication record for this book is available from the British Library.

For electronic access to this publication, please contact: eresources@igi-global.com.

Advances in Digital Crime, Forensics, and Cyber Terrorism (ADCFCT) Book Series

Bryan Christiansen
PryMarke, LLC, USA

ISSN: 2327-0381
EISSN: 2327-0373

MISSION

The digital revolution has allowed for greater global connectivity and has improved the way we share and present information. With this new ease of communication and access also come many new challenges and threats as cyber crime and digital perpetrators are constantly developing new ways to attack systems and gain access to private information.

The **Advances in Digital Crime, Forensics, and Cyber Terrorism (ADCFCT) Book Series** seeks to publish the latest research in diverse fields pertaining to crime, warfare, terrorism and forensics in the digital sphere. By advancing research available in these fields, the **ADCFCT** aims to present researchers, academicians, and students with the most current available knowledge and assist security and law enforcement professionals with a better understanding of the current tools, applications, and methodologies being implemented and discussed in the field.

COVERAGE

- Watermarking
- Cyber Terrorism
- Telecommunications Fraud
- Digital Crime
- Hacking
- Global Threat Intelligence
- Data Protection
- Malicious codes
- Information Warfare
- Malware

IGI Global is currently accepting manuscripts for publication within this series. To submit a proposal for a volume in this series, please contact our Acquisition Editors at Acquisitions@igi-global.com or visit: http://www.igi-global.com/publish/.

Titles in this Series

For a list of additional titles in this series, please visit: www.igi-global.com

National Security and Counterintelligence in the Era of Cyber Espionage
Eugenie de Silva (University of Leicester, UK & Virginia Research Institute, USA)
Information Science Reference • copyright 2016 • 308pp • H/C (ISBN: 9781466696617) • US $200.00 (our price)

Handbook of Research on Civil Society and National Security in the Era of Cyber Warfare
Metodi Hadji-Janev (Military Academy "General Mihailo Apostolski", Macedonia) and Mitko Bogdanoski (Military Academy "General Mihailo Apostolski", Macedonia)
Information Science Reference • copyright 2016 • 548pp • H/C (ISBN: 9781466687936) • US $335.00 (our price)

Cybersecurity Policies and Strategies for Cyberwarfare Prevention
Jean-Loup Richet (University of Nantes, France)
Information Science Reference • copyright 2015 • 472pp • H/C (ISBN: 9781466684560) • US $245.00 (our price)

New Threats and Countermeasures in Digital Crime and Cyber Terrorism
Maurice Dawson (University of Missouri–St. Louis, USA) and Marwan Omar (Nawroz University, Iraq)
Information Science Reference • copyright 2015 • 368pp • H/C (ISBN: 9781466683457) • US $200.00 (our price)

Handbook of Research on Digital Crime, Cyberspace Security, and Information Assurance
Maria Manuela Cruz-Cunha (Polytechnic Institute of Cavado and Ave, Portugal) and Irene Maria Portela (Polytechnic Institute of Cávado and Ave, Portugal)
Information Science Reference • copyright 2015 • 602pp • H/C (ISBN: 9781466663244) • US $385.00 (our price)

The Psychology of Cyber Crime Concepts and Principles
Gráinne Kirwan (Dun Laoghaire Institute of Art, Design and Technology, Ireland) and Andrew Power (Dun Laoghaire Institute of Art, Design and Technology, Ireland)
Information Science Reference • copyright 2012 • 372pp • H/C (ISBN: 9781613503508) • US $195.00 (our price)

Cyber Crime and the Victimization of Women Laws, Rights and Regulations
Debarati Halder (Centre for Cyber Victim Counselling (CCVC), India) and K. Jaishankar (Manonmaniam Sundaranar University, India)
Information Science Reference • copyright 2012 • 264pp • H/C (ISBN: 9781609608309) • US $195.00 (our price)

Digital Forensics for the Health Sciences Applications in Practice and Research
Andriani Daskalaki (Max Planck Institute for Molecular Genetics, Germany)
Medical Information Science Reference • copyright 2011 • 418pp • H/C (ISBN: 9781609604837) • US $245.00 (our price)

www.igi-global.com

701 E. Chocolate Ave., Hershey, PA 17033
Order online at www.igi-global.com or call 717-533-8845 x100
To place a standing order for titles released in this series, contact: cust@igi-global.com
Mon-Fri 8:00 am - 5:00 pm (est) or fax 24 hours a day 717-533-8661

Table of Contents

Section 3
Cyber Forensics and Investigation

Section 4
Visual Information Security

Detailed Table of Contents

Section 1
Digital Sphere Threats and Vulnerabilities

Chapter 1

Digital Sphere is a global network which consists of all the resources that are required for the users, who connected with the digital network. It connects the entire world through the digital technologies. The digital network includes services, applications, and web page files. By connecting, to this network, people from one end in the world can able to communicate and share their knowledge across the world. Global communication and sharing may allow an unknown person which can disrupt the services. This chapter proposes a review on the threats and vulnerabilities related to the digital sphere network with value added security guidelines and countermeasures given to overcome such issues.

Chapter 2

In the recent decade, one of our major concerns in the global technological society of information security is confirmation that a person accessing confidential information is authorized to perform so. Such mode of access is generally accomplished by a person's confirming their identity by the use of some method of authentication system. In present days, the requirement for safe security in storing individual information has been developing rapidly and among the potential alternative is implementing innovative biometric identification techniques. This chapter discusses how the advent of the 20th century has brought forth the security principles of identification and authentication in the field of biometric analysis. The chapter reviews vulnerabilities in biometric authentication and issues in system implementation. The chapter also proposes the multifactor authentication and the use of multimodal biometrics, i.e., the combination of Electrocardiogram (ECG) and Phonocardiogram (PCG) signals to enhance reliability in the authentication process.

In the context of network security, a spoofing attack is a condition in which one person or a program successfully masquerades as another. This is done by providing counterfeit data with the malicious intention of gaining an illegitimate advantage. Spoofing attack which may be generated in various layer of Open Systems Interconnection model (OSI model) is discussed in this chapter. The chapter ends with discussing about the possible spoofing attacks in network layer and the relevant defense mechanism of the same. The detailed analysis and discussion is made on the spoofing attack over the Network layer because, Denial-of-Service (DoS) and Distributed Denial-of-Service (DDoS) attacks more devastating while using network protocol like Internet Protocol (IP) which have become more of a threat than ever for the past few years.

Cybercrimes are those crimes which are associated with the latest technology including internet. There are various forms of committing crimes using the internet. As a result newer forms of crimes have emerged in the society. Some of the newer crimes are traditional crimes which are committed through the internet such as defamation, fraud, harassment, trespass etc. It is necessary to understand what the laws in India suggest towards these kind of newer crimes happening in the society. This paper deals with the types of cybercrimes and also provides the offences and punishments under the Information Technology Act, 2000 in India.

Section 2
Techniques for Combating Security Breaches

Chapter 5

Changing trends in IT industry are opening new avenues. With the scalability, flexibility, and economic advantage offered by cloud computing, more and more organizations are moving towards cloud for their applications. With all the benefits of cloud computing, it poses a danger of digital crime and security breaches. These challenges are compounded by the fact that cybercrime and the transgressors transcend geographical boundaries while the law enforcement does not. This paper tries to focus on how cloud computing is rising to the challenges thrown in from cyber space and recent developments to avoid and mitigate cloud fraud and abuse. Taking counter measures at organizational level, will alleviate and up to an extent eliminate security breaches. With current knowledge on policy and standards adopted by developed nations, the policy makers and law enforcement agencies in developing countries can work towards formulating standards and guidelines for awareness on threats, vulnerabilities and effectiveness of security controls to respond to risk.

Chapter 6

Intrusion Detection Systems (IDS) play a major role in the area of combating security breaches for information security. Current IDS are developed with Machine learning techniques like Artificial Neural Networks, C 4.5, KNN, Naïve Bayes classifiers, Genetic algorithms Fuzzy logic and SVMs. The objective of this paper is to apply Artificial Neural Networks and Support Vector Machines for intrusion detection. Artificial Neural Networks are applied along with faster training methods like variable learning rate and scaled conjugate gradient. Support Vector Machines use various kernel functions to improve the performance. From the kddcup'99 dataset 45,657 instances are taken and used in our experiment. The speed is compared for various training functions. The performance of various kernel functions is assessed. The detection rate of Support Vector Machines is found to be greater than Artificial Neural Networks with less number of false positives and with less time of detection.

Chapter 7

Video surveillance cameras are placed in many places such as bank, hospital, toll gates, airports, etc. To take advantage of the video in real time, a human must monitor the system continuously in order to alert security officers if there is an emergency. Besides, for event detection a person can observe four cameras with good accuracy at a time. Therefore, this requires expensive human resources for real time video surveillance using current technology. The trajectory of one or more targets obtains for object tracking while recording above space and time. By tracking various objects, the burden of detection by human sentinels is greatly alleviated. Efficient and reliable automatic alarm system is useful for many ATM surveillance applications. ATM Video monitoring systems present many challenging research issues in human abnormal behaviors detection approaches. The framework of ATM video surveillance system encompassing various factors, such as image acquisition, background estimation, background subtraction, segmentation, people counting and tracking are briefly discussed in this chapter.

Chapter 8

Advanced Evidence is any data of probative quality that is either put away or transmitted in a double frame. In today's universe of propelling advances, more data is being produced, put away and appropriated by electronic means. This requires numerous offices to build the utilization of advanced proof social affair as a regular or standard instrument in their fight against violations. Computerized proof can be helpful in an extensive variety of criminal examinations. Numerous computerized gadgets productively track client action; it is likewise conceivable to recoup erased records, both of which may influence a criminal examination. Data is similar to the backbone for associations of all sizes, sorts and industry areas. It should be overseen and secured, and when there is a break or wrongdoing conferred including spilled or stolen data, the culprits must be recognized and indicted. Expanded Internet entrance has given exponential ascent in refined assaults on Information Technology framework. Keeping in mind the end goal to make our IT framework versatile against the dangers, there is a requirement for Cyber Security. Digital criminology, likewise called PC legal sciences or advanced legal sciences, is the procedure of extricating data and information from PCs to serve as computerized proof - for common purposes or, by and large, to demonstrate and lawfully indict cybercrime. PC crime scene investigation has as of late increased noteworthy Popularity with numerous nearby law authorization organizations. It is at present utilized in extortion, robbery, drug authorization and each other implementation action. Law implementation organizations confront another test in managing digital wrongdoings. Criminal acts are being perpetrated and the confirmation of these exercises is recorded in electronic structure. Also, wrongdoings are being dedicated in the internet. Proof in these violations is quite often recorded in computerized design. It is critical that PC security experts know about a percentage of the necessities of the lawful framework and comprehends the creating field of PC legal sciences.

Section 3
Cyber Forensics and Investigation

Chapter 9
Poonkodi Mariappan, SRM University, India
Padhmavathi B., SRM University, India
Talluri Srinivasa Teja, SRM University, India

Digital Forensic as it sounds coerce human mind primarily with exploration of crime. However in the contemporary world, digital forensic has evolved as an essential source of tools from data acquisition to legal action. Basically three stages are involved in digital forensic namely acquisition, analysis and reporting. Digital Forensic Research Workshop (DFRW) defined digital forensic as "Use of Scientifically derived and proven method towards the identification, collection, analysis, interpretation, documentation and presentation of digital evidence derived from digital sources for the purpose of facilitating or furthering the reconstruction of event to be criminal". The hard problem in digital forensic is such that the acquired data need to be cleaned and is required to be intelligible for reading by human. As a solution to this complexity problem a number of tools are present which may be repeated until relevant data is obtained.

Chapter 10
Hemalatha J., Thiagarajar College of Engineering, India
Kavitha Devi M. K., Thiagarajar College of Engineering India

In this chapter, a new data conceal technique is anticipated for digital images. The method computes the interpolation error of the image by using histogram shifting method and difference expansion. With the expectation of embedding high payload and less distortion, the undisclosed data has embedded in the interpolating error. Additionally for hiding the data, reversible data hiding technique is used. The histogram deviation is used as evidence for resulting the data conceal in the stereo images. To our best knowledge, by extracting the statistical feature from the image subsample works as steganalysis scheme. To enhance the revealing rate precision the well known support vector machine acts as classifier. In addition to that the experimental results show that the proposed steganalysis method has enhanced the detection exactness of the stego images.

Chapter 11

Geogen G., SRM University, India
Poovammal E., SRM University, India

Why should everyone know about mobile malware? With the introduction of Internet of Things (IoT) and Cloud, you can't survive in a disconnected world. Thus from your home appliances to your window curtains, everything is connected to Internet which can be accessed through your hand held mobile device. Unlike Personal Computers, these devices give Hackers a greater attack landscape. Back in 2004, when the first mobile malware was introduced, we never thought that it would get such a big threat space, as we see today. So, we discuss the History of Mobile malwares and its categories with its motives. We also discuss few signs that indicate the presence of a mobile malware. To conclude we categorize the battle against malware into two namely prevention and response, which is forensically analysed using Static/Dynamic Methods/Tools.

Chapter 12

P. Vetrivelan, VIT University, India
M. Jagannath, VIT University, India
T. S. Pradeep Kumar, VIT University, India

The Internet has transformed greatly the improved way of business, this vast network and its associated technologies have opened the doors to an increasing number of security threats which are dangerous to networks. The first part of this chapter presents a new dimension of denial of service attacks called TCP SYN Flood attack has been witnessed for severity of damage and second part on worms which is the major threat to the internet. The TCP SYN Flood attack by means of anomaly detection and traces back the real source of the attack using Modified Efficient Packet Marking algorithm (EPM). The mechanism for detecting the smart natured camouflaging worms which is sensed by means of a technique called Modified Controlled Packet Transmission (MCPT) technique. Finally the network which is affected by these types of worms are detected and recovered by means of Modified Centralized Worm Detector (MCWD) mechanism. The Network Intrusion Detection and Prevention Systems (NIDPS) on Flooding and Worm Attacks were analyzed and presented.

Section 4
Visual Information Security

Chapter 13

Gayathri RajaKumaran, VIT University, India
NeelaNarayanan Venkataraman, VIT University, India

In the Internet Era, millions of computer systems are connected to the Internet and the number is increasing infinitely. Maintaining proper Control and configuration for all such networked systems has proved to be impossible. This loophole makes the Internet systems vulnerable to various type of attacks. The objective of this research is to systematically identify a wide list of attacks in transport, session and application layers (Host layers). 148 effective controls are identified for the security attacks in addition to the 113 standard controls. The identified controls are analyzed in order to map and categorize them to the corresponding security layers wise.

This chapter deals with the understanding of techniques that are used to create damage to the expert in an investigative process. The name used for these techniques is called anti-forensics, whose mission is to conceal, remove, alter evidence, or make inaccessible a cybercrime. These techniques aim to make the work of the slower expert or difficult to reach a conclusion; however, this chapter will explore some techniques used as measures to subvert digital evidence through anti-forensic measures.

Images are becoming an inevitable part of knowledge in the modern day society. As data is growing at a rapid rate, costs involved in storing and maintaining data is also raising rapidly. The best alternate solution to reduce the storage cost is outsourcing all the data to the cloud. To ensure confidentiality and integrity of the data, a security technique has to be provided to the data even before it is stored on the cloud using cryptography. An attempt is made to explore the possibility of usage of visual cryptography for providing robust security to the secret image. Visual cryptography proves to be more efficient than other cryptography techniques because it is simple and does not require any key management technique.

Visual Sensor Network (VSN) is a network of distributed battery-powered low-cost cameras and CMOS image sensors, each with the capability of capturing, processing, sending, and receiving images. VSN applications include remote monitoring, Security, elderly assistance, Visual Ubiquity, home monitoring, tracking. The highly sensitive nature of images makes security and privacy in VSNs even more important than in most other sensor and data networks. However, the direct use of security techniques developed for scalar WSN will not be suitable for VSN due to its resource constraint. Hence light weight security mechanisms need to be explored. In this chapter the challenging security issues at various layers in VSN are addressed. It also fosters discussion on privacy protection techniques like subjective privacy, Video masking techniques and identifies recent trends in VSN security and privacy. A discussion of open research issues concludes this chapter.

Preface

OVERVIEW

Currently "Cyber Space" happens to be the principal component in the global information and communication infrastructure and hence combating the security breaches in this digital sphere has acquired a more pressing priority in corporations and governments across the globe. Rapidly growing technologies which promote ubiquitous storage and computing facilitate easy and quick access to the Internet leading to its deep integration in everyday life. Consequently the dependence over this digital domain for all our social, personal, economic and political interactions has expanded. The cyber space forms the crux for the critical infrastructure services and sectors like food and water, health care, public safety, finance, information and communication technology, manufacturing, energy and utilities, transportation and government. Hence cyberspace is vital to global economic growth since the digital sphere connectivity supplements all of these critical infrastructure sectors. Unfortunately, the online community faces increased subjectivity to advanced, sophisticated and targeted threats and breaches; our ever- increasing dependence on the digital sphere is attracting avenues for novel and significant vulnerabilities.

Numerous factors magnify this risk of novel attacks and threats on this digital space: large scale storage and processing of confidential and valuable electronic data, especially in the cloud; portable and powerful high end computing devices such as tablets, smartphones, and laptops are progressively coupled with each and every aspect of our daily lifestyle; proliferated sharing, combining and linking of information with other information in a greater frequency; and involving a third - party like outsourcing to a cloud provider, for storage and sharing have become a regular practice. On the contrary, we have skilled cyber criminals who are experts in exploiting the weakness in the digital sphere and thus make the complete system vulnerable. This necessitates that all components involved ought to be equally secure.

Recently, the rate of cybercrimes is increasing because of the fast-paced advancements in computer and Internet technology. Crimes involving a computer can range across the spectrum of criminal activity, from child pornography to theft of personal data to corporate espionage to destruction of intellectual property. Crimes employing mobile devices, data embedding/mining systems, computers, network communications, or any malware impose a huge threat to data security. In internet communications and electronic business, information security is an essential feature, and as of state, there is a pressing need to develop advanced methods to prevent and control these. The interest in cyber forensics and investigations is obvious from the industrial and standardization efforts accomplished in the last years. Cyber forensics and investigations have many challenges, including complexity of the fully connected digital environment, increased sophistication level of the threats, breach preparedness not being the top priority, debate over compliance vs. risk management. The entire breach combating procedure covers a wide range of activities starting from effective evidence collection and following prescribed forensic procedures for evidence preservation, custody of evidence chain, managing the digital evidence and data/image authentication and forensics of the hard disk/any storage device, cryptography and cryptanalysis in forensics, steganography and steganalysis and mobile forensics.

Our intention in editing this book is to offer concepts and various techniques that are employed in combating security breaches and criminal activities in the digital sphere in a precise and clear manner to the research community. In editing the book, our attempt is to provide frontier advancements in digital forensics and investigation, legal view of the cyber crimes and their punishments, security attacks targeting the mobile platform, cloud environment, multimedia – images and videos, network intrusion detection systems, biometric systems etc. along with the conceptual basis required to achieve in depth knowledge in the field of security in computer science and information technology. This book will comprise the latest research from prominent researchers from all over the world. Since the book covers case study-based research findings, it can be quite relevant to researchers, university academics, computing professionals, and probing university students. In addition, it will help those researchers who have interest in this field to keep insight into different concepts and their importance for applications in real life. This has been done to make the edited book more flexible and to stimulate further interest in topics

The topics presented are recent works and research findings in state-of-the-art idea of the problems and solution guidelines emerging in cyber forensics and investigations, thus summarizing the roadmap of current digital forensic research efforts in combating such security breaches. A wide variety of topics of interest are addressed, from the technical views such as advanced techniques for forensic developments in computer and communication-link environments, to legal perspectives - procedures for cyber investigations, standards and policies, to application perspective, such as cloud forensics, mobile malware, multimedia forensics – steganalysis etc., and to user perspective – techniques combating the security breaches through encryptions, authentications, forensic procedures, etc.

The prospective audience for this book will be cyber law policy makers, hackers, cyber forensic analyst, academicians, researchers, advanced-level students, technology developers, and global consortiums for security. This will also be useful to a wider audience of readers in furthering their research exposure to pertinent topics in cyber forensics and assisting in advancing their own research efforts in this field.

The topics in this book are categorized into one of the four sections. The first section provides an insight into the recent threats and vulnerabilities in the digital sphere, cloud environment, advancements in the malware for mobile devices and current trends of the biometric authentication systems. The second section discusses various techniques and strategies for combating the breaches and vulnerabilities using misuse detection systems, intrusion detection systems exclusively against flooding, worm and spoofing attacks and summarizes the comprehensive mapping of security solutions and mechanisms in a network for a variety of attacks. The third section presents the cyber forensics and investigation procedures, legal perspectives of the cybercrime, details the procedure and tools employed for digital evidence collection, forensics and anti-forensics techniques against cybercriminal activities. The final section discusses visual information security, especially on images and videos, systems for securing the physical systems via video surveillance systems and wireless sensor networks. Each section provides the current research trends in the concerned field of study.

Section 1: Digital Sphere Threats and Vulnerabilities

The global acceptability and usability of the network consists of some security breaches which may lead to security attack by the unauthorized users. Since, digital sphere is a widely used cyber space and open for anyone, the analysis of various threats and attacks is essential to determine the appropriate countermeasures and guidelines. Chapter 1 covers the background, possible threats, vulnerabilities and attacks on digital sphere with solutions and recommendations.

Biometrics is described as automatic recognition of individuals through their unique physiological (fingerprint, face, iris etc.) or behavioural (voice, gait, signature etc.) attributes. Biometric attributes cannot be lost, transferred or stolen. It offers better security due to fact that these attributes are very difficult to forge and require the presence of genuine user while granting access to particular resources. Chapter 2 is written with an objective to provide an in-depth overview of advances in biometrics for secure human authentication system technology to the readers. Also a new biometrics system is described which adopts two modalities: ECG and PCG.

Cloud based IT services have been gaining popularity and security in cloud environment needs to be evaluated from different perspectives. Chapter 3 focuses on security and privacy issues raised by the cloud environment, investigation challenges in the cloud environment, different dimensions to cloud security so that organizations can be better prepared for secure information management in the cloud environment.

With the advent of Internet of Things (IoT) and Cloud, everything is connected to Internet which can be accessed through our hand held mobile devices. Unlike Personal Computers, these devices give Hackers a greater attack landscape. Chapter 4 discusses the History of Mobile malwares, its categories with its motives and few signs that indicate the presence of a mobile malware. Also the battle against malware is categorized into two: namely prevention and response, which is forensically analysed using Static/ Dynamic Methods/Tools in this chapter.

Section 2: Techniques for combating Security Breaches

Intrusion detection systems are defined as tools, methods and resources to help identify, assess and report unauthorized or unapproved network or host both due to insider and outsider threats. Misuse detection systems detect intrusions by comparing with previously detected intrusions database through pattern matching technique. A model for misuse detection system which comprises of major components such as data and feature extraction, data processing and classifier is proposed in Chapter 5.

The Network Intrusion Detection and Prevention Systems (NIDPS) on Flooding and Worm Attacks are analyzed and presented in Chapter 6. The objective is to explore new detection mechanisms for the TCP SYN attacks and to detect and recover the network affected by camouflaging worms.

In the context of network security, a spoofing attack is a condition in which one person or a program successfully masquerades as another. Spoofing attack which may be generated in various layer of Open Systems Interconnection model (OSI model) is discussed in Chapter 7. The chapter ends with discussing about the possible spoofing attacks in network layer and the relevant defense mechanism of the same.

A comprehensive study aimed at systematically identifying, analyzing and classifying the security attacks in the host layer is presented in chapter 8. A wide list of attacks in transport, session and application layers (Host layers) are analyzed and mapped to their corresponding security mechanisms. 148 effective controls for the security attacks in addition to the 113 standard controls are identified and discussed in this chapter.

Section 3: Cyber Forensics and Investigation

Cybercrimes are newer classes of crimes committed using the technology and mainly internet. With the introduction of social media such as facebook, twitter etc., there has been havoc created in the society and the crimes using the internet have risen. Chapter 9 deals with the types of cybercrimes and also provides the offences and punishments under the Information Technology Act, 2000 in India.

Computerized proof is "information that is made, controlled, put away or conveyed by any gadget, PC or PC framework or transmitted over a correspondence framework that is significant to the procedure." Chapter 10 gives a brief of how Digital confirmation starts from a large number of sources including seized PC hard-drives and reinforcement media, ongoing email messages, talk room logs, ISP records, site pages, advanced system activity, nearby and virtual databases, computerized catalogs, remote gadgets, memory cards, and computerized cameras. . It also presents the procedure of distinguishing, saving, examining and displaying computerized proof in a way that is legitimately satisfactory. Finally it summarizes how the advanced proofs are gathered and what techniques and apparatuses can be utilized to safeguard the computerized confirmations.

In the digital era, digital data is dominating the analog but however, since the digital edit software is ubiquitous the authenticity of digital data faces a great challenge. Some useful guidelines for the perspective application of machine learning for digital forensics are discussed in Chapter 11.

The difficulty in maintaining the integrity of digital evidence emerges as a challenge, because they depend on a number of appropriate technical knowledge and use of specific tools for analysis and verification of all traces possibly left by the criminal in devices and networks. The counter measures to elucidate anti forensic techniques are discussed and analysed in Chapter 12.

Section 4: Visual Information Security

Every sphere of life has embedded computer vision field. The ability to automatically detect and track objects is of great interest in the field of Security. Tracking a person is a necessary aspect of HCI (Human Computer Interaction), interacting with and within virtual environments, and capturing motion for computer enhanced motion pictures. The framework of ATM video surveillance system encompassing various factors, such as image acquisition, background estimation, background subtraction, segmentation, people counting and tracking are briefly discussed in Chapter 13.

Like all the security techniques, steganography has been propelled to grip the computational power and proliferation in security alertness. In chapter 14, an interpolation based data hiding on the stereo image which ensures greater embedding payload, less distortion, greater perceptual quality has been discussed.

Currently images form an inevitable part of knowledge in the cyber space. Due to the rapid growth rate, there is a rapid rise in cost to store and maintain the image data. Cloud offers an excellent service for storing these huge, massive image files. Medical images, satellite images, personal images stored on the cloud server are highly susceptible to attack by the adversaries. However, ensuring confidentiality and integrity of the image content is upto the owner for which he seeks the application of cryptography. Conventional cryptographic systems could not be straightly applied on images. Visual cryptography proves to be more efficient in this scenario. Chapter 15 describes the successful visual cryptography techniques adapted currently and elaborates various issues, challenges and possible solution to have them implemented in cloud setup.

As Visual sensor networks gain more civilian attention, security becomes a major design issue. The VSN is vulnerable and can be demoralized to compromise the network task or to obtain unconstitutional admission to relevant information. The highly sensitive nature of images makes security and privacy in VSNs even more important. Chapter 16 has elucidated the current state and prominence of security concerns in VSN. It also fosters discussion on privacy protection techniques like subjective privacy, Video masking techniques and identifies recent trends in VSN security and privacy.

We have made a sincere effort to keep the book reader-friendly as well as useful to the information security community. A serious look into the cyber threats, breaches and awareness on how to safeguard oneself in this cyberspace while reaping the maximum benefits out of the digital sphere is the prime motive of this book. The book explains with many real world cases and the current best security practices followed globally. At the same time, it enables the readers to identify the possible vulnerabilities in any of their interaction with the cyber space, discover a feasible solution for the trivial as well as non-trivial aspect of the issue. We trust and hope that the book will help its readers to further carryout their research in different directions.

S. Geetha
VIT University, Chennai Campus, India

Y. Asnath Victy Phamila
VIT University, Chennai Campus, India

Section 1
Digital Sphere Threats and Vulnerabilities

Chapter 1
A Review on Digital Sphere Threats and Vulnerabilities

Muthuramalingam S.
Thiagarajar College of Engineering, India

Thangavel M.
Thiagarajar College of Engineering, India

Sridhar S.
Thiagarajar College of Engineering, India

ABSTRACT

Digital Sphere is a global network which consists of all the resources that are required for the users, who connected with the digital network. It connects the entire world through the digital technologies. The digital network includes services, applications, and web page files. By connecting, to this network, people from one end in the world can able to communicate and share their knowledge across the world. Global communication and sharing may allow an unknown person which can disrupt the services. This chapter proposes a review on the threats and vulnerabilities related to the digital sphere network with value added security guidelines and countermeasures given to overcome such issues.

1. INTRODUCTION

A Global network with full of digital resources are provided to the requested users by connecting them to the digital world is called as digital sphere. It plays a significant role in the IT by shaping up into the reality, due to the increased dependency of users with the recent trends of evolving digital technologies. This sphere contains various varieties of data such as academia, media, social media, journalism, search engines and the computing technologies with enormous data centres, where the data retrieved by the sphere users in the form of web pages, applications, files and other such formats through the browsers with the help of protocols. Several organizations prefer to share or store their resources and run their business completely through digital sphere. By this, the customers of digital sphere are satisfied with variety of resources from various organizations. With the increased usage and the mobility of users, the services provided as applications, which is globally acceptable and accessible by the authorized users at anywhere and anytime.

DOI: 10.4018/978-1-5225-0193-0.ch001

The global acceptability and usability of the network consists of some security breaches which may lead to security attack by the unauthorized users. Cyber incidents are frequently occurred and rises costlier damage. The foremost problem and a challenging issue of the cyberspace (Lehto 2015) is that it has no borders or defined jurisdiction. It provides a open land for actors, who are playing a role of malicious access are left out without any judiciary actions and without being detected. Sophisticated number of recent cyber attacks and the attention given by the media to this arena shows that the importance of security in this sphere. However, the experienced person's interest on the cyber space and the money invested by the industrialist on various aspects does not seem to become more secure. Since, digital sphere is a widely used cyber space and open for anyone, the analysis of various threats and attacks is essential to determine the appropriate countermeasures and guidelines.

The rest of the chapter covers Background, Threats, Vulnerabilities and attacks of digital sphere with Solutions and Recommendations, Future works and Conclusion.

2. BACKGROUND

The security in the cyber space needs to attain a desired state, in-order to grant secure access to the users who are able to travel along the cyber world without having worry about security breaches. The word cyber is originated from the Greek word kybereo it specifies- to steer, to guide, to control. At the end of the 1940's, Norbert wiener an American mathematician, began to use the word cybernetics to describe computerized control systems. According to the wiener's statement cybernetics deals with sciences that address the control of machines and living organisms through their communications and from the given feedback.

Major challenge drivers in the cyber world are time, data and network. In today's world, (i) for a single minute, 2,16,000 photos are shared through instagram, (ii) Upload rate of video into the YouTube site increased in every 3 days (iii) Within a minute 70 new domains are registered and created 572 new websites (iv) At the same time face book, twitter, emails are also posing their increased rate in the internet (Gao, 2011). That is face book receives 1.8 million likes, 1, 80,000 more tweets taken by twitter and 204 million emails are sent and received by Gmail. and (v) Chatting over Skype are taken by the relatives and friends are taken is equivalent to 1.4 million minutes. Compared to the previous year's Internet usage is drastically increased (Woollaston 2013).

According to the U.S News Briefs, unauthorized access to the network becomes a major issue than denial of service attacks. With the increased device usage and growth of cyber space, most of the people needs to access all the services through unauthorized privileges. The FBI investigating that the criminals having target to the selected regional offices computer systems including intrusions into public switched networks, major network intrusions, privacy violations and other crimes (IT Professional 2005).

Recent attacks performed by attackers are using the botnet a kind of unauthorized access. With the botnet, an attacker accessed the user database of an online website T35.net which is a personal and business hosting web services for many users. (Department of Justice 2010, Online).

Botnets are the background process that has collection of software agents that run automatically to command large number of computers that allow the criminals enter into the cyber network to conduct spreading of large scale infection program, spam mails, credential theft and personal information theft. That also performs the transformation of malware from one to other (Pinguelo and Muller, 2011).

A recent study by Clear Swift shows that 58% security incidents results from insider threat activities. (Clear Swift, 2013). It results that Edward Snowden a former CIA employee publishing the secret information's of U.S National Security Agency. It is globally accepted that lot of insider threats are unreported. The organizations are not reporting about this type of attacks (BBC News, 2013).

Social networks are also affected by some kind of malware. One of the famous attack happened in face book was the Koobface virus; it just sent a link of a video to a friend or some person. Once click the link then they were asked to update or install the adobe flash player. If anyone action is performed a Trojan downloaded to their system (Kasperski, 2008)

(Jagatic, 2005) conduct an experiment to find out the people reaction in phishing messages from a popular link. From the social connections they sent an email with fake sender name. More than 80% of people in receivers are clicked and redirected the fake website. Nearly 70% of people enter their personal data. From the categories of respondents includes 77% of women often than 65% of men.

3. DIGITAL SPHERE ISSUES

The issues of digital sphere has been classified as Security Threats, Vulnerabilities and Attacks. Handling the issues of digital sphere can be taken through the guidelines and countermeasures of the cyber space. The Figure 1 shows that the taxonomy of issues in the digital sphere.

4. SECURITY THREATS

Threat is any kind of danger that could exploit a vulnerability of a security system. These threats are associated with the applications, services, products used by the end users. Threats (Marinos 2012) are classified into four major categories such as unauthorized access, malicious threat, Natural threat, and other threat. Figure 2 shows that the taxonomy of threats.

Figure 1. Digital sphere issues

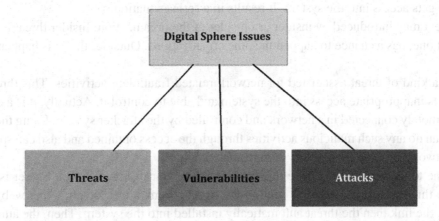

Figure 2. Threat taxonomy

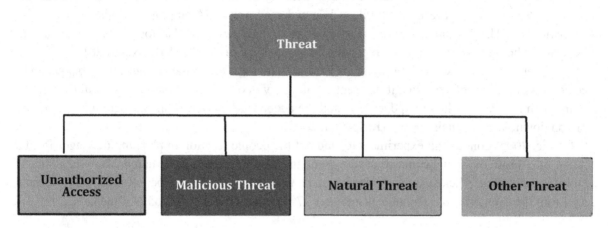

4.1 Unauthorized Access

In digital sphere, data's are stored on the computer system which has to be accessed by the authorized users as useful information. It introduces some security threats to the computer system due to unauthorized person's having access to the system and when transmitting information form one user to another via wired or wireless network.

Threat is a kind of action taken by a user inside in the organization, just taken for fun or for an intended purpose. Someone may try to use their friend's account to know the message details. Others intentionally perform this for money, revenge etc..,

Considering an example of when a user should transmit their data through the wireless network the following actions are possible.

1. By performing unauthorized association the attacker may associate him or herself to the network as a intended user. Then he/she can access the data transmitted over the connected network by the network credentials.
2. Promiscuous client is a threat in the wireless network that offers an irresistibly strong signal intentionally for malicious activities. A person may theft the confidential information of a particular once he gets access into the system. It results in a series situation.
3. The threat may introduced by insider or outsider of the organization. Insider threat is a series and harmful one, has a chance to happen in some organizations. Outsider threat is happened globally.

Botnet is a kind of threat associated for network related fraudulent activities. This threat cause an attacker to gets inappropriate access into the system and able to control it. Actually, it is a collection of computers remotely connected in a network and controlled by the attacker system. Using these systems, the attacker can do any such malicious activities through the access obtained and also can spread viruses across the network. At last, the entire system results in failure.

There some tools available to create this type of threats, for example ProRat Server is a tool used for creating a threat. The created file is send to the target by email or such attracting web links. Once the user click the link then the threat automatically installed into the system. Then, the attacker able to access and control the system remotely.

4.2 Malicious Threats

Malicious Threats is a set of malicious software programs includes malicious activities and propagation routines. This threats are intentionally perform the task why it was created. This may be stealthy, intended to steal the credential information, act as a spy on the system to gather data without the user's knowledge. This threats sends spam mails, spread virus information or to engage distributed denial of service attacks. It includes malware, adware, ransomware, spyware, adware, worms, infected files, Trojan horse, executable codes and scripts.

Virus is a computer program that usually hidden or placed inside a file. It replicates itself, infect other file contents etc.. Trojan horse used to enter into a victim's computer and have unrestricted access. By the gained access the attacker may harm the file contents in victim's storage. Rootkit allows the concealment of malicious program that is hidden from the normal user. It prevents from showing the malicious process in the list of system processes and files. Backdoor are useful for bypassing the normal authentication procedures. It may installed by viruses and Trojans.

Stuxnet is a type of malware with diverse modules and functionalities. It is mostly used to grab the control and reprogramming the industrial control systems by modifying the programmable logic controllers. In which it create a way for an attacker may intrude into a system and launch an attack by making changes in the code and taking control of the entire system.

- It is a self replicate program through removable drives that exploiting a vulnerability allowing auto execution.
- Automatically spreads in a LAN through the vulnerability of windows print spooler.
- Update itself through a peer-peer mechanism within a LAN.
- It contains a windows rootkit that hide its binaries and attempts to bypass security products.
- This threat impact in higher level problems that may causes the entire network of an organization.
- JPS virus maker is software used to create such harmful applications that are viruses, Trojans, etc.., it creates the files as per the users need.

4.3 Natural Threats

Natural threats are raised due to the improper management and lack of planning as well as in the system design. Earthquakes, hurricanes, floods, lightning, and fire can cause huge damage into the computer network. Due to this loss of productivity, damage to hardware are occur. Humans also involved in this threat to damage the system by tampering the cables and other such activities.

4.4 Other Threats

Misconfiguration of web server and the networking devices lead to data theft, intrusion and traversal activities. Credential theft is happened due to the poor password management policy and the usage of less secure cryptography techniques. Tampering the parameter of an application leads to modify the data such as credential and permissions. Open file access leads to access the file and include some malicious contents. Injection of something to the cyber space makes the services inaccessible.

4.5 Threat Countermeasures

Preventive measures need to be followed in order to lessen the possibility of virus infections and data loss. Some of these methods include,

- Install antivirus software that detects and removes infections as they appear.
- Generate an antivirus policy for safe computing and distribute it to the staff.
- Pay attention to the instructions while downloading files or any programs from the internet.
- Update the antivirus software on a monthly basis, so that it can identify and clean out new bugs.
- Avoid opening the attachments received from an unknown sender as viruses spread via email attachments.
- Possibility of virus infection may corrupt data, thus regularly maintain data backup.
- Schedule regular scans for all drivers after the installation of antivirus software.
- Do not accept disks or programs without checking them first using a current version of an antivirus program.
- Ensure the executable code sent to the organization is approved.
- Run disk clean up, registry scanner, and defragmentation once a week.
- Do not boot the machine with infected bootable system disk.
- Keep informed about latest virus and threats.
- Run anti-spyware or adware once in a week.
- Check the DVDs and CDs for virus infection.
- Block the files with more than one file type extension.
- Ensure the pop-up blocker is turned on and use an internet firewall.
- Be cautious with the files being sent through the instant messenger.
- Avoid opening email attachments received from unknown senders.
- Block all unnecessary ports at the host and firewall.
- Avoid accepting the programs transferred by instant messaging.
- Harden weak, default configuration settings.
- Disable unused functionality including protocols and services.
- Monitor the internal network traffic for odd ports or encrypted traffic.
- Avoid downloading and executing applications from untrusted sources.
- Install patches and security updates for the operating systems and applications.
- Scan CDs and floppy disks with antivirus software before using.
- Restrict permissions within the desktop environment to prevent malicious applications installation.
- Avoid typing the commands blindly and implementing pre-fabricated programs or scripts.
- Manage local workstation file integrity through checksums, auditing, and port scanning.
- Run local versions of antivirus, firewall and intrusion detection software on the desktop.
- Educate users regarding the dangers of installing applications downloaded from the internet, and to be cautious if they have to open email attachments.
- Use antivirus tools such as windows defender, McAfee and Norton to detect and eliminate backdoors

Figure 3. Vulnerabilities taxonomy

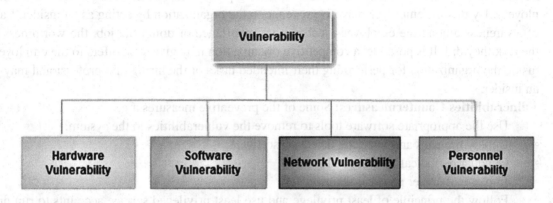

4.6 Summary of Threats

So, Threats can initiated through two important sources: humans and nature. Human threats then can be divided into two sub categories: malicious and non-malicious. The non-malicious attacks usually occurs from users who are not equipped with training on computers or not conscious of various computer security threats. Malicious attacks usually occurs from non-employees or disgruntled employees who have a specific goal or objective to attack.

5. SECURITY VULNERABILITIES

Vulnerability is a weakness which allows an attacker to reduce the assurance of an information system. It is susceptible by a system's flaw that may give an access to the attacker to exploiting it. The vulnerabilities are classified into four major categories are hardware vulnerability, software vulnerability, network vulnerability and personnel vulnerability. Figure 3 shows the taxonomy of Vulnerabilities in the digital sphere.

- **Hardware Vulnerability:** Hardware vulnerabilities are having higher impact in the system failure. The hardware is the basic need of any systems. The system gets initial construction by aligning the hardware parts. The configuration of the hardware makes the storage and performance of the system in a better way. It may harmful from the natural disaster issues.
- **Software Vulnerability:** Vulnerabilities in the software are from improper testing. By this an attacker my controls the application for his intended purpose. The bugs associated with the software are lead to series flaws in future. Design of software includes some errors and bugs in nature. Removal of this form the software is necessary to attain a high level security.
- **Network Vulnerability:** Unprotected communication lines and the insecure network architecture are some vulnerability associated with the network. The network may cause from the unprotected communication lines. Due to the lacking of controls over the network such administration tasks it leads to the failure of a network. Misconfiguration of the Networking devices such as router, switch is leads to the intruder may harm the system by gaining unauthorized access.

- **Personnel Vulnerability:** The inadequate recruiting process results in work burden for the employees. By this the employee may give revenge to the organization by acting as an insider. Lack of awareness among the employees such as the importance of doing the job, the worthiness of the task they did. It is possible, a competitive organization may give such offers to the employees inside the organization for performing their intended tasks or the hiring of a professional may be an insider.

- **Vulnerabilities Countermeasures:** Some of the preventive measures are,
  - Use the appropriate software tools to remove the vulnerabilities in the system.
  - Deploy firewalls and intrusion detection software.
  - Conduct periodical auditing tasks.
  - Implement higher physical security.
  - Follow the principle of least privilege and use least privileged service accounts to run process and access resources.
  - Create secure audit trails and use digital signatures.
  - Use strong authentication and encryption.
  - Use tamper resistant protocols across communication links.
  - Secure communication links with protocols that provide message integrity.
  - Use resource and bandwidth throttling technique.
  - Validate and filter all inputs.
  - Do not pass credentials as plain text over the wire.
  - Do not store secrets as plain text.
  - Protect authentication cookies with secure socket layer.
  - Use data hashing and signing.
  - Provide sensitive data only through the secured access granting mechanisms.
  - Check the parameters in the application forms.

- **Vulnerabilities Summary:** So, Microsoft defined "a security vulnerability is a weakness in a product that could allow an attacker to compromise the integrity, availability, or confidentiality of that product". Confidentiality, Integrity, Availability are the three main goals for security. If one or more of these three goals lacks, then there is said to be a security vulnerability. A single security vulnerability will compromise all these goals at the same time.

6. SECURITY ATTACKS

Security attack is an attempt to break the security of a system by exploiting the threats and vulnerabilities associated with it. In general, attack was performed to destroy or steal the sensitive information. Attack is classified into such types are active and passive attack, inside and outside attack.

Active attack is an attempt to learn, make use of information resources and affect the system operation. Whereas Passive attack is an attempt to learn, make use of information resources and without affecting the system operation.

Attack can be performed by either inside or outside of the organization. Inside attack was initiated by an entity inside the security perimeter. Outside attack was initiated from outside of the security perimeter that was performed by unauthorized or illegitimate users of the system.

Figure 4. Attack taxonomy

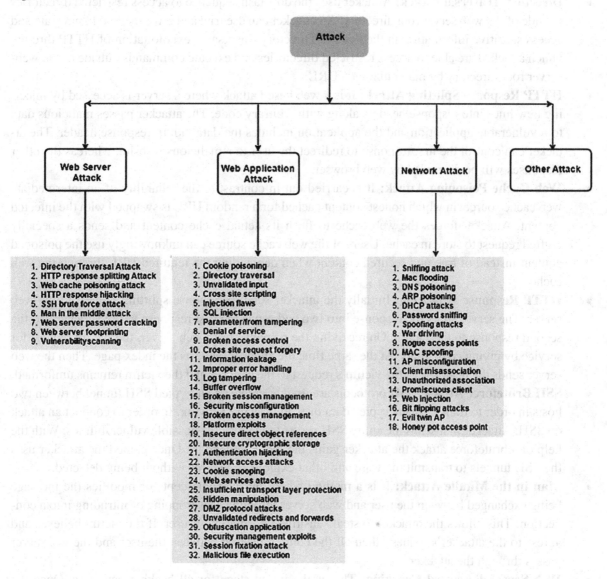

Attacks are classified into the following four categories. They are, web server attacks, web application attacks, network attacks and other attacks. Figure 4 shows that the designed taxonomy of attacks in the digital sphere.

Web Server Attacks

Web server attack was performed for compromised use of accounts, tampering the data, website defacement, secondary attacks from the website, data theft, and root access for other applications or servers. Attacks in the web server are happen because of the servers are installed with default settings, improper permissions assigned for the files and directories. Misconfiguration of an SSL certificate and encryption settings. Unnecessarily enabled services including the content management and remote administration. Here some of web server attacks are discussed,

- **Directory Traversal Attack:** Attacker uses the dot slash sequence to access restricted directories outside of the web server root directory. An attacker can use trial and error method to navigate and access sensitive information in the system. Directory traversal is expoloitation of HTTP through which attacked are able to access restricted directories and execute commands outside of the web-server root directory by manipulating a URL.
- **HTTP Response Splitting Attack:** It is a web based attack where a server is accessed by inject-ing new lines into response headers along with arbitrary code. The attacker passes malicious data to a vulnerable application and the application includes the data in http response header. The at-tacker can control the first response to redirect the user to a malicious website; whereas the other responses will be discarded by web browser.
- **Web Cache Poisoning Attack:** It is carried out in contrast to the reliability of an intermediate web cache source, in which honest content cached for a random URL is swapped with the infected content. Attacker forces the web cache to flush its actual cache content and sends a specially crafted request to store in cache. Users of the web cache source can unknowingly use the poisoned content instead of true and secured content when demanding the required URL through the web cache.
- **HTTP Response Hijacking:** Initially the attacker sends a response splitting request to the web server. The server splits the response into two and sends the first response to the attacker and the second response to the victim. On receiving the response from web server, the victim request for service by giving credentials. At the same time the attacker requests the index page. Then the web server sends the response of the victim's request to the attacker and the victim remains uniformed.
- **SSH Bruteforce Attack:** SSH protocols are used to create an encrypted SSH tunnel between two hosts in order to transfer unencrypted data over an insecure network. In order to conduct an attack on SSH, Attacker first scans the entire SSH server to identify the possible vulnerabilities. With the help of a bruteforce attack the attacker gains the login credentials. Once gained the attacker uses the SSH tunnels to transmit malware and other exploits to victims without being detected.
- **Man in the Middle Attack:** It is a method where intruder intercepts or modifies the message being exchanged between the user and web server through eavesdropping or intruding into a con-nection. This allows the attacker to steal sensitive information of user. If the victim believes and agress to the attacker's request, then all the communication between the user and the webserver passes through the attacker.
- **Web Server Password Cracking:** This is the initial stage for all hacking activities. Once the password is cracked an attacker may login to the system as an unauthorized person. Attacker use different methods such as social engineering, phishing, wiretapping, key loggers, bruteforce at-tacks, dictionary attacks etc.., Attacker target mainly for Web form authentication cracking, SSH Tunnels, FTP Servers, SMTP servers, Web shares.
- **Web Server Footprinting:** It is performed to gather more information about security aspects of a web server with the help of tools or footprinting techniques. The purpose is to know remote access capabilities, its ports and services and the aspects of security.
- **Vulnerability Scanning:** It is a method to find out various vulnerabilities and misconfigurations of a web server. It is done with the help of various automated tools known as vulnerable scan-ners. There are some tools available to perform such web server attacks are ID serve, Nessus, Metasploit, Brutus, and THC- Hydra.

- **Web Server Attack Counter Measures:** The general countermeasures of Web server attack are as follows:
    - Scan for existing vulnerabilities and perform updates and patch management to the software regularly.
    - Apply all updates, regardless of their type, on an "as-needed" basis.
    - Ensure that service packs, hotfixes, and security patch levels are consistent on all domain controllers. Ensure that server outages are scheduled and a complete set of backup tapes and emergency repair disks are available.
    - Have a back-out plan for that allows the system and enterprise to return their original state, prior to the failed implementation.
    - Before applying any service pack, hotfix, or security patch, read and peer review all relevant documentation.
    - Test the service packs and hotfixes on a representative non-production environment prior to being deployed to production.
    - Ensures that server outages are scheduled and a complete set of backup tapes and emergency repair disks are available
    - Schedule periodic service pack upgrades as part of operations maintenance and never try to have more than two service packs behind.
    - Create URL mappings to internal servers cautiously.
    - If a database server such as Microsoft sql server is to be used as a backend databae, install it on a separate server.
    - Do use a dedicated machine as a web server.
    - Don't install the IIS server on a domain controller.
    - Use server side session ID tracking and match connection with time stamps, IP address, etc..,
    - Screen and filter incoming traffic request.
    - Do physically protect the web server machine in a secure machine room.
    - **Protocols:**
        - Block all unnecessary ports, internet control message protocol traffic and unnecessary protocols such as NetBIOS and SMB.
        - Harden the TCP/IP stack and consistently apply the latest software patches and updates to the system software.
        - If using insecure protocols such as Telnet, POP3, SMTP, or FTP take appropriate measures to provide secure authentication and communication.
        - If remote access is denied, make sure that the remote connection is secured properly by using tunneling and encryption protocols.
        - Disable WebDAV if not used by the application or keep secure if it is secured.
    - **User Account:**
        - Remove all unused modules and application extensions.
        - Disable unused default user accounts created during installation of an operating system.
        - When creating a new web root directory, grant the appropriate NTFS permissions to the anonymous user being used from the IIS web server to access the web content.
        - Eliminate unnecessary database users and stored procedures and follow the principle of least privilege for the database application to defend against SQL query poisoning.

- Use secure web permissions, NTFS permissions and .NET framework access control mechanisms including URL authorization.
- Slow down brute force and dictionary attacks with strong password policies and the audit and alert for logon failures.
- Run processes using least privileged accounts as well as least privileged service and user accounts.
  ◦ **Files and Directories:**
    - Eliminate unnecessary files within.jar files.
    - Eliminate sensitive configuration information within the byte code.
    - Avoid mapping virtual directories between two different servers or over a network.
    - Monitor and check all network service logs, website logs, and os logs frequently.
    - Disable serving of directory listings.
    - Eliminate the presence of web application or website files and scripts on a separate partition or drive other than that of the operating system, logs, and any other system files.

Web Application Attacks

There is some attack vectors associated with the web. Some attack vectors are parameter manipulation, XML poisoning, client validation, server misconfiguration, web service routing issues and cross site scripting. The threats and attacks associated with the web application are described as follows.

- **Cookie Poisoning:** By changing the information inside the cookie, attackers bypass the authentication process and once they gain control over the network, then either modify the content and use the system for performing malicious attack or to steal information from the user's system.
- **Directory Traversal:** Attacker exploit http by using directory traversal and they have the ability to access restricted directories and execute commands outside of the webserver root directory by manipulating a URL.
- **Unvalidated Input:** Attacker can gain access to the victim's system using the information present in cookies. Examples of these attacks are SQL injection, cross site scripting.
- **Cross Site Scripting:** An attacker bypasses the client id security mechanism and gain access privileges. Then inject malicious scripts into the web pages of a particular web site. These malicious scripts can even rewrite the html contents of the website.
- **Injection Flaws:** These are web application vulnerabilities that allow untrusted data to be interpreted and executed as part of a command or query.
- **SQL Injection:** It is a type of attack where SQL commands are injected by the attacker via input data, so the attacker can tamper with the data. Using this attack, an attacker logs onto an application without providing valid user name and password and gains administrative privileges and obtains information stored in the database and also the hacker can insert malicious content into web page, or alter the contents of a database.
- **Parameter/from Tampering:** This type of tampering attack is intended to manipulate the parameters exchanged between clients and server in order to modify application data, such as user credentials and permissions. This information's usually stored in cookies, hidden form fields or in URL query strings. Man in the middle attack is one of the examples for this type of attack.

- **Denial of Service:** It is an attacking method intended to terminate the operations of a website or a server and make it unavailable to intended users. For instance a website related to bank or email service is not able to function for a few hours to a few days. This results in loss of time and money.
- **Broken Access Control:** Broken access control is a method used by attackers where a particular flaw has been identified related to the access control, where authentication is bypassed and the attacker compromises the network.
- **Cross Site Request Forgery:** The cross site request forgery method is a kind of attack where an authenticated user in made to perform certain tasks on the web application that an attackers chooses. For example a user clicking on a particular link sent through email or chat.
- **Information Leakage:** Information leakage can cause great losses for a company. Hence, all sources such as systems or other network resources must be protected from information leakage by employing proper content filtering mechanisms.
- **Improper Error Handling:** It is necessary to define how the system or network should behave when an error occurs. Otherwise, it may provide a chance for the attacker to break into the system. Improper error handling may lead to dos attacks.
- **Log Tampering:** Logs are maintained by web applications to track the usage patterns such as user login credentials, admin login credentials, etc. attackers usually inject, delete, or taper with web application logs so that they can perform malicious actions or hide their identities.
- **Buffer Overflow:** A web application's buffer overflow vulnerability occurs when it fails to guard its buffer properly and allows writing beyond its maximum size because boundary checks are not done fully or in most cases, they are skipped entirely. Programming languages such as C have vulnerabilities in them. C functions do not validate buffer size.
- **Broken Session Management:** When security-sensitive credentials such as passwords and other useful material are not properly taken care, these types of attacks occur. Attackers compromise the credentials through these security vulnerabilities.
- **Security Misconfiguration:** Developers and network security administrators should check that the entire stack is configured properly or security misconfiguration can happen at any level of an application stack, including the platform, web server, application server, framework and custom code. Missing patches, misconfigruations, use of default accounts can be detected with the help of automated scanners that attackers exploit to compromise web application security.
- **Broken Access Management:** Even authentication schemes that are valid are weakened because of vulnerable account management functions including account update, forgotten or lost password recovery or reset, password changes, and other similar functions.
- **Platform Exploits:** Various web applications are built on by using different platforms such as BEA web logic and ColdFusion. Each platform has various vulnerabilities and exploits associated with it.
- **Insecure Direct Object References:** When various internal implementation objects such as file, directory, database record or key are exposed through a reference by a developer, then the insecure direct object reference takes place.
- **Insecure Cryptographic Storage:** When sensitive data has been stored in the database, it has to be properly encrypted using cryptography. A few methods are available to perform the secure storage.

- **Authentication Hijacking:** In order to identify the user every web application users have identification details such as user id and password. Once the attacker compromises the system, various things like theft of services, session hijacking, and user impersonation can occur.
- **Network Access Attacks:** Network access attacks can majorly impact web applications. These can have effect on basic level of services within an application and can allow access that standard HTTP application methods would not have access.
- **Cookie Snooping:** Attackers use cookie snooping on a victim's system to analyze their surfing habits and sell that information to other attackers or may sue this information to launch various attacks on the victim's web applications.
- **Web Services Attacks:** Web services are process-to-process communications that have special security issues and needs. An attacker injects a malicious script into a web service and is able to disclose and modify application data.
- **Insufficient Transport Layer Protection:** SSL/TLS authentications should be used for authentication on websites or the attacker can monitor network traffic to steal an authenticated user's session cookie. Various threats such as account theft, phishing attacks, and admin accounts may happen after systems are being compromised.
- **Hidden Manipulation:** These type of attacks are mostly used by attackers to compromise e-commerce websites. Attackers manipulate the hidden fields and change the data stored in them. Several online stores face this type of problem every day. Attackers can alter prices and conclude transactions with the price of their choice.
- **DMZ Protocol Attacks:** DMZ – Demilitarized Zone is a semi trusted network zone that separates the untrusted internet from the company's trusted internal network. An attacker who is able to compromise a system that allows other DMZ protocols has access to other DMZs and internet systems. This level of access can lead to
  - Compromise the web application and data.
  - Defacement of websites
  - Access to internal systems, including databases, backups, and source code.
- **Unvalidated Redirects and Forwards:** Attackers make a victim click an unvalidated link that appears to be a valid site. Such redirects may attempt to install malware or trick victims into disclosing passwords or other sensitive information.
- **Obfuscation Application:** Attackers usually work hard at hiding their attacks and to avoid detection. Network and host intrusion detection systems are constantly looking for signs of well known attacks, driving attackers to seek different ways to remain undetected. The most common method to attack obfuscation involves encoding portions of the attack with Unicode, UTF-8 or URL encoding. Unicode is a method of representing letters, numbers, and special characters so these characters can be displayed properly, regardless of the application or underlying platform in which they are used.
- **Security Management Exploits:** Some attackers target security management systems, either on networks or on the application layer, in order to modify or disable security enforcement. An attacker who exploits security management can directly modify protection policies, delete existing policies, and add new policies, modify applications, system data and resources.
- **Session Fixation Attack:** In a session fixation attack the attacker tricks or attracts the user to access a legitimate web server using an explicit session id value. A session fixation attack is a kind of *session hijacking attack*. The difference between the two attacks is that, in session hijacking the

attack is performed by stealing the established session after the user logs in whereas in session fixation, the attack starts before the user logs in. This attack can be performed by using various techniques. The technique that the attacker needs to choose for the attack depends on how the web application deals with session tokens.

- **Malicious File Execution:** Malicious file execution vulnerabilities had been found on most applications. The cause of this vulnerability is because of unchecked input into the web server. Due to the unchecked input, the files of attacker performs remote code execution, installs the rootkit remotely, and in at least some cases, take complete control over the systems.Tools used for these attacks are httprint, webinspect, burp suite's intruder, OWASP zed attack proxy, wireshark, SQL ninja, etc..,

- **Web Application Attacks Countermeasures:** The following are the countermeasures related to web application attacks.
  - **Cookie/Session Poisoning:**
    - Do not store plain text or weekly encrypted password in a cookie.
    - Implement cookie's timeout.
    - Cookie's authentication credentials should be associated with an IP address.
    - Make logout functions available.
  - **DoS Attacks:**
    - Configure the firewall to deny external internet control message protocol traffic access.
    - Secure the remote authentication and connectivity testing.
    - Prevent use of unnecessary functions such as gets, strcpy and return addresses from being overwritten, etc.
    - Prevent sensitive information from overwriting.
    - Perform thorough input validation.
    - Data processed by the attacker should be stopped from being executed.
  - **Web Service Attacks:**
    - Configure firewall/IDS for a web services anomaly and signature detection.
    - Configure WSDL access control permissions to grant or deny access to an y type of WSDL based SOAP messages.
    - Configure firewall/IDS systems to filter improper SOAP and XML syntax.
    - Use document-centric authentication credentials that use SAML.
    - Implement centralized in-line requests and responses schema validation.
    - Use security tools provided with the web server and scanners that automate and make the process of securing a web server easy.
    - Screen and filter the incoming request.
    - Avoid using redirects and forwards if destination parameters cannot be avoided; ensure that the supplied value is valid, and authorized for the user.
    - Log off immediately after using a web application and clear the history.
    - Do not allow your browser and websites to save login details.
    - Check the HTTP referred header and when processing a POST ignore URL parameters.
    - Use SSL for all authenticated parts of the application,
    - Verifiy whether all the users identities and credentials are stored in a hashed form.
    - Never submit the data as part of GET.
    - Do not create or use weak cryptographic algorithms.

○ **LDAP Injection Attacks:**
- Perform type, pattern and domain value validation of all input data.
- Make LDAP filters a specific as possible.
- Validate and restrict the amount of data returned to the user.
- Implement tight access control on the data in the LDAP directory.
- Perform dynamic testing and source code analysis.

Network Attacks

Network is the medium that connects the users globally in the world. This network caused by such attacks in both the wired and wireless manner. The wired or wireless based network attacks are categorized as follows:

- **Sniffing Attack:** Sniffers are also referred to as network protocol analyzers are used for capturing data that is being transmitted on a network either legitimately or illegitimately. It is a form of wiretap applied to computer networks. When an attacker plugs into a port he can monitor all the broadcast traffic to that port and access sensitive information available in the unencrypted traffic.
- **Mac Flooding:** Mac flooding is a kind of sniffing attack that floods the network switch with the data packets that interrupt the usual sender to recipient data flow that is common with MAC addresses. The data, instead of passing from sender to recipient, blasts out across all the ports. Thus attackers can monitor the data across the network.
- **DNS Poisoning:** It is a process in which the user is misdirected to a fake website by providing fake data to the DNS server. The website looks similar to the genuine site but it is controlled by the attacker.It allows attacker to replace DNS entries for a target on a given DNS server with IP addresses of the server he/she controls. Attacker can create fake DNS entries for files(containing malicious content) with same names as that of target server.
- **ARP Poisoning:** ARP poisoning is an attack in which the attacker tries to associate his or her own MAC address with victim's IP address so that the traffic meant for that IP address is sent to the attacker. Using fake ARP messages, an attacker can divert all communications between two machines so that all traffic is exchanged via his/her PC.
- **DHCP Attacks:** DHCP starvation is a process of attacking a DHCP server by sending a large amount of requests to it. Rogue DHCP server attack is a method in which an attacker sets up a rogue DHCP server to impersonate a legitimate DHCP server on the LAN, the rogue server can start issuing leases to the network's DHCP clients. The information provided to the clients by this rogue server can disrupt their network access, causing DoS.
- **Password Sniffing:** Password sniffing is a method used to steal passwords by monitoring the traffic that moves across the network and pulling out data including the data containing passwords. At times, passwords inside the systems are displayed in plain text without encryption, which makes easy to identified by an attacker and match them with the usernames.
- **Spoofing Attacks:** A spoofing attack is a situation where an attacker successfully pretends to be someone else by falsifying data and thereby gains access to restricted resources or steals personal information. The spoofing attacks can be performed in various ways. An attacker can user the victim's IP address illegally to access their accounts, to send fraudulent emails and to setup fake

websites for acquiring sensitive information such as passwords, account details etc.., attackers can even set up fake wireless access points and simulate legitimate users to connect through the illegitimate connection.

- **War Driving:** In a war driving attack, wireless LANs are detected either by sending probe requests over a connection or by listening to web beacons. Once a penetration point is discovered, further attacks can be launched on the LAN. some of the tools that can be used to perform wardriving are kisMAC, NetStumber and Wavestumber.

- **Rogue Access Points:** In order to create a backdoor into a trusted network, an unsecure access point or fake access point is installed inside a firewall. Any software or hardware access points can be used to perform this kind of attack. Rogue wireless access point placed into an 802.11 network can be used to hijack the connections of legitimate network users. When the user turns on the computer, the rogue wireless access point will offer to connect with the network user's NIC. All the traffic the user enters will pass through the rogue access point, thus enabling a form of wireless packet sniffing.

- **MAC Spoofing:** Using the MAC spoofing technique the attacker can reconfigure the MAC address to appear as an authorized access point to a host on a trusted network. This can be done by changing the information in the packet's header. Though it is intended for the purpose of legitimately requiring connectivity after hardware failure, it is associated with server security risks. Thus an attacker can gain access to the network and take over someone's identity who is already on the network.

- **AP Misconfiguration:** If any of the critical security settings is improperly configured at any of the access points, the entire network could be open to vulnerabilities and attacks. The AP can trigger alerts in most intrusion systems, as it is authorized as a legitimate device on the network.

- **Client Misassociation:** The client may connect or associate with an AP outside the legitimate network either intentionally or accidentally. This is because the WLAN signals travel through walls in the air. This kind of client misassociation thus can be lead to access control attacks. An attacker set up a rogue access point outside the corporate perimeter, this can be potentially used as a channel by the attacker to bypass enterprise security policies. Once a wi-fi client connects to the rogue access point, an attacker can steal the sensitive information by launching man-in-the-middle kind of attacks.

- **Unauthorized Association:** Unauthorized association is the major threat to wireless network. Prevention of this kind of attack depends on the method or technique that the attacker uses in order to get associated with the network. It may be accidental association or malicious association. Malicious association is performed with Soft APs. Attacker connect to organization network through soft APs instead of actual AP.

- **Promiscuous Client:** The promiscuous client offers an irresistibly strong signal intentionally for malicious purposes. Wireless cards often look for a stronger signal to connect to network. In this way the promiscuous client grabs the attention of the users towards it by sending strong signal.

- **Web Injection:** Creating and sending forged WEP encryption keys

- **Bit Flipping Attacks:** Captures the frame and flips random bits in the data payload, modifies ICV, and sends to the user.

- **Evil Twin AP:** Evil Twin is a wireless AP that pretends to be a legitimate AP by imitating another network name Masquerading as an authorized AP by beaconing the WLAN's service set identifier to lure users.

- **Honey Pot Access Point:** Setting service set identifier to be the same as an access point at the local hotspot assumes the attacker as the legitimate hotspot. Attackers can set up an unauthorized wireless network by controlling an in the region of multiple WLANs. These APs mounted by the attacker are called honeypot APs. These APs transmit a stronger signal, hence an authorized user may conncet to this malicious honeypot AP; Tools used for performing this attacks are inSSIder, NetSurveyor, NetStumbler, WirelessMon.

- **Countermeasures:**
  - **Wireless Attacks Countermeasures:**
    - Change the default SSID after WLAN configuration.
    - Set the router access password and enable firewall protection.
    - Disable SSID broadcasts.
    - Disable remote router login and wireless communication.
    - Enable MAC address filtering on your access point or router.
    - Enable encryption on access point and change passphrase often.
    - Choose WPA instead of WEP.
    - Disable the network when required.
    - Place wireless access points in a secured location.
  - **Sniffing Countermeasures:**
    - Restrict the physical access to the network media to ensure that a packet sniffer cannot be installed.
    - Use encryption to protect confidential information.
    - Permanently add the MAC address of the gateway to the ARP cache.
    - Use static IP addresses and static ARP tables to prevent attackers from adding the spoofed ARP entries for machines in the network.
    - Turn off network identification broadcasts and if possible, restrict the network to authorized users in order to protect network from being discovered with sniffing tools.
    - Use ipv6 instead of ipv4 protocol.
  - **Firewalls and IDS Countermeasures:**
    - Administratively shut down a switch port interface associated with a system from which attacks are being launched.
    - Perform bifurcating analysis, in which the monitor deals with ambiguous traffic streams by instantiating separate analysis threats for each possible interpretation of the ambiguous traffic.
    - Maintain security vulnerability awareness, patch vulnerabilities as soon as possible and wisely choose the IDS based on the network topology and network traffic received.
    - Generate TCP RST packets to tear down malicious TCP session any issues of several available ICMP error code packets in response to malicious traffic UDP traffic.
    - Interact with the external firewall or router to add a general rule to block all communication from individual IP addresses or entire networks.
    - Keep updating the IDS systems and firewall software regularly.
    - Implement a traffic normalizer a network forwarding element that attempts to eliminate ambiguous network traffic and reduce the amount of connection state that the monitor must attain.

Figure 5. Interaction model of threats, vulnerabilities, risks, and countermeasures

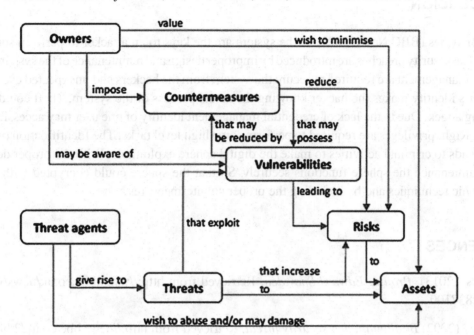

Other Attacks

- With the open nature of digital sphere, anyone can breach the security system and may perform any illegal activities to change the actual work flow of it.
- By performing such Illegal activities an attacker may perform such intrusion attacks. This kind of attack may lead to failure the security of an entire system.
- Cryptographic methods are used to safeguarding the access management. Insecure storage of cryptographic encryption details makes the credential theft easier for the attackers.
- Failed to Protect Transport layer, URL access, File execution, Network access helps to breach the security system.

Attack Summary

The Figure 5 shows that interaction model of threats, vulnerabilities, risks and countermeasures.

7. FUTURE WORK

This chapter gives a broader view of the threats, vulnerabilities and attacks associated with the digital sphere. From the reviewed threats and the corresponding countermeasures, it is possible to secure the digital sphere in effective way. Further the problems are reviewed and experimented to analyze the performance. From this additional security controls are added up to strengthen the digital sphere from these kinds of unwanted situations.

8. CONCLUSION

Security Breaches (BBC News, 2002) of the system are the keys to an attacker to perform such illegal activities. The security breaches are introduced by improper design and maintenance of the system. Identity and access management are required to secure the system from the hackers and unexpected events. Theft of one user's identity makes the hacker knowing the actual process of the system. Theft could perform by spoofing attack. Due to the lack of credential management identity of one user may accessible by the other user. Right privileges are required to perform some high level tasks. The Identification of security breaches leads to criminal activities to make the digital sphere exploitable. With the proper design and control maintenance the sphere functions securely. So that the sphere could encrypted with the right cryptographic techniques and by including the proper countermeasures.

REFERENCES

BBC News. (2013). *Profile: Edward Snowden.* Retrieved from http://www.bbc.co.uk/news/world-us-canada-22837100

BBC News. (2002) *Battling the net security threat.* Retrieved from http://news.bbc.co.uk/2/hi/technology/2386113.stm

Clearswift. (2013). *The enemy within.* Retrieved from http://www.clearswift.com/sites/default/files/images/ blog/enemy-within.pdf

Department of Justice. (2010). *Another pleads guilty in botnet hacking conspiracy.* Retrieved from http://www.cybercrime.gov/smithPlea2.pdf

Gao, H., Hu, J., Huang, T., Wang, J., & Chen, Y. (2011). Security issues in online social networks. *IEEE Internet Computing, 15*(4), 56–63. doi:10.1109/MIC.2011.50

Jagatic, T., Johnson, N., Jakobsson, M., & Menczer, F. (2005). Social phishing. *Communications of the ACM, 50*(10), 94–100. doi:10.1145/1290958.1290968

Kasperski. (2008). *Kaspersky Lab Detects New Worms Attacking MySpace and Facebook.* Retrieved from http://www.kaspersky.com/news?id=207575670

Lehto. (2015). Phenomena in the Cyber World. InCyber Security: Analytics, Technology and Automation. Academic Press.

Marinos. (2012). *ENISA threat landscape: Responding to the evolving threat environment.* ENISA.

Pinguelo & Muller. (2011). Virtual crimes, Real damages. *VJLT, 16*(1).

10. th CSI/FBI Survey Shows "Dramatic Increase in Unauthorized Access". (2005). *IT Professional Magazine.*

Woollaston, V. (2013, July 30). Revealed, what happens in just ONE minute on the internet. *Daily Mail Online.*

KEY TERMS AND DEFINITIONS

Attack: An attempt to break the security of a system by exploiting the threats and vulnerabilities associated with it. In general, attack was performed to destroy or steal the sensitive information.

Threat: Any kind of danger that could exploit a vulnerability of a security system. These threats are associated with the applications, services, products used by the end users.

Vulnerability: Vulnerability is a weakness which allows an attacker to reduce the assurance of an information system. It is susceptible by a system's flaw that may give an access to the attacker to exploiting it.

Chapter 2
Advances in Biometrics for Secure Human Authentication System:
Biometric Authentication System

Jagannath Mohan
VIT University, India

Adalarasu Kanagasabai
PSNA College of Engineering and Technology, India

Vetrivelan Pandu
VIT University, India

ABSTRACT

In the recent decade, one of our major concerns in the global technological society of information security is confirmation that a person accessing confidential information is authorized to perform so. Such mode of access is generally accomplished by a person's confirming their identity by the use of some method of authentication system. In present days, the requirement for safe security in storing individual information has been developing rapidly and among the potential alternative is implementing innovative biometric identification techniques. This chapter discusses how the advent of the 20th century has brought forth the security principles of identification and authentication in the field of biometric analysis. The chapter reviews vulnerabilities in biometric authentication and issues in system implementation. The chapter also proposes the multifactor authentication and the use of multimodal biometrics, i.e., the combination of Electrocardiogram (ECG) and Phonocardiogram (PCG) signals to enhance reliability in the authentication process.

DOI: 10.4018/978-1-5225-0193-0.ch002

INTRODUCTION

Security plays an important part in contemporary day situation where identity fake and radicalism possesses biggest risk. These continually increasing criminal and terrorist acts in government/private properties, public places resulted in chaotic scenarios thereby making the existing security systems questionable – "How effective is the security system to prevent unlawful activities?", "Does the existing system guarantee the required level of security?", "Is the system user friendly?". In early stages, the identity management systems relied on cryptographic methods (knowledge based) requiring the users to remember a secret text (password) or keep something with them (token, card) or a combination of both to prove their identity. Consequently, the population is flooded with passwords and tokens to gain access to required resources for instance; access control, computer logins, e-mail checking, making internet banking, conflict zones etc. However, the users challenged the efficacy of such systems through the queries such as, "What happens, if I forget/lost my password/token?", "How many passwords/cards I have to remember/keep?". As an answer, from the middle of the 20th century, the rise of new technologies in order to assess bodily or behavioural features of human has given the word, Biometry, a newer connotation for security applications. The idea of human identification and authentication based on bodily (physiological) or behavioural attributes of individuals is proposed and very often termed as Biometrics. Biometrics is described as programmed recognition of persons based on their unique bodily (iris, face, fingerprint, etc.) or behavioural (voice, signature, gait, etc.) characteristics (Jain et al., 2004; Jain & Kumar, 2012). In modern decade, the need for improvement in security for personal information storage has grown steeply and among the expedient alternatives is one which employs inventive biometric system. Although biometrics is not the perfect solution but it offers several advantages over knowledge and possession based approaches in the way that there is no need to remember anything, biometric attributes cannot be lost, transferred or stolen, offer better security due to fact that these attributes are very challenging to falsify and involve the manifestation of honest user while permitting access to specific resources. Inspired from the development of Bertillon's system in 1883 to Sir John Galton's elementary fingerprint recognition system in 1903, the research community devoted their efforts to discover several biometric modalities.

Any physiological or behavioral attribute can qualify for being a biometric trait unless it satisfies the criteria such as:

1. **Universality:** Possessed by all humans,
2. **Distinctiveness:** Discriminative amongst the population,
3. **Invariance:** The selected biometric attribute must exhibit invariance against time,
4. **Collectability:** Easily collectible in terms of acquisition, digitization and feature extraction from the population,
5. **Performance:** Pertains to the availability of resources and imposition of real constraints in terms of data collection and guarantee to achieve high accuracy,
6. **Acceptability:** Willingness of population to submit that attribute to recognition system, and
7. **Circumvention:** Prone to imitation or mimicry in case of fraudulent attacks against the recognition system (Jain et al., 2004).

Based on the criteria, several distinctive human characteristics are identified and tested. Instead of the broad categories (physiological, behavioral and soft attributes), for convenience the physiological modalities can be further sub-divided into different sub-categories according to their respective position in human body such as:

1.   Hand region attributes,
2.   Facial region attributes,
3.   Ocular and periocular region attributes,
4.   Behavioral attributes, and
5.   Medico-chemical attributes.

The sub-division is illustrated in Figure 1.

The chapter is written with an objective to provide an overview of advances in biometrics for secure human authentication system technology to the readers.

Figure 1. Classification of biometric modalities
Adapted from Unar et al., 2014.

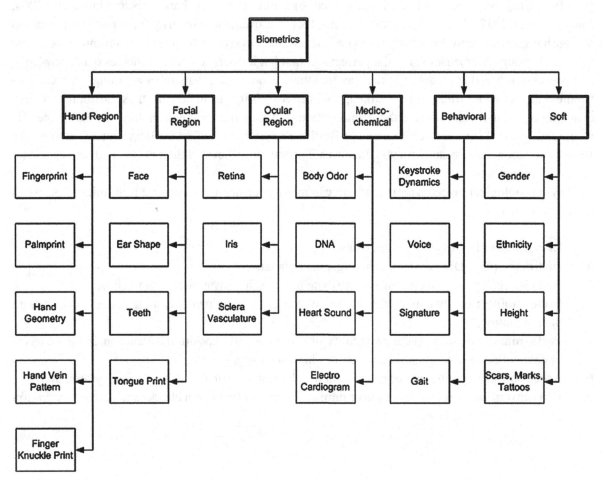

BACKGROUND

The term "biometrics" came from Greek word. The word "bio" means life and "metrics" means to measure (Rood & Hornak, 2008). Biometrics is the process of authenticating the individual that he is claimed to be real. Authentication of an individual can be performed in three ways:

1. One the individual has (key and smart card),
2. One that individual remembers (password), and
3. Something the person is (fingerprints, palmprints and footprint).

Biometrics utilizes anatomic distinctiveness of an individual and as trail it can be used for identification of an individual. Such distinctive features from automated biometrics system can be used to avoid unofficial access to specific system by examining unique physiological or behavioural features that identifies the individual.

Based on the application context, any biometric recognition system can be functioned in any of the modes: authentication mode and identification mode (Kyoso & Uchiyama, 2001; Jain et al., 2008; O'gorman, 2003). The authentication of an individual involves verifying the identities they declare; and the identification of an individual corresponds to recognizing those declared identities, while the individual may be known or not about this identification mode being performed. Biometric has become a leading light in identification systems which are slowly supplementing the well-established security codes like passwords. A biometric application consists of three phases (Pal et al., 2015):

1. Enrolment phase, where biometric data from a person is stored,
2. Recognition phase, where a person gets connected to working environment and biometric data is detected and matched with data stored at enrolment time, and
3. Decision phase.

The identification process involves analysis of similarity between the different samples and estimation of the equality by means of matching scores. Biometric models having high scores show that they originate from same person.

The workflow of general biometric system is depicted as in Figure 2. Biometric process uses pattern recognition method by extracting distinctive features which is generally refered as biometric models (recognition phase) and comparing these models with information stored in the authentication system (enrolment phase). The identification operation executes equality analysis between the models and estimates the matching scores.

Historical Eras of Biometrics

The concepts of biometrics have been evolved since many decades. The momentary historical eras of biometrics systems is shown in Table 1. The first indications of biometrics acted in 29,000 BC as the cavemen get involved their fingerprints to create a logo on their drawings. Babylonians used their fingerprints to sign in their business transaction accounts in clay tablets. The first documented substantiation of usage of biometrics system was in early Egypt. During the course of construction of Khufu pyramid, one officer in a group suggested to systemize the food providing system to workers. He documented all

Figure 2. Biometric matching process between recognition and enrolment models which generates score based on the similarity analysis

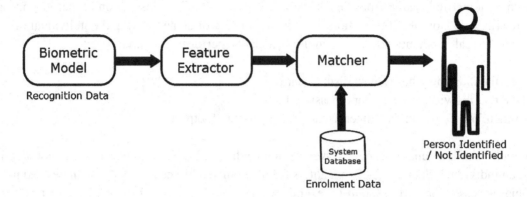

details about the construction workers (name, age, position, work unit, etc.). But in the later stage, many workers started cheated him; then the officer created a system of recording their bodily and behavioral features. In 14th century, biometrics was very famous among merchants in China. Technology of premature biometrics system was pretty simple. People used paper and ink to take children's palmprints and footprints to distinguish them from one another. Such biometrics system is the most widespread across the world and is quiet in use in all time due to its simplicity.

Biometrics Modalities

This section provides an overview of different biometric modalities. Physiological systems of identification are more reliable when specific features of an individual do not alter by stimulus of psycho-emotional state. Such systems involve with statistical features of an individual: fingerprints, palmprint, hand geometry, iris and facial recognition, DNA.

Table 1. Momentary historical eras of biometrics systems

Year	Event
1965	North American Aviation developed the first automatic signature recognition system
1985	The US Defense Department in the Naval Postgraduate School used the first retinal scanning system for secure access
1990	Daugman of Cambridge University developed the iris recognition system
1993	Palm System created the first automated Fingerprint Identification System (AFIS)
2000	The US Government agencies performed the first face recognition vendor test
2003	Fujitsu Laboratories Limited, Vietnam introduced the first palm vein recognition system
2004	The US Government agencies deployed the first state-wide automated palmprint database
Present	On-going research on bio-signal based biometrics systems

Figure 3. A typical hand region biometric modality: fingerprints

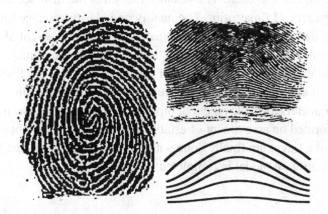

Fingerprints

Fingerprints are considered as the most first-born and popular biometrics system. Fingerprint biometrics system is also recognized as dactyloskopy. The dactyloskopy is the process of matching two samples of skin imprint from human fingers, palm or toes (Jain & Feng, 2011). The fingerprint biometrics system aids police to perform investigation on crimes during extensive period. The interesting fact numerous particulars about an individual can be identified using fingerprints (Figure 3).

Moreover the variety of fingerprints is grounded on distinctiveness of papillary pattern, fingerprints can be varied based on the pace of taken and/ or where it can be applied (Jain & Feng, 2011; Liu, 2010):

- Examplar prints are termed as known prints which intentionally collected to apply them for number of uses: to register to working environment, also when an individual is under arrest. It is observed that the way of taking fingerprints using ink and white paper is generally applied here.
- Latent prints are unintentionally missing on some surface. Technologies in the form of physical, chemical, electronic can make latent unseen print visible.
- Patent prints are noticeable to the naked eyes due to transfer of external material from human finger to the surface. They require no additional technologies due to their visibility.
- Plastic prints are embossed in the material that rests their profile. They are noticeable and there is no requirement of any extra technologies.
- Electronic recording: In present days, many sophisticated techniques appear to be easy accessible. For example, stolen cell phones, I-pads and notebooks can transmit information to the nearby police station with offender's photo and so on.

The goal of all fingerprint readers is to evaluate the physical variance between the pattern of ridges and the valleys. The technique of capturing the fingerprint comprises of sensor made with rolling and touching mechanism. The sensor senses the pattern of ridges and valleys between two persons based on their physical attributes. The reliability of the results from this technique shows varying and non-uniform appearance. This is based on the fact that the difference in the direction of finger impression, applied pressure and skin tone. In order to overcome these difficulties, innovative three-dimensional (3-D) fingerprint scanner was developed in 2010. The 3-D scanner performs the operation of rolling the finger by means of digital approach. The scanner measures the distance between adjacent points and creates the image pattern of fingerprint. The quality and clarity enhanced image pattern allows to gather all the necessary details. In order to authenticate a person, it is essential to obtain the image of papillary pattern by means of special scanner. Additionally, the obtained image needs to be processed and special features like end of lines, bifurcation of lines and crossing the lines are to be found. The comparative arrangement and related parameters are recorded for each feature. The cumulative results of such features and parameters form the model of biometric characteristic. The method of identification and verification is performed on assessment of established model with the obtained one. The verification and identification of a finger are finally done with the help of the confident level of accord and the inference about identification of model is completed.

Palmprint

Palmprint discusses about an image taken from the palm area of the individual hand. The palmprint is generally refered as a technique of biometrics with fingerprints and iris recognition techniques. The palmprint is a unique technique that can easily be attained with low resolution scanning machine. The scanning machine is inexpensive. However this mechanism is similar to others that are followed for fingerprints technique but its size is somewhat bulky which makes the restriction of implementing in mobile devices. The palmprint technique is compatible for everybody and moreover it has got one big advantage: it needs no personal data. The palm of each individual comprises of principle lines, secondary lines, wrinkles, valley and ridges. The palm of the hand also covers information such as texture, marks and indents which are considered during comparison process of the palmprint with other palmprints.

The palmprinting has its particular benefits as compared to other techniques of biometrics system. The age of a person does not affect the palmprint (the ageing factor is the foremost problem for facial recognition). Many people choose palmprint technique to iris recognition technique because the palmprinting is harmless to the health of people (Huang et al., 2008). The palmprinting is considered to be one of the rapidly developed techniques of biometrics system. Recognizing veins of the palm is one of the alternatives of palmprinting. This technique uses infra-red scanning camera that captures the photo of inner and external side of the palm. The infra-red light is absorbed by the haemoglobin and veins are shown as black outlines (Kong et al., 2009). This technique is touch-less and reliable. The major disadvantage of this technique is that we should perform scanning only in dark environment.

Hand Geometry

Hand geometry technique uses the anthropometric of the hand for biometrics. This technique has been used for more than ten years ago but in present days it is rarely in practice. The technique follows the fact that the hand shape of an individual varies from the hand shape of another individual. Moreover, the shape of the hand does not alter after the certain age group but the technique is not distinctive. The major features of this technique are determining and recording the length, width of the fingers, hand surface area, proximal and distal joints distance and knuckles shape.

The technique of hand geometry has its own merits and demerits. Simplicity and user friendly are the core merits of this technique. The scanning device is cheap. It is comparatively very easy to gather hand geometry information that makes this technique superior than fingerprinting. Factors like skin tone, texture, color, etc. does not make any impact in the results. The weaknesses of the technique are that it cannot be applied in identification process and has huge data storage. The hand geometry technique is more suitable for grown-ups but not appropriate for budding kids as their hand features changes regularly over time.

Iris Recognition

Iris is a distinctive feature of an individual. The trabecular meshwork is the main feature of iris which divides the iris in a circular manner. Iris is shaped in the gestation period of eighth month. Iris recognition is the precise technique of biometrics as the iris is unchanging during the entire life time. Iris is sheltered by aqueous humour, cornea and eyelid that accomplish the likelihood harm nominal not like fingerprint technique (Santos & Hoyle, 2012). Different people follow different steps; certain people split the method of iris recognition into two phases, and many into three (capturing the eye image, locating the iris and recognizing the localized region). The process is very similar to the facial recognition technique.

Iris recognition technique is convenient for enrolment, accomplishing the procedure less time consuming and safe. If any individual used to wears optical glass need to remove it at the time of initial enrolment procedure to prevent reflection. And it is not required for those who wear contact lenses because wearing lens will not create any effect on the procedure, they will not create reflection. This technique provides no physical contact between the user and vision of the camera. This technique also provides high degree of accuracy with incredible high speed and scalability. However, the iris recognition technique has some disadvantages. The iris organ is small in size and it is very difficult to perform scanning from long distance. People with eye problems such as cataracts and blindness will have difficulty in undergoing the procedure followed in the course of iris recognition (Marsico et al., 2012). This procedure also requires appropriate illumination to capture iris image.

Facial Recognition

Human being has the tendency to differentiate one individual from the other by looking at the face (Abate et al., 2007). Facial (face) detection is a surveillance application that automatically recognizes or detects an individual by means of an image or a video from the digital camera. The simplest way to perform this is to do comparison of the given image with the images already stored in the database. Each person's face has a various unique characteristics. Face IT contains eighty (80) nodal points and the specialized software can be used to measure some of these points (Zhang & Gao, 2009):

- Eyes distance,
- Nose width,
- Eye sockets depth,
- Cheekbones shape,
- Jaw line length.

A special code is formulated by quantifying these nodal points. Such code is termed as face print that denotes the actual face in the primary information database. We can classify the facial detection technologies into two methods (Figure 4):

Figure 4. Facial recognition: 2-D and 3-D technologies

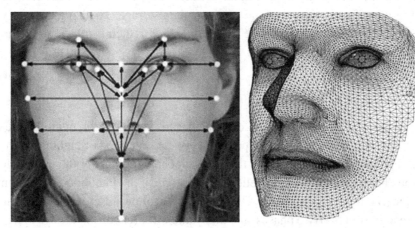

1. **Two-Dimensional (2-D) Face IT:** It was considered to be the most unreliable method of biometrics. This technique is widely applied in criminalistics. The computer form of the 2-D technique seemed creating this reasonably reliable now. This technique does not require any costly device, but intensely be determined by the incident light. There are some limitations to this method that needs to be addressed. Difficulties may arise if the individual has worn sun-glass, beard, etc. The facial expression should be unbiased and sitting posture should be straight to the vision of the camera.

2. **Three-Dimensional (3-D) Face IT:** There are numerous techniques existing for 3-D facial detection. We cannot compare these techniques because they all have diverse scanning mechanisms and databases. The benefit of this technique is that it does not require any contact and it is less sensitive to factors such as sun-glass, beard, hair style, hair colour. This 3-D facial detection technique demonstrates the statistical reliability that can be used as supportive tool with fingerprinting. However, the detriment of the technique is the costly device; change in the facial expression decreases the high degree of reliability of the technique.

The conventional technique of facial detection is the construction of projection model of the human face. Initially, a human face is projected onto the flexible grid. Further, it is captured by camera that creates photos of ten frames per second and the captured photos are processed and analyzed with the developed program. The ray incidents onto the curved surface, that creates bending of ray. The visible bright light is initially used, but at the later stage it is transformed to the infra-red light. At pre-stage level, the program erases all the stored photos wherever the face is not perceived at all. The sun-glass, beard and other needless things is also deleted. Further, the 3-D model of the face is then constructed. The next phase is the examination of the 3-D model which includes different anthropometrical features are extracted and assigned to the unique code.

Typically, face recognition method involves four steps:

1. **Detection:** Human being finds no difficulty in differentiating the individual from another by looking at the face. But the computer finds it hard to differentiate the face. The computer programme need to take decision on what portion of the image is required and what is not required. It is very easy if the photo's background is plain white, rather it tends to be tougher if some other colour complex background is present.

2. **Normalization:** Once the face detection step is over, normalization step is followed. It needs to be homogeneous in relation with position, size, and aspect ratio of the image in the stored database. The computer program localizes the facial points. Based on these points the program can generate a minor deviation of the image. The recognition step gets fail if facial points are not able to be located.

3. **Feature Extraction:** Biometric model is produced using recognition algorithm. This algorithm transforms the facial image to a mathematical expression to accomplish a recognition task. This model is kept in the information database and considered to be the key element of any recognition process. It is essential that detailed information need be reserved for effective recognition. The algorithm cannot produce effective recognition if the above condition is not valid, and the process will get unsuccessful.

4. **Recognition:** In this process, we have two steps: one is identification and the other is verification. The verification step involves matching of the image with only one stored image in the information database. The identification step involves comparing the image with all stored images in the information database.

Deoxyribonucleic Acid (DNA)

Deoxyribonucleic acid (DNA) is the portion of a cell which holds genetic data distinctive for each individual. DNA typing is one of the productive techniques that identifies and analyses sample of DNA to differentiate individuals with high probability degree. This technique of recognizing a person is relatively common in criminalistics. DNA technique is the only technique of biometrics which has manual procedures and the test takes hours to generate the result. However this technique is well taken to be the most consistent technique. This technique solves many complicated cases and unsolved crimes. In comparison with other techniques of biometrics those are dependent on the distinctive parts of the individual, for example, fingerprints, iris, etc., the technique of DNA is unique one. The same DNA results arise from the twins. The DNA result remains unchanged over time. The DNA sample can be extracted from various bases: blood, hair, urine, ear wax, chewed gum, glass, paper or plastic cups, socks, sweat T-shirt, etc.

The key benefit of DNA technique is that it detects detailed kinds of syndromes, identifies the tendency to various categories of breast cancer. DNA is also an essential test in finding foreign bodies. The DNA sample is easily stolen one; this is probably the demerit of this technique. In consideration with the recent trends of DNA testing in areas such as physical and network security, the factor purely based on the specialists and their capability to allow the technique more efficient. The DNA sample test is pretty expensive these days.

Biometrics Prospects

We have several biometric devices that are commercially inexpensive and standard in the marketplace such as keystroke, speech, iris, facial, fingerprinting and gait (Jain et al., 2004; Faundez-Zanuy, 2004; O'gorman, 2003; Peter, 2003). The most popular four aspects of physical characteristics that are being applied in person authentication are:

- **Fingerprint:** Has been in practice for several years by legal administration and other government and non-government organizations. It is considered as reliable and distinctive identifier.
- **Speech Recognition:** Analyses a speech print (voice) that helps to examine how an individual pronounces a particular vocabulary or sentence distinctive to other person (Dustor & Szwarc, 2010).
- **Iris:** Used to check an individual's identity by examining the characteristics of blood vessels in the retinal area and color patterns of the iris (Palaniappan & Raveendran, 2002).
- **Facial Recognition:** Captures distinctive facial characteristics to recognize a person.

The above mentioned modalities or techniques are not completely reliable with respect to identification accuracy. They are also not robust against falsifications. Table 2 depicts the demerits of various traditional biometric modalities.

The forecasted revenue share for each modality (Acuity, 2007) is illustrated in Figure 5. Nevertheless, USA and most of the European countries are in a leading position due to early adoption of biometric based identity management in terms of visa enrolments, passports, border control, criminal identification along with e-commerce and e-banking. However, the analysts are predicting the biometric market shift towards Asia Pacific region in near future due to the continuous efforts from governments in terms of citizen registration, passports and driving licenses. Besides Japan, Singapore and Taiwan which are already leading the way in biometrics based surveillance and access control management in the region, the substantial demands from financial institutions in China, India and Malaysia are growing (Lane, 2011). The exemplary evidences include issuance of multi biometric National Identity Card like Indian government's Aadhaar/Unique ID project which has been ranked as world's largest biometric project (Romero, 2012) through Unique Identification authority of India (UIDAI).

Multifactor Human Authentication

Instead of the tremendous advances in biometric technology the recognition systems based on the measurement of single modality cannot guarantee 100% accuracy (Unar et al., 2014). This is due to influence of several factors such as noisy information, intra-class disparities, spoof attacks and individuality. In fact, these factors laid the foundation of the systems which use multiple independent evidences of biometric information from either single or different biometric modalities, very often termed as multimodal

Table 2. Traditional biometric modalities and their demerits

Biometric Modality	Vulnerability
Signature	Can be reproduced by professional forger
Speech Recognition	Can be simply imitated or pre-recorded and playback
Fingerprint	Can be falsified by using gypsum based plaster (latex) or acquired the impression from the surface played by the individual and restored in latex
Iris Recognition	Can be replicated using contact lens by copying iris topographies on it
Facial Recognition	Can be exposed to artificial mask or captured by cam recorder
Deoxyribonucleic acid (DNA)	Can be stolen from an unsuspecting person

Figure 5. Global market by biometrics technology

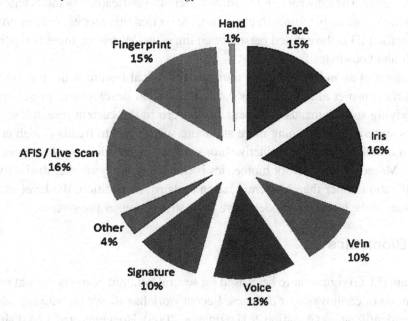

biometric systems. Keeping in view the bottlenecks attached with mono-modal systems, it is obvious that multimodal systems offer more robustness in terms of recognition accuracy as well as handling the poor quality of biometric attributes.

These systems use multiple uncorrelated biometric signatures acquired through different imaging sensors. For example, iris and palm print of an individual is combined to establish the identity. Such systems offer better accuracy and show robustness against illumination conditions, sensor operating conditions, and improper contact with the imaging sensors. However, they require effective dimensionality reduction techniques. In addition, the multiple modalities must be selected from different regions containing biometric features. For example, fingerprint along with face or iris etc. Selecting the modalities requiring different image resolution will help to overcome the problem of improper illumination. For instance, face combined with palm print, or iris combined with fingerprint.

A multimodal biometric system functions in two modes; (i) Serial/cascaded mode: the acquired multiple traits are processed one after another. The output of one trait serves as an input to the processing of next trait. Within the frame of this scheme, the first modality is normally used as an index to narrow down the search space before the next modality is processed which in turn results in the reduction of recognition time, (ii) Parallel mode: multiple modalities are processed simultaneously and the obtained results are combined together to obtain a final match score. This architecture provides better accuracy but requires more time to establish the identity.

FUTURE RESEARCH DIRECTIONS

Human recognition is increasingly becoming important process in our day-to-day lives. In modern days, the practice of a robust and reliable biometrics system to identify the legality of the person is pretty essential particularly in personnel security, military, commercial use, economics, airfield, clinic, and several other vital areas. The drawback of the current identity verification methods based on knowledge factors such as token system, pin number, password, etc. is that this process cannot prove whether the holder of the specified ID is the entitled person or an imposter. Moreover, there is no direct connection between the user and knowledge factor.

The identification of an individual using a unique biological feature is the need of the hour in the society now-a-days (Phua et al., 2008). Hence, the design and development of automatic biometrics systems for satisfying such demands is a focus of concern in the current research scenario. Conventional biometrics systems are becoming more and more susceptible to frauds (Singh et al., 2012). The recognition of an individual using a distinctive biometric characteristic is very essential in the world at the present time. Moreover, this type of biometrics is characterized by smaller distinctiveness; they are used in the verification rather than in identification systems. In addition, the level of security is also increased, because all the biometric models have to be stolen to enter the system.

ECG Based Biometrics

Electrocardiogram (ECG) signals have been used for several hundred years for patient well-being monitoring and diagnosis of cardiovascular diseases. Recent work has shown the validity of the cardiogram signal for human identification (Agrafioti & Hatzinakos, 2009). Hoekema et al. (2001) have analytically stated that every person has a unique ECG which characterizes the electrical impulse generated from the heart and that is being proposed in the field of biometrics. The new biometrics techniques have been investigated, like the heartbeat rhythm picked up by ECG signal. According to Agrafioti & Hatzinakos (2009), the ECG signal has been explored as a biometry since ten years ago. The study has revealed favourable outcomes. The procedure to acquire the ECG signal is very simple and non-invasive. This enables us to employ ECG as a biometric tool.

The ECG indicates life so it is used as a liveness detector. The ECG of every individual is highly unique and personal. Therefore, it is hard to be mimicked and simulated. In recent times, many researchers have initiated to examine the usage of ECG as a biometric tool (Kyoso & Uchiyama, 2001; Sörnmo & Laguna, 2005). The opportunity to apply ECG as a biometric tool is sustained by the fact that there is distinctiveness in the individual ECG due to the geometrical and physiological changes of the heart of different individuals. The individual's ECG reading shows the heterogeneous patterns, typically due to alteration in amplitudes and time intervals of the ECG waveform. This heterogeneous pattern among persons is due to the fact that there is a difference in dimensions, location and bodily state of their heart. The way in which the electrical phenomenon of the heart hints to changes in person's myocardium which as well shows a vital role in generating distinctive rhythm of heartbeat (Simon & Eswaran, 1997).

PCG Based Biometrics

Like ECG, phonocardiogram (PCG) which represents the heart sounds as well have evidence about a person's body functioning. A PCG signal possesses a distinctive identity of each individual (Phua et al., 2008; Kumar & Jagannath, 2015). ECG and PCG signals are hard to mask and hence minimizes forgery in human identification system. PCG shares its source with the ECG, but conveys distinctive information of an individual that can be used in biometric applications. However, exhibition of the feasibility in using ECG signal for person recognition is under progress in terms of commercial product. This conceptual idea has drawn the considerations in using PCG signal also as a biometric tool.

Figure 6. Block diagram of proposed human authentication system

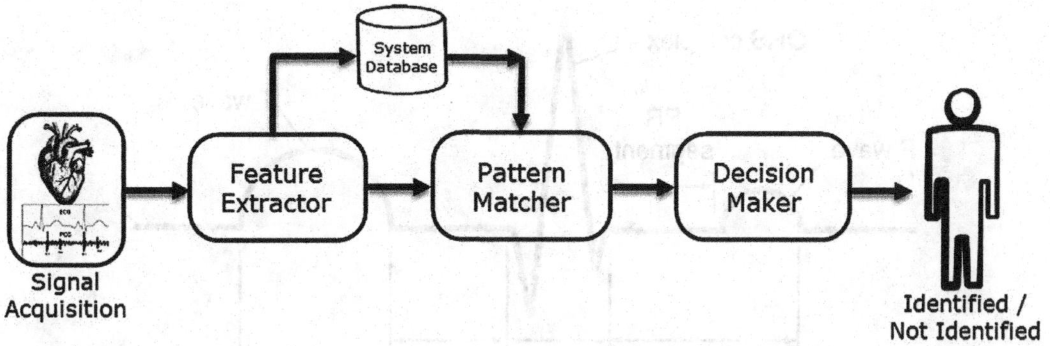

Proposed Secure Human Authentication System

In the proposed system authentication methods comprises of two steps (phases). In the first step, the information database is formed where the biometric model which defines each person is stored (enrolment phase). In the second step (authentication phase), the comparison of the extracted feature sets is made with the biometric model stored in the information database to perceive the similarity (identification mode) or compared with the feature template of the claimed identity (verification mode).

The general approach to the proposed ECG and PCG based human authentication system consists of five functional elements (modules) (Figure 6):

1. Data/ signal acquisition element which contains the ECG electrode system and electronic stethoscope used to acquire the heart's electrical activity and heart sound of an individual. The acquired signals typically span 10-60 seconds.
2. Feature extraction element used to extract a set of prominent and discriminatory features from the acquired signals after processing.
3. Pattern matching element performs the comparison between the features extracted during recognition step and the stored models to produce a similarity score. The similarity score is a measure of the match of the input extracted feature set to the stored database biometric model.
4. Decision making element confirms the user's claimed identity (verification) or establishes the user's identity (identification) depends on the similarity score.
5. Database element stores the biometric models of the registered (enrolled) users.

In this chapter, a new biometrics system is described which adopts two modalities: ECG and PCG. The first one is chosen because it is a source of physical features and behavioral ones. The main advantages of this modality are that it can be acquired only from a living person and that it is very hard to steal or forge someone ECG. The second modality is the PCG, which is another source of biometric features. Furthermore, measurement of the heart sound is entirely non-invasive and socially acknowledged.

Once the ECG and PCG signals are obtained from the user, filtering from baseline wander and power line interference, body movement, myogram artifact, etc. has to be performed to prevent incorrect estimation of biometric features that might ultimately cause misclassification (Kyoso & Uchiyama, 2001). Visual trace of each ECG signal exposes three projections from baseline. These projections are named

Figure 7. A typical ECG waveform with fiducial points

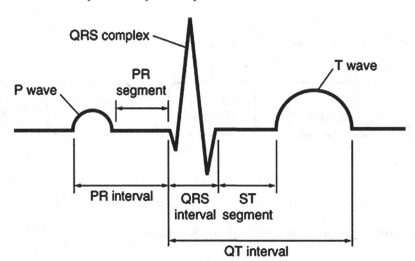

as waves and are labeled as P, QRS and T waves (Figure 7). Each individual has certain distinctiveness in their ECG based on the functional and geometrical variations of the heart (Israel et al., 2005). This allows for recommending ECG as a new biometric approach and it is difficult to be spoofed or falsified.

The feature extraction methods of ECG based biometric approach fall into two major categories namely,

- Methods based on fiducial points (time domain techniques).
- Methods not based on the fiducial points (frequency domain techniques).

In this chapter, the fiducial method is proposed where individual parameters are extracted using some characteristic points (called fiducial points) because they are widely used in medical diagnosis. The eleven (11) fiducial points from each heartbeat in an ECG waveform consists of P, R and T (three peak points), Q and S (two valleys) and the six onsets and offsets for the three waves. Henceforth fiducial features characterize the temporal and amplitude distances between fiducial points. In this method, two techniques would be used for feature extraction. The first method uses the linear predictive coding. The second method uses the wavelet packet decomposition (WPD) where the features would be extracted using the second order Daubechies (db2) wavelet in 5-level decomposition. Then classification would be performed using three-layer back propagation neural network for user authentication.

The possibility of using PCG signal is also investigated as a biometric tool for identifying a person based on the succeeding objectives:

- **Universal:** All living individual's heart beats until their death.
- **Quantifiable:** We can measure the PCG signal by means of an electronic stethoscope. Two sounds (S1 and S2) are typically generated as blood streams through the heart valves in the course of each cardiac cycle (Figure 8). We can hear the sounds associated with the opening and closing of four valves by positioning a microphone on the various auscultation points on the chest wall.
- **Uniqueness and Vulnerability:** The bodily condition of a person's well-being, age, size, structure, height, weight of the heart and also the genetics aspects all contribute to a person's distinctive heart sound. The heart sounds of two individuals having the identical heart diseases also differ.

Figure 8. Waveform of first heart sound S1 and second heart sound S2

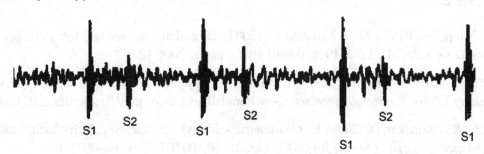

We need to design an artificial pumping mechanism with the same anatomy of the heart that requires to be reconstructed to replicate the same heart sound of a person; the physical characteristic surrounding the artificial heart should also match the same characteristics of the individual. Henceforth, the fact is that heart sound cannot be easily simulated accurately.

- **Usability:** With the development in sensor technology that the sensor can eventually be positioned on the individual to record his heart signals when he is moving or doing some activities. These signals can be sent to remote location using wireless communication with internet of things to determine the accessibility and identification of the person. Therefore, authentication of an individual can be completed even earlier the individual reaches the gate, thereby causing time consumption.
- **Variability:** In a controlled environment and recording procedure, the human ECG and PCG remain adequately invariant over a specific period of time.

CONCLUSION

Biometrics has been evolved from the ancient period and is extensively applied in the present days. It is a challenging and interesting area because many people consider that biometrics is just used in criminalistics. But the fact is that the foremost improvement of biometrics is security, that demonstrates how truthful and courteously people give importance to their private materials. Biometrics is now wide spread all over the world. The key authorization of this is biometric passports, aadhar card and voter identity card. Almost all the countries, biometric passports have the same details: digital image of the person (owner), surname and given names, nationality, date of birth, sex, number of the passport, date of issue, date of expiry and country code.

In this chapter, the synopsis of the existing biometric systems is discussed in addition with their classification and performance analysis. This chapter also provides an overview on several biometric attributes with their potential merits and limitations. Despite the challenges, the market trend presented in the chapter portrays a keen interest in biometric solutions to a number of identity management tasks. However, the limitations of mono-modal biometric systems forced the researchers to search for more options. Consequently, the multimodal biometrics system is proposed. Multimodality based systems offer better accuracy as compared to mono-modal systems.

REFERENCES

Abate, A., Nappi, M., Riccio, D., & Sabatino, G. (2007). 2D and 3D face recognition: A survey. *Pattern Recognition Letters, 28*(14), 1885–1906. doi:10.1016/j.patrec.2006.12.018

Acuity. (2007). *Market intelligence, biometrics market development: Mega trends and meta drivers.* Retrieved January 2, 2016, from http://www.acuity-mi.com/hdfsjosg/euyotjtub/ Biometrics 2007 London.pdf

Agrafioti, F., & Hatzinakos, D. (2008). ECG biometric analysis in cardiac irregularity conditions. *Signal. Image and Video Processing SIViP, 3*(4), 329–343. doi:10.1007/s11760-008-0073-4

Dustor, A., & Szwarc, P. (2010). Spoken language identification based on GMM models.*International Conference on Signals and Electronic Systems (ICSES),* (pp. 105–108).

Faundez-Zanuy, M. (2004). On the vulnerability of biometric security systems. *IEEE Aerosp. Electron. Syst. Mag., 19*(6), 3–8.

Hoekema, R., Uijen, G., & Oosterom, A. (2001). Geometrical aspects of the interindividual variability of multilead ECG recordings. *IEEE Trans. Biomedical Engineering, 48,* 551–559.

Huang, D., Jia, W., & Zhang, D. (2008). Palmprint verification based on principal lines. *Pattern Recognition, 41*(4), 1316–1328. doi:10.1016/j.patcog.2007.08.016

Israel, S., Irvine, J., Cheng, A., Wiederhold, M., & Wiederhold, B. (2005). ECG to identify individuals. *Pattern Recognition, 38*(1), 133–142. doi:10.1016/j.patcog.2004.05.014

Jain, A., & Feng, J. (2011). Latent fingerprint matching. *IEEE Trans. Pattern Anal. Mach. Intell., 33*(1), 88–100. doi:10.1109/TPAMI.2010.59

Jain, A., Flynn, P., & Ross, A. (2008). *Handbook of biometrics.* New York: Springer. doi:10.1007/978-0-387-71041-9

Jain, A., & Kumar, A. (2012). Biometric recognition: An overview. *The International Library of Ethics, Law and Technology Second Generation Biometrics: The Ethical, Legal and Social Context, 11,* 49–79.

Jain, A., Ross, A., & Prabhakar, S. (2004). An introduction to biometric recognition. *IEEE Transactions on Circuits and Systems for Video Technology, 14*(1), 4–20. doi:10.1109/TCSVT.2003.818349

Kong, A., Zhang, D., & Kamel, M. (2009). A survey of palm print recognition. *Pattern Recognition, 42*(7), 1408–1418. doi:10.1016/j.patcog.2009.01.018

Kumar, S., & Jagannath, M. (2015). Analysis of phonocardiogram signal for biometric identification system.*International Conference on Pervasive Computing (ICPC),* (pp. 154-157).

Kyoso, M., & Uchiyama, A. (n.d.). Development of an ECG identification system. In *2001Conference Proceedings of the 23rd Annual International Conference of the IEEE Engineering in Medicine and Biology Society.* doi:10.1109/IEMBS.2001.1019645

Lane, L. (2011). Analyst finds thriving local markets in Asia Pacific. *Biometric Technology Today, 2011,* 2–2.

Liu, M. (2010). Fingerprint classification based on Adaboost learning from singularity features. *Pattern Recognition, 43*(3), 1062–1070. doi:10.1016/j.patcog.2009.08.011

Marsico, M., Nappi, M., & Riccio, D. (2012). Noisy iris recognition integrated scheme. *Pattern Recognition Letters, 33*(8), 1006–1011. doi:10.1016/j.patrec.2011.09.010

O'gorman, L. (2003). Comparing passwords, tokens, and biometrics for user authentication. *Proceedings of the IEEE, 91*(12), 2021–2040. doi:10.1109/JPROC.2003.819611

Pal, A., Gautam, A., & Singh, Y. (2015). Evaluation of bioelectric signals for human recognition. *Procedia Computer Science, 48*, 746–752. doi:10.1016/j.procs.2015.04.211

Palaniappan, R., & Raveendran, P. (2002). Individual identification technique using visual evoked potential signals. *Electron. Lett. Electronics Letters, 138*(25), 1634–1635. doi:10.1049/el:20021104

Peter, P. (2003). Biometrics continue to evolve. *Biometric Technology Today, 11*(9), 1–7.

Phua, K., Chen, J., Dat, T., & Shue, L. (2008). Heart sound as a biometric. *Pattern Recognition, 41*(3), 906–919. doi:10.1016/j.patcog.2007.07.018

Romero, J. (2012). *Fast start for world's biggest biometrics ID project*. Retrieved January 2, 2016, from http://spectrum.ieee.org/computing/it/fast-start-for-worlds-biggest-biometrics-id-project

Rood, E. P., & Hornak, L. A. (2003). Are you who you say you are? *World & I, 18*(8), 142.

Santos, G., & Hoyle, E. (2012). A fusion approach to unconstrained iris recognition. *Pattern Recognition Letters, 33*(8), 984–990. doi:10.1016/j.patrec.2011.08.017

Simon, B., & Eswaran, C. (1997). An ECG classifier designed using modified decision based neural networks. *Computers and Biomedical Research, an International Journal, 30*(4), 257–272. doi:10.1006/cbmr.1997.1446 PMID:9339321

Singh, Y., Singh, S., & Gupta, P. (2012). Fusion of electrocardiogram with unobtrusive biometrics: An efficient individual authentication system. *Pattern Recognition Letters, 33*(14), 1932–1941. doi:10.1016/j.patrec.2012.03.010

Sörnmo, L., & Laguna, P. (2005). EEG signal processing. *Bioelectrical Signal Processing in Cardiac and Neurological Applications,* (pp. 55-179).

Unar, J., Seng, W., & Abbasi, A. (2014). A review of biometric technology along with trends and prospects. *Pattern Recognition, 47*(8), 2673–2688. doi:10.1016/j.patcog.2014.01.016

Zhang, X., & Gao, Y. (2009). Face recognition across pose: A review. *Pattern Recognition, 42*(11), 2876–2896. doi:10.1016/j.patcog.2009.04.017

KEY TERMS AND DEFINITIONS

Authentication: A process in which the credentials provided are compared to those on file in a database of authorized users' information on a local operating system or within an authentication server. If the credentials match, the process is completed and the user is granted authorization for access. The permissions and folders returned define both the environment the user sees and the way he can interact with it, including hours of access and other rights such as the amount of allocated storage space.

Biometry: A measurement and statistical analysis of people's physical and behavioral characteristics. The technology is mainly used for identification and access control, or for identifying individuals that are under surveillance. The basic premise of biometric authentication is that everyone is unique and an individual can be identified by his or her intrinsic physical or behavioral traits. (The term "biometrics" is derived from the Greek words "bio" meaning life and "metric" meaning to measure).

DNA: Deoxyribonucleic acid; A nucleic acid that carries the genetic information in cells and some viruses, consisting of two long chains of nucleotides twisted into a double helix and joined by hydrogen bonds between the complementary bases adenine and thymine or cytosine and guanine. DNA sequences are replicated by the cell prior to cell division and may include genes, intergenic spacers, and regions that bind to regulatory proteins.

Electrocardiography: The process of recording the electrical activity of the heart over a period of time using electrodes placed on a patient's body. These electrodes detect the tiny electrical changes on the skin that arise from the heart muscle depolarizing during each heartbeat. It is commonly a non-invasive procedure for recording electrical changes in the heart. The record, which is called an electrocardiogram, shows the series of waves that relate to the electrical impulses which occur during each beat of the heart. The results are printed on paper or displayed on a monitor. The waves in a normal record are named P, Q, R, S, and T and follow in alphabetical order. The number of waves may vary, and other waves may be present.

Fingerprint: An impression or mark made on a surface by a person's fingertip, able to be used for identifying individuals from the unique pattern of whorls and lines on the fingertips.

Palmprint: A study of the structure of cutaneous designs of the palmar surface of the hand for identification purposes. In criminalistics it is used along with dactyloscopy (fingerprinting) in the identification of individuals. Four groups of relief formations are differentiated on the palm: papillary lines, flexion folds of skin, wrinkles, and pores. In identifying a palm print, the configuration, dimensions, and designs on the plam are examined.

Phonocardiography: The graphic recording of heart sounds and murmurs; by extension, the term includes pulse tracings (carotid, apex, and venous pulse). Phonocardiography involves picking up, through a highly sensitive microphone, sonic vibrations from the heart which are then converted into electrical energy and fed into a galvanometer, where they are recorded on paper. The procedure is most useful when there is evidence of heart murmurs or unusual heart sounds, such as gallops that are difficult to discern by the human ear.

Chapter 3
Against Spoofing Attacks in Network Layer

Kavisankar L.
SRM University, India

Chellappan C.
GKM College of Engineering and Technology, India

Poovammal E.
SRM University, India

ABSTRACT

In the context of network security, a spoofing attack is a condition in which one person or a program successfully masquerades as another. This is done by providing counterfeit data with the malicious intention of gaining an illegitimate advantage. Spoofing attack which may be generated in various layer of Open Systems Interconnection model (OSI model) is discussed in this chapter. The chapter ends with discussing about the possible spoofing attacks in network layer and the relevant defense mechanism of the same. The detailed analysis and discussion is made on the spoofing attack over the Network layer because, Denial-of-Service (DoS) and Distributed Denial-of-Service (DDoS) attacks more devastating while using network protocol like Internet Protocol (IP) which have become more of a threat than ever for the past few years.

INTRODUCTION

It is essential to impose the network security, which can achieve control over access from intruders and malicious users. According to Cisco (2012), network security consists of the provisions and policies adopted by a network administrator to prevent and monitor unauthorized access, misuse, modification, or denial of a computer network and network-accessible resources.

Security is considered as an integral part of internet browsing. It is one of the most important quality attributes in the field of networking. Due to the gradually increasing number of vulnerabilities, the identification of an attack is essential. Network attacks, must thus be defined in order to measure security.

DOI: 10.4018/978-1-5225-0193-0.ch003

In the context of network security, a spoofing attack is a situation in which one person or a program successfully masquerades as another. This is done by providing counterfeit data with the malicious intention of gaining an illegitimate advantage. Spoofing attack which may be generated in various layer of Open Systems Interconnection model (OSI model) is discussed in this chapter. The chapter ends with discussing about the possible spoofing attacks in network layer and the relevant defense mechanism of the same.

We start our discussion in application layer on the vulnerabilities of application protocols towards spoofing attacks. The application protocols like Simple Mail Transfer Protocol (SMTP), Hypertext Transfer Protocol (HTTP), Domain Name System (DNS) and Dynamic Host Configuration Protocol (DHCP) are vulnerable to spoofing attacks. The very essential application like biometric is also vulnerable to spoofed attacks. The biometric like fingerprint and iris suffers spoofing by the attackers. The concentration is on presentation layer now, where the Multi-Purpose Internet Mail Extensions (MIME) is vulnerable to Spoofing attacks. While in the Session layer we have major vulnerability of session hijacking. The Session hijacking is closely related to the session spoofing attack. The like Transmission Control Protocol (TCP) and User Datagram Protocol (UDP) are vulnerable to synchronization (SYN) Spoofing and UDP Spoofing respectively. This is done by exploiting the vulnerabilities of the transport layer protocols.

The Data Link layer uses the protocol like Address Resolution Protocol (ARP). The ARP which is used to translate internet protocol addresses to hardware interface addresses. Because ARP does not provide methods for authenticating ARP replies on a network, ARP replies can be spoofed by hosts on a network other than the one from which a reply was expected. A malicious user may leverage ARP spoofing to perform a man-in-the-middle or denial-of-service attack on other users on the network. Various software exists to both detect and perform ARP spoofing attacks, though ARP itself does not provide any methods of protection from such attacks. We also have attack on the Media Access Control (MAC) address i.e. MAC spoofing is a technique for changing a factory-assigned MAC address of a network interface on a networked device. Finally, the Physical layer the location Spoofing works in two ways impersonation of access points (from one location to another) and elimination of signals sent by legitimate access points.

The detailed analysis and discussion is made on the spoofing attack over the Network layer because, denial-of-service (DoS) and distributed denial-of-service (DDoS) attacks more devastating while using network protocol like Internet Protocol (IP) which have become more of a threat than ever for the past few years.

The Network layer is used to router the packets from source to destination based on the IP address of the destination System. Because the router does not have any knowledge about the source address of the packet the attacker use this vulnerability to attack the destination system by using the forged or spoofed IP address. The spoofed IP address with flooding increases the intensity of the attack denial of service attack.

According to IBM (2014), a DDoS attack is launched from hundreds or even thousands of sources simultaneously. A DDoS attack appears like normal traffic coming from a large number of sources rather an excess of traffic coming from a single source. The identify and mitigation is difficult even more difficult is to trace back to its original origin. To add to it the address spoofing or IP spoofing is programmed by the attackers which are done by putting the fake source addresses in the packets. In such cases tracing to its origin becomes ever more difficult.

According to Brian (2013), and Ronen (2013) Criminals nowadays increase in the volume of attacks, using multi-vector attacks. According to Incapsula's report the attackers are more successful by varying the attack methods which creates "A smoke screen effect" which is justified by the report with 81% of the network attack methods. Out of 81%, 39% are using 3 or more difficult attack methods simultaneously. In addition botnets are also being used with 29%, hitting more than 50 targets over the 90 day period. The powerful botnets are typically rented on per hour basis by the Cybercriminals which is used to knock competitor websites offline for a specific period. Unlike network attacks, the DDoS attacks can easily knock most mid-size websites offline by increasing the frequency of the requests per second. The latest trend of attackers is the multi-vector approach which can overcome or bypass the strongest of DDoS protection methods which are currently available.

VARIOUS SPOOFING ATTACKS

The taxonomy in Figure 1 gives us a clear picture of various spoofing attacks in each and every layers of OSI model. The application layer spoofing attacks are SMTP, HTTP, DNS, DHCP and also biometric spoofing. Session layer suffers from session spoofing. In transport layer SYN spoofing, UDP spoofing is possible. In network layer, IP spoofing is possible. In data link layer, MAC and ARP spoofing are done. In the same way, in the physical layer location spoofing is possible.

Figure 1. Spoofing attacks in various layer of OSI model

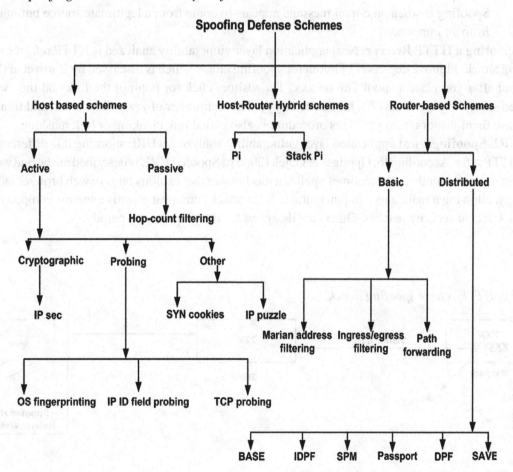

Application Layer Spoofing Attacks

1. **E-Mail Spoofing:** According to Kruck & Kruck (2006) the technique called E-Mail spoofing is done by attackers to conceal the identities of the real sender which in turn fakes to be a legitimate user. These kind vulnerabilities may cause hazardous effects such as spam, phishing and confidential data leakage etc. The vulnerabilities points in the email system are in both client applications and email protocols.

   a. **Email Client Vulnerabilities:** Earlier Email clients were designed for sending and receiving only text-based emails. But, nowadays Email clients have become more features enhanced which supports scripting languages, address books, and integration with other desktop applications. These enhanced features have increased vulnerabilities with are exploited by viruses, worms, and other forms of malware.

   b. **Protocol Vulnerabilities:** A key vulnerabilities in SMTP is that users are not authenticated that is the servers do not verify the origin of a message. Since, the origin of a message is assumed to be trusted. The sending server substitute fake addresses (spoofing) in the message and send it to the receiving client. The receiving server continues to handle the message from this spoofed address. The sending server can put any origin address in the message and send it. The receiving server accepts this address and continues to handle this message which allows spammers to substitute fake addresses (spoofing) and hide the true identity of the sender. Spoofing is when an e-mail message appears to come from a legitimate source but in fact is from an impostor.

2. **Spoofing a HTTP Referer:** Next application layer vulnerability analyzed is HTTP referrer spoofing attack. Figure 2 depicts HTTP Referer spoofing attack which is discussed by Barth et al (2008) that after you place a spoof link on xxx. The visitors click (or pop-up) the link and they will be redirected to page zzz with a fake referrer yyy. The webmaster of zzz will be stung and think you gave them visitors from yyy. This procedure is also called link cloaking or link masking.

3. **URL Spoofing:** Next application layer vulnerability analyzed is URL spoofing it is different from HTTP refer. According to, Oppliger & Gajek (2005) a Spoofed URL is described as the one website that poses as another. It sometimes applies a mechanism that exploits bugs in web browser technology, allowing a malicious computer attack. Such attacks are most effective against computers that lack recent security patches. Others are designed for the purpose of a parody.

Figure 2. HTTP referer spoofing attack

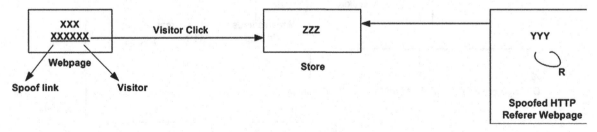

During such an attack, a computer user innocently visits a web site and sees a familiar URL in the address bar such as http://www.xxx.org but is, in reality, sending information to an entirely different location that would typically be monitored by an information thief. When sensitive information is requested by a fraudulent website, it is called phishing.

The user is typically enticed to the false website from an email or a hyperlink from another website.

In another variation, a website may look like the original, but is in fact a parody of it. These are mostly harmless, and are more noticeably different from the original, as they usually *do not* exploit bugs in web browser technology.

This can also take place in a hosts file. It can redirect a site(s) to another IP, which could be a spoofed website.

4. **Biometric Spoofing:** Biometric is one of the important factors in the secure authentication in the applications. It's important to analyze the vulnerabilities of this biometric spoofing. An early report into fingerprint devices and their susceptibility to acceptance of "lifted" fingerprints or fake fingers was published by Network Computing in 1998. They found that four out of six devices tested were susceptible to fake finger attacks.

Further research was undertaken by Tsutomu Matsumoto who published a paper on "gummy" fingers in 2002. In this research, finger sleeves were made from gelatine, designed to cover a fingertip and with a fingerprint on the outer surface. In testing, these had a high acceptance rate from fingerprint readers using optical or capacitive sensors. In addition, fake fingers could be enrolled in the system (68 to 100% acceptance).

In November 2002 c't magazine published the results of the testing of a variety of biometric devices. A number of spoofing attacks were successful, as "man-in-the-middle" attacks on datastreams. Tests were conducted on fingerprint, facial recognition and iris scan biometric devices. The facial recognition devices were spoofed by playing back a video of a person's face. Iris scanners were spoofed with a high resolution photograph of an iris held over a person's face and with a hole cut in the photograph to reveal a live pupil. Another method of spoofing iris scanners is to replay a high resolution digital image of the iris.

In August 2003, two German hackers claimed to have developed a technique using latent prints on the scanner and converting them to a latex fingerprint replacement, small enough to escape all but the most intense scrutiny. This method uses graphite powder and tape to recover latent prints which are digitally photographed, and the image enhanced using graphics software. Where complete fingerprints are not available, the graphics software is used to compile a fingerprint from overlapping portions recovered from the scanner.

The image is photo-etched to produce a three-dimensional reproduction of the fingerprint. This etch is then used to as a mould for the latex fingerprint. More recently (December 2005) research undertaken at Clarkson University revealed that it was possible to demonstrate a 90% false verification rate in the laboratory. This included testing with digits from cadavers, fake plastic fingers, gelatine and modelling compounds.

However, Roberts (2007) discusses when "liveness" detection was integrated into the fingerprint readers, the false verification rate fell to less than 10% of the spoofed samples. Much of the activity in spoofing biometric systems has, up until now, been confined to researchers. However, as biometric systems become more widespread, the incentives to misuse or attack biometric systems will grow. Understanding the nature and risk of such attacks it will become increasingly important to systems architects administrators and security managers.

5. **DNS Spoofing:** Another application layer spoofing attack is DNS spoofing which is defined by Hanley (2000), as the successful insertion of incorrect resolution information by a host that has no authority to provide that information. It may be conducted using a number of techniques ranging from social engineering through to exploitation of vulnerabilities within the DNS server software itself. Using these techniques, an attacker may insert IP address information that will redirect a customer from a legitimate website or mail server to one under the attacker's control – thereby capturing customer information through common man-in-the-middle mechanisms. According to the most recent "Domain Health Survey" (Feb 2003), a third of all DNS servers on the Internet are vulnerable to spoofing.

    a.   **The Attack:** Normally, a DNS server discover the IP address of the named host the customer wish to connect to.

        i.   The customer request the DNS server the IP address of www.xxxxxx.com?"

        ii.   The DNS responds to the customer query request with "The IP address of www.xxxxxx. com is xxx.xx.xx.xx"

        iii.   The Customer then connects to the host at xxx.xx.xx.xx – expecting it to be www.xxxxxx. com.

Here, with help of a successful DNS spoofing attack, the process has been altered. The Figure 3 reflects this process.

        i.   The attacker targets the DNS service used by the customer and adds/alters the entry for www.xxxxxx.com – changing the stored IP address from xxx.xx.xx.xx to the attackers fake site IP address (yyy.yy.yy.yy).

        ii.   The customer request the DNS server the IP address of www.xxxxxx.com?"

        iii.   The DNS responds to the customer query with "The IP address of www.xxxxxx.com is yyy.yy.yy.yy" – not the real IP address.

        iv.   The Customer then connects to the host at yyy.yy.yy.yy– expecting it to be www.xxxxxx. com, but in fact reaching the attackers fake site.

Figure 3. DNS spoofing attack the DNS resolution process

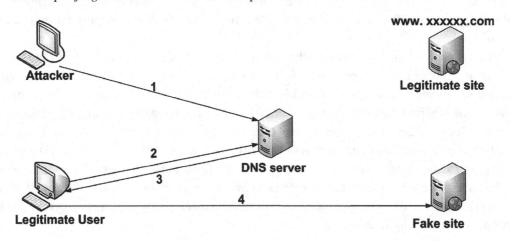

6. **DHCP Spoofing:** Though the application layer has various other vulnerabilities this discussion on the application layer spoofing ends with the DHCP spoofing. According to, Kruck & Kruck (2006) the DHCP spoofing is a type of attack on DHCP server to obtain IP addresses using spoofed DHCP messages. Normally, this is done when a request for an IP address from a PC on the network to supply access to the network, it responds with a packet containing the configured (spoofed) IP address along with a renewal time, which is set to a few seconds. The requester then has access to the DHCP server and gets a real IP address. Other variations exist in environments where the APP server utility is running. In this type of environment represented in the Figure 4, the Ascend Password Protocol (APP) server must first authenticate a user before a call to the remote network can be made. APP authentication requires an IP address, but will accept a temporary (spoofed) address supplied by the Pipeline.

7. **Session Spoofing:** According to Yang et al. (2005) the session layer vulnerability like session spoofing, Session hijacking occurs at the TCP level. According to Internet Security Systems, "TCP session hijacking is when a hacker takes over a TCP session between two machines. Since most authentications only occur at the start of a TCP session, this allows the hacker to gain access to a machine."

The thing is that in other parts of the site (such as profile changing), the editing of the users profile is done by getting their row of data in the SQL database with the username that was stored in the session when the user logged in.

After doing this will make us think, that there a way the session can be spoofed so it will be like they are logged in as a different user? Then edit other peoples information in the profile since that is my only means of getting the users row.

So, is this possible to do an hacker change a server side value with an injection of some sort in the directory that stores sessions is protected.

8. **ARP Spoofing:** Altunbasak et al. (2004), discusses about the vulnerabilities in the data link layer. A computer connected to an IP/Ethernet LAN has two addresses. One is the address of the network card, called the MAC address. The MAC, in theory, is a globally unique and unchangeable address which is stored on the network card itself. MAC addresses are necessary so that the Ethernet protocol can send data back and forth, independent of whatever application protocols are used on top of it. Ethernet builds "frames" of data, consisting of 1500 byte blocks. Each frame has an Ethernet header, containing the MAC address of the source and the destination computer.

Figure 4. DHCP server passing the IP address

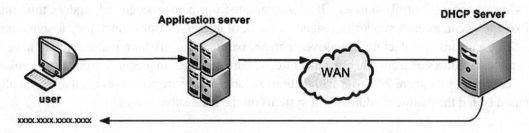

The second address is the IP address. IP is a protocol used by applications, independent of whatever network technology operates underneath it. Each computer on a network must have a unique IP address to communicate. IP addresses are virtual and are assigned via software.

IP and Ethernet must work together. IP communicates by constructing "packets" which are similar to frames, but have a different structure. These packets cannot be delivered without the data link layer. In our case they are delivered by Ethernet, which splits the packets into frames, adds an Ethernet header for delivery, and sends them down the cable to the switch. The switch then decides which port to send the frame to, by comparing the destination address of the frame to an internal table which maps port numbers to MAC addresses.

When an Ethernet frame is constructed, it must be built from an IP packet. However, at the time of construction, Ethernet has no idea what the MAC address of the destination machine is, which it needs to create an Ethernet header. The only information it has available is the destination IP from the packet's header. There must be a way for the Ethernet protocol to find the MAC address of the destination machine, given a destination IP.

This is where ARP, the Address Resolution Protocol, comes in.

ARP operates by sending out "ARP request" packets. An ARP request asks the question, "Is your IP address x.x.x.x? If so, send your MAC back to me." These packets are broadcast to all computers on the LAN, even on a switched network. Each computer examines the ARP request, checks if it is currently assigned the specified IP, and sends an ARP reply containing its MAC address.

To minimize the number of ARP requests being broadcast, operating systems keep a cache of ARP replies. When a computer receives an ARP reply, it will update its ARP cache with the new IP/MAC association. As ARP is a stateless protocol, most operating systems will update their cache if a reply is received, regardless of whether they have sent out an actual request.

ARP spoofing involves constructing forged ARP replies. By sending forged ARP replies, a target computer could be convinced to send frames destined for computer A to instead go to computer B. When done properly, computer A will have no idea that this redirection took place. The process of updating a target computer's ARP cache with a forged entry is referred to as "poisoning".

9. **MAC Spoofing:** Another vulnerability of data link layer is MAC spoofing. According to, Joshua et al. (2003), Sheng et al. (2008) the MAC spoofing is a technique for changing a factory-assigned Media Access Control (MAC) address of a network interface on a networked device.

The changing of the assigned MAC address may allow the bypassing of access control lists on servers or routers, either hiding a computer on a network or allowing it to impersonate another network device. A user may wish to legitimately spoof the MAC address of a previous hardware device in order to reacquire connectivity after hardware failure.

Traffic can be disrupted on a network if two Ethernet adapters have exactly the same hardware (or MAC – Media Access Control) addresses. If all adapters are from major, recognized vendors, this problem is unlikely to occur, as each vendor is assigned a block of addresses from which they assign a unique address to each card manufactured. However, bargain basement or offshore manufacturers have been known to hijack addresses from other manufacturer's address ranges. In practice, even this is unlikely to cause a conflict, as there are 2^{48} (over 280 trillion) separate hardware addresses available, and all that is required is that the hardware addresses of systems on the local subnet be unique

Most people are surprised to discover that practically every Ethernet adapter can be reprogrammed to have any desired hardware address. Although this reprogramming is rarely done, except in cases where a software license is tied to the hardware address, hackers can reprogram the Ethernet adapter on a system to spoof that of another system on the network (hence the term MAC spoofing), which typically will result in neither system being able to communicate. If the hacker chooses the same hardware address as the local router, all communication outside the subnet will be disrupted.

The changing of the assigned MAC address may allow the bypassing of access control lists on servers or routers, either hiding a computer on a network or allowing it to impersonate another network device. A user may wish to legitimately spoof the MAC address of a previous hardware device in order to reacquire connectivity after hardware failure. IP address spoofing, where senders spoofing their address in a request direct the receiver into sending the response elsewhere, in MAC address spoofing the response is usually received by the spoofing party.

10. **IP Spoofing:** IP spoofing is one of the vulnerabilities of Network layer. An *IP address spoofing* attack, according to Gonzalez et al. (2011), Manusankar et al. (2010), consists of packets injected into the network with an IP address that is different than the actual IP address of the system sending out these packets.

Figure 5 depicts the IP address spoofing attack. Here the attacker initially sends a spoofed packet with fake source address. The middleman return packet with destination address of spoofed sender. It is generally possible to assume that an unsolicited response is likely caused by spoofing.

Figure 5. IP address spoofing attack

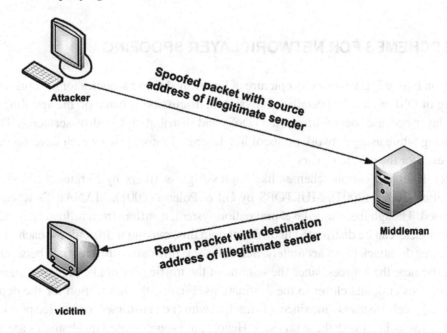

Figure 6. SYN flood attack

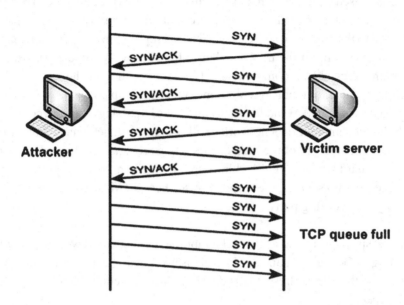

11. **SYN Spoofing:** According to, Kavisankar & Chellappan (2011), Joshua Wright & Joshua (2003) a SYN Flood is where an attacker sends TCP SYN packets with a spoofed source IP Address to the server (victim). This attack exploits a vulnerability of the TCP protocol, by the way in which the TCP three-way connection is established. This is shown in Figure 6.

12. **Location Spoofing:** The Location spoofing is done in using various method by impersonation of access points (from one location to another) and elimination of signals sent by legitimate access points according to Zeng et al. (2013).

DEFENSE SCHEMES FOR NETWORK LAYER SPOOFING

The taxonomy in Figure 7, gives us a clear picture of Spoofing defense schemes for network and transport layer spoofing of OSI model. The detailed analysis and discussion is made on the spoofing attack over the Network layer because, denial-of-service (DoS) and distributed denial-of-service (DDoS) attacks more devastating while using network protocol like Internet Protocol (IP) which have become more of a threat than ever for the past few years.

The Source level prevention schemes like Ingress/Egress filters by Ferguson (2000), D-WARD by Mirkovic et al (2002), (2003), MULTOPS by Gil & Poletto (2001), MANAnet's Reverse Firewall (2012) were used. Though the source level prevention system, it suffers from following issues. First, the sources of the attacks can be distributed in different domains, making it difficult for each of the sources to detect and filter the attack flows accurately. Secondly, it is difficult to differentiate between legitimate and attack traffic near the sources, since the volume of the traffic may not be big enough, as the traffic typically aggregates at points closer to the destinations. Finally, the motivation for the deployment of the source-based mechanisms is low, since it is unclear who (i.e., customers or service providers) would pay the expenses associated with these services. Hence, pure source-based mechanisms are not efficient and effective against DDoS flooding attacks.

Figure 7. Taxonomy for spoofed request flooding DDoS attacks defense schemes

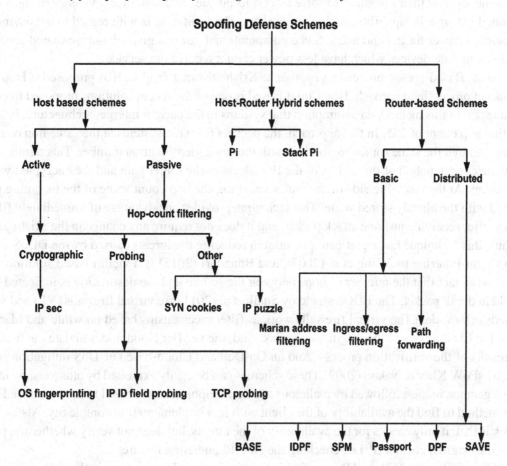

The intermediate router level defense scheme, like Zhang & Dasgupta's (2003) and Duan et al's (2008), proposed a router based solution in which the flooding is stopped at the router level itself. They make use of hardened routers, which provide digital signatures and encryption. Even though this system provides more secure and private communications between the routers involved, a tremendous amount of implementation complexity is involved. Establishing hardened routers increases the cost of the system. In addition to that, the last router is critical as it decrypts the initial packet; thus a single point of failure, and consequently, a less reliable information system is created.

A destination level defense scheme, like the StackPi method proposed by Yaar et al (2006) performs marking and filtering for the detection of attack packets; the attackers are considerably reduced using this method, but a router may mistakenly drop the legitimate packets, if it simply drops all packets with an "attack path" marking. The server requires a evidence of work from the client, before assigning its resources to the client. The challenge response method like Completely Automated Public Turing test to tell Computers and Humans Apart (CAPTCHA) proposed by Von et al (2003) and the IP puzzling discussed by Feng & Kaiser (2011) and Ma (2005) are used to find the legitimate user. The graphical Turing is used to decide on whether a client is allowed to get connected to a trusted approved location so as to access the web server using the Secure Overlay Services (SOS) and WebSOS proposed by Keromytis et al (2002), and Stavrou et al (2005) respectively, to protect a web service against DDoS attacks. Clients expend their resources to solve a "crypto-puzzle" and submit an evidence of the solution as an embedded signal (capability) within the packets. The limitation is with regard to the asymmetric computational power for the end users. Since computational puzzles give advantage to end-users with faster CPUs, mobile devices which have less power cannot receive the services.

Hop count Based packet processing approach: KrishnaKumar et al (2010) proposed a Hop count Based packet processing approach. Hop Count Based is one of the recent solutions proposed to counter DDOS attacks. In this method, an assumption that systems in the current internet architecture, is located max with a hop count of 255. In this approach, the packets from the systems at the same hop count and traversing through the same router are marked with the same identification number. This number is derived by the concatenation of the 32 bits of the IP address of the router path and the encrypted value of the hop count. At the receiving side of the router interface, the hop count value of the incoming packet is checked with the already stored value. This technique provides an advantage of immediately filtering the traffic after receiving just one attack packet, and it does not require any change in the existing protocols. Thus, this technique has significant potential in reducing the threats caused by the DDoS attacks.

Hop Count Filtering by Wang et al (2007), and Bhandari (2013) is a victim-based solution, and it is based on the fact that the number of hops between the source and the destination is indicated by the TTL field in the IP packet. The EDOS shield by Sqalli et al (2011) are virtual firewalls (VF) and verifier cloud nodes (V-Nodes).The virtual firewalls work as filter mechanisms based on white and black lists that hold the IP addresses of the originating nodes. And, the verifier cloud nodes update the lists based on the results of the verification process. And an On-Demand Cloud-based eDDoS mitigation scheme is given by sPoW Khor & Nakao (2009).These schemes can be easily exploited by attackers, by initially sending a genuine request followed by malicious attacks. Delphinanto et al (2011) have proposed a TCP probing method to find the availability of the client with less implementation complexity. Also, another drawback is that, it only checks for the availability of the clients, but does not verify whether the packets are from the original client's IP, i.e., checking the Non-Repudiation feature.

According to Brian (2013), and Ronen (2013) Criminals nowadays increase in the volume of attacks, using multi-vector attacks. According to Incapsula's report the attackers are more successful by varying the attack methods which creates "A smoke screen effect" which is justified by the report with 81% of the network attack methods. Out of 81%, 39% are using 3 or more difficult attack methods simultaneously. In addition botnets are also being used with 29%, hitting more than 50 targets over the 90 day period. The powerful botnets are typically rented on per hour basis by the Cybercriminals which is used to knock competitor websites offline for a specific period. Unlike network attacks, the DDoS attacks can easily knock most mid-size websites offline by increasing the frequency of the requests per second. The latest trend of attackers is the multi-vector approach which can overcome or bypass the strongest of DDoS protection methods which are currently available.

CONCLUSION

This chapter discussed the existing works related to the various forms of Spoofing attacks, such as Simple Mail Transfer Protocol (SMTP) spoofing, Hypertext Transfer Protocol (HTTP) spoofing, Domain Name System (DNS) spoofing, Dynamic Host Configuration Protocol (DHCP) spoofing, Multi-Purpose Internet Mail Extensions (MIME) spoofing, session spoofing, Transmission Control Protocol (TCP) spoofing, User Datagram Protocol (UDP) spoofing, Address Resolution Protocol (ARP) spoofing, MAC spoofing, denial-of-service (DoS) and distributed denial-of-service (DDoS) with help of spoofing the IP address which in turn creates multi-vector DDoS attacks are discussed. Due to the increase in number of attack and devastating effect of DDoS attack with help of IP spoofing is discussed in depth. It also addressed the limitations of the existing mitigation schemes for DDoS attacks with help of IP spoofing. This chapter conclude with the note that the multi-vector approach, which is already used by the vast majority of all network attacks, is a clear indication of the attackers' familiarity with current DDoS protection methods and the ways in which these methods are defended.

REFERENCES

Abhishek Singh. (2010). *Demystifying Denial-Of-Service attacks*. Retrieved 02 November, 2010, from http://aka-community.symantec.com/connect/es/articles/demystifying-denial-service-attacks-part-one

Adelsbach, A., Gajek, S., & Schwenk, J. (2005, January). Visual spoofing of SSL protected web sites and effective countermeasures. In ISPEC (Vol. 3439, pp. 204-216). doi:10.1007/978-3-540-31979-5_18

Altunbasak, H., Krasser, S., Owen, H., Sokol, J., Grimminger, J., & Huth, H. P. (2004, November). Addressing the weak link between layer 2 and layer 3 in the Internet architecture. In *Null* (pp. 417-418). IEEE.

Anomalous. (2012). *session-hijacking-explained*. Retrieved 15 July, 2012 http://hackingalert.blogspot.com/2011/05/session-hijacking-explained.html

Barth, A., Jackson, C., & Mitchell, J. C. (2008, October). Robust defenses for cross-site request forgery. In *Proceedings of the 15th ACM conference on Computer and communications security* (pp. 75-88). ACM. doi:10.1145/1455770.1455782

Bhandari, N. H. (2013). DDoS Attack Prevention In Cloud Computing Using Hop Count Based Packet Monitoring Approach. *International Journal of Advanced and Innovative Research*, 2(4), 954–956.

Brian. (2013). *Multi-vector DDoS Attacks Grow in Sophistication*. Retrieved 29January 2013 from: http://www.securityweek.com/multi-vector-ddos-attacks-grow

Brian. (2014). *2013-2014 DDoS Threat Landscape Report*. Retrieved 27 March 2014 from: http://threatpost.com/ntp-amplification-syn-floods-drive-up-ddos-attack-volumes

Chothia, T., & Chatzikokolakis, K. (2005, January). A survey of anonymous peer-to-peer file-sharing. In Embedded and Ubiquitous Computing–EUC 2005 Workshops (pp. 744-755). Springer Berlin Heidelberg. doi:10.1007/11596042_77

Cisco. (2012). *What is Network security*. Retrieved 5 July 2012 from: http://www.cisco.com/cisco/web/solutions/small_business/resource_center/articles/secure_my_business/what_is_network_security/index.html

Decker, M. (2009, July). Prevention of Location-Spoofing-A Survey on Different Methods to Prevent the Manipulation of Locating-technologies. In ICE-B (pp. 109-114).

Delphinanto, A., Koonen, T., & den Hartog, F. (2011). Real-time probing of available bandwidth in home networks. *IEEE Communications Magazine*, 49(6), 134–140. doi:10.1109/MCOM.2011.5783998

Duan, Z., Yuan, X., & Chandrashekar, J. (2008). Controlling IP spoofing through interdomain packet filters. *IEEE Transactions on Dependable and Secure Computing, 5*(1), 22–36. doi:10.1109/TDSC.2007.70224

Eddy, W. M. (2007). *TCP SYN flooding attacks and common mitigations*. Academic Press.

Ehrenkranz, T., & Li, J. (2009). On the state of IP spoofing defense. *ACM Transactions on Internet Technology, 9*(2), 6. doi:10.1145/1516539.1516541

Endorf, C. F., Schultz, E., & Mellander, J. (2011). *Network Protocol Abuses*. Retrieved 12 May, 2011, from http://flylib.com/books/en/2.352.1.31/1/

Feng, W. C., & Kaiser, E. (2011). *System and methods of determining computational puzzle difficulty for challenge-response authentication*. U.S. Patent Application 13/050,123.

Ferguson, P. (2000). *Network ingress filtering: Defeating denial of service attacks which employ IP source address spoofing*. RFC 2267.

Gil, T. M., & Poletto, M. (2001). MULTOPS: a data-structure for bandwidth attack detection. *Proceeding 10th Usenix Security Symposium*.

Gonzalez, J. M., Anwar, M., & Joshi, J. B. (2011, July). A trust-based approach against IP-spoofing attacks. In *Privacy, Security and Trust (PST), 2011 Ninth Annual International Conference on* (pp. 63-70). IEEE.

Groß, T. (2003, December). Security analysis of the SAML single sign-on browser/artifact profile. In *Computer Security Applications Conference, 2003. Proceedings. 19th Annual* (pp. 298-307). IEEE.

Hanley, S. (2000). *DNS overview with a discussion of DNS spoofing*. Academic Press.

IBM. (2014). *X-Force Mid-year Trend and risk report*. Retrieved 5 July2014 from: http://www-03.ibm.com/security/xforce

Jakobsson, M., & Stamm, S. (2006, May). Invasive browser sniffing and countermeasures. In *Proceedings of the 15th international conference on World Wide Web* (pp. 523-532). ACM. doi:10.1145/1135777.1135854

Joshua Wright, G. C. I. H., & Joshua, C. C. N. A. (2003). *Detecting Wireless LAN MAC Address Spoofing*. Cisco Certified Network Associate.

Kavisankar, L., & Chellappan, C. (2011). *CNoA: Challenging Number Approach for uncovering TCP SYN flooding using SYN spoofing attack*. arXiv:1110.1753

Kavisankar, L., & Chellappan, C. (2011, June). A Mitigation model for TCP SYN flooding with IP Spoofing. In *Recent Trends in Information Technology (ICRTIT), 2011 International Conference on* (pp. 251-256). IEEE. doi:10.1109/ICRTIT.2011.5972435

Keromytis, A. D., Misra, V., & Rubenstein, D. (2002). SOS: Secure overlay services. *Computer Communication Review, 32*(4), 61–72. doi:10.1145/964725.633032

Khor, S. H., & Nakao, A. (2009). sPoW: On-Demand Cloud-based eDDoS mitigation mechanism. *Proceeding of HotDep (Fifth Workshop on Hot Topics in System Dependability)*, (pp. 1-6).

Kong, Z., & Jiang, X. Z. (2010). DNS Spoofing Principle and Its Defense Scheme. *Computer Engineering, 3*, 43.

Kost & Kanter. (2006). *Spoofing Oracle session Information*. Integrigy Corporation.

KrishnaKumar, B., Kumar, P.K., & Sukanesh, R. (2010). Hop Count Based Packet Processing Approach to Counter DDoS Attacks. *International Conference on Recent Trends in Information, Telecommunication and Computing*, (pp. 271- 273).

Kruck, G. P., & Kruck, S. E. (2006). Spoofing-a look at an evolving threat. *Journal of Computer Information Systems, 47*(1), 95.

Ma, M. (2005). Mitigating denial of service attacks with password puzzles. *International IEEE Conference on Information Technology: Coding and Computing*. doi:10.1109/ITCC.2005.200

MANAnet's Reverse Firewall. (2012). *Reverse Firewall*. Retrieved 15 January 2012 from: http://www.cs3-inc.com/pubs/Reverse_FireWall.pdf

Manusankar, C., Karthik, S., & Rajendran, T. (2010, December). Intrusion Detection System with packet filtering for IP Spoofing. In *Communication and Computational Intelligence (INCOCCI), 2010 International Conference on* (pp. 563-567). IEEE.

Mirkovic, J., Prier, G., & Reiher, P. (2002). Attacking DDoS at the source. In *Proceedings 10th IEEE International Conference on Network Protocols*, (pp. 312-321). doi:10.1109/ICNP.2002.1181418

Mirkovic, J., Prier, G., & Reiher, P. (2003). Source-end DDoS defense. *Second IEEE International Symposium on Network Computing and Applications*. doi:10.1109/NCA.2003.1201153

Mirkovic, J., & Reiher, P. (2004). A taxonomy of DDoS attack and DDoS defense mechanisms. *Computer Communication Review, 34*(2), 39–53. doi:10.1145/997150.997156

Noureldien, N. A., & Hussein, M. O. (2012). Block Spoofed Packets at Source (BSPS): a method for detecting and preventing all types of spoofed source IP packets and SYN Flooding packets at source: a theoretical framework. *International Journal of Networks and Communications, 2*(3), 33–37. doi:10.5923/j.ijnc.20120203.03

Oppliger, R., & Gajek, S. (2005, January). Effective protection against phishing and web spoofing. In *Communications and Multimedia Security* (pp. 32–41). Springer Berlin Heidelberg. doi:10.1007/11552055_4

Ornaghi, A., & Valleri, M. (2003). Man in the middle attacks. In Blackhat Conference Europe.

Ramachandran, V., & Nandi, S. (2005). Detecting ARP spoofing: An active technique. In *Information Systems Security* (pp. 239–250). Springer Berlin Heidelberg. doi:10.1007/11593980_18

Reveron, D. S. (Ed.). (2012). *Cyberspace and national security: threats, opportunities, and power in a virtual world*. Georgetown University Press.

Roberts, C. (2007). Biometric attack vectors and defences. *Computers & Security, 26*(1), 14–25. doi:10.1016/j.cose.2006.12.008

Ronen. (2013). *An Inside Look at One of the Most Complex DDoS Attacks to Date*. Retrieved 22 October 2013 from: http://www.incapsula.com/blog/ funded-persistent-multi-vector-ddos-attack.html

Rush, H., Smith, C., Kraemer-Mbula, E., & Tang, P. (2009). *Crime online: Cybercrime and illegal innovation*. Academic Press.

Sheng, Y., Tan, K., Chen, G., Kotz, D., & Campbell, A. (2008, April). Detecting 802.11 MAC layer spoofing using received signal strength. In *INFOCOM 2008. The 27th Conference on Computer Communications*. IEEE.

Sheng, Y., Tan, K., Chen, G., Kotz, D., & Campbell, A. (2008, April). Detecting 802.11 MAC layer spoofing using received signal strength. In *INFOCOM 2008. The 27th Conference on Computer Communications*. IEEE.

Sqalli, M. H., Al-Haidari, F., & Salah, K. (2011). EDoS-Shield -a two-steps mitigation technique against EDoS attacks in cloud computing. *2011 Fourth IEEE International Conference on Utility and Cloud Computing (UCC)*, (pp. 49-56). doi:10.1109/UCC.2011.17

Stavrou, A., Cook, D.L., Morein, W.G., Keromytis, A.D., Misra, V., & Rubenstein, D. (2005). WebSOS: an overlay-based system for protecting web servers from denial of service attacks. *Computer Networks, 48*(5), 781-807.

Von Ahn, L., Blum, M., Hopper, N.J., & Langford, J. (2003). CAPTCHA: Using hard AI problems for security. In *Advances in Cryptology—EUROCRYPT 2003*. Springer Berlin Heidelberg.

Wagner, R. (2001). *Address resolution protocol spoofing and man-in-the-middle attacks*. The SANS Institute.

Wang, H., Jin, C., & Shin, K.G. (2007). Defense against spoofed IP traffic using hop-count filtering. *IEEE/ACM Transactions on Networking, 15*(1), 40-53.

Wang, H., Zhang, D., & Shin, K. G. (2002). Detecting SYN flooding attacks. *Proceedings INFOCOM 2002. Twenty-First Annual Joint Conference of the IEEE Computer and Communications Societies*. IEEE.

Wang, H., Zhang, D., & Shin, K. G. (2004). Change-point monitoring for the detection of DoS attacks. *IEEE Transactions on Dependable and Secure Computing, 1*(4), 193–208. doi:10.1109/TDSC.2004.34

Yaar, A, Perrig, A, & Song, D. (2006). StackPi: New packet marking and filtering mechanisms for DDoS and IP spoofing defense. *IEEE Journal on Selected Areas in Communications, 24*(10), 1853-1863.

Yang, C. C., Wang, R. C., & Liu, W. T. (2005). Secure authentication scheme for session initiation protocol. *Computers & Security, 24*(5), 381–386. doi:10.1016/j.cose.2004.10.007

Yang, C. C., Wang, R. C., & Liu, W. T. (2005). Secure authentication scheme for session initiation protocol. *Computers & Security, 24*(5), 381–386. doi:10.1016/j.cose.2004.10.007

Zeng, Y., Cao, J., Hong, J., Zhang, S., & Xie, L. (2013). Secure localization and location verification in wireless sensor networks: a survey. *Journal of Supercomputing, 64*(3), 685-701.

Chapter 4
Classification of Cybercrimes and Punishments under the Information Technology Act, 2000

Sree Krishna Bharadwaj H.
National Law School of India University, India

ABSTRACT

Cybercrimes are those crimes which are associated with the latest technology including internet. There are various forms of committing crimes using the internet. As a result newer forms of crimes have emerged in the society. Some of the newer crimes are traditional crimes which are committed through the internet such as defamation, fraud, harassment, trespass etc. It is necessary to understand what the laws in India suggest towards these kind of newer crimes happening in the society. This paper deals with the types of cybercrimes and also provides the offences and punishments under the Information Technology Act, 2000 in India.

INTRODUCTION

Cybercrimes are newer classes of crimes committed using the technology and mainly internet. With the introduction of social media such as facebook, twitter etc., there has been havoc created in the society and the crimes using the internet have risen. Some of the newer crimes are traditional crimes which are committed through the internet such as defamation, fraud, harassment, trespass etc. The Information Technology Act, however, deals with these offences and also provides punishments for the offences committed.

DOI: 10.4018/978-1-5225-0193-0.ch004

BACKGROUND

There are various laws which exist in India on the subject of cybercrimes. Various tries to analyse the various provisions of the Indian Penal Code, 1860 and how they are trying to combat the problems created by the cybercrimes in India (Gupta, 2015).

LAWS RELATED TO CYBER CRIMES IN INDIA

Definition of Cyber Crimes

Cybercrime is defined as a crime in which a computer is the object of the crime (hacking, phishing, spamming) or is used as a tool to commit an offense (child pornography, hate crimes). Cybercriminals may use computer technology to access personal information, business trade secrets, or use the Internet for exploitive or malicious purposes. Criminals can also use computers for communication and document or data storage. Criminals who perform these illegal activities are often referred to as hackers. (Techopedia, 2015). The Tech Terms Computer Dictionary defines Cybercrime as a criminal activity done using computers and the Internet. This includes anything from downloading illegal music files to stealing millions of dollars from online bank accounts. Cybercrime also includes non-monetary offenses, such as creating and distributing viruses on other computers or posting confidential business information on the Internet. (The Tech Terms Computer Dictionary, 2015). The Encyclopaedia Britannica defines Cybercrime, also called computer crime, the use of a computer as an instrument to further illegal ends, such as committing fraud, trafficking in child pornography and intellectual property, stealing identities, or violating privacy. Cybercrime, especially through the Internet, has grown in importance as the computer has become central to commerce, entertainment, and government (Encyclopaedia Britannica, 2015).

Classification of Cyber Crimes

1. **Crimes against Individuals:** There are certain offences which affects the personality of individuals can be defined as:
   a. **Harassment:** Harassments could be through wrongful use of social media or photoshopping, emailing etc. It also includes blackmailing and extortion and other kinds of offences under the Indian Penal Code, 1860.
   b. **Cyber-Stalking:** With the introduction of social media such as facebook, twitter etc. cyber stalking has increased day by day. One's movement can be easily traced and violation of privacy is committed.
   c. **Publishing of Obscene Material:** Applications like coral draw, photoshop is being misused and pictures of females are being edited in an obscene manner and published online.
   d. **Defamation:** The social media has created unlimited number of controversies. Social media has become a platform for individual revenge through defamation.
   e. **Hacking:** Accessing another's personal computer without the permission of the owner is termed as hacking and it is punishable under the Information Technology Act, 2000.

f.   **Spoofing:** E-mail spoofing refers to sending of e-mails in the name of others and gathering the sensitive information of others. Spoofing is also used to hack a person's computer and remote access it.

g.   **Cheating and Fraud:** These are the traditional crimes which also occur in the IT world as well. It is mainly through the use of internet and could be through many ways such as spoofing, spamming etc.

2.   **Crimes against Property of an Individual:**

a.   **Intellectual Property Crimes:** These may include unethical use of copyrighted material, wrongful use of any design or research work or patented item etc.

b.   **Squatting:** It is done through creating a similar website with minor changes which are unnoticeable. For example, if google.com is a website, googlee.com would be a squat. It is a threat to sensitive information such as credit card details, accounts details etc.

c.   **Trespass:** Trespass means unauthorised entry into an individual's property which is an offence. It is done through hacking, spamming, spoofing, squatting etc.

3.   **Crimes against the Government:** There are certain offences done by group of persons intending to threaten the international governments by using internet facilities. It includes:

a.   **Cyber Terrorism:** Terrorism has reached higher levels with the use of internet for passing on messages across the globe, and spreading of hatredness between communities and nations.

b.   **Pirated softwares and CDs:** It is although not directly against the government but the selling of pirated softwares and CDs is against the government in several aspects including tax evasion.

c.   **Unauthorized Information:** Possessing and selling of information which an individual obtains either through position in the government or through criminal activities including hacking and defacing the government websites is an offence.

4.   **Crimes against Society:**

a.   **Child Pornography:** It is the worst form of crime using the internet. Offering money for the virginity of girl children for watching and distribution of such content against children are crime against society.

b.   **Cyber Trafficking:** Using the internet as a media for trafficking the women and children to different parts of the world is a crime and government needs to take stringent action against this type of crime.

c.   **Online Gambling:** Many websites offer gambling through cards play such online rummy and poker. Gambling creates debts in the families and has the potential to destroy a family.

d.   **White Collar Crimes:** These include hacking the banks and obtaining sensitive information, embezzling etc. which mainly include the financial gains.

Offences and Punishments under the Information Technology Act, 2000

It is an Act which aims to provide legal recognition for transactions carried out by means of electronic data interchange and other means of electronic communication, commonly referred to as "electronic commerce", which involve the use of alternatives to paper-based methods of communication and storage of information, to facilitate electronic filing of documents with the Government agencies and further to amend the Indian Penal Code, the Indian Evidence Act, 1872, the Bankers' Books Evidence Act, 1891 and the Reserve Bank of India Act, 1934 and for matters connected therewith or incidental thereto. However there are many provisions which categorises the offences and also provides punishment.

If any person without permission of the owner or any other person who is incharge of a computer, computer system or computer network:

1. Accesses or secures access to such computer, computer system or computer network or computer resource;
2. Downloads, copies or extracts any data, computer data base or information from such computer, computer system or computer network including information or data held or stored in any removable storage medium;
3. Introduces or causes to be introduced any computer contaminant or computer virus into any computer, computer system or computer network;
4. Damages or causes to be damaged any computer, computer system or computer network, data, computer data base or any other programmes residing in such computer, computer system or computer network;
5. Disrupts or causes disruption of any computer, computer system or computer network;
6. Denies or causes the denial of access to any person authorised to access any computer, computer system or computer network by any means;
7. Provides any assistance to any person to facilitate access to a computer, computer system or computer network in contravention of the provisions of this Act, rules or regulations made thereunder;
8. Charges the services availed of by a person to the account of another person by tampering with or manipulating any computer, computer system, or computer network,
9. Destroys, deletes or alters any information residing in a computer resource or diminishes its value or utility or affects it injuriously by any means;
10. Steal, conceals, destroys or alters or causes any person to steal, conceal, destroy or alter any computer source code used for a computer resource with an intention to cause damage; he will be liable to pay damages by way of compensation to the person so affected.

If any person without permission of the owner or any other person who is incharge of a computer, computer system or computer network:

1. Accesses such computer, computer system or computer network or computer resource;
2. Downloads, copies or computer system or computer network or computer resource;
3. Downloads, copies or extracts any data, computer data-base or information;
4. Introduces or causes to be introduced any computer contaminant or computer virus;
5. Damages or causes to be damaged any computer, computer system or computer network data, computer database or any other programmes;
6. Disrupts or causes disruption;
7. Denies or causes the denial of access to any person authorised to access;
8. Provides any assistance to any person to facilitate access in contravention of the provisions of this Act;
9. Charges the services availed of by a person to the account of another person by tampering with or manipulating any computer, computer system or computer network;

10. Destroys, deletes or alters any information residing in a computer resource or diminishes its value or utility or affects it injuriously by any means;

11. Steal, conceals, destroys or alters or causes any person to steal, conceal, destroy or alter any computer source code with intention to cause damage; he will be liable to pay damages by way of compensation to the person so affected.

Information Technology Act, 2000: Section Details

- **Section 43A:** Compensation for failure to protect data. Where a body corporate, possessing, dealing or handling any sensitive personal data or information in a computer resource which it owns, controls or operates, is negligent in implementing and maintaining reasonable security practices and procedures and thereby causes wrongful loss or wrongful gain to any person, such body corporate will be liable to pay damages by way of compensation to the person so affected.

- **Section 44:** Penalty for failure to furnish information, return, etc. If any person who is required under this Act or any rules or regulations made thereunder to-
  - Furnish any document, return or report to the Controller or the Certifying Authority fails to furnish the same, he will be liable to a penalty not exceeding one lakh and fifty thousand rupees for each such failure;
  - File any return or furnish any information, books or other documents within the time specified therefor in the regulations fails to file return or furnish the same within the time specified therefor in the regulations, he will be liable to a penalty not exceeding five thousand rupees for every day during which such failure continues;
  - Maintain books of account or records, fails to maintain the same, he will be liable to a penalty not exceeding ten thousand rupees for every day during which the failure continues.

- **Section 45:** Residuary penalty. Whoever contravenes any rules or regulations made under this Act, for the contravention of which no penalty has been separately provided, will be liable to pay a compensation not exceeding twenty-five thousand rupees to the person affected by such contravention or a penalty not exceeding twenty-five thousand rupees.

- **Section 65:** Tampering with computer source documents. Whoever knowingly or intentionally conceals, destroys or alters or intentionally or knowingly causes another to conceal, destroy, or alter any computer source code used for a computer, computer programme, computer system or computer network, when the computer source code is required to be kept or maintained by law for the time being in force, will be punishable with imprisonment up to three years, or with fine which may extend up to two lakh rupees, or with both.

- **Section 66:** Computer related offences. If any person, dishonestly or fraudulently, does any act referred to in section 43, he will be punishable with imprisonment for a term which may extend to three years or with fine which may extend to five lakh rupees or with both.

- **Section 66B:** Punishment for dishonestly receiving stolen computer resource or communication device. Whoever dishonestly received or retains any stolen computer resource or communication device knowing or having reason to believe the same to be stolen computer resource or communication device, will be punished with imprisonment of either description for a term which may extend to three years or with fine which may extend to rupees one lakh or with both.

- **Section 66C:** Punishment for identity theft. Whoever, fraudulently or dishonestly make use of the electronic signature, password or any other unique identification feature of any other person, will be punished with imprisonment of either description for a term which may extend to three years and will also be liable to fine with may extend to rupees one lakh.

- **Section 66D:** Punishment for cheating by personation by using computer resource. Whoever, by means for any communication device or computer resource cheats by personating, will be punished with imprisonment of either description for a term which may extend to three years and will also be liable to fine which may extend to one lakh rupees.

- **Section 66E:** Punishment for violation of privacy. Whoever, intentionally or knowingly captures, publishes or transmits the image of a private area of any person without his or her consent, under circumstances violating the privacy of that person, will be punished with imprisonment which may extend to three years or with fine not exceeding two lakh rupees, or with both.

- **Section 67:** Punishment for publishing or transmitting obscene material in electronic form. Whoever publishes or transmits or causes to be published or transmitted in the electronic form, any material which is lascivious or appeals to the prurient interest or if its effect is such as to tend to deprave and corrupt persons who are likely, having regard to all relevant circumstances, to read, see or hear the matter contained or embodied in it, will be punished on first conviction with imprisonment of either description for a term which may extend to three years and with fine which may extend to five lakh rupees and in the event of second or subsequent conviction with imprisonment of either description for a term which may extend to five years and also with fine which may extend to ten lakh rupees.

- **Section 67:** Publishing of information which is obscene in electronic form. Whoever publishes or transmits or causes to be published in the electronic form, any material which is lascivious or appeals to the prurient interest or if its effect is such as to tend to deprave and corrupt persons who are likely, having regard to all relevant circumstances, to read, see or hear the matter contained or embodied in it, will be punished on first conviction with imprisonment of either description for a term which may extend to five years and with fine which may extend to one lakh rupees and in the event of a second or subsequent conviction with imprisonment of either description for a term which may extend to ten years and also with fine which may extend to two lakh rupees.

- **Section 67A:** Punishment for publishing or transmitting of material containing sexually explicit act, etc., in electronic form. Whoever publishes or transmits or causes to be published or transmitted in the electronic form any material which contains sexually explicit act or conduct will be punished on first conviction with imprisonment of either description for a term which may extend to five years and with fine which may extend to ten lakh rupees and in the event of second or subsequent conviction with imprisonment of either description for a term which may extend to seven years and also with fine which may extend to ten lakh rupees.

- **Section 67B:** Punishment for publishing or transmitting of material depicting children in sexually explicit act, etc., in electronic form. Whoever:
  - Publishes or transmits or causes to be published or transmitted material in any electronic form which depicts children engaged in sexually explicit act or conduct; or
  - Creates text or digital images, collects, seeks, browses, downloads, advertises, promotes, exchanges or distributes material in any electronic form depicting children in obscene or indecent or sexually explicit manner; or

- ◦ Cultivates, entices or induces children to online relationship with one or more children for and on sexually explicit act or in a manner that may offend a reasonable adult on the computer resource; or
- ◦ Facilitates abusing children online, or
- ◦ Records in any electronic form own abuse or that of others pertaining to sexually explicit act with children, will be punished on first conviction with imprisonment of either description for a term which may extend to five years and with fine which may extend to ten lakh rupees and in the event of second or subsequent conviction with imprisonment of either description for a term which may extend to seven years and also with fine which may extend to ten lakh rupees. But provisions of section 67, section 67A and this section does not extend to any book, pamphlet, paper, writing, drawing, painting representation or figure in electronic form:
    - ▪ The publication of which is proved to be justified as being for the public good on the ground that such book, pamphlet, paper, writing drawing, painting representation or figure is in the interest of science, literature, art or learning or other objects of general concern; or
    - ▪ Which is kept or used for bona fide heritage or religious purposes.
- **Section 71:** Penalty for misrepresentation. Whoever makes any misrepresentation to, or suppresses any material fact from the Controller or the Certifying Authority for obtaining any licence or Electronic Signature Certificate, as the case may be, will be punished with imprisonment for a term which may extend to two years, or with fine which may extend to one lakh rupees, or with both.
- **Section 72:** Penalty for breach of confidentiality and privacy. Except as otherwise provided in this Act or any other law for the time being in force, if any person who, in pursuance of any of the powers conferred under this Act, rules or regulations made thereunder, has secured access to any electronic record, book, register, correspondence, information, document or other material without the consent of the person concerned discloses such electronic record, book, register, correspondence, information, document or other material to any other person will be punished with imprisonment for a term which may extend to two years, or with fine which may extend to one lakh rupees, or with both.
- **Section 72A:** Punishment for disclosure of information in breach of lawful contract. Save as otherwise provided in this Act or any other law for the time being in force, any person including an intermediary who, while providing services under the terms of lawful contract, has secured access to any material containing personal information about another person, with the intent to cause or knowing that he is likely to cause wrongful loss or wrongful gain discloses, without the consent of the person concerned, or in breach of a lawful contract, such material to any other person, will be punished with imprisonment for a term which may extend to three years, or with fine which may extend to five lakh rupees, or with both.
- **Section 73:** Penalty for publishing Electronic Signature Certificate false in certain particulars.
    - ◦ No person will publish an Electronic Signature Certificate or otherwise make it available to any other person with the knowledge that-
        - ▪ The Certifying Authority listed in the certificate has not issued it; or
        - ▪ The subscriber listed in the certificate has not accepted it; or
        - ▪ The certificate has been revoked or suspended, unless such publication is for the purpose of verifying a electronic signature created prior to such suspension or revocation.

- ◦ Any person who contravenes the provisions of sub-section (1) will be punished with imprisonment for a term which may extend to two years, or with fine which may extend to one lakh rupees, or with both.
- **Section 74:** Publication for fraudulent purpose. Whoever knowingly creates, publishes or otherwise makes available an Electronic Signature Certificate for any fraudulent or unlawful purpose will be punished with imprisonment for a term which may extend to two years, or with fine which may extend to one lakh rupees, or with both. If any person knowingly creates, publishes or otherwise makes available an Electronic Signature Certificate for any fraudulent or unlawful purpose, he will be punished with imprisonment upto two years, or with fine upto one lakh rupees, or with both.
- **Section 77:** Penalties or confiscation not to interfere with other punishments. No penalty imposed or confiscation made under this Act will prevent the imposition of any other punishment to which the person affected thereby is liable under any other law for the time being in force.
- **Section 85:** Offences by companies.
  - ◦ Where a person committing a contravention of any of the provisions of this Act or of any rule, direction or order made thereunder is a company, every person who, at the time the contravention was committed, was in charge of, and was responsible to, the company for the conduct of business of the company as well as the company, will be guilty of the contravention and will be liable to be proceeded against and punished accordingly: But nothing contained in this sub-section will render any such person liable to punishment if he proves that the contravention took place without his knowledge or that he exercised all due diligence to prevent such contravention.
  - ◦ Notwithstanding anything contained in sub-section (1), where a contravention of any of the provisions of this Act or of any rule, direction or order made thereunder has been committed by a company and it is proved that the contravention has taken place with the consent or connivance of, or is attributable to any neglect on the part of, any director, manager, secretary or other officer of the company, such director, manager, secretary or other officer will also be deemed to be guilty of the contravention and will be liable to be proceeded against and punished accordingly.

The Indian Penal Code, 1860

The Indian Penal Code was amended by inserting the word 'electronic' thereby treating the electronic records and documents on a par with physical records and documents. The Sections dealing with false entry in a record or false document etc. (e.g. Section 192, 204, 463, 464, 464, 468 to 470, 471, 474, 476 etc.) have since been amended as 'electronic record and electronic document' thereby bringing within the ambit of IPC. Now, electronic record and electronic documents has been treated just like physical records and documents during commission of acts of forgery or falsification of physical records in a crime. After the above amendment, the investigating agencies file the cases/ charge-sheet quoting the relevant sections from IPC under section 463,464, 468 and 469 read with the Information Technology Act, 2000 under Sections 43 and 66 in like offences to ensure the evidence and/or punishment can be covered and proved under either of these or under both legislation (Gupta, 2015).

SOLUTIONS AND RECOMMENDATIONS

The solution to the problem is not that simple. The laws in the paper must come into action. The implementation issues are always to be removed from the societal side as well as the administration side. Things like corruption, incapable officials, lack of equipment etc. should not hamper the justice to an ordinary man who is already victimized by the offender.

FURTHER RESEARCH DIRECTIONS

The indicators include the implementation and effectiveness of Information Technology Act, 2000 which has been passed in the year 2000 itself. An evaluation of the Act empirically which reveal the extent to which the Act has been useful for deterring the offenders.

CONCLUSION

It can be said that the measures taken up by the laws in ensuring the cybercrime free society is overwhelming. There are various provisions for various crimes occurring through the wrong use of web. The law is highly deterrent but also required to curb these crimes in the society. However, there are certain technical issues in the implementation of the Act which needs to be sorted out at the Governmental level. The technical glitches should not be a reason for injustice to any person.

REFERENCES

Cybercrime. (2015a). *Definition of Cybercrime*. Retrieved November 25, 2015 from https://www.techopedia.com/definition/2387/cybercrime

Cybercrime. (2015b). *Definition of Cybercrime*. Retrieved November 25, 2015 from http://techterms.com/definition/cybercrime

Cybercrime. (2015c). *Definition of Cybercrime*. Retrieved November 25, 2015 from http://www.britannica.com/topic/cybercrime

Gupta, K. R. (2015). *An Overview Of Cyber Laws vs. Cyber Crimes: In Indian Perspective*. Retrieved November 25, 2015 from http://www.mondaq.com/india/x/257328/Data+Protection+Privacy/An+Overview+Of+Cyber+Laws+vs+Cyber+Crimes+In+Indian+Perspective

Information Technology Act (2000)

KEY TERMS AND DEFINITIONS

Companies: Companies means a registered company such as company defined under the Companies Act, 2013.

Crime: A punishable offence under criminal laws of a country.

Cybercrime: A crime committable through internet or a crime which involves internet.

Defamation: Defamation includes both libel and slander.

Fraud: A common generic term which means deception.

Internet: A global computer network.

Penalty: Penalty not only includes monetary compensation only and not imprisonment for an offence under the criminal laws.

Section 2
Techniques for Combating Security Breaches

Chapter 5

Cloud Crime and Fraud:
A Study of Challenges for Cloud Security and Forensics

Nimisha Singh
Birla Institute of Management Technology, India

ABSTRACT

Changing trends in IT industry are opening new avenues. With the scalability, flexibility, and economic advantage offered by cloud computing, more and more organizations are moving towards cloud for their applications. With all the benefits of cloud computing, it poses a danger of digital crime and security breaches. These challenges are compounded by the fact that cybercrime and the transgressors transcend geographical boundaries while the law enforcement does not. This paper tries to focus on how cloud computing is rising to the challenges thrown in from cyber space and recent developments to avoid and mitigate cloud fraud and abuse. Taking counter measures at organizational level, will alleviate and up to an extent eliminate security breaches. With current knowledge on policy and standards adopted by developed nations, the policy makers and law enforcement agencies in developing countries can work towards formulating standards and guidelines for awareness on threats, vulnerabilities and effectiveness of security controls to respond to risk.

INTRODUCTION

Cloud based IT services have been gaining popularity as they do not require big investments. Ford (2011) described the cloud as "in which dynamically scalable and often-virtualized resources are provided as a service over the internet" whereas Knorr & Gruman (2009) described it as "any IT resources outside of the firewall including conventional outsourcing". Cloud services are based on a new business model of on demand service where customers can choose what they want, how much they want and pay only for those services, which they require and has been rendered to them. The shared use of resources like - storage, servers, and applications and services- has led to potential cost saving.

DOI: 10.4018/978-1-5225-0193-0.ch005

Even though the cloud technology is not mature, there is an increased confidence in its adoption by businesses owing to lower running costs and ease in deployment. Cloud computing offers flexibility, efficiency and cost saving and at the same time poses challenges of security not only to users but also to regulatory and law enforcement agencies. The cloud service provider is entrusted with hosting, maintaining and has general access to customer data. Outsourcing and global dispersion of cloud service providers raises jurisdiction issue for law enforcement agencies since the service provider may have data centres in multiple countries, each with their unique laws on data usage and privacy. The layered architecture and multi-tenacy opens a large surface for attack from outsiders. With increasing trend towards adoption of cloud based services, there is a need for secure cloud services. Also, organizations are required to follow data governance law of their country which emphasize maintaining data privacy and confidentiality. The security in cloud environment needs to be evaluated from different perspectives:

- Cross border jurisdiction as the service provider may be in a different jurisdiction than the customer.
- Technical solution to make architecture more robust and difficult to penetrate by intruders.
- Compliance by organizations to maintain data privacy and confidentiality.

The paper looks at current state of affairs, cloud demand and risks; and offers advice on cloud adoption by incorporating technical, organizational and legal dimension to combat security issues. With technology available to today and process improvement, organizations can make themselves better prepared to tackle privacy and security breaches.

The chapter focuses on security and privacy issues raised by the cloud environment, investigation challenges in the cloud environment, different dimensions to cloud security so that organizations can be better prepared for secure information management in the cloud environment.

BACKGROUND

With Information technology playing a strong role in today's global economy, organizations are adopting cloud based services to develop and protect their market share in their core business. The survey of cloud service market indicates inexorable shift to cloud with IDC predicting public IT cloud service spending to grow to $127 billion by 2018 (Leopold 2014). IDC also predicts that "public IT cloud services will account for more than half of global software, server, and storage spending growth by 2018" (Leopold 2014). Driving this growth will be use of cloud based applications. Using cloud service, data will be outsourced to a cloud service provider which requires higher security standards to protect customer's data from losses due to technical malfunction, external intrusion and maintain confidentiality. As dispersion of cloud service providers enables low cost, flexibility and data availability, it also brings in jurisdiction issues in case of a security breach.

To understand how cloud environment has brought cost saving and flexibility, it is necessary to understand its characteristics, deployment model and service models. the As given by NIST, cloud computing is defined as a collection of five essential characteristics, three service models and four deployment models (Mell, 2011).

The essential characteristics are:

1. **On Demand Self-Service:** Provisioning of computing capabilities such as network storage, server time by consumer without human intervention by the service provider.
2. **Network Access:** The capabilities provided are accessible through standard mechanisms over network.
3. **Resource Pooling:** Multiple consumers use the pooled computing resources in multi-tenant model.
4. **Rapid Elasticity:** Based on the need, capabilities can be elastically upgraded or downgraded at any time.
5. **Measured Service:** Cloud systems leverage capability for monitoring, controlling and reporting the usage of resources giving transparency to both the provider and consumer.

The cloud service models deployed on cloud infrastructure are:

1. **Private Cloud:** The cloud resources are owned, managed and controlled by an enterprise and services are offered to their internal users only.
2. **Public Cloud:** Cloud services are offered to the general public.
3. **Community Cloud:** owned and operated by organizations of a specific community with shared interests.
4. **Hybrid Cloud:** composition of two or more clouds (private, public, community) eg academic clouds.

The three service models are:

1. **Infrastructure as a Service (IAAS):** Computing hardware such as networks, servers and storage create a resource pool, a portion of which is give to the customer on a pay per usage model.
2. **Platform as a Service (PAAS):** Provides web accessible platform to developers to code and test new software. Using services such as Amazon's EC2 or Microsoft Azure, customers do not have to deal with the complexity of development and production servers.
3. **Software as a Service (SAAS):** Typically an application hosted by a provider where the customer does not need to install any application locally, for example: salesforce.com, and Google Docs.

Taken collectively, it can be as described as in Figure 1

Gartner (2012) forecasted that spending on cloud computing will double by 2016. But a wide adoption of this emerging technology has raised security concerns as the services are outsourced. Though cloud computing, just like any other technological development, was aimed at mass convenience and adoption, there are those who see these advances as platforms for fraud and abuse. Ernst and Young (2011) reiterated this perceived risk in adopting cloud technologies.

Cloud environment is prone to security and operational risks including hardware and software failure, power outages, server mis-configuration, malware as well as insider threat. In addition to the security issues faced by traditional systems, multi-tenancy, virtual machine infrastructure (Grispos et al 2013), architecture, network dependency, third party outsourcing, and scale make it more vulnerable to threats which may have disastrous impact leading to data loss and corruption, tampering with data and breach of confidentiality (Jules, Opera 2013).

Figure 1. NIST cloud definition framework
Source: Created by authors from information from National Institute of Standards and Technology, US Department of Commerce.

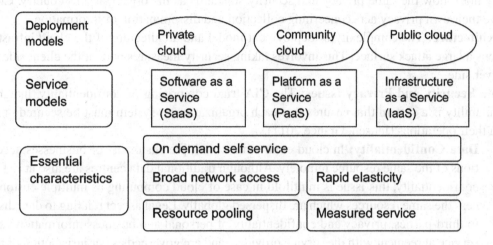

Even though the private cloud is meant for a single organization, and the organization has the control over security system, data flow and storage policies; the system is at risk similar to that of a non-cloud hosting. The challenge in such a scenario is that the organization should have the expertise to create and implement a security strategy for a complex system.

SECURITY AND PRIVACY ISSUES

Cloud computing has brought a paradigm shift by displacing data and applications of an organization to be maintained and operated by another organization. An investigation by Condon (2012) revealed serious security problems in cloud environment including ability for customers to access each other's data. Breach of personal information is one of the big problems in cloud environment. Privacy refers to the right of an individual to be aware of information stored about them and prevent its abuse (Guilloteau, Mauree 2012). Maintaining privacy through secure management and control of personal information is important as it promotes user confidence and economic development as well as to meet legal compliance set forth by national laws and regulations. Although it is not possible to draw a holistic picture of current issues in cloud environment, one method of classification could be attempted by dividing security and privacy issues under the given categories (Jansen, Grance 2011).

1.   **Governance:** An organization's control over standards, policies procedures set forth for an application development and monitoring diminishes when cloud computing services are used. The organization will be at a risk if policies related to privacy and security are overlooked.
2.   **Compliance:** There are security and privacy laws and regulations at national, state and local level for compliance but in case of cloud computing these may get ignored due to cross-border flow of data. In case of an in-house computing centre, the data is stored and safeguard as per the organization's governance policy. In contrast, cloud service providers' do not disclose the data location to their subscribers. In such a situation, it is difficult to establish whether legal and compliance requirements

are met. Also laws and jurisdictions of the country where data is stored will be applicable which may not follow the same privacy and security standards as the organization's country. Countries have their own privacy acts concerning collection and dissemination of information.

3. **Architecture:** The complexity of deployment model and architecture of the cloud infrastructure opens a large attack surface. This involves taking security measures both at the client side and the server side.

4. **Data Security and Privacy Issues:** The CIA triad comprising of confidentiality, integrity and availability is a system that ensures that each organization or system must be secured enough to run their operations (Jansen, Grance 2011).

    a. **Data Confidentiality:** In cloud environment multiple customers or businesses access portions of the same resource remotely. Although traditional data centres are also at risk of data confidentiality, this issue is multifold in case of cloud computing as multiple customers access the same resources which are dispersed globally. Legal aspect relating to data disclosure to third-parties, privacy and confidentiality of personal and business information vary with service agreement with the service providers and are governed as per jurisdiction of physical location of data storage. It also brings loss of policy level control as customers do not have a physical access to their cloud service provider.

    b. **Data Integrity:** For any business trustworthiness of information is utmost priority. In a public cloud which is multi-tenant, multiple access points make the system more vulnerable to software manipulation putting both storage and processing at a risk affecting data integrity. Since cloud hosts data from multiple customers, it is more enticing for hackers. Besides the external attacks, the multi-tenant public cloud is vulnerable to attacks from other tenants in the same cloud.

    c. **Availability:** Cloud computing like traditional computing can experience outages and performance slowdown due to hardware, software or any other external issue not in control of the service provider. Multiple layers and multiple access points in cloud expose it to attacks from multiple points eventually disrupting services to its clients.

5. **Trust:** Confidentiality, integrity and accessibility are easy to maintain in traditional computing environment as the owner has physical and policy control over data and services. In traditional architecture, an efficient security policy ensures trust and the owner can make infrastructure and policy changes for any weak point. By moving data and services to cloud environment, the customer is relinquishing its control over security aspects and entrusting the cloud service provider with ensuring audits and control mechanisms to mitigate threats that the customer data and processes are now exposed to. At times cloud services are nested and layered with other cloud services e.g. an application may be built upon PaaS and IaaS. At times, a service provider may involve a third party for outsourcing or subcontracting some of its services without disclosing it to the customer.

Division of responsibility differs based on the cloud service model under consideration. In SaaS model, a consumer uses provider's application running on a cloud infrastructure. With this model, consumer has no control over how data is processed and stored and relies completely on the service provider to take security measures. PaaS provides tools that enable developers to develop and deploy applications. Here developer needs to use best practices and privacy friendly tools. In IaaS model, the consumer uses computing resources and service provider is responsible for securing the data centres, network and systems and ensures that its operations and procedures comply with the applicable law and regulations.

Challenges to Privacy in Cloud

The expanding quantity of personal data and promise by cloud computing to deliver on lower costs has driven the demand for cloud services. The complexity of cloud services and data flow crossing national boundaries raises questions that need to be addressed to maintain data security and privacy

1. Who are the stakeholders and what is their role and responsibility?
2. What is the location of data storage?
3. What legal rules apply to data processing?
4. What are the measures taken by service providers to meet the expected level of security and privacy?

Investigation Challenges in Cloud

In digital forensics investigation, the hard disk is acquired, verified and analyzed. The same techniques can be applied for virtual disks associated with cloud model but there are some challenges since the data is stored on the cloud. In traditional forensics investigation, the main source of information is the suspect's or victim's computer. Not only is it easy to get hold of the computers, it is also easy to analyze recently opened files and data which are stored locally on the suspect's computer.

Data stored on cloud spans gigabytes which is too much data for law enforcement agencies to process or store. To overcome this issue, selective data acquisition may be used by reducing the dataset that investigator is interested in. But ensuring that no evidence is missed will become a challenge if the data set is reduced. With multi-tenant model and multiple access points, association of the data with the suspect is impractical. Even though the Cloud Service Providers maintain a log, the data and log files are stored in more than one geographical location (Grispos et al 2013).

In case of an incident at CSP end, the CSP will be more interested in restoring the service than preserving the evidence. The CSP may not report the incident for the sake of reputation or may start its own investigation without proper measures to preserve evidence. In cloud computing, since the data is not stored locally but is on cloud, direct evidence is not available for the investigators. For evidence, the investigator is dependent on the cloud service provider who may be out of investigators' jurisdiction. Law enforcement agencies are finding it challenging to investigate when suspect computer is in one jurisdiction and data stored in cloud is in another jurisdiction. This gets even more complicated with different cyber laws in different countries. Another challenge is physically accessing the cloud service provider compared to traditional environment where a computer or server is acquired and imaged for investigation. Acquiring servers in cloud environment will affect services to multiple customers which may raise a liability issue for the service provider.

Another challenge in cloud environment is international communication and cooperation which is not yet in place for cloud investigation. Although many countries are connected by INTERPOL's I-24/7 network or the G8 24/7 network, their structure and organization are a hindrance to real time attacks such as DDoS (Joshua et. Al, 2013).

Investigation in cloud environment not only faces technical challenges but also challenges of policy, guidance, and standard (Badger et al 2011). There is a growing acceptance for cloud technology due to lower cost and operational efficiency but at the same time the technology has not matured enough to counteract the threats. There is a great deal of work required to deal with security, privacy, and compliance monitoring, given the fact that the people who are concerned with these issues are not the ones who own this technology, which is where the attack may be manifested.

Digital Investigation in Cloud Environment

Although there are geopolitical and technological challenges when it comes to cloud computing, digital forensics investigation process model can still be employed to acquire and analyze the data (Joshua et al 2013). Digital forensics is a set of processes to acquire digital evidence. Typically digital evidence includes, files stored on the disk, data items stored in memory, audio or video files, data transmitted over network. Digital evidence once collected must be authentic, reliable, complete, believable and admissible to common law and legislative rules (Reilly et al. 2011). Preservation of evidence is very crucial to the forensic investigation. Joshua et al. (2013) gave a four phase digital forensic investigation process model which is comprised of Readiness phase, physical crime scene investigation, digital crime scene investigation and analysis of data.

1. **Readiness Phase:** For successful forensic investigation, certain measures are required to be taken before the actual incident occurs. This involves procurement of equipment, training of technical staff and first responders. Taking this approach to cloud computing would mean education about cloud related technologies, know-how of infrastructure, platform and software and tools and methods to collect relevant data and legal staff familiar with multi jurisdiction and multi tenant issues.

2. **Physical Crime Scene Investigation:** Digital forensics requires access to possible sources of evidence such as victim's computer, hacker's device and the data centre. In case of cloud computing, the devices containing the evidence may be difficult to get hold of due to geographical and jurisdiction spread. For ensuring cost effectiveness and service availability, cloud service providers have their data centres around the world in different jurisdictions. Data is replicated in multiple locations to reduce the risk of multiple point of failure.

3. **Digital Crime Scene Investigation:** Next phase is digital crime scene investigation which again is spread over different locations. Different cloud service models and deployment models require different set of tools and procedures to acquire data sources. For example, in public cloud, provider side data sources needto be segregated among multiple tenants whereas there is no such need in case of private cloud. The first step in digital scene investigation is preserving the scene which involves removing victim's computer and taking disk image. Here again, cloud computing throws in some peculiar challenges. Isolating a victim's computer is possible but isolating a cloud service provider for investigation will affect services provided to many other customers. Preservation of crime scene is followed by acquisition of potential evidence which is easier to do with the victim's computer. But in case of cloud computing live data, forensics will need to be used since services of other customers cannot be suspended for the sake of investigation.

4. **Analysis of Acquired Data:** The last phase is analysis of acquired data to produce reasoned conclusions and present it to jury or court. This requires explaining how the evidence was acquired and what exactly the evidence means which may be challenging when dealing with cloud data centres with multiple servers, spread all over the world and accessed by thousands of tenants. To satisfy legal requirements, digital evidence must be authentic, reliable, complete, believable and admissible to legislative rules.

Considering the complexity of cloud deployment, service models and amount of data that CSPs hold in addition to distribution of cloud servers, CSPs and law enforcement agencies need to work together to identify potential risks, model threats and their impact. Not only will it train personnel involved, it will also help in timely acquisition of relevant data and efficient response and how to handle data when such an incident occurs.

SOLUTIONS AND RECOMMENDATIONS

As cloud innovations heat up, so will the competition. To win their customers, cloud service providers need to enable customers

- To use and pay for services as per their need and enjoy secure access to their data anytime and from anywhere.
- Access to high class products and services to be used in a simple, reliable and secure way.
- Access to quality service from a trusted vendor.
- Exceptional network availability for easy data access.
- Solutions integrating centralized computing, mobile access and high speed network.

At the heart of successful cloud adoption is having a secure cloud management to avoid any failures whether technical or man-made.

The features of cloud computing that made possible saving operational costs have also put the risk for data confidentiality and security. The complex layered architecture has opened up a large attack surface, access of services over the network opens it for network threats and conferring data processing and management to another organization raises the concern for privacy. At the same time, features of cloud computing such as centralized data, compute intensive resources and inbuilt hash authentication assist in digital investigation.

Digital forensics investigation starts with collecting digital evidences which are in the form of documents, photographs, spreadsheets, internet history, email etc. which are stored locally on suspect or victim's computer. In case of cloud computing, these files are no longer stored locally hence it is difficult to collect evidence. The process of cyber forensics investigation remains the same but the challenge is to identify where the relevant data is actually stored and how it can be obtained and analyzed for forensics investigation (Singh, Rishi 2015). One way is to see possible fraud and abuse scenarios and consider possible mitigations. In her work, Webb-Hobson (2013) has put forward possible scenarios such as criminal fraud investigation, intellectual property theft, breach of acceptable use policy, contractual dispute with CSP, civil dispute between corporations and proposed avoidance and mitigation strategies which can help in efficient investigation. Some of the important things to notice when moving data to cloud is to check contractual agreements and the forensics readiness in procedures to gather and preserve digital evidence. Not only will it help to deter and detect crime but also prepare the organization for using digital evidence in its defense.

The existing digital forensic investigation models, practices and tools are meant for off line investigation of storage media where the investigator has control of the storage medium. In contrast, cloud environment storage media may be beyond control of the investigator (Grispos et al 2013). From technology point of view, there is a lack of maturity in cloud service model. From regulatory point of view, there is not much support to deal with international jurisdiction (Singh, Rishi, 2015). Security issues, requirements and challenges that the cloud environment is posing calls for security standards and management models. One way is to look at cloud environment from both technology and business perspective model (Grispos et al 2013) emphasizing improvement on current prevention mechanism, improved standard for corporate security professionals, increased awareness of current vulnerabilities and prevention measures (Al-Fadaghi, Al-Babtain, 2012).

Multi-Dimensional Approach to Cloud Security

Cloud security involves multiple stakeholders- the cloud service provider, the user and the security software provider each with their own security, privacy and trust requirements (Takabi et al 2010). Cloud security is not just a technical issue but a multi dimensional issue that requires collaboration between, CSP, customer, multiple tenants sharing same resources, and among international law enforcement agencies. The three dimensions of cloud forensic are – technical, organizational and legal (Ruan et al, 2011)

Technical Dimension

Technical dimension covers the tools and procedures to investigate in cloud environment. Some of the key features are

1. Forensic data collection- identifying and acquiring data from client premises and service provider infrastructure.
2. Evidence segregation- sharing of resources makes evidence segregation impractical.
3. Investigations in virtualized environment- in cloud environment, operations are mostly virtualized whereas investigation requires physical acquisition of the device for evidence retrieval.

Organizational Dimension

Forensic investigation in the cloud involves both the cloud service provider and the customer. To be forensic ready, both the provider and customer of cloud services need to collaborate in the investigation. One way is to define the roles of internal staff as investigators; IT professionals to facilitate the investigators in accessing crime scene; is also referred to as business continuity plan that documents set of procedures, set of actions to be taken before, during and after a disaster to recover and protect IT infrastructure. The plan specifies precautions to be taken and procedures an organization needs to follow to minimize the effects of disaster and to quickly resume mission-critical functions.

Legal Dimension

Legal dimension includes multi-jurisdiction and multi-tenancy as well as service level agreement (SLA). Cloud investigation at times spans multiple jurisdiction which calls for regulations and agreements to ensure that forensic activities do not breach any laws or regulations under any jurisdiction(s), and the confidentiality of other tenants sharing the same infrastructure does not get compromised, during the investigation.

Service level agreements (SLA) between the service provider and customer need to address issues related to forensic investigation in case of an incident such as techniques supported, access granted for investigation, roles and responsibilities of service provider and customer etc. SLA terms need to address data security policy emphasizing legal, regulatory and security controls for incident management. Although SLA addresses these issues, they vary with respect to terms, resources covered, time period and guarantees.

The multiple stakeholder approach will enhance the security and forensic investigation readiness of the organization using the cloud services. Further, the security requirements can be divided as process oriented requirements and technical requirements (Badger et al 2011). Process oriented requirements will include cloud privacy guideline, security control roles and responsibilities, trustworthiness of cloud operators, business continuity and disaster recovery whereas technical requirements will include continuous monitoring capabilities, data protection, identity and access management, authorization and cloud based denial of service (Badger et al 2011). Another way would be real-time auditing either by organization using cloud service or any third party to evaluate security visibility and assure correct cloud service operations (Jules, Opera 2013). A shared security responsibility approach involving all stakeholders to cover multidisciplinary approach will be effective in dealing with cloud security.

The accountability for security and privacy in public cloud environment does not just lie with cloud provider. Public cloud is a choice for many organizations. Organizations should carefully evaluate technology risks and threats when outsourcing data, applications and other computing resources to public cloud environment. Hence they need to

- Analyze and plan security and privacy aspects of cloud computing before using them.
- Ensure that organizational security and privacy requirements are met when using services offered by cloud environment.
- Take measures to maintain privacy and security of data and applications implemented in cloud environment.

In the absence of defined regulations regarding cloud computing, organizations need to take a careful approach to identify laws and regulations and how they will affect cloud business model and then choose a technical architecture model and implement service management for cloud services (Zota, Fratila 2013). One way is to consider solutions for security and privacy issues from technical, organizational or legal point of view as described in Table 1.

Table 1. Addressing security and privacy issues

Sr. No.	Security/ Privacy Issue	Dimension	Solution
1	Governance	Organization	Privacy and security policies in SLA to accommodate monitoring capabilities in cloud.
2	Compliance	Organization, legal	• SLA need to address the compliance issues related to security and privacy law and regulations. • Cloud security and privacy need to be addresses at national and international level to have common standards for compliance
3	Architecture	Technical	Secure architecture to combat attacks which may be due to multi-tenancy, deployment model or layered architecture
4	Data confidentiality	Organization, legal, technical	• SLA needs to address the issues related to data disclosure to third parties, data governance as specified by jurisdiction where the service is located; physical location of data storage • International regulation needed to resolve the jurisdiction issues related to data confidentiality • Secure technical architecture to avoid the breach of security
5	Data integrity	Technical	• Data retrieval procedure in case of failure of storage and processing • Notification to the client in case of such an incident
6	Availability	Technical	• Backup system to manage outage and performance slowdown • Instant notification to client in case of such an incident
7	Trust	Technical, organizational	Transparent audit and control mechanism and to be conducted and shared with client periodically

International Privacy Protection Principles/ Laws

Organization for Economic Cooperation and Development (OECD) has developed guidelines governing protection, privacy and transborder flow of personal data. The principles in these guidelines serve as basic standards which should be supplemented by additional measures for data privacy whether in public or private sectors. Guiding principles of OECD are:

- Collection limitation principle,
- Data quality principle,
- Purpose specification principle,
- Use limitation principle,
- Security safeguard principle,
- Openness principle,
- Individual participation principle,
- Accountability principle,
- Implementing accountability,
- Basic principles of international application: free flow and legitimate restrictions.

In addition to the principles, OECD emphasizes national implementation and international cooperation to facilitate cross border privacy law enforcement.

Many countries around the world have data protection laws as well as guides for private and public organizations and individuals. The privacy principles and frameworks are aimed at preventing harm to individuals:

- National Institute of Standards and Technology guidelines on security and privacy in cloud computing environment,
- European Union Data protection Directive 95/46/EC,
- Asia pacific Economic Cooperation (APEC) privacy framework,
- Organization for Economic Cooperation and Development (OECD) principles,
- Madrid resolution- every responsible person should have transparent policies with regard to processing personal data,
- European Network and Information Security Agency (ENISA)-recommendation to facilitate understanding of balance of responsibility and accountability for key functions,
- Privacy by design-EU directive 95/ 46/ EC and e-privacy directive 2002/ 58/EC are main legal instrument in Europe for privacy and processing of personal data.

Although EU member states have implemented 1995 directive, they have done so differently resulting in difficulties in enforcement across member states. The conflicting data protection regulations among countries could hamper transfer of data across borders. Efficiency of cloud computing will not be achieved if coordination at international level on government policies is not taken up.

Countries in developing world are also introducing privacy and data protection laws.

Privacy Laws in India

With the digital revolution in India public and private sector are collecting huge amount of an individual's personal information. India being a major IT hub for outsourced projects, needs to have strong data protection mechanism as well as governance for privacy protection as organizations collecting data need to comply with international standards. As compared to developed nations, laws regarding cloud computing and privacy issues are evolving in India. Many countries are putting geographical restrictions which disallow cross border data exchange. In such a situation, India will be at a disadvantage in absence of cloud computing law governing the cyberspace. Indian Information Technology Act 2000 lays down penalty for breach of confidentiality and privacy. The concept of due diligence prescribed by the Information technology (Intermediaries Guidelines) Rules 2011 requires all organizations to maintain privacy in cloud environment. These provisions safeguard the privacy interests and are thus a deterrent in nature. There are no dedicated legislations for cloud environment which deals with cross border data flow. In absence of a dedicated legislation, organizations need to take a proactive approach to deal with incidents in cloud environment i.e. secure cloud adoption for data protection and secure cloud management for business continuity (Singh, Rishi 2015).

Applying privacy principles to cloud computing

1. **Contracted Service Provider Requirements:** Negotiate cloud provider's standard terms and conditions to prevent privacy breach in cloud
2. **Transfer of Data Out of India Rules:** The current Information Technology Act does not address issues pertaining to the transborder flow of data.
3. **Protection and Security:** Organization using cloud service need to ensure that personal information stored in the cloud is protected against unauthorized access and loss to comply with the privacy principles.
4. **Use and Disclosure:** Since the organization will be liable for misuse of data, it needs to ensure that the agreement with the cloud provider does not allow the cloud provider to access information.
5. **Mandatory Notification of Security Breach:** To minimize the negative impact of a breach, the organization relies on the cloud provider which means the organization should consider including a mandatory breach notification in the agreement.
6. **Lawful Access in Other Countries:** Information stored in a server located in another country will be governed by the laws and regulation of that country. The impact of any such laws on the data should be carefully analyzed by the organization using the cloud service.

Information Management and Data Security

The organization using cloud services needs to evaluate and expand its information security documentation as well as use technical and procedural interventions for mitigating future exposure (Grispos et al 2013). NIST (Dempsey et al 2011) has developed guideline for organizations to develop strategy and implement Information System continuous Monitoring for awareness on threats and vulnerabilities, effectiveness of deployed security controls which will provide information to respond to risk.

The Cloud Service Providers must have an information management and data security policy emphasizing the legal, regulatory and security controls in place in case of an incident (Grispos et al 2013). Although these issues are addressed in SLA (Service Level Agreement), they differ widely in terms of different terms, covering different resources, time periods and different guarantees (Badger et al 2011). This ambiguity leaves customer at risk. Even though, data in cloud environment is in shared environment, the owner should have full control over data with a standard based security approach (Takabi et al 2010). NIST Cloud Computing program has identified strategic and tactical security, interoperability requirements as high priority requirements to meet the objectives of Federal Cloud Computing Strategy. Some of the initiatives of NIST cloud computing program are

- CAESARS (Continuous Asset Evaluation, Situational Awareness & Risk Scoring) provides architectural system monitoring and reporting.
- SCAP (Security Content Automation protocol) provides specifications for security configurations & events, event management & incident handling.
- FISMA (Federal Information Security Management) provides baseline security controls.

FUTURE RESEARCH DIRECTIONS

Cloud computing is an emerging technology but is gaining wide acceptance by organizations as well as individuals owing to flexibility, ease of use, location independent services and cost savings. The paper has tried to bring out the privacy and security issues in cloud environment and existing legislations as deterrent to breach of privacy and security. The paper has analyzed challenges posed by cloud computing and work done by standard development organizations and the role of organizations using cloud services. Although there are challenges of maintaining privacy in cloud environment, a multi stakeholder approach can be adopted to prepare organizations to deal with security and privacy breach. The paper has described international legislations and privacy principles observed by developed nations and also the Acts and legislations in the Indian context. These principles still do not address the accountability issue over cross border data flow. In absence of an international legislation, adopted by all the countries, organizations need to take measures to maintain data confidentiality and privacy. There is a need for further work to develop a framework for organizational readiness for cloud security and forensic to prepare them for pre incident and post incident management.

Another area for future work is to compare the national laws for enforcing and protecting privacy with international laws, standards to identify gaps that hinder interoperability. Development of internationally comparable standards for privacy framework will give practical effect to these guidelines.

CONCLUSION

Some of the security challenges in the cloud environment are traditional computing challenges and some are unique to cloud computing. In addition to the traditional computing security concerns such as hardware and software malfunction; the complex cloud model, the way of service delivery and access to shared resources make the cloud more vulnerable to threats leading to breach of privacy and security. Each layer in the cloud model can be a potential point of attack. Although cloud computing may be prone to crime and misuse of systems and data but right tools, professional support and international legislation are all that are needed to fight cloud abuse and fraud. Taking a multi-stakeholder approach emphasizing awareness of current vulnerabilities, improved standards for data security, and improvement on current prevention mechanism will make the organization secure its information assets from security breaches.

REFERENCES

Agarwal, A., Gupta, M., Gupta, S., & Gupta, S. (2011). Systematic digital investigation model. *International Journal of Computer Science and Security, 5*(1).

Al-Fedaghi, A., & Al-Babtain, B. (2012). Modeling the forensic process. *International Journal of Security and its Applications, 6*(4).

Badger, L., Bernstein, D., Bohn, R., Vaulx, F., Hogan, V., Mao, J., & Leaf, D. et al. (2011). *High priority requirements to further USG agency cloud computing adoption. In US Government Cloud Computing Roadmap* (Vol. I). NIST.

Badger, L., Bernstein, D., Bohn, R., Vaulx, F., Hogan, V., Mao, J., & Leaf, D. et al. (2011). *Useful Information for Cloud Adopters. In US Government Cloud Computing Roadmap* (Vol. 2). NIST.

Birk, D., & Wegener, C. (2011). Technical issues of forensic investigations in cloud computing environments. *Systematic Approaches to Digital Forensic Engineering,IEEE Sixth International Workshop.* doi:10.1109/SADFE.2011.17

Carrier, B., & Spafford, E. (2003). Getting Physical with the Investigative Process. *International Journal of Digital Evidence, 2*(2).

Cloud Computing Issues and Impact. (2011). Ernst & Young.

Condon, R. (2012). *Investigation reveals serious cloud computing data security flaws.* Retrieved on February 17, 2014 from http://www.computerweekly.com/news/2240148943/Investigation-reveals-serious-cloud-computing-data-security-flaws

Daryabar, F., Deghantanha, A., Udzir, N. I., Sani, N. F., Shamsuddin, S., & Norouzizadeh, F. (2013). A survey about impacts of cloud computing on digital forensics. *International Journal of Cyber-Security and Digital Forensics, 2*(2), 77–94.

Dempsey, K., Chah, N., Johnson, A., Johnston, R., Jones, A., Orebaugh, A., … Stine, K. (2011). *Information System Continuous monitoring for federal information Systems and Organizations.* NIST Special Publication 800-137.

Ford, S. (2010, October). Managing Your Global Business with Cloud Technology. *Financial Executive.*

Grispos, G., Glisson, W. B., & Storer, T. (2013). *Cloud Security Challenges: Investigating Policies, Standards, and Guidelines in a Fortune 500 Organization.* Paper presented at 21st European Conference on Information Systems, Utrecht, The Netherlands

Grispos, G., Glisson, W. B., & Storer, T. (2013). *Calm before storm: the challenges of cloud computing in digital forensics.* Retrieved on March 27, 2014 from http://www.dcs.gla.ac.uk/~grisposg/Papers/calm.pdf

Grobauer, B., Walloschek, T., & Stocker, E. (n.d.). *Understanding clud computing vulnerabilities.* Retrieved on March 23, 2014 from http://www.infoq.com/articles/ieee-cloud-computing-vulnerabilities

Guilloteau, S., & Mauree, V. (2012). *Privacy in cloud computing.* ITU-T Technology Report.

Hare-Brown, N., & Douglas, J. (1995). *Digital Investigations in the Cloud*. Digital Forensics Laboratories. Retrieved on July 10, 2013 from www.qccis.com/

Helland, P. (2013). Condos and cloud. *Communications of the ACM, 56*(1), 50. doi:10.1145/2398356.2398374

Jansen, W., & Grance, T. (2011). *Guidelines on Security and Privacy in Public Cloud Computing*. NIST Special Publication 800-144.

Joshua, J. I., Shosha, A. F., & Gladyshev, P. (2013). Digital Forensic Investigation and Cloud Computing. In K Raun (Ed.), Cybercrime and Cloud Forensics: Applications for Investigation Processes (pp 1-41). IGI Global. doi:10.4018/978-1-4666-2662-1.ch001

Juels, A., & Opera, A. (2013). New Approaches to Security and Availability for Cloud Data. *Communications of the ACM, 66*(2).

Kent, K., Chevalier, S., Grance, T., & Dang, H. (n.d.). *Guide to Integrating Forensics into Incident Response*. Special Publication 800-86, Computer Security Division Information Technology Laboratory, NIST.

Knorr, E., & Gruman, G. (2008). *What cloud computing really means*. Retrieved on July 31, 2010 from http://www.infoworld.com/d/cloudcomputing/what-cloud-computing-really-means-031

Kobrin, S. (2001). Territoriality and the governance of cyberspace. *Journal of International Business Studies, 32*(4), 687–704. doi:10.1057/palgrave.jibs.8490990

Koops, B. J., Leenes, R., Hert, P., & Olislaegers, S. (2012). *Crime and criminal investigation in the clouds; threats and opportunities of cloud computing for Dutch criminal investigation*. Retrieved on March 23, 2014 from http://english.wodc.nl/onderzoeksdatabase/cloud-computing.aspx?cp=45&cs=6796

Leopold, G. (2014). *Forecasts Call For Cloud Burst Through 2018*. Retrieved on March 22, 2015, from http://www.enterprisetech.com/2014/11/03/forecasts-call-cloud-burst-2018/

Madrid Resolution, International Standards on the Protection of Personal Data and Privacy, International Conference of Data Protection and Privacy Commissioners. (2009, November 5). Retrieved on July 3, 2015 from www.privacyconference2009.org/dpas_space/space_reserved/documentos_adoptados/common/2009_Madrid/estandares_resolucion_madrid_en.pdf

Marinescu, D. (n.d.). *Cloud computing: cloud vulnerabilities*. Retrieved on February 17, 2014 from http://technet.microsoft.com/en-us/magazine/dn271884.aspx

Mell, P., & Grance, T. (2011). *The NIST Definition of Cloud Computing*. NIST Special Publication, 800-145.

Oliveira, A. M. (2013). Cloud forensics- best practice and challenges for process efficiency of investigations and digital forensics. In *Proceedings of The Eighth International Conference on Forensic Computer Science*.

Reilly, D., Wren, C., & Berry, T. (2011). Cloud computing: pros and cons for computer forensic investigations. *International Journal Multimedia and Image Processing, 1*(1).

Ruan, K., Carthy, J., Kechadi, T., & Crosbie, M. (2011). Cloud Forensics: An overview. *Advances in Digital Forensic, 7.*

Saxena, A., Shrivastava, G., & Sharma, K. (2012). Forensic investigation in ccoud Computing environment. *International Journal of Forensic Computer Science, 2*(2), 64–74. doi:10.5769/J201202005

Singh, N., & Rishi, A. (2015). Pyramid- A case study of cyber security in India. *South Asian Journal of Business and Management Cases, 4*(1), 135–142. doi:10.1177/2277977915574046

Takabi. H., Joshi, J., & JoonAhn, G. (2010, November-December). Security and privacy challenges in cloud computing environment. *IEEE Computer and Reliability Societie,* 24-31.

The Future of Privacy. (n.d.). Retrieved from http://ec.europa.eu/justice/policies/privacy/docs/wp-docs/2009/wp168_en.pdf

Webb-Hobson, E. (2013). *Digital Investigation in Cloud.* Retrieved on July 10, 2013 from http://www.gartner.com/newsroom/id/707508

Zota, R., & Fraatila, L. (2013). Cloud standardization: consistent business process and information. *Informatica Economică, 17*(3).

KEY TERMS AND DEFINITIONS

Access Control: Information security access control refers to selective restriction of access to resources by authorized users thus regulating who can view or use computing resources. Two commonly used access control mechanisms are locks and logons.

Authentication Mechanism: An essential element of the computer network security model to confirm the identity of user trying to logon to the system to access resources. There are a number of different authentication mechanisms such a logon authentication, network access authentication, IP security authentication, remote authentication etc.

Availability: To ensure availability, rigorous maintenance of all hardware, correct functioning of operating system environment free of software conflicts is needed. To prevent data loss from unpredictable events, to mitigate consequences from hardware failure, fast adaptive disaster recovery plan needs to be in place including redundancy, failover, high availability clusters. Authentication mechanisms ensure availability of data when needed.

CIA Triad: Confidentiality Integrity Availability triad is a model designed for development of policies for information security. The elements of the triad are confidentiality- a set of rules limiting access to information; integrity- assuring trustworthiness and accuracy of information; availability- guaranteeing information access to authorized people.

Cloud Service Provider (CSP): A cloud provider is a company offering components of cloud computing: Infrastructure as a Service, Software as a Service or Platform as a Service through private, public or hybrid cloud. The resources are accessed through the internet.

Confidentiality: Refers to measures undertaken to prevent information from reaching the wrong people. To safeguard data confidentiality, special training may be given to familiarize security risks that can threaten information, familiarize with risk factors and how to guard against them, password related best practices.

Disaster Recovery Plan: Also referred to as business continuity plan that documents set of procedures, set of actions to be taken before, during and after a disaster to recover and protect IT infrastructure. The plan specifies precautions to be taken and procedures an organization needs to follow to minimize the effects of disaster and to quickly resume mission-critical functions.

Integrity: Refers to maintaining and assuring consistency and accuracy of data throughout its life cycle. In order to do so, no unauthorized person should get access stored in cloud. Steps must be taken to ensure that the data can not be altered by unauthorized people. Some of the measures include file permission, access control, version control to prevent erroneous changes or accidental deletion by authorized users. There should be some means of detecting changes in data due to non-human caused events such as server crash or any other technical failure.

Service Level Agreement (SLA): SLA is part of a contract which is formally negotiated specifying what services the service provider will furnish. The document also defines the terms of service being offered which may include service hours, service availability, information on security, charges and service levels to be provided in case of contingency. Some of the technical interventions to ensure confidentiality are data encryption, password, two factor authentication, biometric verification, security tokens. Protecting confidentiality needs defining and enforcing appropriate information access mechanisms.

Version Control: Records changes made to a file over time which is time stamped and also records the person who made the change. The mechanisms tracks and provides control over changes which can later be used in case of disaster recovery and digital investigation.

Chapter 6
Combating Cyber Security Breaches in Digital World Using Misuse Detection Methods:
Misuse Detection

Subbulakshmi T.
VIT University, India

ABSTRACT

Intrusion Detection Systems (IDS) play a major role in the area of combating security breaches for information security. Current IDS are developed with Machine learning techniques like Artificial Neural Networks, C 4.5, KNN, Naïve Bayes classifiers, Genetic algorithms Fuzzy logic and SVMs. The objective of this paper is to apply Artificial Neural Networks and Support Vector Machines for intrusion detection. Artificial Neural Networks are applied along with faster training methods like variable learning rate and scaled conjugate gradient. Support Vector Machines use various kernel functions to improve the performance. From the kddcup'99 dataset 45,657 instances are taken and used in our experiment. The speed is compared for various training functions. The performance of various kernel functions is assessed. The detection rate of Support Vector Machines is found to be greater than Artificial Neural Networks with less number of false positives and with less time of detection.

1. INTRODUCTION

This paper focuses on Network Intrusion detection systems and related issues in identifying and monitoring attacks and the causes of attacks. A significant challenge in the area of Information security is to provide security both physically and technically to the information which may be stored either in the network (Network Intrusion Detection Systems) or host (Host Intrusion Detection Systems). Intrusion (Endorf et al., 2006) is defined as an active sequence of related events that deliberately cause harm or attack attempts both successful and unsuccessful such as rendering the system unusable, accessing unauthorized information or manipulating such information. Intrusion detection systems are defined as

DOI: 10.4018/978-1-5225-0193-0.ch006

(Endorf et al., 2006) tools, methods and resources to help identify assess and report unauthorized or unapproved network or host both due to insider and outsider threats. The placement of IDS in the network can be after the firewall and before the router. Another place of IDS may be before the firewall to completely stop external intrusions. On every system of the network the Host IDS can be placed along with the Network IDS to have more effective protection.

Based on the mode of detection Intrusion detection systems are categorized into two types. Misuse detection systems detect intrusions by comparing with previously detected intrusions database through pattern matching technique. Anomaly Intrusion Detection Systems are capable of detecting both known and unknown intrusions using the behaviour profiles by applying more sophisticated statistical techniques (Zhang et al., 2001)or Machine learning techniques (Mukkamala et al., 2005).

2. BACKGROUND

Soft computing was first proposed by Lotfi Zadeh to construct new generation computationally intelligent hybrid intelligent systems including Neural networks, Fuzzy logic, approximate reasoning and derivative free optimization techniques like Genetic algorithms for most of the real world applications like function approximation, Image processing and Intrusion detection.

Neural Networks are applied to effectively find out the intrusions by Martin Botha, Rossouw von solms. Next Generation Proactive Identification Model is used to protect the system using neural networks. This model is based on the assumption that each user's behaviour is unique and when he leaves the system it could be recorded for further comparison. Fuzzy Default Logic(FDL) (Jian et al., 2003)is applied to Intrusion Detection using reasoning and FDL-IDS was developed which increases detection speed and accuracy which reduces the cumulative cost of developing an traditional Intrusion Detection Expert System (Denning, 1987). A Novel attack detection method is proposed to detect intrusions using fuzzy logic and data mining. The proposed system is designed as both misuse and anomaly detection system by combining well-formed fuzzy if-then rules and simple data mining.

ANN and SVM are employed for intrusion detection using (Mukkamala & Sung, 2005) DARPA dataset and it is observed that SVMs are superior to ANN in three critical respects. SVM train and run an order of magnitude faster; SVM scale much faster; and SVMs give high classification accuracy. Feature selection and ranking is presented using two methods: first is Performance Based Ranking Method using performance metrics and 34 out of 41 features are selected for classification by a Multilayer FF ANN. Second using SVMs with support vector decision function. 23 out of 41 features are selected in this method for classification. SVMs prove higher classification accuracy.

NN and SVM are applied for misuse detection using DARPA data with (Mukkamala et al., 2005) all 41 features. The key idea is to discover useful patterns or features that can describe user behavior on a system and use them to build classifiers that can recognize known intrusions and anomalies in real time. The SVM IDS was developed for binary classification. The two classes are Normal (1) and Attack or intrusive patterns (-1). Attacks belong to 22 different attacks out of 25 which belong to four classes DoS, R2U, U2S and Probing. Data consists of 14292 points where 7312 for training and 6980 for testing. RBF kernel is used. The accuracy got in this is 99.50% with only 6 misclassifications. Three Multilayer FF

NN IDS was developed with scaled conjugate descent training function with the following architecture and efficiency. Network A, B, C (A: 4 layer, 41-20-20-20-1, 99.05%, B: 3 layer, 41-40-40-1,99.25%, C: 3 layer, 41-25-20-1,99%). The results show that SVMs training time is shorted than NNs with good accuracy. 17.77 sec vs 18 min. SVMs are suitable for binary classification. And NNs are suitable for Multiclass classification.

Three anomaly detection approaches are presented (Ghosh et al.,1999) for profiling program behavior. Initially a simple equality matching approach is used to determine anomalous behavior and FF Neural Network is evolved for learning program behavior. Finally an Elman network is used to recognize recurrent features in program execution traces. 1998 DARPA Intrusion Detection Evaluation Program is used to provide BSM audit data of system calls which is used as the dataset for evaluating this research.

In Equality matching method, instead of 'strace' of Linux to capture the system calls Sun Microsystem's Basic Security Module (BSM) is used to capture the events and there by the system calls. The system calls captured during online are compared with those of the database and for the anomalous behavior and intrusive alarm is raised. The results of this method are 86.4% with the FPR of 4.3%. Next step is FF MLP Neural Networks are implemented in this study which is trained with several network architectures and with several hidden nodes. The architecture with best DR is kept and others are left. The DR in this case is 77.3% with the FPR of 2.2%.The final step is getting results from an Elman network. In order to maintain the state information between inputs a recurrent ANN topology is employed. Elman networks has input nodes, output nodes, hidden nodes and context nodes (receives input from a single hidden node and sends its output to each node in the layer of its corresponding hidden node) Elman networks were able to detect 77.3% of Intrusions with no false positives.

3. DATA SET USED IN THIS RESEARCH

The data used in our experiment were got from kddcup'99 dataset. This is a version of the original dataset of 1998 DARPA Intrusion detection Evaluation program. A LAN was simulated like U. S. Air force LAN to collect raw TCP/IP dump packets. The LAN is operated in a normal environment but blasted with multiple attacks. For each TCP/IP connection 41 various qualitative and quantitative features were extracted. Nearly 32 different types of attacks are identified. The total number of records in the dataset is 4898431. In these 20% are normal records.

4. PROPOSED MODEL FOR MISUSE DETECTION SYSTEM

Figure 1 shows the proposed model for misuse detection system which comprises of major components such as data and feature extraction, data processing and classifier.

1. **Data and Feature Extraction:** Author has used two different types of features in our Experiment. The first one contains all the 41 features and the second one contains 15 important features from the overall 41. 31418 records are taken as training data set and 14239 records are taken as testing data set from the total of 48,984,31 records. The testing data set contains records which are not present in the training data set. In data extraction phase the 45,657 records are extracted from the full dataset into two different files with 41 features namely input_train1 with 31418 records, in-

Figure 1. Misuse detection system design

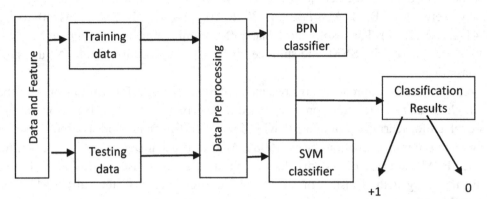

put_test1 with 14239 records. In feature extraction phase, from the two input files which contains 41 features, 15 important features were extracted and two new files are produced input_train2 and input_test2.

2. **Data Preprocessing:** In data preprocessing all the four files containing various data types for various features will be converted into binary formats which again produce another four files: binary_train1, binary_test1, binary_train2, and binary_test2, so that they can be directly fed to the Classifier. All the data values are converted into binary and the last value will be either 0 or 1. 0 represents attack and one represents normal. The input files are converted into training feature vectors with their training inputs and training targets and testing feature vectors with their testing inputs and testing targets. This feature vectors is stored in the binary files so that they can be directly fed to the classifiers.

3. **The BPN Classifier:** The BPN classifier is described using the following steps:
   a. **Selection of Training Functions and Parameters:** The training function is chosen from nine training functions. The nine training functions are as follows.
   b. **Design of BPN Classifier:** Neural Network is a powerful data classification tool. The tool can acquire knowledge through learning and can represent complex input output relationships. A Multi-layer Feed forward Back Propagation Network is used in this paper. The no of nodes in each layer are for 41 feature experiments are (41-15-11-1) and for 15 feature experiment are (15-13-11-1).
   c. **Training and Testing with 41 Features:** A multilayer feed forward network with 41-15-11-1 is created. The preprocessed file binary_train1 is fed to the BPN. The network was trained using different training functions to improve the efficiency. The preprocessed file binary_test1 is fed to the BPN and the network was tested.
   d. **Training and Testing with 15 Features:** A multilayer feed forward network with 15-13-11-1 is created. The preprocessed file binary_train2 is fed to the BPN. The network was trained using different training functions to improve the efficiency. The preprocessed file binary_test2 is fed to the BPN and the network was tested.

4. **SVM Classifier:** The SVM classifier is described using the following steps.
   a. **Selection of Kernel Function and Parameters:** They are six no of different kernels available which are linear, polynomial, Gaussian RBF, linear spline, linear BSpline and exponential RBF. If the kernel function is selected differently, then SVM will produce different outputs. To select the SVM kernel, the function 'svkernal' is used.
   b. **Design of SVM Classifier:** The results produced as a result are summarized as
      i. Execution time,
      ii. Status,
      iii. Margin,
      iv. Sum alpha,
      v. Support Vectors,
      vi. Classification accuracy.
   c. **Training and Testing with 41 Features:** Support Vector Classification is done using the function

[nsv alpha bias] = svc(X,Y,ker,C)

where

X - Training inputs.
Y - Training targets.
ker - Kernel function.
C - Upper bound (non-separable case).
nsv - Number of support vectors.
alpha - Lagrange Multipliers.
b0 - Bias term.

   d. **Training and Testing with 15 Features:** The preprocessed file is fed to the classifier. The network was trained using different training functions to improve the efficiency. The preprocessed is fed to the SVM and the network was tested.

5. CLASSIFICATION RESULTS

Table 1 shows the number of epochs, goal and accuracy of the various training functions using 41 features. The number of epochs are increased or decreased according to the training function The results of the Experiment Number 2 are given in Table 1.

Table 1 s hows the results of 15 and 41 features Experiments. It is observed that the goal is reached in minimum number of epochs for 15 features.

After the training is over the trained network should be tested with the preprocessed files (Table 2).

The files binary_train1, binay_test1 tested in the (41-15-11-1) Network and the overall detection rate for this network obtained was 85%. The files binary_train2, binay_test2 were tested in the (15-13-11-1) Network and the overall detection rate for this network obtained was 83%.

Table 1. BPN classifier training results of 41 and 15 features

Training Function	Goal	41 Features		15 Features	
		No. of Epochs	Accuracy	No. of Epochs	Accuracy
traingd	100	1000	69.45	500	78.34
triaingdm	100	900	75.43	300	51.37
traingda	100	500	66.78	200	57.57
traingdx	100	500	96.74	300	94.56
trainrp	100	50	98.78	45	98.45
traincgf	100	400	92.49	200	89.38
traincgp	100	500	89.56	300	80.34
traincgb	100	400	95.12	200	90.11
trainscg	100	300	85.39	200	79.27

Table 2. BPN classifier testing results of 41 and 15 features

Input Files	Detection Rate	Misclassification Rate	
		FPR	FNR
binary_train1(41 features)	85.68	7.15	4.17
binay_test1(41 features)	83.93	8.31	4.76
binary_train2 (15 features)	85.82	9.32	4.86
binay_test2 (15 features)	83.93	7.35	5.72

Table 3. SVM classifier training results of 41 and 15 features

Kernal Function	41 Features		15 Features	
	NSV	Accuracy	NSV	Accuracy
Linear	110	87.76	90	89.66
Polynomial	45	88.15	37	86.15
Gaussion RBF	34	74.56	54	77.53
Exponential RBF	120	78.47	101	79.44
Linear Spline	134	56.72	112	67.76
Linear BSpline	112	76.78	110	78.68

Table 4. SVM classifier testing results of 41 and 15 features

Input Files	Detection Rate	Misclassification Rate	
		FPR	FNR
binary_train1(41 features)	86.04	6.25	3.41
binay_test1(41 features)	85.26	7.27	3.23
binary_train2 (15 features)	87.64	7.51	2.56
binay_test2 (15 features)	83.01	5.32	3.11

Table 5. Speed comparison of BPN and SVM classifiers for 41 features

Attack Category	Training Time		Testing Time		Accuracy	
	BPN	SVM	BPN	SVM	BPN	SVM
Normal	694.583	394.276	0.151	0.091	99.8	95.3
Probe	456.342	203.182	0.241	0.027	91.9	90.2
DoS	1164.365	500.998	0.150	0.019	70.3	85.3
U2R	307.257	110.724	0.161	0.011	61.6	77.2
R2L	110.898	55.743	0.281	0.192	74.1	82.2

Table 6. Speed comparison of BPN and SVM classifiers for 15 features

Attack Category	Training Time		Testing Time		Accuracy	
	BPN	SVM	BPN	SVM	BPN	SVM
Normal	250.115	134.567	0.053	0.032	98.8	96.3
Probe	160.564	73.388	0.078	0.009	90.9	92.2
DoS	532.345	183.567	0.045	0.007	72.3	87.3
U2R	123.451	78.459	0.076	0.004	63.6	79.2
R2L	54.274	34.567	0.012	0.070	76.1	83.2

6. COMPARISON OF PERFORMANCE

For comparison of performance, see Table 5 (41 features) and Table 6 (15 features).

7. CONCLUSION AND FUTURE WORK

Multilayer Feed forward BPN is used in this research with two different architectures, one with 41 input nodes and next with 15 input nodes. The results indicated that the resilient BPN and conjugate learning training functions gave faster training than the other algorithms. Over all accuracy of Experiment 1 is 85% and overall accuracy of experiment 2 is 83%. By using SVM the classification accuracy can still be improved. Thus, an analysis of the classifier in two different experiments aids in detecting the security breaches in the digital sphere and provides protection to critical infrastructure.

REFERENCES

Denning, D. E. (1987). An Intrusion Detection Model. *IEEE Transactions on Software Engineering*, *13*(2), 222–232. doi:10.1109/TSE.1987.232894

Endorf, C., Schultz, E., & Melander, J. (2006). *Intrusion detection and Prevention*. Tata McGraw Hill.

Ghosh, A. K., Schwartzbard, A., & Schatz, M. (1999). Learning Program Behavior Profiles for Intrusion Detection. In *Proceedings of Workshop on Intrusion Detection and Network Monitoring*. Academic Press.

Jian, Z., Yong, & Jian, G. (2003). Intrusion Detection System based on Fuzzy Default Logic. In *Proceedings of IEEE International Conference on Fuzzy Systems* (*vol. 2,* pp. 1350-1356). IEEE.

Mukkamala, S., Janoski, G., & Sung, A. H. (2002). Intrusion Detection Using Neural Networks and Support Vector Machines. In *Proceedings of IEEE International Joint Conference on Neural Networks* (pp.1702-1707). IEEE Computer Society Press. doi:10.1109/IJCNN.2002.1007774

Mukkamala, S., & Sung, A. H. (2005). Feature Selection for Intrusion Detection using Neural Networks and Support Vector Machines. In *Proceedings of Second International Symposium on Neural Networks*. Academic Press.

Mukkamala, S., Sung, A. H., & Abraham, A. (2005). Intrusion Detection using an ensemble of Intelligent Paradigms. *Journal of Network and Computer Applications, 28*(2), 167–182. doi:10.1016/j.jnca.2004.01.003

Zhang, Z., Li, J., Manikopoulos, C. N., Jorgenson, J., & Ucles, J. (2001). HIDE: A Hierarchical NIDS using statistical preprocessing and Neural Network classification. In *Proceedings of IEEE workshop on Information Assurance and Security*. Academic Press.

Chapter 7
Critical Video Surveillance and Identification of Human Behavior Analysis of ATM Security Systems

M. Sivabalakrishnan
VIT University, India

R. Menaka
VIT University, India

S. Jeeva
VIT University, India

ABSTRACT

Video surveillance cameras are placed in many places such as bank, hospital, toll gates, airports, etc. To take advantage of the video in real time, a human must monitor the system continuously in order to alert security officers if there is an emergency. Besides, for event detection a person can observe four cameras with good accuracy at a time. Therefore, this requires expensive human resources for real time video surveillance using current technology. The trajectory of one or more targets obtains for object tracking while recording above space and time. By tracking various objects, the burden of detection by human sentinels is greatly alleviated. Efficient and reliable automatic alarm system is useful for many ATM surveillance applications. ATM Video monitoring systems present many challenging research issues in human abnormal behaviors detection approaches. The framework of ATM video surveillance system encompassing various factors, such as image acquisition, background estimation, background subtraction, segmentation, people counting and tracking are briefly discussed in this chapter.

DOI: 10.4018/978-1-5225-0193-0.ch007

INTRODUCTION

Every sphere of life has embedded computer vision field. The increased level of global terrorism and life threatening activities in public places increase the demand for object tracking which is the core objective in the computer vision field. The availability of computers with high efficiency in terms of quality, cameras and cost for fully automized object tracking algorithms. Surveillance cameras are installed in airports, parking lots, train stations and banks etc. To take advantage of the video in real time, a human must monitor the system continuously in order to alert security officers if there is an emergency. Moreover, manually a human can observe only four cameras at a single instance of time for event detection. Therefore, this requires expensive human resources for real time video surveillance using current technology. Object tracking aims to automatically record trajectories of one or more targets across time and space. By tracking various objects, the burden of detection by human sentinels is greatly alleviated.

The fundamental step in object tracking is video analysis. Detecting and tracking the moving object frame wise is the key point for analyzing the object's behavior. The object must be tracked in a two dimensional image plane as the object moves in the frame. The image tracking algorithm should labels for the tracked object in the consecutive image frames of the video. The tracker needs to provide the information regarding the area, shape, orientation of the object also. The issues in projecting the 3D image into 2D space as image, noise in the transformation process, Complexities in the object motion, non rigidity in objects, full human occlusion, complex shapes of the object, changes in scene lightening details during real time processing makes tracking complex.

Many different approaches are available for object tracking. Modeling the object, the suitability of object representation for tracking, selection of features from images are the key requirements of an object tracking algorithms. The choice is made based on two factors: environment and use when tracking is performed. The significance of object tracking are realized in various activities like automated surveillance, motion-based recognition, traffic monitoring, video indexing, industrial applications, medical applications etc.

- **Motion Based Recognition:** It basically deals with object recognition, pattern matching and motion analysis. Nowadays, Motion recognition is used in design of augmented reality based video games, where the player controls the navigation by using their body movements. Another interesting application includes design of a virtual dance or aerobics instructor, which would inspect different dance movements or exercises and provides feedback based on the performance. Other applications include automated control of home appliances through gesture, design of assistive devices for elderly people etc.
- **Automated Surveillance:** The primary is to reduce human intervention by including software in a surveillance which works effectively to analyze behavior changes automatically. High resolution cameras are ideal to distinguish indoor and outdoor activities of various real world environments to spot suspicious behavior. Other applications include facility protection, managing parking lots, event monitoring etc.
- **Traffic Monitoring:** Application of video sensors in traffic applications is getting significant attention because of its speed case in installation, operation and maintenance, and its good monitoring capacity. Furthermore, the speed measurement, count of multiple point vehicles, classification of vehicle categories, assessment in highways during congestion or incidents are its advantages.

- **Video Indexing:** Some application of video indexing comprise of fast retrieval of videos during browsing, visual electronic commerce analysis, by speculating internet activities of people, remote instruction, news event, scrutiny, insightful web video management and surveillance of videos.

- **Medical Applications:** Plays a crucial role in medical field for assisting clinical diagnosis, image oriented theory planning and various phases. Resilient tracking in deformable anatomical objects which mainly includes the prime organ of life heart and several other pivotal organs is also carried out with higher efficacy. Another widely used application of video tracking in medicine is tracking of eye ball. Recent technological advancements have made its use with clinical populations, including autism spectrum disorder.

- **Industrial Applications:** Using high speed video cameras, one can monitor and analyze defects, inefficiencies or malfunctions in production machines in industries which produce sports, health and other mechanical equipments. The data and video analysis and storage devices for monitoring these equipments include: triggering device, sensors, high speed and resolution camera and data acquisition components. The analysis helps to improve the design of devices with higher optimacy.

- **Security Applications:** The ability to automatically detect and track objects is of great interest in the field of Security. Applications which scrutinize exact information on count, position and behavior of people are very helpful for checking authentication and automization of services in its real world environments. Tracking a person is a necessary aspect of HCI(human computer interaction), interacting with and within virtual environments, and capturing motion for computer enhanced motion pictures.

- **Issues in ATM:** The possible attacks involved in ATM could be listed as follows:
  - Network and System based attacks against ATM in order to obtain card related: information.
  - Dedicated effort to acquire customer bank card related information.
  - Physical attacks against ATM.

- **Card Skimming:** This attack is usually launched with a special device called as skimming device or skimmed card reader. This could be placed over the ATM machine so that it usually hides it presence to the external user. But it collects the card related information by observing the magnetic stripe of the card and the customer's PIN. Then PIN information is usually collected by placing a very small camera at an appropriate location. The card information is compromised by the skimming device placed over the mouth of the card reader. These attacks are generally difficult to detect and handle.

- **Phishing:** Scam and spam mails were the usual ways to launch this phishing attack. The intruders will usually send mail in the form of bank representatives and requests for confidential information like customer card number, PIN etc. The typical way is that, user will be given a link to enter all these information. However, as the link is fraudulent, the end user's information is compromised.

- **Physical Attacks:** These attacks were generally made with the motive of obtaining access to the cash inside ATM or the ATM security enclosures. Robbery attacks were also reported nowadays, when the ATMs are restocked or being serviced. Incidents were also reported where the technician is held up while servicing the machines. In order to handle these attacks, several measures were taken with the help of biometrics and related techniques (Graevenitz, 2007). The procedure is to capture the face portion of the user and compare it with the database (Zhang, et al, 2014). But it also suffers from a bottleneck in handling these suspects, if their face portion was occluded or hidden through some ways.

- **Frightening Attacks:** Frightening attacks usually involve threatening of customers inside the ATM premises to disclose their confidential information. Numerous incidents were reported in the recent days, where the customers were generally either physically attacked or threatened by the attacker to reveal their information. Though, there was a rule to allow only person at a time inside the ATM, it is violated for many reasons which results in all these abnormal events.
- **Shoulder Surfing:** Shoulder surfing is an act where a person notices over another person's shoulder when they feed in any data into a computer or any device. A typical example is a situation where an attacker observes the action of a customer during the time when he/she enters confidential information like ATM PIN, card number etc. These attacks are generally difficult to detect and handle, as the customer would be busy with their transactions.

Beyond these straightforward tasks, the information extracted from multi-object tracking is essential for recognizing many human activities. For instance, the task of a surveillance system might be to warn an operator when it detects events which require human intervention, such as an accident or vandalism. To be reliable, these warnings must be able to detect and understand human behavior, and this requires reliable detection and tracking. Also through tracking, many types of behavior analysis can be performed. For instance, if some of the people are detected moving at a higher than normal rate of speed, it might indicate some sort of emergency. A person loitering about a restricted area for a long period of time might indicate that he is engaged in a suspicious activity. A person intentionally placing an object in a crowded place might indicate that he is involved in an anomalous activity. Hence early detection of such anomalous events could potentially decrease the rate of emergency and can launch appropriate rescue measures like issuing alerts to the control terminal.

FUNDAMENTAL ELEMENTS IN VIDEO TRACKING

Efficient and reliable automatic alarm system is useful for many ATM surveillance applications. There are basically two kinds of crimes possible in ATM sectors. The violent crime leaves question to our life such s killing and robbing, the little deprecated non violent crime involves fraudulent actions of thieving ATM cards or passwords. Apart from the crime some time human may be affected abnormal behavior such as heart attack, fits and so forth. ATM Video monitoring systems present many challenging research issues in human abnormal behaviors detection approaches. The architecture for the surveillance based video monitoring system is shown in Figure 1.

Image Acquisition

The camera used for security purpose should be capable of capturing the picture during day and night, in any environments, under changing circumstances. Hence camera with special infrared LED's and advanced HDR technologies with expensive components are usually a must. Once, Dealt with capturing the image, next deal with storing the captured data into drives (disk drive, USB flash drive, SD memory card or other mass storage device) in a computer. Specific software program such as network video recorder (NVR), Digital video recorder (DVR) or hybrid program with both the functionalities of NVR and DVR are used. These enable alert message and notification to the concerned person.

Figure 1. ATM video surveillance system architecture

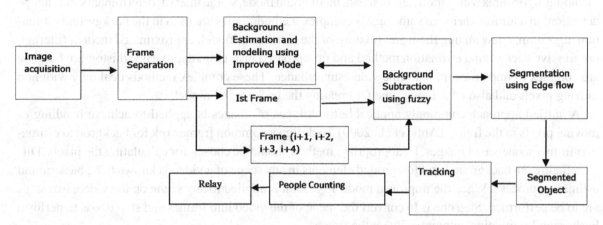

Estimation and Subtraction of the Background from Video Objects

The aim is to build a preliminary step for an automatic background estimation and subtraction, which accepts different types of image sequences. (piccardim,2009) The block diagram of the author methodology is shown in Figure 2.

The author method consists of the following stages: Background estimation, and background subtraction.

Background Estimation

Tracking a moving object is a confronting task in the field of computer vision. The conventional approach evolves in finding the changes between current and background image. People counting include background estimation, background subtraction, segmentation and tracking. To estimate the background in real time is the first important step for many video surveillance applications. Background extraction surface has lots of challenges in handling low resolution color, foreground and complex background element details. Recently, researchers have come up classical algorithms for background Estimation,

Figure 2. Block diagram of background estimation and subtraction method

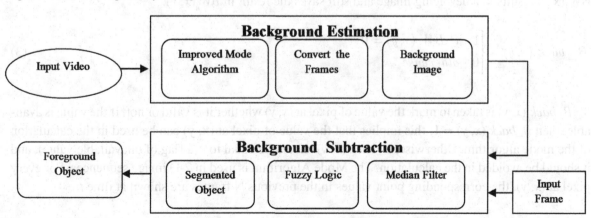

including algorithms with parameters of mean, median and mode, stable interval determinants and change detection. In addition, there are some highly complex methodologies are used in the background estimation algorithm, a few among them are: mixture of the Gaussians model, approximated median filtering, progressive background estimation method and group-based histogram approaches /histogram but they are complex to implement in real time video surveillance. These complex methods deal only with non moving pixels and also take a long time for creating the background model.

A unified approach commonly applicable to all types of images is applied to achieve handling of moving pixels in the frame. (Antic et al., 2009) To design a common framework for background estimation from a sequence of images, an appropriate method should be chosen for calculating the pixels. Differentiating the background and foreground elements in any scene of a video is known to be background estimation process. When the improved mode algorithm is applied to any scene on the video, two steps are to be performed. Step one is to convert the scene of the video into frames and step two is to perform background estimation automatically on the frames.

Current approaches for estimating the background consider the pixel to be a non- moving object. The motivation for the improved mode algorithm is to use the distinguishing pixel to separate the unchanging background and the moving object. The frame differentiation method categories the pixels into two: a static background and the moving objects, and then it calculate the unchanged background pixels through the mode algorithm. In the Frame difference algorithm, whenever an object moves in the video, it's grey level will change significantly. $I_n(x,y)$ is the value of pixel at (x, y) in frame $t = t_n$. Likewise, $I_{n+1}(x,y)$ is the value of pixel at (x, y) in frame $t = t_{n+1}$. The simple difference image $D(x,y)$ between these two frames is:

$$D(x,y) = \left| I_{n+1}(x,y) - I_n(x,y) \right| \forall (x,y) \in [1,N] \times [1,M] \tag{1}$$

where N×M is the image frame dimension. Applying a suitable threshold T on $D(x,y)$ results in a binary image, which classifies all the pixels into two classes: static background and moving objects.

$$BW_n(x,y) = \begin{cases} 0 = unchanged\ background\ if\ D(x,y) < T \\ 1 = moving\ object\ otherwise \end{cases} \tag{2}$$

After image binarization, applying the opening and closing of the mathematical morphology on $BW_n(x,y)$ results in a devoicing image and still saves the result in $BW_n(x, y)$.

$$B\_back_n(x,y) = \begin{cases} 1 & if\ BW_n(x,y) = 0 \\ 0 & otherwise \end{cases} \tag{3}$$

$B\_back_n(x, y)$ is taken to mark the value of pixel at (x, y) whether it is valid or not. If the value is available, then $B\_back_n(x, y) = 1$; this implies that the value of pixel at (x, y) can be used in the calculation of the mode algorithm. Otherwise, $B\_back_n(x, y)$ should be equal to 0(a flag of unavailable value), and it should be avoided in the calculation. The Mode Algorithm is used in 2-D image sequences. For every pixel at (x, y), the corresponding point values in the previous N frames are shown at time t:

$$B_{t-N}(x,y), B_{t-N+1}(x,y), B_{t-N+2}...B_{t-2}(x,y), B_{t-1}(x,y)$$

the sequence of values through the mode algorithm is calculated and the background value of the current image is taken as the result. The computing formula of the background value is:

$$B(x,y) = mode\left(I_{t-N}(x,y), I_{t-N+1}(x,y)...I_{t-2}(x,y), I_{t-1}(x,y)\right) \qquad (4)$$

To eliminate the deficiency of the mode algorithm, an improvement is done on it. This method can eliminate the deficiency in the mode method. The computing formula of the new method is:

$$BG(x,y) = mode\begin{vmatrix} B_{t-N}(x,y) \times \alpha_{i-N}, B_{t-N+1}(x,y) \times \alpha_{i-N+1}, B_{t-N+2}(x,y) \\ \times \alpha_{i-N+2}...B_{t-2}(x,y) \times \alpha_{t-2}, B_{t-1}(x,y) \times \alpha_{i-1} \end{vmatrix} \qquad (5)$$

$$\alpha_n = \begin{cases} 1 & if\ B\_back_n(x,y) = 1 \\ 0 & otherwise \end{cases}$$

where α_n determine the pixel (moving or background). Background can be estimated from this formula. And then proceed to the background subtraction model.

Background Subtraction

Background subtraction is a general term for a process which aims to separate foreground objects from a relatively stationary background. This process generates a foreground mask for each frame. The background image is subtracted from the current frame. Background view excludes the foreground; it is obvious that foreground objects are projected out after the comparison on the background image in the video. This approach is applied to each frame, to achieve the moving object tracking. Background subtraction is a very famous and effective technique applicable to static surveillance scenarios. Difficulties in this task arise from camera noise caused due to same colors in both background and foreground objects. In addition, there are some highly complex methods that are used in background subtraction, like the pfinder, codebook and MOG. Background subtraction algorithm samples values over a long period, without the need of parametric assumptions. Mixed backgrounds can be modeled by multiple codewords and also while illumination various false positive rate increased.

So author is designed to estimate the background from a sequence of frames, and a pure background image is obtained. Using this background image the current frame is subtracted to get a segmented foreground image. To design a common framework for background subtraction from current images, appropriate methods should be chosen for subtracting. The major contributions of the background estimation / subtraction method are as follows:

- Background estimation using the improved mode algorithm for getting a pure background.
- Background subtraction using a fuzzy based system for getting the foreground mask by separating the foreground from the background.

Detection is achieved in some approaches (Sivabalakrishnan et al., 2009) using only background subtraction, and by predicting the background intern using the next update interval. In these approaches the background is not estimated but detected. Here, the background image was generated by the improved mode algorithm. In the standard background method, it is hard to determine whether a pixel is actually a moving object or not. Illumination variations occur in the scenes which generate a false classification of the image pixels. The fuzzy logic inference system acts multiple information sources together for deci- sion- making. To determine the foreground object, the proposed binarization of the fuzzy background subtraction is done, after passing through the median filter. The method detects moving objects even if their gray level is similar to the background gray level. In addition, it can remove small noise because of the median filter.

In the adaptive background modeling and classification scheme, the image data in the past frames is used to compute the joint distribution of the images to build a background model. Based on the background model, the image block is classified as the foreground or the background. If a new object is introduced into the background or a background object is moved, before it is updated, this object will be classi- fied as a foreground object and hence becomes part of the silhouette. To solve this problem, high-level knowledge about the object motion is utilized to guide the adaptive update of the background model.

The prime thing is the need for a methodology to detach the objects which are moving. Which is a challenging task due to lack of automated reasoning on which is, and which is not, the target object, referenced from the video sequence? Sophisticated object recognition and identification algorithms can be deployed. Which are computationally intensive and not robust, an effective yet simple algorithm for object segmentation is designed. Fuzzy logic inference used for object segmentation for this system. Suppose one is working on frame n and the object in frame $n - 1$ has been correctly extracted. Let the foreground image region in frame n be O_n, which might contain the human body and moving objects. The fuzzy logic inference system is based on the following observations:

1. If an image block in O_n belongs to the object, it should have a high possibility of finding a good match in O_{n-1}. The sum of absolute difference (SAD) is used to measure the "goodness" of matching.
2. If many of the blocks in its neighborhood have good matches in O_{n-1}, it is highly possible that this block also belongs to the object.
3. If this block is far from the predicted position of the object centroid, the possibility that this block belongs to the object is low.
4. SAD in motion matching. For each block in O_n, the best match in frame $n - 1$ is found.

The SAD between this block and its best match form the first feature variable is the distance between the new block and the predicted object centroid.

This algorithm is based on image differencing techniques. It is mathematically represented using the following equation:

$$D(t) = \frac{1}{N}\sum \left| I\left(t_i\right) - I\left(t_j\right)\right| \tag{6}$$

where N is the number of pixels in the image used as a scaling factor, $I(t_i)$ is the image I at time i, $I(t_j)$ is the image I at time j and $D(t)$ is the normalized SAD for that time.

In an ideal case, when there is no motion

$$I\left(t_i\right) = I\left(t_j\right) \tag{7}$$

and $D(t) = 0$. However, noise is always present in images and a better model of the images in the absence of motion will be

$$I\left(t_i\right) = I\left(t_j\right) + n(p) \tag{8}$$

where n(p)is a noise signal.

The value D(t), which represents the normalized SAD is used as reference for comparing the threshold value. To estimate the membership functions of these features, a set of membership functions are defined from these distribution data.

An fuzzy inference system has the following parameters:

Rule 1: If SAD is medium, AND the Neighborhood is small, THEN the Object is low.
Rule 2: If SAD is high, AND the Neighborhood is small, THEN the Object is high.
Rule 3: If SAD is high AND the Neighborhood is high, THEN the Object is high.

According to the above rules, if an object is recognized to be in foreground, it is uses the fuzzy inference system to detach the moving objects and will erode the object from misclassification. The proposed binarization of the fuzzy background subtraction, after performing morphological operations and neighborhood information, would find out the missing parts. The motion images are subjected to morphological operations. noise reduction is a trivial step considered like pre-processing of results. Median filter usage eliminates the effect of input noise with an extremely large value of magnitudes. The motion across the boundary is also removed. This removal is done to avoid ambiguity in recognizing the moving object. At last, the targeted object is fitted in the block. If there is no moving object in the scene, then this object can be taken to be an optimal object for background subtraction. Let the pixel coordinates of the reference background image and the scene image at frame, be gray levels.

Algorithm: Background Estimation/Subtraction

From the current image, (Sivabalakrishnan et al., 2010) the automatic background estimation starts by processing the estimated background as in the following steps: According to the discussion given above, the various steps are:

Step 1: A movie is taken and converted into a number of successive frames (images).

Step 2: Two frames are obtained at fixed intervals from the video and saved in $I_n(x,y)$ and $I_{n+1}(x,y)$. For the purpose of simple calculation and real-time speed, these two frames should be converted into grey images.

Step 3: Using $I_n(x,y)$ and $I_{n+1}(x,y)$ the frame difference image can be obtained as $D_n(x,y)$. And then, the opening and closing operation of the mathematical morphology on D(x, y) is applied and the computed result using Equation 2 is saved in $BW_n(x,y)$.

Step 4: According to the value of pixels in $BW_n(x, y)$, the pixels are classified into either background moving objects or unchanging objects. According to Equation 3, make a flag as the pixel whether it is the moving objects or background. If the flag value is 1, it implies that the pixel belongs to a moving object and it's unavailable in mode calculation; otherwise its background is available. These values of the flag are saved in $B\_back_n(x, y)$.

Step 5: If n reaches the maximum set up, the procedure goes on to step 6; else the procedure should go to step 1.

Step 6: $B_n(x, y)$ should be calculated including the video and saved as $B(x,y,z)$, namely, the values of the background of all frames. Through the steps above, the background image can be estimated accurately. As a result of the pixels of moving objects being removed, even if the pixel background value just emerges once, it can be estimated accurately by the new method.

Step 7: The estimated background should be subtracted from the current image and the resulting image is filtered.

Step 8: Fuzzy based background subtraction is applied and the segmented foreground image is obtained from the input image.

Step 9: The resulting foreground image is compared with the ground truth image and the accuracy of the detected image using different metrics, is evaluated.

Step 10: The fuzzy based background subtraction method is compared with the other methods.

This algorithm was implemented in MATLAB and various metrics have been evaluated from the test results. These data set images have been gathered from the sites of several research groups.

- EC Funded CAVIAR Project, IST 2001.
- For sequences belonging to (Toyama et al.,1999; Brown et al., 2005), the ground truth is available as a binary detection mask for one reference frame.
- http://perception.i2r.a-star.edu.sg/bk_model/bk_index.html.

Edge Detection for Image Segmentation

Among the diversified problems persisting in image processing, image segmentation has found its application either directly or indirectly in many tasks including object detection, tracking, recognition, retrieval and image analysis. Edge detection is the process of identifying and locating sharp discontinuities in an image and is considered to be very interesting and important. It acts more intriguing when color images are taken due to their multi-dimensional nature. Color images portray exact information about the object; it is more useful rather than gray scale images. Due to some inescapable reasons such as deformation, long suit variation, noise, segmentation errors, convergence, and object occlusion in images, it is usually inconceivable to segment whole objects. Lack of object edge information leads to visual defects in the output image. The output of the image segmentation algorithm is handed over to higher level processing tasks and hence has to be done very carefully. Discontinuity found in the intensity, gradient is considered to be the key for edge detection in most methods. In typical images, edges characterize the object boundaries, which are useful for segmentation, registration and identification of objects in a scene. For edge detection many techniques are used; some of them are Canny edge detection, Marr–Hildreth algorithm, Sobel Operator, Prewitt, LoG.

In this book, it is decided to apply the enhanced edge flow method. The major contributions of the improved edge flow vector detection systems are as follows:

- An effective segmentation technique based on an edge field computed directly from the images.
- The flow field can be computed from various image features, including colour, texture and intensity edges.
- A new edge function that is more precise than the commonly used gradient magnitude, based on the scalar potential of the edge flow field.

Edge Flow

On the contrary the detection and localization of edges (or more general sense for image boundaries) are computed indirectly. First, by identifying a flow direction at each pixel location that points to the closest boundary, followed by the detection of locations that encounter two opposite directions of the edge flow. Since any image attributes such as color, texture and their combination is useful to define the edge flow, this scheme serves as a general framework for shouldering different types of image information in boundary detection.

Enhanced Edge Flow Method

In this topic, the processing steps of the enhanced edge flow vector approach are presented. The algorithm consists of six stages of image acquisition: Gaussian Kernel Smoothing, Gabor filtering and Smoothing, Edge Flow vector, Edge Detection, and post-processing. Figure 3 shows process flow of human motion detection algorithm. In detailed description of each stages is given below. The problem of achieving a robust tracking is solved by designed rule base, using the erroneous and sparse data from the image processing algorithms.

Image Acquisition and Frame Separation

Image acquisition is to get the frames of image which is taken by a camera or by the various cameras. Before the work starts, a video is sub sampled into a sequence of images. Which is called frame separation and it is done by the frame grabber.

Figure 3. Block diagram of the enhanced edge flow method

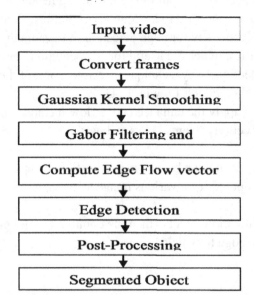

Gaussian Kernel Smoothing

For each data point in the time series a kernel function is applied by some of efficient smoothing algorithms. This process is called Kernel smoothing which will be categorized under weighted moving average class. In that time series all the points are weighted and they are used to compute the result of the kernel function. This function should have the following properties:

- The kernel functions are usually symmetric.
- Kernel values should be non-negative integers.
- These values are decreased from maximum to zeros.

To find the object's nature or noise this might be observed by Gaussian probable form. Gaussian kernel smoothing technique is used often for image processing. This is used to remove the image noise that image is smoothened by Gaussian filter like techniques.

Gabor Filtering and Smoothing

To find the illustory boundaries or to build n edge flow field gabor filter approach is used. The complex Gabor filtered image can be written as

$$O(x,y) = \mathrm{Re}(x,y) + \mathrm{Im}(x,y) \tag{9}$$

where Re(x,y) and Im(x,y) represent the real and imaginary parts of the Gabor filtered output, respectively. The phase of the filtered image can be expressed as

$$\varphi(x,y) = a\tan\left[\frac{\text{Im}(x,y)}{\text{Re}(x,y)}\right] \tag{10}$$

The Gabor filter is basically a Gaussian (with variances sx and sy along x and y-axes respectively) modulated by a complex sinusoid (with centre frequencies U and V along x and y-axes respectively) and described by the following equation:

$$G(x,y) = \frac{1}{2*pi*sx*sy} * \exp\left(\frac{-1}{2}\left\{\left[\frac{x}{sx}\right]^2 + \left[\frac{y}{sy}\right]^2\right\} + 2*pi*i*(Ux+Vy)\right) \tag{11}$$

where

I : Input image.
Sx & Sy: Variances along x and y-axes respectively.
U & V : Centre frequencies along the x and y-axes respectively.
G : is the output filtered image.

Edge Flow Vector Method

To detect the boundary, combine the various edges energies and their probabilities to get a single edges flow field. Consider

$$E\left(s,\theta\right) = \sum_{a\in A} E_a\left(s,\theta\right)\cdot w\left(a\right) \text{ and } \sum_{a\in A} W\left(a\right) = 1 \tag{12}$$

$$P\left(s,\theta\right) = \sum_{a\in A} P_a\left(s,\theta\right)\cdot w\left(a\right) \tag{13}$$

where $E_a(s, \theta)$ and $P_a(s, \theta)$ represent the energy and probability of the edge flow computed from the image attribute a, a\{intensity/colour, texture, phase\}.$w(a)$ is the weighting coefficient associated with the image attribute. For each of the RGB color band, the edge flow intensity is calculated by using the texture information is the combined color for boundary detection. Compute the flow direction also. Each location of the image contains, $\{[E(s, \theta), P(s, \theta), P(s, \theta+\pi)]|_{0\leq\theta<\pi}\}$. To maximize the sum of probabilities of the corresponding half plane, identify the continuous range of flow directions:

$$\Theta\left(s\right) = \underset{\theta}{\text{argmax}}\left\{\sum_{\theta\leq\theta'<\theta+\pi} P\left(s,\theta'\right)\right\} \tag{14}$$

The edge flow vector is then defined to be the following vector sum:

$$\vec{F}\left(s\right) = \sum_{\Theta(s)\leq\theta<\Theta(s)+\pi} E\left(S,\theta\right)\cdot\exp\left(j^{\theta}\right) \tag{15}$$

where $\vec{F}(s)$ is a complex number with its magnitude representing the resulting edge energy, and the angle representing the flow direction.

The edge flow vector properties are given as follows:

- Points of the vectors are naturally towards the nearest edge.
- The magnitude of the vectors is small away from the edges and increases near the edges.
- The flow vectors from opposite directions cancel each other on the edges.

Identify the directional flow of each pixel location which points the closest boundary that is pursued by the location detection to concern the edge flow application direction. At each location of the image, there are some direction changes in its attributes like texture, color and phase discontinuities which are to be identified and integrated for predictive coding model that is used by edge flow method.

Edge Detection

In image processing and computer vision, edge detection is a basic tool mainly used in the field of feature extraction and detection that aims to identify points in a image brightness which the digital image changes more formally, or sharply has lack of sequence. The object is to recognize objects in a complicated image. Usually detect accurate change of state in intensity and/or color within an image by edge detection algorithm. These changes of state are feature of object edges. Region segmentation and object recognition can take place before edges of the object are detected. So edges of object act as prime role to precede other processes.

The development of optimal edge detectors has most emerging research for detecting edge, which leads to the best trade-off between the localization performance and detection. An approach is to scheming such edge operator is to find the filter which can reduce the performance with high opinion to the three divisions: good localization, unique response, and good detection to a single edge. On hand algorithms

(Canny 1994) the first derivative of a Gaussian is approximated for the optimal detector. This filter is used to convolving the image; the edge detection is correspondent to discover and the appropriate direction for the maxima in the gradient magnitude of a Gaussian-smoothed image. Another important issue in edge detection is to Detecting and combining edges at many scales and multiple resolutions. (Witkin, 1983) was initiated scale-space technique which entails to generating coarser resolution images, and then Gaussian smoothing kernel for convolving the novel images.

Post-Processing

A number of image regions can be identified by connecting the disjoint boundaries until to get closed contours obtain before that boundary detection can be recognized. After that compute the edge flow of an image, the edge flow can be computed with help of boundary detection and repeat iteratively propagating method to find frame where two conflicting direction of flows come across each other. At each position, the local edge flow is broadcasted to its neighbor in the direction of the flow, if they also have same flow path. The steps are

1. Set n=0 and $\vec{F}_0\left(s\right) = \vec{F}\left(s\right)$.

2. Set the initial Edge flow $\vec{F}_{n+1}\left(s\right)$ at time n+1 to zero.

3. At each image location, identify the neighbor $s' = \left(x', y'\right)$ which is in the direction of the edge flow $\vec{F}_n\left(s\right)$.

4. Propagate the edge flow if $\vec{F}_n\left(s'\right) \cdot \vec{F}_n\left(s\right) > 0$: $\vec{F}_{n+1}\left(s'\right) = \vec{F}_{n+1}\left(s'\right) + \vec{F}_n\left(s\right)$ otherwise the edge flow stays at its original location. $\vec{F}_{n+1}\left(s\right) = \vec{F}_{n+1}\left(s\right) + \vec{F}_n\left(s\right)$.

5. If nothing has been changed, stop the iteration. Otherwise, set n=n+1 and go to step 2 and repeat the process.

Once the edge flow proliferation reaches a steady state, detect the image borders by recognizing the positions where the non-zero edge flows to be coming from two contrasting directions. Let the edge signals *V(x,y)* and H(x,y) be the vertical and horizontal edge maps between the image pixels, and let

$$\vec{F} = \left(h(x,y), v(x,y)\right) = \left(re\left[\vec{F}(s)\right], \mathrm{Im}\left(\vec{F}(s)\right)\right) \tag{16}$$

Then, the edge signals $V(x, y)$ and $H(x, y)$ will be turned on, is equivalent to, the two neighboring edge flows point at each other. Its energy is distinct to be the summation of the ledges of those two edge flows towards it before this edge signal is on. Summarizing:

- Turn on the edge $V(x, y)$ if and only if $H(x-1, y) > 0$ and $H(x, y) > 0$; then

$$V\left(x, y\right) = H(x-1, y) - H(x, y) \tag{17}$$

- Turn on the edge $H(x, y)$ if and only if $V(x, y-1) > 0$ and $V(x, y) > 0$ then

$$H(x, y) = V(x, y-1) - V(x, y) \tag{18}$$

After detected the edge signals, Edge signals $V(x, y)$ and $H(x, y)$ can be identified by average of energy of connected edges to form boundaries. A number of image regions can be identified by connecting the disjoint boundaries until to get closed contours obtain before that boundary detection can be recognized. A half circle with its center located at the unconnected end of the contour is called neighbourhood. The basic approaches for linking the boundaries are recapitulated as pursue.

- For each open contour, link a neighbourhood search size comparative to the length of the contour.
- Within the half circle is identified by the nearest boundary element.
- If the boundary element is identified, then smooth boundary segment is get to attach the unwrap contour to the nearest boundary element.
- Repeat this process few times (typically 2-3 times), till the contour is completely closed.

At the end, a region merging algorithm is used to merge similar regions, based on a measurement that evaluates the sizes of the regions, the percentage of the unique boundary between the two adjacent regions and the distances of region texture and color features. This algorithm sequentially reduces the total number of regions can be reduced by sequentially applying this algorithm at each time, by inspection if the user's ideal number has been drawn near.

TRACKING AND PEOPLE COUNTING SYSTEM

Moving object tracking is one of the difficult tasks in computer vision problems, such as human computer interactions, visual surveillance etc. On especially in monitoring large scale environments such as security sensitive areas and public has becoming an important task in video surveillance. An object of interest would be identified and then monitored or tracked kind of operations performed in this field of video surveillance. A numerous methods for tracking an object and to handled or overcome the problem in tracking such as occlusion (Bird et al., 2005), and noise in surveillance videos, but required the robust tracking method for an improvement. From the video sequence frames are spitted for performing Tracking objects and it consists of two main steps: from each frame background objects can be separated, and find relationship between objects in successive frames to trace them. For the detection of motion object, background subtraction can be used that is to find the distance between incoming frame and then reference frame to get the foreground object. This technique can be used for many real-time vision surveillance applications.

This book describes the novel and secure tracking framework for counting people for ATM surveillance. A novel human motion detection algorithm that identifies moving blob regions by using a fuzzy rule-based classification scheme, In addition, this chapter also discusses the integration of background estimation, subtraction and edge flow based segmentation with this people counting framework, to build a complete people tracking system and also based on the people count relay unit arise the alarm.

TRACKING AND COUNTING SYSTEM ARCHITECTURE

This system consists of five stages; image acquisition, RGB to HSV conversion, BitXOR operation, preprocessing and blob identification. Figure 4 shows the proposed people counting algorithm and its process flow. (Barandiaran J et al., 2008) The detailed description of each stage is given below.

Image Acquisition and Segmentation

In any motion-based vision application as a common preliminary step is Image acquisition, image frames are obtained from a stationary or multiple cameras, or moving camera. Before the actual processing begins, frame grabber is used to sampling the image from the video at certain frame rate. Usually, video sequence can be a low frame rate (< 10 *fps)* or high frame rate (10-30*fps)* that can be maintained by the threshold. Based on the type of video system used then only suitable segmentation method can be implemented. Later than the image acquisition, Background subtraction for image segmentation can be performed, based on the frame rate of the video sequences.

Figure 4. Tracking and counting system architecture

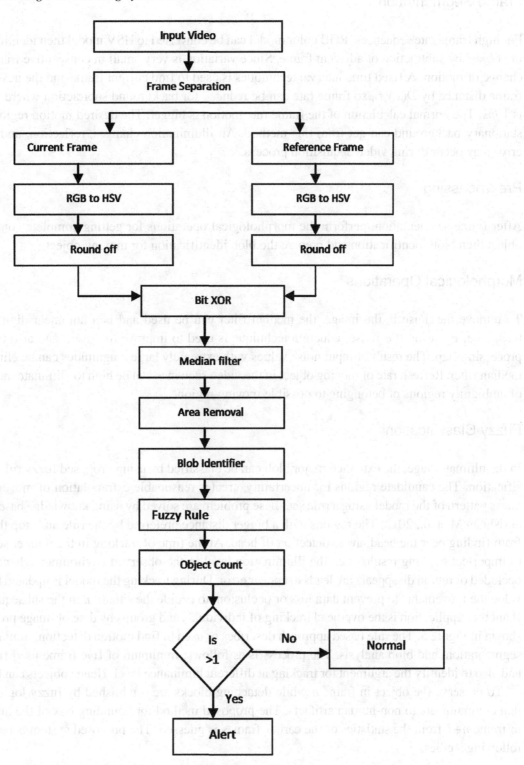

Frame Segmentation

For high frame rate sequences, RGB color model can be converted to HSV model then identify the moving object by subtraction of adjacent frame. Since variation is very small in consecutive frames for the change of motion. A fixed time interval techniques is used to find current frame and the next acquiring frame distance by $D(x,y,t)$, so frame rate can be reduced for background subtraction where the change is 1 *fps*. The normal calculation of the frame rate motion is bigger. The desired motion region from the stationary background can get from this method. An illumination changes, reflection, and noise like error may occur during video acquisition process.

Preprocessing

After frame segmentation, perform the morphological operations for getting complete contour of the object then blob Identification and prepare the blob identification for moving object.

Morphological Operations

To remove the noise in the image, the median filter can be used and is a nonlinear digital filtering technique. By using this noise reduction technique is used to improve the result and also typical preprocessing step. The result of input noise values with extremely large magnitudes can be eliminated by median filter. Refresh rate of moving object in the video sequence can be high to eliminate the boundary of ambiguity regions of belonging to possible moving region.

Fuzzy Classification

In the ultimate stage, the extracted major blob can be classified by using proposed fuzzy rule base classification. The candidate regions for uncertainty, creates reasonable extrapolation of movements, and guess pattern of the model using a rule set, these problem are solved by using knowledge base. (Sivabalakrishnan M et al., 2012) The regions with a bigger distance preferred by the rule and stop the tracking from finding near the head, avoid detection of head. At the time of tracking in the pointer section, due to imperfect tracking results; i.e., the illumination level in the observed environment changes or gets occluded or region disappears are leads to appear error. During tracking the model is updated to estimate value the movements to prevent data loss or occlusion, to decide the situation in the subsequent frame. If another application is the overhead tracking of individuals and groups by date of image processing as shown in Figure 5. The rule based approach describes or used to find motion detection, luminance-level segmentation, and blob analysis. The process is as follows: minimum of five frame used find motion and also to identify the argument for tracking at different luminance level. Hence objects can be tracked.

To preserve the object in frame n while detaching blocks are established by fuzzy logic inference that communicate to non-human artifacts. The proposed method for bounding box of the human body in frame $n+1$ from the statistics of the earlier frames is guessed. The proposed system is based on the following studies:

1.   The training of each and every silhouette is identified.
2.   The bounding box is calculated for each and every individual.

Figure 5. Silhouette of the user shown with search regions

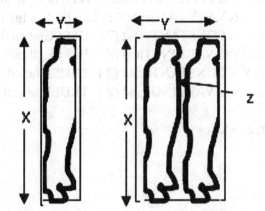

3. The person entering the focused screen is taken as an object and proceeds with a unique identify number until the object leaves the frame.
4. Continuous monitoring of the width and height of the silhouette is done.
5. Counting is done as to whether there is a new unique identifier number entering.
6. Counting memory of the unique identify number is resized and fuzzy is processed.
7. Width & height are the inputs of the silhouette for the bounding boxes.

The 6 rules given below, are used in the fuzzy logic and are exemplify in Figure 5 and the set of membership functions for these rule are illustrated in Figure 6 in a MATLAB implementation. The fuzzy rule is based on three input variables (X, Y, and Z) and one output variable Count (Figure 7).

Figure 6. Surface viewer of the fuzzy system

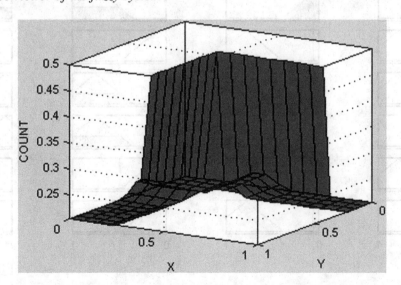

1. If (X is CONSTANT) and (Y is CONSTANT) and (Z is FALSE) then the (COUNT is ONE)
2. If (X is VARYING) and (Y is VARYING) and (Z is TRUE) then the (COUNT is TWO)
3. If (X is VARYING) and (Y is CONSTANT) and (Z is FALSE) then the (COUNT is ONE)
4. If (X is CONSTANT) and (Y is VARYING) and (Z is FALSE) then the (COUNT is ONE)
5. If (X is VARYING) and (Y is CONSTANT) and (Z is TRUE) then the (COUNT is TWO)
6. If (X is CONSTANT) and (Y is VARYING) and (Z is TRUE) then the (COUNT is TWO)

where X = width, Y = height, Z = holes.

CASE STUDY

This section deals with the integration of various factors, such as Background Subtraction, Segmentation, Tracking and counting system together, to produce a complete people counting system for videos.

Integration of Background Subtraction with Segmentation

Initially, background subtraction is integrated with Segmentation. When a video is applied as input to the system, it separated the frames and also identifies the background reference image, using the Improved Mode Algorithm and reports the various frames with their background reference image as the output. Later these blocks are passed on for background subtraction, using fuzzy, which isolates the image/

Figure 7. Membership functions of 6 rules of the fuzzy logic inference system

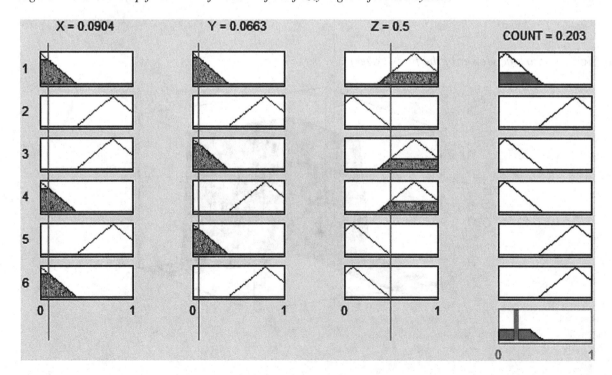

picture blocks to accumulate the foreground regions as of the video progression. Next, the foreground regions which communicate to humans are given as input to the segmented method based on edge flow techniques Segmentation has been applied over the foreground images to recognize the images.

Algorithm to Read Video

Step 1: Read the AVI format video file.
Step 2: Declare two global variables row and columns, which store the Width and Height values of video frames respectively.
Step 3: For $i = 1$ to No of_Frames in steps of 1 with an interval of 4 frames

Read each frame of video clip and store it.
Store the video frames into img_1d
Increment variable k which stores the total number of frames in img_1d .
end for

Step 4: For $i = 1$ to frame_cnt$k$ Convert images obtained in step 3 from RGB to gray format and store.

Automatic Background Extraction

A set of successive frames is a pre-condition for carrying out the background extraction process automatically. This process initially starts with two successive frames as already described in the algorithm. The output of the background extraction method is the background reference image.

Algorithm Background Subtraction using Fuzzy

Step 1: Read the input, background reference image and ground truth image.
Step 2: Convert the input, background reference RGB image to a Gray image.
Step 3: Subtract the input, background reference image and store the result.
Step 4: Apply the fuzzy rule.
Step 5: Subtracted image should be evaluated through fuzzy.
Step 6: Apply median filter and store the result.
Step 7: Stop.

Algorithm for Segmentation using the Edge Flow Vector

Step 1: Input image can be read.
Step 2: Compute number of rows and columns using the size function.
Step 3: Remove the lonely Pixels from the input image.
Step 4: Read the ground truth image.
Step 5: Find the number of connected objects in the input image.
Step 6: Measure the properties of the image regions (blob analysis).
Step 7: Remove the unwanted area using the area properties.
Step 8: Find the number of connected objects in the input image after the blob analysis.

Table 1. Number of people appearing in each frame

F1	F2	F3	F4	F5	F6	F7	F8	F9	F10	F11	F12	F13	F14	Total
1	2	0	2	1	0	2	0	2	2	1	3	2	2	20

Table 2. Comparison of fuzzy people counting and other methods

	Ground Truth	Barandiaran et al (2008)	Antic et al (2009)	Proposed
In+Out	11+10	11+9	10+10	11+9
TP	21	19	20	20.5
FP+FN	0+0	1+2	0+1	1+1
Precision	1.00	0.95	1.00	1.00
Recall	1.00	0.90	0.95	0.97
F-Score	1.00	0.92	0.97	0.99

Step 9: Display the resulting image.
Step 10: Stop.

Integration of Background Subtraction with Segmentation and Tracking and Counting System

A complete people counting system has a tracking and counting system. This tracking and counting system is integrated with Background subtraction and Segmentation. In this integration the segmented output will be the input of the people counting system. Then, the blobs are calculated, and the human emergence models in every frame are updated until they occlude each other or merge into a group. The performance of the people counting framework has been evaluated by integrating the background subtraction and segmentation results, which are shown in Figure 9.

Table 1 shows the number of objects in the video sequence in each frame. Figure 8 shows the graphical representation of the objects in the video sequence. Then implement the fuzzy-based rule for the occluted frame. Based on precise human body location prediction, the algorithm uses a huge temporal modernize window size unit in its frames for image blocks inside the bounding box, while using a relatively small size for those outside. The most common interaction patterns are observed in test cases that formerly led to tracking errors. The fuzzy-based system can resolve these cases, and continuously track the user's body. On comparison, it is evident that improved one's give a better result than the other methods. An increase in tracking ability was spotted after adaption using the fuzzy method, failure rate also improved than in conventional tracking (Table 2). To make a solid comparison using numbers is an unclear way (Figure 10).

A repetitive target detection scheme and motion prediction technique can uses propose algorithm and their results are shown that do not rely on spatial immediacy. Figure. 9 shows the people segmentation, tracking and counting results, and Figure 9(a) shows the Original frame. Figure 9 (b) our proposed extraction method can identify the background image. Figure 9 (c) shows the Ground truth. Figure 9(d) shows

Figure 8. Results of people appearing in each frame

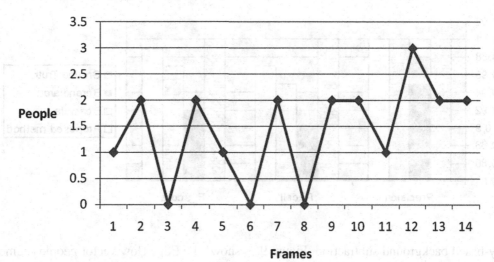

Figure 9. Open results and processing steps for background estimation, background subtraction, people segmentation, tracking and counting: a) original frame; b) background image generated by our proposed extraction method; c) ground truth; d) fuzzy based background subtraction; e) edge flow vector people segmentation; f) tracked image with occlusion

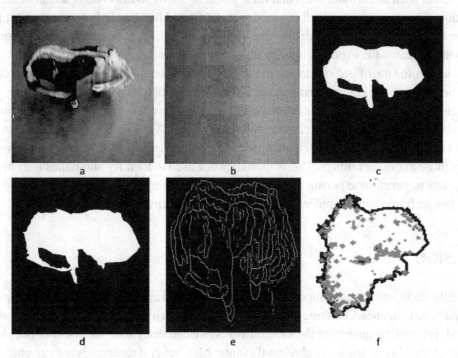

Figure 10. Comparison of the performance measures for the people counting system

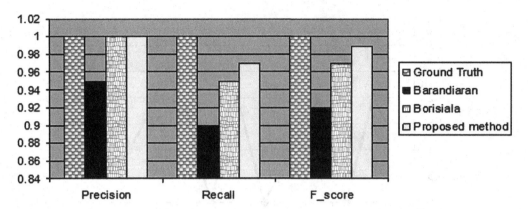

the fuzzy-based background subtraction. Figure 9(e) shows the Edge flow vector people segmentation Figure 9(f) gives the results for tracking with blobs. The people segmentation algorithm shows good performance. The fuzzy permutation of motion-based tracking has improved the tracking performance under different luminance. In complex luminance and environment with modeled backgrounds, our method allowed tracking where it was not possible before, as well as in critical first application cases.

All these attacks could not be detected manually and controlled. But through video analytics, it is possible to detect such abnormal events and raise potential alerts to the control terminal for taking immediate action. Also it is quite difficult in practice to detect and handle all these attacks. But the last two attacks namely frightening and shoulder surfing could be handled by tracking the people count through the sensed video streams. i.e. From the input of the surveillance cameras placed inside the ATM premises, the crowd count or the no. of persons inside the ATM premises could be determined and accordingly an alert could be raised to the control terminal for handling these two attacks.

In this study performance of people counting has been improved. Based on the people count the relay trigger the alarm. So this framework can be used for real time ATM video surveillance. On account of ATM has lot of anomalies action to be performed in ATM centers, so this framework can used to track and identify those anomalies things. The Way framework used to identify anomalies is as per the law in ATM center has to permit one person at a time if more than one person entered into the center means. It's against law so framework identifies, track and arise the alarm to the administrator.

CONCLUSION

Video surveillance is getting more importance in various critical applications like Automatic monitoring of ATM Systems, Unmanned auditing activities, Several Security based solutions and so forth. In the case of ATM Systems, by analyzing the video streams, we can determine the count of people inside the ATM facility at any time to track any abnormal events. Also, several researches are currently carried out in video processing for crowd detection and tracking of abnormal events in the crowded places. Hence through automatic analysis of these video streams, In future we can anticipate solutions which would alarm the control person, in case of any abnormal events in the public places. Also in the course of recent decades, significant efforts have been made in video analysis prompting the improvement of numerous propelled innovations. In addition, the development in the Internet, online networking, and video capture devices, combined with the needs of security applications, has prompted the demand for storage of video streams. Inspection of such huge volume of video streams is opening up new research issues, which will likely call for novel solution strategies. As opposed to completely self-ruling applications, the meeting of man and machine may be the future trend in many video processing solutions.

REFERENCES

Antic, B., Letic, D., Culibrk, D., & Crnojevic, V. (2009). K-means based segmentation for real-time zenithal people counting. *2009 16th IEEE International Conference on Image Processing (ICIP), 1*(1), 2565-2568. doi:10.1109/ICIP.2009.5414001

Barandiaran, J., Murguia, B., & Boto, F. (2008). Real-Time People Counting Using Multiple Lines.*2008 Ninth International Workshop on Image Analysis for Multimedia Interactive Services, 1*(1), 159-162. doi:10.1109/WIAMIS.2008.27

Bird, N., Masoud, O., Papanikolopoulos, N., & Isaacs, A. (2005). Detection of Loitering Individuals in Public Transportation Areas. *IEEE Transactions on Intelligent Transportation Systems, 6*(2), 167–177. doi:10.1109/TITS.2005.848370

Brown, L. M., Senior, A. W., Tian, Y., Connell, J., Hampapur, A., Shu, C., & Lu, M. et al. (2005). Performance Evaluation of Surveillance Systems under Varying Conditions. In *Proc. IEEE PETS Workshop*, (pp. 1-8). IEEE.

Canny, J. (1986). A Computational Approach to Edge Detection. *IEEE Transactions on Pattern Analysis and Machine Intelligence,* 679-698.

Graevenitz, G. (2007). Biometric authentication in relation to payment systems and ATMs. *DuD Datenschutz Und Datensicherheit - DuD,* 681-683.

Piccardi, M. (2004). Background subtraction techniques: A review.*IEEE International Conference on Systems, Man and Cybernetics (IEEE Cat. No.04CH37583).*

Sivabalakrishnan, M., & Manjula, D. (2009). An Efficient Foreground Detection Algorithm for Visual Surveillance System. *International Journal of Computer Science and Network Security, 9*(5), 221–227.

Sivabalakrishnan, M., & Manjula, D. (2010a). Adaptive Background subtraction in dynamic environments using fuzzy logic. *International Journal on Computer Science and Engineering, 2*(2), 270–273.

Sivabalakrishnan, M., & Manjula, D. (2010b). Human Tracking Segmentation using color space conversion. *International Journal of Computer Science Issues, 7*(5), 285–289.

Sivabalakrishnan, M., & Manjula, D. (2010c). RBF Approach to Background Modelling for Background subtraction in Video Objects. *International Journal of Computer Science and Research, 1*(1), 35–42.

Sivabalakrishnan, M., & Manjula, D. (2010d). Fuzzy Rule-based Classification of Human Tracking and Segmentation using Color Space Conversion. *International Journal of Artificial Intelligence & Applications IJAIA, 1*(4), 70–80. doi:10.5121/ijaia.2010.1406

Sivabalakrishnan, M., & Manjula, D. (2010e). Adaptive background subtraction using fuzzy logic. *IJMIS International Journal of Multimedia Intelligence and Security*, *1*(4), 392–401. doi:10.1504/IJMIS.2010.039239

Sivabalakrishnan, M., & Manjula, D. (2011a). Novel Segmentation Method using improved edge flow vectors for people tracking. *Journal of Information and Computational Science*, *8*(8), 1319–1332.

Sivabalakrishnan, M., & Manjula, D. (2011b). Background extraction using improved mode algorithm for visual surveillance applications. *IJCSE International Journal of Computational Science and Engineering*, *6*(4), 275–282. doi:10.1504/IJCSE.2011.043927

Sivabalakrishnan, M., & Manjula, D. (2012). Performance analysis of fuzzy logic-based background subtraction in dynamic environments. *The Imaging Science Journal*, *60*(1), 39–46. doi:10.1179/1743131X11Y.0000000008

Toyama, K., Krumm, J., Brumitt, B., & Meyers, B. (1999). Wallflower: Principles and practice of background maintenance.*Proceedings of the Seventh IEEE International Conference on Computer Vision*, (pp. 255-261). doi:10.1109/ICCV.1999.791228

Witkin, A. (1983). Scale-Space Filtering. In *Proceedings 8th International Joint Conference* (pp. 1019-1022). Academic Press.

Zhang, X., Zhou, L., Zhang, T., & Yang, J. (2014). A novel efficient method for abnormal face detection in ATM.*2014 International Conference on Audio, Language and Image Processing*. doi:10.1109/ICALIP.2014.7009884

KEY TERMS AND DEFINITIONS

ATM Surveillance: ATM room based frauds to be increased such as shoulder surfing, frightening attacks. For monitoring such activity system can be developed.

Background Estimation: To identify the region of interest system much known things this is irrelevant. For background estimation is more important.

Background Subtraction: The removal of background and identify region interest or foreground from the scene image.

Computer Vision: System automatically diagnoses the situation of the region and act accordingly.

Object Tracking: Human object detect in the frame or scene the blog can move along with that object.

People Counting: System will identify number of people present in the given frame.

Security: The system can be used for more secured areas like server rooms, data centers. These places system framework can use.

Video Surveillance: For security monitoring region of interest and surveillance location.

Chapter 8
Digital Evidence in Practice:
Procedure and Tools

Uma N. Dulhare
MJCET, India

Shaik Rasool
MJCET, India

ABSTRACT

Advanced Evidence is any data of probative quality that is either put away or transmitted in a double frame. In today's universe of propelling advances, more data is being produced, put away and appropriated by electronic means. This requires numerous offices to build the utilization of advanced proof social affair as a regular or standard instrument in their fight against violations. Computerized proof can be helpful in an extensive variety of criminal examinations. Numerous computerized gadgets productively track client action; it is likewise conceivable to recoup erased records, both of which may influence a criminal examination. Data is similar to the backbone for associations of all sizes, sorts and industry areas. It should be overseen and secured, and when there is a break or wrongdoing conferred including spilled or stolen data, the culprits must be recognized and indicted. Expanded Internet entrance has given exponential ascent in refined assaults on Information Technology framework. Keeping in mind the end goal to make our IT framework versatile against the dangers, there is a requirement for Cyber Security. Digital criminology, likewise called PC legal sciences or advanced legal sciences, is the procedure of extricating data and information from PCs to serve as computerized proof - for common purposes or, by and large, to demonstrate and lawfully indict cybercrime. PC crime scene investigation has as of late increased noteworthy Popularity with numerous nearby law authorization organizations. It is at present utilized in extortion, robbery, drug authorization and each other implementation action. Law implementation organizations confront another test in managing digital wrongdoings. Criminal acts are being perpetrated and the confirmation of these exercises is recorded in electronic structure. Also, wrongdoings are being dedicated in the internet. Proof in these violations is quite often recorded in computerized design. It is critical that PC security experts know about a percentage of the necessities of the lawful framework and comprehends the creating field of PC legal sciences. It will clarify why Digital Evidence is a vital part of any crime scene investigation examination and why strict approaches and methodology must exist to manage the administration of confirmation. Digital examination conventions

DOI: 10.4018/978-1-5225-0193-0.ch008

offer specialists some assistance with gathering computerized proof in a forensically substantial manner. Computerized proof is "information that is made, controlled, put away or conveyed by any gadget, PC or PC framework or transmitted over a correspondence framework that is significant to the procedure." The section will give a brief of how Digital confirmation starts from a large number of sources including seized PC hard-drives and reinforcement media, ongoing email messages, talk room logs, ISP records, site pages, advanced system activity, nearby and virtual databases, computerized catalogs, remote gadgets, memory cards, and computerized cameras. The advanced confirmation is not virtual exist, but rather there are some different components to search for, the computerized proof can be duplicated with boundless contrasts, can be altered effortlessly, difficult to be distinguished the first asset, can be incorporated information check, and can't be seen straightforwardly without specialized procedure. The trust value of this computerized information is a basic question that advanced scientific analysts must consider. For this reason, part "advanced proof" partitioned into seven classifications. This part gives the learning important to handle advanced confirmation in its numerous structures, to utilize this proof to construct a case, to manage the difficulties connected with this kind of confirmation and ways to deal with taking care of computerized proof put away and transmitted utilizing systems as a part of a way that is well on the way to be acknowledged by law. The section presents the procedure of distinguishing, saving, examining and displaying computerized proof in a way that is legitimately satisfactory. It will clarify why Digital Evidence is an imperative part of any crime scene investigation examination and why strict arrangements and techniques must exist to manage the administration of proof. The section will give a brief of how Digital confirmation starts from a huge number of sources including seized PC hard-drives. Further the part will contain order of computerized confirmations where Digital proof can be grouped, looked at, and individualized in a few ways. One of those courses is by the substance of the confirmation. The later Section in the part will contain how the advanced proofs are gathered, what techniques and apparatuses can be utilized to safeguard the computerized confirmations.

1. INTRODUCTION

Digital devices are all over the place in today's reality, peopling correspond neighborhood and universally easily. A great many people promptly consider PCs, mobile phones and the Internet as the main hotspots for computerized proof, yet any bit of innovation that procedures data can be utilized as a part of a criminal way. For instance, hand held diversions can convey encoded messages in the middle of lawbreakers and even more up to date family apparatuses, for example, an icebox with an inherent TV, could be utilized to store, view and offer unlawful pictures in Figure 1. The critical thing to know is that responders need (ECSI, 2008).

Computerized proof incorporates all advanced information that can set up that a wrongdoing has been carried out or can give a connection between a wrongdoing and its casualty or a wrongdoing and its culprit. Interruption Detection Systems are an extraordinary wellspring of advanced confirmation (Casey, 2000). They gather data from an assortment of framework and system sources then investigate the data for indications of interruption and abuse.

Since the most recent couple of years have seen a sensational increment in the quantity of assaults, interruption recognition has turned into the standard of data affirmation. While firewalls do give some assurance, they don't give full insurance and still should be complimented by an interruption identification framework. The motivation behind interruption location is to offer PC frameworks some assistance with

Figure 1. Digital evidence

preparing for and manage assaults. Interruption recognition frameworks gather data from an assortment of sources inside of PC frameworks and systems. For most frameworks, this data is then contrasted with predefined examples of abuse to perceive assaults and vulnerabilities. There are two sorts of Intrusion Detection Systems – Host-Based and Network-Based (Bace & Rebecca, 1998)

In the host-based interruption recognition structural engineering, the framework is utilized to investigate information that begins on PCs (has) as appeared in Figure 2. In this manner, this construction modeling is utilized for distinguishing insider assaults and abuse. For instance, and representative who manhandle their benefits, or understudies changing their evaluations. Host-based frameworks analyze occasions like what records are gotten to and what applications are executed. Logs are utilized to assemble this occasion information. In any case, the review arrangement is vital on the grounds that it characterizes which end-client activities will bring about an occasion record being composed to an occasion log, for instance, logging all gets to of mission-basic documents. Host-construct interruption discovery frameworks dwell in light of each framework and more often than not answer to a headquarters console. To recognize abuse, marks, or predefined examples of abuse are contrasted and the information from the log documents. At the point when there is a relationship, either the security overseer is advised of the potential abuse, or a predefined reaction to the abuse is instituted.

Figure 2. Host based IDS

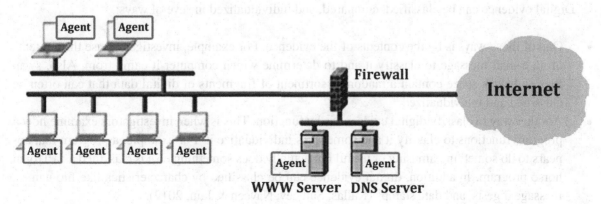

Figure 3. Network based IDS

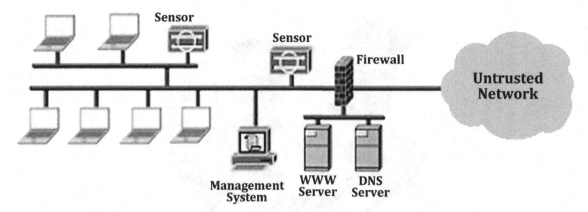

In the network-based intrusion detection architecture, the system is used to analyze network packets. Network-based architectures are used to detect access attempts and denial of service attempts originating outside the network. This architecture consists of sensors deployed throughout a network as shown Figure 3. These sensors then report to a central command console. Similar to host-based architectures, packet content signatures are used to identify misuse. These signatures are based on the contents of packets, headers and flow of traffic. However, it is important to note that encryption prevents detection of any patterns in the contents of the packet (Kurose, Keith & Ross, 2002).

However, because network-based intrusion detection can relate information like IP addresses which can be spoofed, a valid user could be wrongly attributed to perpetrating the misuse of the system. This makes network-based intrusion detection data invalid, which also makes most, but not all network digital evidence invalid. However, host-based intrusion detection data can be valid digital evidence.

2. CLASSIFICATION OF DIGITAL EVIDENCE

Computer forensic evidence is just like any other evidence in the sense that it must be: authentic, accurate, complete, convincing to juries, and in conformity with common law and legislative rules (admissible). To ensure authenticity, the must be proven to come from where it purports. The evidence is accurate and reliable if the substance of the story the material tells is believed and is consistent, and there are no reasons for doubt. Evidence is complete if the story that the material purports to tell is complete. That is, there are no other stories that the material also tells that might have a bearing on the legal dispute or hearing.

Digital evidence can be classified, compared, and individualized in several ways:

- One of those ways is by the contents of the evidence. For example, investigators use the contents of an e-mail message to classify it and to determine which computer it came from. Also, swap files and slack space contain a random assortment of fragments of digital data that can often be classified and individualized.
- Another way to classify digital evidence is by function. This is when investigators examine how a program functions to classify it and sometimes individualize it. For example, a program that appears to do something amusing or useful but actually does something else is classified as a Trojan horse program. In addition, digital evidence can be classified by characteristics like file names, message digests, and date stamps (Kailas, Sanjeev, Naveen & Jain, 2012).

3. COLLECTION OF DIGITAL EVIDENCE

3.1 Digital Evidence Collection Process

There is a general four step procedure to follow when collecting evidence:

- First the evidence has to be identified. Evidence must be distinguished from junk data. For this purpose, what the data is should be known, where it is located, and how it is stored should also be known.
- Next, the evidence should be preserved. The evidence must be preserved as close as possible to its original state. Any changes made during this phase must be documented and justified.
- Also, all procedures used in the examination should be audible, that is, a suitably qualified independent expert appointed by the other side of a case should be able to track all the investigations carried out by the prosecution's experts.
- Subsequently, all evidence must be analyzed. That is, the stored evidence must be analyzed to extract the relevant information and recreate the chain of events. Finally, the evidence must be presented. Communicating the meaning of the evidence is vitally important; otherwise you can't do anything with it. The manner of presentation is important, and it must be understandable by a layman to be effective.

Through each progression of the system, it is essential to record and report everything that is done and everything that is utilized. This guarantees the system is repeatable. Nonetheless, these records and archives are broad. Who at first reported the suspected episode alongside the time, date, and circumstances encompassing the suspected occurrence ought to be recorded. Additionally, points of interest of the introductory evaluation prompting the formal examination ought to be recorded. What's more, it is critical to record the names of all persons directing the examination. The case number of the episode and the explanations behind the examination ought to additionally be recorded. Moreover, a rundown of every single PC framework incorporated into the examination, alongside complete framework particulars ought to be recorded. System graphs and applications running on the PC frameworks beforehand recorded ought to be recorded. Additionally, a duplicate of the arrangement or approaches that identify with getting to and utilizing the frameworks already recorded ought to be recorded. A rundown of overseers in charge of the standard upkeep of the framework and additionally a point by point rundown of steps utilized as a part of gathering and breaking down confirmation ought to be recorded. At long last, an entrance control rundown of who had entry to the gathered proof at what date and time ought to be recorded (Priyanka, Kayarkar, Prashant & Anand, 2014):

- With knowing the rules and guidelines surrounding the identification and collection of evidence, some collection steps can be introduced.
- First the evidence has to be found. This is a very dynamic step that changes on a case by case basis. However, it is helpful to use a checklist to double-check that everything that is being looked for is there.
- Next, the relevant data needs be found out of the collected data. Once the data has been found, the part that is relevant to the case needs to be figured out. In general, err should be on the side of over-collection.

- After that an order of volatility needs to be created. Now that what to gather is known, a best order needs to be worked out in which to gather it. This ensures the minimized loss of uncorrupted evidence.
- Next, external avenues of change need to be removed. It is essential that alterations to the original data are avoided. Preventing anyone from tampering with the evidence helps you to create as exact an image as possible.
- Then it is time to collect the evidence. The evidence needs to be collected using the appropriate tools for the job. During the collection it is beneficial to re-evaluate the evidence that has already been collected. It may be the case that something important may be missed. Finally, everything should be documented. The collection procedures may be questioned later, so it is important that everything is documented.

With the evidence collected, before going any further, it is important to compare digital evidence with physical evidence. Digital evidence can be duplicated exactly and a copy can be examined as if it were the original. Also, examining a copy will avoid the risk of damaging the original. With the right tools, it is very easy to determine if digital evidence has been modified or tampered with by comparing it with the original. Digital evidence is relatively difficult to destroy. Even is it is "deleted", digital evidence can be recovered. When criminal attempt to destroy digital evidence, copies can remain in places they were not aware of (Essays, 2013).

The focus of digital evidence is on the contents of the computer as opposed to the hardware. With that in mind, there are two kinds of copies:

- Copy everything,
- Or just copy the information needed.

When there is plenty of time and uncertainty about what is being sought, but a computer is suspected to contain key evidence, it makes sense to copy the entire contents.

When collecting the entire contents of a computer, the general concept is the same in most situations:

- All related evidence should be taken out of RAM, and then the computer should be shutdown.
- Next, the hardware configuration of the system should be documented as well as the time and date of the CMOS.
- The computer should be booted using another operating system that bypasses the existing one and does not change data on the hard drive(s).
- Finally, a copy of the digital evidence from the hard drive(s) should be made.

While gathering the whole substance of a PC, a bit stream duplicate of the computerized confirmation is generally alluring. So, a bit stream duplicate duplicates what is in slack space and unallocated space, though a customary duplicate does not. Slack space is characterized to be the unused space in a plate bunch. The DOS and Windows document frameworks use settled size bunches. Regardless of the fact that the genuine information being put away requires less capacity than the bunch estimate, a whole group is saved for the document. This unused space is known as the slack space.

Making information accumulation one stride promote, a motivation for duplication and safeguarding can be portrayed. There are numerous apparatuses to make bit stream reinforcements of hard circles and floppy plates. Among them are devices like Encase, dd, ByteBack, and SafeBack. It is dependably to record the apparatus that used to make the duplicate. While making the bit stream picture, note and report how the picture was made. It is alluring to additionally take note of the date, time and analyst.

The observational law of computerized gathering and protection expresses that if one and only duplicate of the advanced confirmation is made, that proof will be harmed or totally lost. In this way, no less than two duplicates of the proof are taken. One of these is fixed in the vicinity of the PC proprietor and afterward put in secure stockpiling. This is the expert duplicate and might be opened for examination under direction from the Court in the case of a test to the proof exhibited after scientific investigation on the second duplicate.

3.2 Case Study

3.2.1 Collection Concealing Information

The most evident approach to conceal data on a plate is giving a document of interest anvague name or sparing it into a rare area. This trap is so clear and gives so little assurance that no sensible security arrangement would ever give it a chance to pass; however why is regardless it being utilized by the offenders, and, above all, why does despite everything it work?

The answer is agonizingly straightforward: specialists are time-compelled up to the fact they're obstructed with cellular telephones, tablets and seized hard drives to be investigated. They frequently have twenty minutes to a couple of hours, max, keeping in mind the end goal to separate all conceivable proof. To make things considerably more convoluted, examiners are bound by strict principles. By breaking any of the principles, specialists might refute all removed proof (Yuri, 2012).

One ought not expect finding all client data sitting in the default organizer, or being situated in whatever the default area is for a given sort of document. Figure 4. Demonstrates looking the whole hard circle are required to find all decoded log and history documents. This may create a sure number of false positives so extra checks are regularly required.

In reality, locating any one of the files is an obvious exercise. As applications such as instant messengers or email clients have to have access to their working files, they store files' locations somewhere in Windows registry or in their own configuration files. One sure must know a lot of things about each and every application being analyzed, which includes literally hundreds of messengers, email clients, peer-to-peer applications and browsers.

3.2.2 Hidden and Inaccessible Files and Folders

PC clients regularly ensure data by appointing document properties and authorizations avoiding unapproved access. Shrouded documents and ensured in the framework can be view by empowering the required alternatives as appeared in the Figure 5 a Hidden records and figure 5b.protected framework records and envelopes are a typical spot nowadays; these will be shown and even highlighted by each scientific investigation apparatus in presence. Most scientific investigation apparatuses can sidestep security traits and authorization control administration (yet not encryption) set by the document framework, for example, NTFS access control rights. Unique consideration ought to be paid to difficult to reach records and organizers; generally one can miss proof in envelopes having entry limitations.

Figure 4. Searching entire location and files

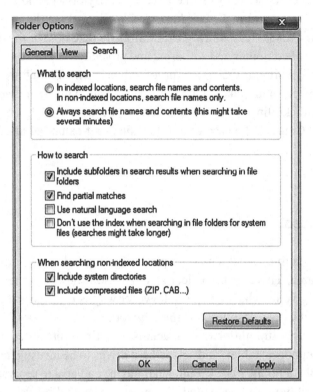

Figure 5. a) Enabling hidden files; b) Enabling protected files

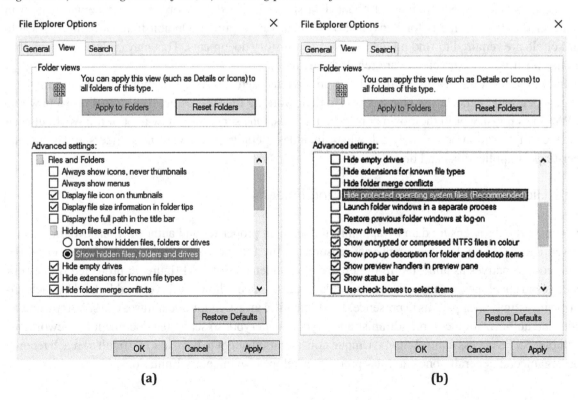

3.2.3 Deleted Files

Critical confirmation frequently winds up in the reuse receptacle. This is particularly valid for Windows PCs. Actually, erased documents can frequently be effectively recovered by investigating the substance of the Recycle Bin, a provisional stockpiling they're put before being deleted.

On the off chance that erased records don't appear in the Recycle Bin, there are still great opportunities to recuperate them by utilizing one of the numerous business information recuperation devices. The rule of erased record recuperation depends on the way that Windows does not wipe the substance of the document when it's being erased. Rather, a document framework record putting away the definite area of that record on the plate is being stamped as "erased". The plate space beforehand involved by the record is then promoted as accessible - yet not overwritten with zeroes or other information just yet (on the other hand, see the accompanying part, "The Issue of SSD Drives"). A decent illustration of such information recuperation instruments are items created by Disk Internals (www.diskinternals.com) e.g. Circle Internals Partition Recovery.

By investigating the record framework and/or examining the whole hard drive searching for trademark marks of known record sorts, one can effectively recoup not just documents that were erased by the client, additionally find confirmation, for example, interim duplicates of Office archives (counting old variants and corrections of such reports), makeshift documents spared by numerous applications, renamed documents et cetera (see "Information Carving").

Data put away in erased documents can be supplemented with information gathered from different sources. For instance, Skype stores its talk sign in the history database, and keeps interior information that may contain pieces and bits of client discussions in the "chatsync" envelope. The configuration is not authoritatively unveiled, but rather there are apparatuses accessible that can dissect such records (e.g. Belkasoft Evidence Center 2012). In this manner, if chatsync envelope exists, there are clear opportunities to recuperate Skype talks regardless of the fact that one have neglected to recoup an erased Skype database.

3.2.4 Retrieving Logs and History Files

Logs and history records contain a lot of key confirmation. Visit correspondences are frequently went with timestamps and handles of alternate gatherings, permitting making sense of precisely who the respondent was. Deciding the accurate area and name of these records is a key initial step required to perform further examination.

Late forms of Windows regularly keep client made and application-produced information in AppData, Program Files, and Documents and Settings organizers. In Windows Vista and Windows 7, the AppData envelope does not have a settled area on the plate, which encourage confuses the hunt. Likewise, these frameworks keep up a virtualized stockpiling for applications dispatched with lower than authoritative consents (AppData \ Local\Virtual Store). These areas are usually neglected by specialists. Indeed, even the surely understood Documents and Settings can tolerate diverse names relying upon the default area of a specific adaptation of Windows. For instance, it can be names "Мои документы" or "Dokumente und Einstellungen." PC clients can confound the investigation significantly encourage by moving or renaming normal records.

After you've discovered documents of enthusiasm by investigating Windows Registry and applications' design records or performing a manual/computerized look, you need to concentrate information out of them. To do as such, you need to know the definite arrangement of each of the source documents. Today, a huge number of distinctive organizations exist, calling for specialized information of arrangement specifics - or essentially for an instrument to computerize the errand. Luckily, numerous cutting edge applications use very much reported organizations that simple to investigate. For instance, SQLite databases are utilized by Skype and ICQ, the prevalent XML organization is used by MSN ambassador, Mirc visit utilizes straightforward content records, et cetera.

SQLite databases can be researched with free SQLite Database Viewer system, while XML records can be effectively opened with Internet Explorer.

In any case, there are numerous more organizations in presence that are way less legal amicable. The mysterious, personality inspiring "mork" position used by Firefox, or the exclusive PST group by Outlook, or even Blowfish-scrambled OLE-holders utilized by QQ Messenger are only a couple of illustrations. This is precisely the motivation behind why measurable examiners lean toward utilizing computerized scientific devices rather than manual pursuit and

3.3 Integrity of Evidences

Since the evidence has been collected, it is important to ensure the integrity of the evidence. That is, pollution should controlled. Firsts ought to never be utilized as a part of scientific examination – confirmed copies ought to be utilized. When information has been gathered, it must broke down to separate the confirmation to introduce and revamp precisely what happened. Remember that everything that is done must be completely archived, the work will be addressed and it must be demonstrated that the outcomes are reliably realistic from the systems performed. To reproduce the occasions that prompted the framework being adulterated, a course of events must be made. Log records utilized time stamps to demonstrate when a section was included, and these must be synchronized to bode well. Additionally remember that the information on the reinforcements needs to likewise be free from tainting. Thus, while investigating reinforcements it is best to have a committed host for the employment. This examination host ought to be secure, clean, and separated from any system. Once more, everything that is done should be reported to guarantee that what is done is repeatable and able to do continually giving the same result

4. VALIDATION OF DIGITAL EVIDENCE

There are five properties that confirmation must have keeping in mind the end goal to be helpful. The principal property is that computerized proof must allowable. That is, proof must have the capacity to be utilized as a part of court. Inability to follow this principle is identical to not gathering the confirmation in any case, expect the expense is higher. Another property is realness. Proof must be fixed to the occurrence keeping in mind the end goal to demonstrate something. Additionally, the confirmation must be appeared to identify with the occurrence relevantly. Culmination is additionally another property that manages the acceptability of advanced proof. It's insufficient to gather confirm that just demonstrates to one point of view of the occurrence. Not just ought to confirmation be gathered that can demonstrate an assailant's activities, additionally confirm that could demonstrate their purity. Case in point, on the off chance that it can be demonstrated that the aggressor was signed in at the season of the episode, it likewise should be indicated who else was signed in or not in order to perhaps demonstrate the blamelessness of someone else. This is called exculpatory proof, and is an essential piece of demonstrating a case. Another property is unwavering quality. All the more particularly, the proof accumulation and examination techniques must not give occasion to feel qualms about the confirmation's validness and veracity. One more decide is that of authenticity. The confirmation that is displayed ought to be obviously justifiable and convincing by a jury. All things considered, there's no reason for displaying a parallel dump of procedure memory if the jury has no clue what everything implies.

Utilizing the former five standards, some essential do's can be inferred. It is critical that the taking care of and along these lines the debasement of unique information be minimized. Once an expert duplicate of the first information is made, it ought not be touched nor the first. Optional duplicates ought to be taken care of. Furthermore, any progressions made to the firsts will influence the results of any examination later done to duplicates. For instance, no projects that adjust the entrance times of documents ought to be run. Additionally, any progressions ought to be represented, and point by point logs ought to be kept of the moves made. On the other hand, when proof modification is unavoidable it is completely key that the nature, degree, and explanations behind the progressions need be reported. Besides, as exact a picture of the framework ought to be caught as could be allowed. Catching an exact picture of the framework is identified with minimizing the taking care of or defilement of the first information. Contrasts between the first framework and the expert duplicate consider a change to the information. These distinctions must be represented. Additionally, the individual who gathered the proof ought to be arranged to affirm. Without the authority of the confirmation arriving to approve the reports made amid the proof gathering prepare, the proof gets to be noise, which is unacceptable. What's more, it is essential to guarantee the moves made on the information are repeatable. In the event that the activities can't be duplicated and the same results can't be come to, those unique activities won't be accepted. This tenets out any experimentation activities. At long last, it is essential to work quick. The quicker the work happens, the more improbable the information is going to change. Unstable proof may vanish totally in the event that it is not gathered in time. Mechanization of specific undertakings makes gathering continue significantly quicker.

Utilizing those same five principles, a few don'ts can likewise be determined. The framework ought not be shutdown before gathering proof. There is the likelihood of loss of unpredictable proof and the aggressor might have trojaned the startup and shutdown scripts, Plug and Play might change the framework design and provisional documents frameworks may be wiped out. Additionally, no projects ought to be keep running on the influenced framework. There is the likelihood of unintentionally activating something that could change or wreck proof. Any projects utilized ought to be on perused just media and ought to be statically connected.

5. PRESERVING THE DIGITAL EVIDENCE

1. **Message Digests:** A message digest calculation can be considered as a black box, that acknowledges a computerized object as information and produces a number as yield. A message process dependably creates the same number for a given information. Moreover, a great message digest calculation will deliver an alternate number for distinctive inputs. Along these lines, a precise will have the same message digest as the first however in the event that a document is changed even somewhat it will have an alternate message digest from the first. The MD5 calculation can be utilized for figuring message digests. The calculation utilizes the information as a part of an advanced article

to ascertain a mix of 32 numbers and letters. It is very impossible that two records will have the same message digest unless the documents are copies. Message digests give a strategy for close individualization and thusly, are in some cases alluded to as computerized fingerprints and are valuable for figuring out whether a bit of advanced confirmation has been messed around with. Generally, message digests represent the respectability of the document (Rivest, 1992).

2. **Log Files:** PC log documents are made routinely and contain data about acts and occasions made at particular times by, or from data transmitted by, a man with learning. Some PC created data has been seen as so solid that it has been acknowledged as immediate proof. Direct confirmation is generally something unmistakable that is displayed to demonstrate a reality. It is critical to keep these log records secure and to back them up intermittently. Since logs are consequently time stamped, a solitary duplicate ought to suffice, in spite of the fact that they ought to be digitally marked and scrambled when essential, to shield them from defilement. There are many different log files that are potential sources for digital evidence. Among them are:

    a. Acct, which contains every command typed by every user on the computer. Loginlog records failed logins.

    b. Syslog contains the main system log file that contains a wide range of messages from many applications.

    c. Sulog records every attempt to log in as the administrator of the computer.

    d. Utmp contains a record of all users currently logged into a computer. The 'who' command accesses this file.

    e. Wtmp contains a record of all of the past and current logins and records system startups and shutdowns. The 'last' command accesses this file.

    f. xferlog contains a record of all files that were transferred from a computer using the file transfer protocol.

6. TOOLS

The sleuth pack – http://www.sleuthkit.org – is an as good as ever Coroner's Toolkit. It is an open source criminological toolbox for dissecting Microsoft and UNIX record frameworks. After a picture has been made from a segment utilizing the dd charge, the sleuth unit can go to work. It empowers examiners to recognize and recuperate proof from pictures gained amid occurrence reaction or from live frameworks. There are four layers of capacities which break down the picture record that are in the unit. To begin with, the record framework layer cooperates with the document framework the plate picture was made in. Illustrations of records frameworks incorporate, Extended 2 document framework, record portion table, and new innovations documents framework. One approach to arrange and recollect works better is that any instrument that starts with the letter "f" is identified with the document framework. The substance layer of a record framework contains the genuine document content, or information. Information is put away in expansive lumps, with names, for example, squares, pieces and bunches. All devices in this layer start with the letter 'd'. The metadata layer portrays a document or index. This layer contains unmistakable information, for example, dates and estimate and also the location of the information units. This layer depicts the information in wording that the PC can prepare proficiently. The structure that the information is put away in has names, for example, hub and catalog section. All devices in this layer start with the letter 'i'. At long last, the human interface layer permits one to associate with records in a way that is more helpful than specifically through the metadata layer. In some working frameworks there are discrete structures for the metadata and human interface layers while others consolidate (Brian, 2003; TSK, 2008).

- **The Autopsy Forensic Browser (http://www.sleuthkit.org/dissection, http://autopsy.source-forge.net/):** A graphical interface to utilities found in the sleuth unit. It permits the apportioned and erased records, indexes, information units, and metadata of document framework pictures to be broke down in a read-just environment. Pictures can be hunt down strings and consistent expressions to recoup erased material. It additionally permits one to make a definite timetable of the Modified, Access, and Changed times of documents. Hash databases are utilized to recognize if a document is known not great or awful. Records can likewise be composed taking into account their document sort – rather than simply seeing them by catalog postings. Post-mortem examination won't adjust the first pictures and the honesty of the pictures can be checked in Autopsy utilizing MD5 val

- **First (foremost.sourceforge.net):** A Linux system to recoup records in view of their headers and footers. Chief can take a shot at picture records, for example, those produced by 'dd', or straightforwardly on a drive. The headers and footers are indicated by a setup document so you can pick and pick which headers you need to search for. A full depiction of preeminent and the setup record are incorporated into its man page.

- **Impression (www.webglimpse.net):** A capable indexing and question framework that permits a speedy pursuit through records. It can be utilized by people for their own document frameworks and by substantial associations for vast information accumulations. Glimpseindex manufactures a record of all content documents in the tree established at DIR. With it, impression can look through all records similarly as agrep, anticipate that you don't have will determine document names and the pursuit is quick.

- **Wipe (wipe.sourceforge.net):** A device that safely deletes records from attractive media. Recuperation of as far as anyone knows deleted information from attractive media is less demanding than what numerous individuals might want to accept. A system called Magnetic Force Microscopy permits any modestly financed rival to recoup the last a few layers of information kept in touch with circle. Wipe more than once overwrites exceptional examples to the documents to be decimated. In ordinary mode, 34 examples are utilized. These examples were prescribed in an article from Peter Gutmann entitled "Secure Deletion of Data from Magnetic and Solid-State Memory". A snappy mode permits you to utilize just 4 goes with arbitrary examples, which is obviously substantially less secure.

- **Etherape (etherape.sourceforge.net/):** A graphical system activity program. Etherape shows system action graphically. It utilizes GNOME libraries as its client interface, and libpcap, bundle catch and separating library. Highlighting join layer, IP and TCP modes, it shows system action graphically. Shading coded conventions are likewise shown. It underpins Ethernet, FDDI, Token Ring, ISDN, PPP, and SLIP conventions. It can channel activity to be appeared, and can read movement from a document and additionally live from the system.

- **Fenris-Razor (bindview.com/devices/fenris/) :** An apparatus that examines program execution. Fenris is a multipurpose tracer, GUI debugger, stateful analyzer and fractional decompiler expected to rearrange bug following, security reviews, code, calculation, convention investigation and PC legal sciences - giving a basic system follow, intuitive troubleshooting capacities, general data about inner developments, execution way, memory operations, I/O, contingent expressions and considerably more. Since it doesn't require sources or a specific gathering strategy, this multi-segment task can be exceptionally useful for black-box tests and assessments - yet it will likewise be an awesome instrument for open source venture reviews, as an unmatched ongoing observation device - particularly when sources are excessively unpredictable or too seriously composed, making it impossible to be broke down by hand reliably and sensible time. Fenris does not depend on GNU libbfd for any basic errands, and due to that, it is conceivable and attainable to follow and examine doubles changed to trick debuggers, crypted, or generally changed.

- **Honeyd (http://www.citi.umich.edu/u/provos/honeyd/):** A charge line honeypot program. Honeyd makes virtual hosts for IP addresses coordinating the particular net. It can reproduce any TCP and UDP administration. It answers to ICMP reverberation demands. Right now, all UPD ports are shut as a matter of course and sweet will answer with an ICMP inaccessible port message if the arrangement identity allows that. This empowers a solitary host to claim addresses on a LAN for system reproduction. The net contention might contain numerous locations and system ranges. With the goal honeyd should get system movement for IP addresses that it ought to recreate, it is important to either unequivocally course activity to it, use intermediary arp or run arpd for unassigned IP addresses on a common system.

- **Grunt (http://www.snort.org):** An open source system interruption recognition framework, fit for performing constant activity investigation and parcel signing on IP net-works. It can perform convention examination, content looking/coordinating and can be utilized to distinguish an assortment of assaults and tests, for example, support floods, stealth port outputs, CGI assaults, SMB tests, OS fingerprinting endeavors, and significantly more. Grunt utilizes an adaptable tenets dialect to depict activity that it ought to gather or go, and also a recognition motor that uses a particular module structural engineering. Grunt additionally has a secluded ongoing cautioning capacity, fusing alarming and logging modules for syslog, an ASCII content documents, UNIX attachments, WinPopup messages to Windows customers utilizing Samba's smbclient, database (Mysql/PostgreSQL/Oracle/ODBC) or XML. Grunt has three essential employments. It can be utilized as a straight parcel sniffer like tcpdump(1), a bundle lumberjack (helpful for system activity investigating, and so on), or as an all out system interruption location framework. Grunt logs bundles in tcpdump(1) paired configuration, to a database or in Snort's decoded ASCII organization to a progressive system of logging catalogs that are named in light of the IP location of the "remote" host.

- **Dsniff (www.monkey.org/~dugsong/dsniff):** An order line system examining and entrance testing device. Dsniff is a gathering of devices for system examining and infiltration testing. dsniff, filesnarf, mailsnarf, msgsnarf, urlsnarf, and webspy inactively screen a system for intriguing information (passwords, email, documents, and so forth) arpspoof, dnsspoof, and macof encourage the capture of system activity ordinarily inaccessible to an aggressor (e.g, because of layer-2 exchanging). sshmitm and webmitm actualize dynamic monkey-in-the-center assaults against diverted SSH and HTTPS sessions by abusing frail ties in impromptu PKI. John the Ripper - www. openwall.com/john/ - is a secret key splitting apparatus. John can utilize a word reference or some pursuit designs and additionally a watchword record to check for passwords. John bolsters distinctive breaking modes and comprehends numerous figure content arrangements, similar to a few DES variations, MD5 and blowfish. It can likewise be utilized to remove AFS and Windows NT passwords. To utilize John, you simply need to supply it a secret key record and the sought choices. On the off chance that no mode is chosen, john will attempt "single" in the first place, then "wordlist" lastly 'incremental'. "Single" implies that John will utilize the principles from (List.Rules:Single). "Wordlist" implies that John will utilize a client characterized word list. At long last, "incremental" implies that John will utilize the predefined ~/john.ini definition.

- **Nikto (www.cirt.net/code/nikto.shtml):** A web server scanner. It checks for things like treats, http ports, and conceivable CGI registries. It appears like nikto likewise has an instrument of interruption recognition framework avoidance. There is little documentation on nikto, perhaps the page will be more useful.

- **Nbtscan (www.unixwiz.net/instruments/nbtscan.html):** An order line apparatus that outputs for open NetBIOS namservers. Put another way, nbtscan is a project for examining IP systems for NetBIOS name data. It sends NetBIOS status question to every location in supplied go and records got in comprehensible structure. For every reaction host it records the IP address, NetBIOS PC name, signed in client name and MAC address.

- **Xprobe (www.sys-security.com):** An order line remote working framework fingerprinting device.

- **Ngrep (www.packetfactory.net/ventures/ngrep/):** An order line system grep capacity. Ngrep endeavors to give the vast majority of GNU grep's basic components, applying them to the system layer. Ngrep will permit determination of stretched out customary expressions to coordinate against information payloads of bundles. It at present perceives TCP, UDP, and ICMP crosswise over Ethernet, PPP, SLIP, FDDI, and invalid interfaces, and comprehends bpf channel rationale in the same manner as more basic bundle sniffing apparatuses, for example, tcpdump, and snoop.

- **Foe (www.packetfactory.net/Projects/foe/):** A charge line system parcel injector. The foe task is intended to be a summon line-based, compact human IP stack for UNIX/Linux. The suite is separated by convention, and ought to take into account helpful scripting of infusing parcel streams from basic shell scripts. Bolstered conventions incorporate ARP, DNS, ICMP, IGMP, OSPF, RIP, TCP, and UDP.

- **Fragroute (monkey.org/~dugsong/fragroute/):** A charge line system interruption testing apparatus. Fragroute captures, changes, and modifies departure activity bound for the particular host, actualizing the vast majority of the assaults portrayed in the Secure Networks "Insertion, Evasion, and Denial of Service: Eluding Network Intrusion Detection" paper of January 1998.

- **Ethereal (www.ethereal.com):** A graphical system analyzer project. It takes into consideration intuitive searching of bundle information from a live system or from a formerly spared catch document. Ethereal's local catch record configuration is libpcap position, which is likewise the organization utilized by tcpdump and different instruments. Furthermore, Ethereal can read catch records from snoop and atmsnoop, Shomiti/Finisar Surveyor, Novell LANalyzer, Network General/Network Associates DOS-based Sniffer (compacted or uncompressed), Microsoft Network Monitor, AIX's iptrace and Cinco Networks

- **Netcat (www.atstake.com/research/tools/network_utilities/):** A command line tool to read and write over the network using the TCP or UDP protocol. It is designed to be a reliable 'back-end' tool that can be used directly or easily driven by other programs and scripts. At the same time, it is a feature-rich network debugging and exploration tool, since it can create almost any kind of connection you would need and has several interesting built-in capabilities. In the simplest usage, 'nc host port' creates a TCP connection to the given port and the given target host. The standard input is then sending to the host, and anything coming back across the connection is sent to the standard output. This continues indefinitely, until the network side of the connection shuts down. Note that this behavior is different from most other applications which shut everything down and exit after an end of file on the standard input. Netcat can also function as a server, by listening for inbound connections on arbitrary ports and then doing the same reading and writing.

- **Tcpdump (www.tcpdump.org/):** A charge line apparatus that dumps system movement. Tcpdump prints out headers of bundles on a system interface that match the Boolean expression. It can likewise be keep running with the - w banner, which makes it spare the parcel information to a record for later investigation, and/or with the - b banner, which makes it read from a spared bundle document as opposed to peruse parcels from a system interface. In all cases, just parcels that match expression will be handled by tcpdump. At the point when tcpdump completes it will report numbers of bundles got by channel, the significance of this relies on upon the OS on which you're running tcpdump. Tcpdump will likewise report the quantity of bundles dropped by the part. This is the quantity of bundles that were dropped because of absence of cradle space, by the parcel catch system in the OS on which tcpdump is running.

- **Hping2 (www.hping.org):** A summon line parcel constructing agent and analyzer. Hping2 is a system device ready to send custom TCP/IP parcels and to show target answers like ping projects do with the ICMP answers. Hping2 handle discontinuity, discretionary bundles body and estimate and can be utilized as a part of request to exchange records typified under bolstered conventions. There are numerous utilizations for hping2. Among them are: test firewall rules, propelled port filtering, test system execution utilizing distinctive conventions, parcel size, TOS, and discontinuity, follow course under diverse conventions, firewall-like utilization, remote OS fingerprinting, TCP/IP stack examining, and substantially more.

- **Ettercap (ettercap.sourceforge.net):** A summon line sniffer, interceptor and lumberjack, for Ethernet systems. It started as a sniffer for exchanged LAN, yet amid the improvement process it has increased more components that have transformed it to an intense and adaptable instrument for man-in-the-center assaults. It underpins dynamic and detached analyzation of numerous conventions and incorporates numerous components for system and host examination. It has five sniffing systems. The primary is IPBASED, where the parcels are separated coordinating IP: PORT source and IP:PORT destination. Next is MACBASED, where parcels are separated coordinating the source and destination MAC address. At that point there is ARPBASED, which utilizes arp harming to sniff as a part of exchanged LAN between two hosts. Next there is SMARTARP, which utilizes arp harming to sniff as a part of changed LAN from a casualty host to every other host knowing the whole rundown of hosts. At last there is PUBLICARP, which additionally utilizes arp toxic substance to sniff as a part of changed LAN from a casualty host to every single other host. With this system the ARP answers are sent in show, however in the event that ettercap has the complete host list (on startup it has filtered the LAN) SMARTARP strategy is naturally chosen, and the arp answers are sent to every one of the hosts yet the casualty, abstaining from clashing MAC addresses as reported by win2K. There are additionally various components that accompany ettercap.

- **Openssh (www.openssh.com):** A protected remote association utility. It is a free form of the SSH convention suite of system availability instruments that expanding quantities of individuals on the Internet are coming to depend on. Numerous clients of telnet, rlogin, ftp, may note understand that their secret word is transmitted over the Internet uncrypted. Openssh encodes all movement to adequately wipe out listening in, association seizing, and other system level assaults. Furthermore, openssh gives a horde of secure burrowing abilities, and additionally an assortment of confirmation techniques.

- **Kismet (www.kismetwireless.net):** A graphical remote system sniffing instrument. Kismet is a 802.11b remote system sniffer. It is equipped for sniffing utilizing any remote card bolstered by Linux, including cards taking into account the Prism/2 chipset with the wlan-ng driver, cards in light of the Lucent chipset, and a couple of different cards. Kimset bolsters logging tot hewtapfile bundle design and spares recognized system data as plaintext, XSV, and XML. Kimset is equipped for utilizing any GPS upheld by gpsd and logs and plots system information.

- **Airsnort (airsnort.shmoo.com):** A graphical remote system interruption apparatus. Airsnort is a remote LAN device which recoups encryption keys. Airsnort works by inactively observing transmissions, processing the encryption key, when enough bundles have been accumulated. 802.11b, utilizing the Wired Equivalent Protocol (WEP), has numerous security defects. Airsnort endeavors to secure these vulnerabilities.

- **GPG (www.gnupg.org/):** An encryption and marking utility. Essentially the GNU variant of PGP.

- **Openssl (www.openssl.org/):** A cryptography toolbox executing the Secure Sockets Layer and Transport Layer Security system conventions and related cryptography measures required by them. The openssl system is a summon line instrument for utilizing the different cryptographic elements of openssl's crypto library from the shell. It can be utilized for: Creation of RSA, DH, and DSA key parameters, computation of message condensations, encryption and unscrambling with Ciphers, and SSL/TLS customer and server tests.

- **Lsof:** An order line utility that rundowns every single open record that a particular project is utilizing. An open record possibly a customary document, an index, a piece exceptional document, or a character uncommon record, an executing content reference, a library, a stream or a system record. A particular document or all records in a document framework may be chosen by way.

- **Chase (lin.fsid.cvut.cz/~kra/index.html) :** A charge line TCP/IP abuse scanner. Chase is a system for interfering into an association, watching it and resetting it. Note that chase is working on Ethernet and is best utilized for associations which can be viewed through it. Nonetheless, it is conceivable to accomplish something notwithstanding for hosts on another section or have that is on exchanged ports.

- **Stunnel (Stunnel.mirt.net) :** An assl association bundle. The stunnel system is intended to act as SSL encryption wrapper between remote customers and neighborhood or remote servers. The idea is that having non-SSL mindful daemons running on your framework you can without much of a stretch set them up to speak with customers over secure SSL channels. Stunnel can be utilized to add SSL usefulness to regularly utilized inetd daemons like POP-2, POP3, and IMAP servers, to standalone daemons like NNTP, SMTP, and HTTP, and clamor burrowing PPP over system attachments without changes to the source code.

- **Arpwatch:** A summon line Ethernet screen. Arpwatch follows along for Ethernet/IP address pairings. It syslogs movement and reports certain progressions by means of email. Arpwatch utilizes pcap to listen to arp bundles on a nearby Ethernet interface.

- **Burrow:** An order line apparatus for questioning space name servers. Burrow (area name groper) is an adaptable apparatus for cross examining DNS name servers. It performs DNS lookups and shows the answers that are come back from the name server(s) that were questioned. Most DNS directors use burrow to investigate DNS issues as a result of its adaptability, convenience and clarity of yield.

- **Chkrootkit (www.chkrootkit.org):** Searches for indications of a root pack. It looks at specific components of the objective framework and figures out if they have been mess.

7. STANDARDS FOR THE EXCHANGE OF DIGITAL EVIDENCE

The Scientific Working Group on Digital Evidence (SWGDE) was established in February 1998 through a collaborative effort of the Federal Crime Laboratory Directors. SWGDE, as the U.S.-based component of standardization efforts conducted by the International Organization on Computer Evidence (IOCE), was charged with the development of cross-disciplinary guidelines and standards for the recovery, preservation, and examination of digital evidence, including audio, imaging, and electronic devices(DESP, 2000).

The following information was drafted by SWGDE and presented at the International Hi-Tech Crime and Forensics Conference (IHCFC) held in London, United Kingdom, October 4-7, 1999. It proposes the establishment of standards for the exchange of digital evidence between sovereign nations and is intended to elicit constructive discussion regarding digital evidence. This document has been adopted as the draft standard for U.S. law enforcement agencies.

7.1 Standards

Principle 1: In order to ensure that digital evidence is collected, preserved, examined, or transferred in a manner safeguarding the accuracy and reliability of the evidence, law enforcement and forensic organizations must establish and maintain an effective quality system. Standard Operating Procedures (SOPs) are documented quality-control guidelines that must be supported by proper case records and use broadly accepted procedures, equipment, and materials.

Standards and Criteria 1.1: All agencies that seize and/or examine digital evidence must maintain an appropriate SOP document. All elements of an agency's policies and procedures concerning digital evidence must be clearly set forth in this SOP document, which must be issued under the agency's management authority.

Discussion: The use of SOPs is fundamental to both law enforcement and forensic science. Guidelines that are consistent with scientific and legal principles are essential to the acceptance of results and conclusions by courts and other agencies. The development and implementation of these SOPs must be under an agency's management authority.

Standards and Criteria 1.2: Agency management must review the SOPs on an annual basis to ensure their continued suitability and effectiveness.

Discussion: Rapid technological changes are the hallmark of digital evidence, with the types, formats, and methods for seizing and examining digital evidence changing quickly. In order to ensure that personnel, training, equipment, and procedures continue to be appropriate and effective, management must review and update SOP documents annually.

Standards and Criteria 1.3: Procedures used must be generally accepted in the field or supported by data gathered and recorded in a scientific manner.

Discussion: Because a variety of scientific procedures may validly be applied to a given problem, standards and criteria for assessing procedures need to remain flexible. The validity of a procedure may be established by demonstrating the accuracy and reliability of specific techniques. In the digital evidence area, peer review of SOPs by other agencies may be useful.

Standards and Criteria 1.4: The agency must maintain written copies of appropriate technical procedures.

Discussion: Procedures should set forth their purpose and appropriate application. Required elements such as hardware and software must be listed and the proper steps for successful use should be listed or discussed. Any limitations in the use of the procedure or the use or interpretation of the results should be established. Personnel who use these procedures must be familiar with them and have them available for reference.

Standards and Criteria 1.5: The agency must use hardware and software that is appropriate and effective for the seizure or examination procedure.

Discussion: Although many acceptable procedures may be used to perform a task, considerable variation among cases requires that personnel have the flexibility to exercise judgment in selecting a method appropriate to the problem.

Hardware used in the seizure and/or examination of digital evidence should be in good operating condition and be tested to ensure that it operates correctly. Software must be tested to ensure that it produces reliable results for use in seizure and/or examination purposes.

Standards and Criteria 1.6: All activity relating to the seizure, storage, examination, or transfer of digital evidence must be recorded in writing and be available for review and testimony.

Discussion: In general, documentation to support conclusions must be such that, in the absence of the originator, another competent person could evaluate what was done, interpret the data, and arrive at the same conclusions as the originator.

The requirement for evidence reliability necessitates a chain of custody for all items of evidence. Chain-of-custody documentation must be maintained for all digital evidence.

Case notes and records of observations must be of a permanent nature. Handwritten notes and observations must be in ink, not pencil, although pencil (including color) may be appropriate for diagrams or making tracings. Any corrections to notes must be made by an initialed, single strikeout; nothing in the handwritten information should be obliterated or erased. Notes and records should be authenticated by handwritten signatures, initials, digital signatures, or other marking systems.

Standards and Criteria 1.7: Any action that has the potential to alter, damage, or destroy any aspect of original evidence must be performed by qualified persons in a forensically sound manner.

Discussion: As outlined in the preceding standards and criteria, evidence has value only if it can be shown to be accurate, reliable, and controlled. A quality forensic program consists of properly trained personnel and appropriate equipment, software, and procedures to collectively ensure these attributes.

7.1.1 International Organization on Computer Evidence (IOCE)

The International Organization on Computer Evidence (IOCE) was established in 1995 to provide international law enforcement agencies a forum for the exchange of information concerning computer crime investigation and other computer-related forensic issues. Comprised of accredited government agencies involved in computer forensic investigations, IOCE identifies and discusses issues of interest to its constituents, facilitates the international dissemination of information, and develops recommendations for consideration by its member agencies. In addition to formulating computer evidence standards, IOCE develops communications services between member agencies and holds conferences geared toward the establishment of working relationships.

In response to the G-8 Communiqué and Action plans of 1997, IOCE was tasked with the development of international standards for the exchange and recovery of electronic evidence. Working groups in Canada, Europe, the United Kingdom, and the United States have been formed to address this standardization of computer evidence.

During the International Hi-Tech Crime and Forensics Conference (IHCFC) of October 1999, the IOCE held meetings and a workshop which reviewed the United Kingdom Good Practice Guide and the SWGDE Draft Standards. The working group proposed the following principles, which were voted upon by the IOCE delegates present with unanimous approval.

7.1.2 IOCE International Principles

The international principles developed by IOCE for the standardized recovery of computer-based evidence are governed by the following attributes:

- Consistency with all legal systems;
- Allowance for the use of a common language;
- Durability;
- Ability to cross international boundaries;
- Ability to instill confidence in the integrity of evidence;
- Applicability to all forensic evidence; and
- Applicability at every level, including that of individual, agency, and country.

These principles were presented and approved at the International Hi-Tech Crime and Forensics Conference in October 1999. They are as follow:

- Upon seizing digital evidence, actions taken should not change that evidence.
- When it is necessary for a person to access original digital evidence, that person must be forensically competent.
- All activity relating to the seizure, access, storage, or transfer of digital evidence must be fully documented, preserved, and available for review.
- An individual is responsible for all actions taken with respect to digital evidence while the digital evidence is in their possession.
- Any agency that is responsible for seizing, accessing, storing, or transferring digital evidence is responsible for compliance with these principles.

8. CONCLUSION

Digital evidence can be valuable in an extensive variety of criminal examinations. Computerized information are surrounding us and ought to be gathered in any examination routinely. This Chapter talked about a few Digital evidence frames which can be broke down to reinforce the linkage evidence in Cyber examinations. Given the boundless utilization of PCs and the wide utilization of systems, it would be a grave blunder to neglect them as a wellspring of evidence in any wrongdoing. Digital evidence as a type of physical evidence makes a few difficulties for measurable analysts. Having the capacity to keep the trustworthiness of all put away evidence is imperative. The procedure of taking care of Digital evidence or electronic evidence must be led in a forensically solid way to guarantee court suitability. Computerized evidence or electronic evidence is profoundly affecting the future routine of law, as norms for getting overseeing and utilizing data accumulated through this procedure keep on being built up. Computerized evidence and electronic evidence will keep on being a basic component of a wide range of legitimate matters and also non-lawful. The Chapter underscored that Collection and conservation of this evidence is the way to its utilization in a court of law. The importance and rules of Standard Operating Procedures (SOPs) help to archived quality-control rules that must bolstered by legitimate case records and utilize extensively acknowledged strategies, hardware, and materials. The section expounded diverse Digital evidence toolbox which empower the accumulation and conservation of computerized evidence.

REFERENCES

Bace, R. (1998). *An Introduction to Intrusion Detection and Assessment: for System and Network Security Management.* ICSA White Paper.

Carrier, B. (2003). *The Sleuth Kit Informer*. Retrieved from http://www.sleuthkit.org/informer/sleuthkit-informer-3.html

Casey, E. (2000). *Computer Evidence and Computer Crime: Forensic Science, Computers, and the Internet.* Cambridge, UK: Cambridge University Press.

Digital Evidence Standards and Principles. (April 2000). Forensic Science Communications. Retrieved from https://www.fbi.gov/about-us/lab/forensic-science-communications/fsc/april2000/swgde.htm/

Electronic CSI: A Guide for First Responders. (2008). Department of Justice, Office of Justice Programs, National Institute of Justice. Retrieved from http://www.nij.gov/pubs--sum/219941.htm

Gubanov, Y. (2012). *Retrieving Digital Evidence: Methods, Techniques, and Issues: Part 1.* Retrieved from http://www.forensicmag.com/articles/2012/05/retrieving-digital-evidence-methods-techniques-and-issues-part-1

Kayarkar, Ricchariya, & Motwani. (2014). Mining Frequent Sequences for Emails in Cyber Forensics Investigation. *International Journal of Computer Applications, 85*(17), 1-6.

Kumar, Sofat, Agarwal, & Jain. (2012). Identification of User Ownership in Digital Forensic using Data Mining Technique. *International Journal of Computer Applications, 50*(4), 1-5.

Kurose, J. F., & Ross, K. W. (2002). *Computer Networking, A Top Down Approach* (6th ed.). Pearson Education.

Rivest, R. (1992). *The MD5 Message Digest Algorithm, RFC 1321*. Retrieved from http://www.rfc-editor.org/rfc/rfc1321.txt

Sleuth Kit. (2008). *The Sleuth Kit*. Retrieved from https://github.com/coriolis/vmxray/tree/master/src/tools/sleuthkit

UK Essays. (2013). *The Information Technology Act Information Technology Essay*. Retrieved from http://www.ukessays.com/essays/information-technology/the-information-technology-act-information-technology-essay.php?cref=1

Section 3
Cyber Forensics and Investigation

Chapter 9
Digital Forensic and Machine Learning

Poonkodi Mariappan
SRM University, India

Padhmavathi B.
SRM University, India

Talluri Srinivasa Teja
SRM University, India

ABSTRACT

Digital Forensic as it sounds coerce human mind primarily with exploration of crime. However in the contemporary world, digital forensic has evolved as an essential source of tools from data acquisition to legal action. Basically three stages are involved in digital forensic namely acquisition, analysis and reporting. Digital Forensic Research Workshop (DFRW) defined digital forensic as "Use of Scientifically derived and proven method towards the identification, collection, analysis, interpretation, documentation and presentation of digital evidence derived from digital sources for the purpose of facilitating or furthering the reconstruction of event to be criminal". The hard problem in digital forensic is such that the acquired data need to be cleaned and is required to be intelligible for reading by human. As a solution to this complexity problem a number of tools are present which may be repeated until relevant data is obtained.

INTRODUCTION TO FORENSIC COMPUTING

Typically any company's top level deals with ethical/cultural considerations. These considerations directly map to the law on hand which in turn to be the policies. These policies generate procedures which lead to technical implementations (Figure 1).

An organizational view at its core part has storage processing where all information's are collected and stored using some storage devices. Required operations are performed over the collected data to discover any hidden information. Administrative concerns take the appropriate decisions according to the attorney suggestions based on the ethical and cultural moralities.

DOI: 10.4018/978-1-5225-0193-0.ch009

Figure 1.

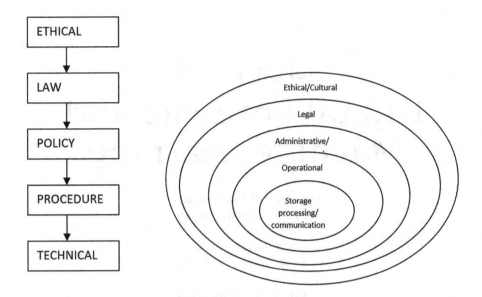

NEED FOR DIGITAL FORENSIC

Today's world communication is through computers or any handheld devices over world wide web. Military secrets, banking, personal information exchange are conducted electronically. A study in the University of California has shown that more than 95% of all information generated in digital form. Among these only few documents that all exchanged over the internet are only and never could be printed on paper.

In the digital era, digital data is dominating the analog predecessors (Witten, Frank, & Hall 2000) but however, since the digital edit software is ubiquitous the authenticity of digital data faces a great challenge. It has aroused the suspicion on the reliability of digital data especially when the digital data renders to the court as the digital evidence. In order to make the judiciary verdict right and objective the probability of the digital evidence produced is expected to be the accurate one.

Digital Forensic as it sounds coerce human mind primarily with an exploration of a crime. However in the contemporary world, digital forensic has evolved as an essential source of tools from data acquisition to legal action. Tampering is done long back where Photoshop can do wonders. Trust in these photographs are the major point of research where authentication has to be provided.

Layers of Abstraction

Data acquired irrespective of application inside on a disc or network in the form of zeros and ones (binary), must be translated to the requirement of the application on hand. At an outset, an abstraction layer may be an input output system with a set of rules for processing and finally error rate margin to be intelligible (Figure 2).

Digital Forensic Research Workshop (DFRW) defined digital forensic as "Use of scientifically derived and proven method towards the identification, collection, analysis, interpretation, documentation and presentation of digital evidence derived from digital sources for the purpose of facilitating or furthering the reconstruction of the event to be criminal".

Figure 2.

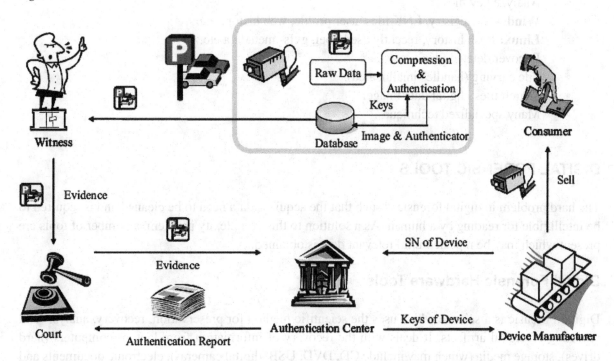

Acquisition Strategies

Forensic Science is a reactive science for which it was introduced especially used in court case analysis, any incident response system and so on. On its evaluation, it has been extended towards proactive means supporting mobile applications, security audits, continuous forensic monitoring (Markman, 2000). Normally information is extracted in the following ways:

- **Backup Files:** Normally there is information provided by the "custodian" which may include backup software from corporations, PST files etc.
- **Logical Acquisition:** A copy of existing file system is created. Here, data and time are being preserved.
- **Physical Acquisition:** Here bit by bit data is extracted and thus creates an exact digital replica of the storage medium. This process requires specialized analysis tools and techniques.
- **Verification of Data:** A calculated hex signature based on a set of data is done. A Hash Value normally verifies forensic image integrity, as a small change in source causes 'avalanche' effect in Hash Value. For two data sets to be proved to be identical their hash values must match. Few used Hash Techniques are MD5(a 128-bit value), SHA(a 256-bit value).
- **Typical Forensic Analysis Steps:** Create timeline of events (Hongliang Jiang, 2012):
  - Obtain metadata from files (images, documents, flash cookies, etc).
  - File system modified, accursed, changed and created.
  - Mount digital data image read-only.
  - Generate a list of all files (allocated and deleted).

- ○ Analyze key files
- ○ **Windows:** Registry, LNK files, user profile, web history etc.
- ○ **Linux:** Bash history, recently used.xbel, gvfs- metadata etc.
- ○ Recover deleted files.
- ○ File carving (handles unallocated).
- ○ Search files, digital data image.
- ○ Many specialized techniques.

DIGITAL FORENSIC TOOLS

The hard problem in digital forensic is such that the acquired data need to be cleaned and is required to be intelligible for reading by a human. As a solution to this complexity problem, a number of tools are present which may be repeated until relevant data is obtained.

Digital Forensic Hardware Tools

Digital Forensic is a science which uses the scientific method for preservation, recovery, analysis and reporting of digital artifacts. It deals with the recovery of information from laptops/computers (hard drives), storage media (which may include CD, DVD, USB, digital cameras), electronic documents and mobile phone.

Forensic Hardware is any hardware device which is specially designed to be used in the gathering, preservation or analysis of digital evidence. It is normally used by trained professionals who are mainly involved in investigations of any crime.

Hardware may be such that one job may be done by a single hardware may be acquiring image acquisition alone whereas other may be a hardware where computer professionals may do their analysis. This hardware is designed in order to safeguard data integrity in spite of software codes which uses these data collected through hardware for analysis.

TYPES OF FORENSIC HARDWARE

- **Forensic Computers:** Computers which are built with a great effort like MacPro for capturing and analyzing data from specific devices like mobile phones, hard disks, flash drives (Figure 3).
- **Write Blocking Devices:** If data integrity is the first priority for digital forensic then protecting such data without any contamination becomes the prime job. These devices are designed in such a way where data would be extracted from original media without any alteration or painting of the data evidence. This device is essential to be write protected. Some examples are Flash Devices, SIM Cards, and SD Cards etc (Figure 4).
- **Imaging Devices:** An exact copy of data from one hard drive to another is made possible with the help of imaging Devices. This is hence called as one to one copy written as '1:1'. Instead of removing the hard drive for data analysis a duplicate copy is made. Here also, digital evidence integrity is maintained (Figure 5).

Figure 3.

Figure 4.

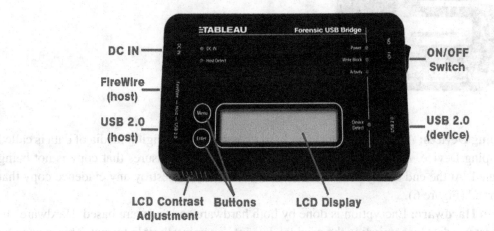

Figure 5.

Figure 6.   *Figure 7.*

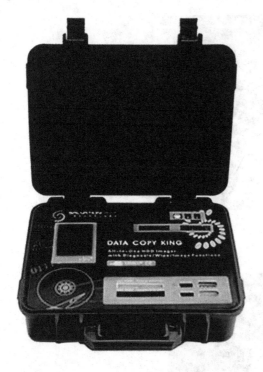

- **Data Wiping Devices:** A device which cleans hard drives and other digital media of data is called a Data Wiping Device. Any information copied from a hard disk ensures that copy is not being contaminated. At the end of any investigation, it is mandatory to destroy any evidence copy that was preserved (Figure 6).
- **Encryption Hardware:** Encryption is done by both hardware and software based. Hardware encryption protects data by converting the original data into an unintelligible format. This is done by an encryption algorithm and a key which may be public or private. The data made as a cipher may be broken by brute force attack which may involve all possible combinations of the key in finding the original data from the cipher. Sometimes backdoor is also there and digital forensic could be done through them or else only brute force is possible (Figure 7).

DIGITAL FORENSIC INVESTIGATION SOFTWARE TOOLS

- **SansSift:** Software designed for Ubuntu which allows the conduct of in-depth trend set and incident response investigation.
- **Sleuthkit:** It comes in a package which does timeline analysis, hash filtering, file system analysis and keyword searching
- **FTK Imager:** It allows view finding in windows explorer. It locates files on local and network drives and view the content of memory downloads.
- **DEFT:** It includes mobile forensic, data recovery and hashing.

- **Last Activity View:** It is used if we want to know the least activity occurred on a machine. The information could be exported to a CSV,SML and HTML files.
- **HxD:** They can be used on oldest main memory. It has features supporting exporting, file sharing and splitting a file.
- **CAINE:** A user-friendly way to be used in an investigation and the best of all forensic tools.
- **Plain Sight:** A live CD that allows you to perform forensic tasks such as looking into internet history, gathering data on USB devices, extracting password hashes and others.
- **Acquiring a Forensic Image:** Connect drive to physical write blocks which prevent any further writes to the drive. This normally done by software techniques also but not effective as a hardware used. As the image is obtained perform verification of source and target image with hash signature and record in chain custody.

```
Command to match source and target image using hash signature
dc3dd if=<source.device>of=derive001.dc3dd verb=on hash=sha256 hlog=drive001.
hashlog log=drive001.log rec=off
rec=off determines how to handle I/O errors(recover=off)
```

MACHINE LEARNING

Machine learning is an Artificial intelligence branch which deals with developing algorithms, that learn from the raw data given as input and thus, adapt to the changes that can improve their performances with experience. Learning approaches are advantageous because they tend to deal with a large data set which are practically too complex for hand-crafted solutions. The asset of learning can potentially be subverted by malicious manipulation of learners environment. Thus, we use machine learning algorithms to solve complex security problems by including training and testing on large databases.

Machine learning has applications in several industries and problems where there is a need to understand and interpret the past and existing problems to identify newer and advanced issues even before they can occur by analyzing the trajectory or the sequence of actions occurring by looking into the given data set. Whether the area it is being used is Behavior prediction of users, learning real world scenarios or the automobile industry where several defects and errors are being detected even before they occur based on the actions happening in the assembly line. With the techniques that have already been developed in the field of machine learning, we can deeply understand complicated problems that have several factors that result in generating errors in many levels.

DIGITAL FORENSIC AND MACHINE LEARNING

In the field of forensics, we find several problems that could have occurred in multiple ways and these kinds of problems could be explained in several scenarios and this imposes a grave problem when it comes to making a system as secure as possible in the eyes of a security analyst. These kinds of problems usually have several key factors that come into play when they occur and they are especially hard to be spotted during inspections as they are hidden within huge amounts of data which cannot be analyzed even by an experienced security expert. In problems like this, Machine Learning proves to be the most efficient and useful method of detection and analyzing with the least amount of error percentage. Using Machine Learning, we can analyze large amounts of data to initially learn the system and then the new Machine Learning system itself can analyze the new incoming data and security threats that are hard to find even today with traditional systems used in a majority of applications and transactions.

Depending on the area of forensics where Machine Learning is being used, there are several methods that can be applied. The most obvious and efficient method that can instantly be used are:

- **Supervised Learning:** Supervised learning is the machine learning task of inferring a specifically defined function from labeled training data. The training data which is initially given to the function consist of a set of training examples in different scenarios. In supervised learning, each example is a pair consisting of an input object (typically a vector) or an input stimuli and the desired output value (also called the supervisory signal) which is a result based on the given function. A supervised learning algorithm analyzes the training data and produces an inferred function, which can be used for mapping new examples. An optimal scenario will allow for the algorithm to correctly determine the class labels for unseen instances. This requires the learning algorithm to generalize from the training data to unseen situations in a "reasonable" way which can be applied to several different problems occurring within the same scenario.
- **Unsupervised Learning:** In machine learning, the problem of unsupervised learning is that of trying to find hidden structure or unknown scenario where the working and the reason behind the results are unknown in unlabeled data. Since the examples given to the learner are unlabeled, there is no error or reward signal to evaluate a potential solution. This distinguishes unsupervised learning from supervised learning and reinforcement learning. This is used to first find out the right way to evaluate the problems by initially learning about the given system.
- **Reinforced Learning:** Reinforcement learning is an area of machine learning inspired by behaviorist psychology, concerned with how agent sought to take actions in an environment so as to maximize some notion of cumulative reward. The problem, due to its generality, is studied in many other disciplines, such as game theory, control theory, operations research, information theory, simulation-based optimization, multi-agent systems, swarm intelligence, statistics, and genetic algorithms.

Existing Machine Learning in Digital Forensic

Machine Learning techniques have been used in several real-time applications such as banking transactions which include credit card transactions, debit card transactions, net- banking transactions, ATM transaction and In-Bank transactions where they have shown a very high success rate when compared to several other techniques and methods. Many of the latest applications now use sophisticated state-of-the- art machine learning algorithms and techniques to identify and report intrusions and varied unusual patterns of users worldwide without any errors. Several of them have adapted themselves to learn the behaviors of individual users which is unthinkable if it needed to be done in any other method.

While we are at a point where several digital revolutions are taking place, there has been no other day in the history than today where we have as many harmful threats that are occurring today than any other day before in history. As the current statistics say 80% of the world data had been created in the last 2 years. We have accomplished several marvelous wonders with this much amount of data that were unimaginable before.

Today we perform several operations on data of all types that had been gathers from several sources to answer specific questions. We use data to take smart decisions during complicated problems where several events act as a crucial factor. At every second and minute Gigabytes of data is being generated in the most spectacular ways. But, there is something that many of the data generators and analysts did not anticipate initially when this revolution was happening.

With the creation of big data, we had created several other harmful ways to perform illegal and unauthorized actions on this data. Many ways where any type of data can be manipulated and exploited in possible ways there is.With different kinds of data such as text, images, video, audio, etc.. image data was the one which had been most exploited and manipulated. It was during this time when there was a boom in Digital data forensics. A lot of practical and publishable methods were being developed by world renowned computer and forensic scientists but they were not able to keep up with specialized black hat hackers.

At the rate at which different kinds of software applications were being made, most of them were not protected well from intrusions and were severely affected during massive attack leaving the users data at a risk. More software was being developed within a particular than there was time to keep up with security flaws and loopholes.Several social networking sites like Facebook and Google+ who operate massive data centers consists of more than 50% images as content. Today, Facebook has the world's largest image repository and it is also a place where a lot of data is been taken away to illegitimate websites where it is being used for different reasons without the consent of the owner.

As time went, the existing methods had become very inefficient and had a huge error percentage and were just wasting the time and resources of users and service providers.

Revolution in Digital Forensic

This was the time when a new kind of revolution started taking place in Digital Forensic Analysis. Several scientists at different academic institutions had started to think about the idea and possibility to use Machine Learning techniques in Digital Forensic.

After several experiments and iterations, they were able to successfully create a system which had alarmingly low error percentages than traditional methods and were also highly efficient in terms of resource utilization and adaptability. These algorithms were able to start learning and adapting to newer and advanced techniques and intrusions(Sommer 1999) without or minimal help from the developer side. Soon these methods were found in several security systems with banks being the first to start implementing them in transactions like a credit card, debit card, net transactions and In-store transactions. Later these algorithms found their way into social networking applications such as Facebook, Google+, Stack overflow, etc..But at the base of all applications was a core part Digital Forensics where all the threats, vulnerabilities and attacks were being monitored.

After the wide adaptation of these techniques had taken place and once their efficiency was validated, even government courts started using these image results and predictions in their court of law. One of the primary problems faced by government courts is the legitimacy of these photos. As reports of morphed or edited photos came under light these images had to be tested.

Case Study 1

The evolution of modern digital devices is outpacing the scalability and effectiveness of Digital Forensics techniques. Digital Forensics Triage (Gomez, 2004) is one solution to this problem as it can extract evidence quickly at the crime scene and provide vital intelligence in time critical investigations. Similarly, such methodologies can be used in a laboratory to prioritize deeper analysis of digital devices and alleviate examination backlog. Developments in Digital Forensics Triage methodologies have moved towards automating the device classification process and those which incorporate Machine Learning principles have proven to be successful. Such an approach depends on crime-related features which provide a relevant basis upon which device classification can take place. In addition, to be an accepted and viable methodology, it should be also as accurate as possible.

Previous work has concentrated on the issues of feature extraction and classification, where less attention has been paid to improving classification accuracy through feature manipulation. In this regard, among the several techniques available for the purpose, we concentrate on feature weighing, a process which places more importance on specific features.

DF Management Framework (DFMF)

DFMF involves in preparing organizations for DF investigations by the proactive identification and the availability of enough admissible evidence, and the restructuring of relevant processes to be forensically sound.

DF software tools and techniques are used in order to enhance governance frameworks in organizations. It helps in gathering and analyzing live evidence during ongoing attacks; and Root cause of an incident is successfully investigated by using DFMF. The components will provide the backbone in the formulation of a comprehensive DFMF, which is part of a broader study. The paper discusses the different components of DF by

- Defining and discussing the goals of ProDF;
- Defining and discussing the goals of ReDF,
- Defining and discussing the goals of ActDF; and
- Discuss how the different components interact to provide a high-level overview of DF.

SOLUTION

A practical solution to these problems is represented by Digital Forensic Triage (DFT), a branch of DF whose aim is to extract evidence to provide vital intelligence in a timely manner. Automated DFT classification aims to remove any manual actions by incorporating Machine Learning (ML) to classify a devices relevance to an investigation. According to Gomez, Marturana et al., and, and Garfinkel et al. the favored method in forensic triage methodologies(Rogers, Goldman, Mislan, Wedge, & Debrota, 2000) is supervised ML. Essential to this process are attributes, which are also known in ML terminology as features, which provide a platform upon which classification can take place. The terms attribute and features are interchangeable and for the purposes of this paper, the term feature will be used. While there has been much work done in DFT on the issues of feature extraction and device classification to speed up the crime investigation, recently a movement towards improving accuracy is taking place. Automated DFT classification is judged, indeed, by classification accuracy and various techniques have been experimented with so far to improve performance. The reason is simple: low accuracy and mis-triaging could result in wasted time and resources for a forensic analysis(Grillo, Lentini, Me, & Ottoni 2009) team which defeats the purpose of using such methodologies in the first place. It has been shown that one such method is known as feature selection, which reduces the feature space complexity by the reducing the number of features with both automated and manual methods. Another solution, which is the one adopted in this work, is known as feature manipulation which encompasses both automated and manual feature weighting methods.

In this research, we use Automated Feature Weighting (AFW) and ML algorithms to remove any manual methods during the DFT process and Manual Feature Weighting (MFW) methods through interaction with forensic experts to make a performance benchmark. The intended aim is to build a comprehensive DFT methodology which enables manipulation of features through weighting in auto-mated classification of digital devices. In this specific context, we will use Kullback-Leibler measure to quantify weights in AFW whereas manual weights in MFW will be determined with the invaluable contribution of digital forensic experts who have been properly surveyed and interviewed. MFW methods are, indeed, perceived important to the proposed methodology as they introduce investigator's ability to influence the process. An investigators knowledge and experience of similar cases is translated to the methodology through applying a weighting to features based on their perceived importance in the case at hand. In a child pornography investigation, for instance, an investigator knows from experience that any picture files on the system could potentially be of child abuse so would place a high importance on this feature. Whereas, the presence of documents is less important but may still provide valuable information. Therefore, features are not removed, as would be in the case in feature selection, but merely less importance is placed on them.

As a result, classification accuracy resulting from AFW and MFW methods will be calculated and benchmark testing will be performed using standard corpora and data from real-life investigations to validate the methodology (Figure 8).

Figure 8.

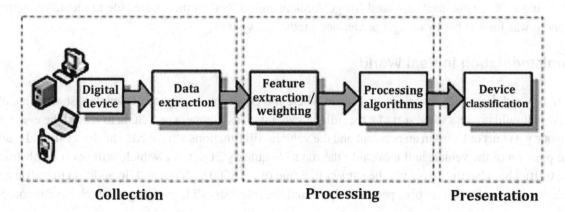

151

A SUMMARIZED WORKFLOW OF THE METHODOLOGY

1. **Collection:**
   a. A digital device is identified and collected at a crime scene for forensic analysis.
   b. Data is extracted from the digital device using an appropriate tool.
2. **Processing:**
   a. The extracted data is transformed to features according to the crime-related state vector.
   b. Each feature is allocated either a manual or automatic weighting according to the chosen method, MFW or AFW respectively.
   c. The manipulated features are inputted to the appropriate supervised ML algorithm and processed.
3. **Presentation:** According to the training set, the digital device is given a binary classification.

Significance of the Methodology Used

This methodology extracts and pre-processes relevant features, and classifies a digital device in relation to the specific crime under investigation. The state vector contains a set of variables which define a concept. The vector can contain a number of variables and can be represented. A set of values pertaining to the variables is represented by an instance of data. Multiple instances are required to define the training set upon which classification can take place.

Our model's dependent variable, i.e. the class, is a binary random variable with two possible values: relevant or non-relevant. When a relationship exists between the digital device and the criminal case under investigation the class is given the relevant value otherwise the non-relevant value is assigned.

The available corpus is split into two cases, namely copyright infringement and child pornography exchange. The copyright infringement case contains 45 variables in the state vector and 13 instances. The child pornography case contains 114 variables in the state vector and 23 instances.

It is noteworthy that this entire process is completed within a matter of minutes and not hours.

One of the many methods used were initially published in a scientific paper titled "A DCT Quantization-based Image Authentication System for Digital Forensics". This paper introduced a new method for detecting photos that were earlier edited using any photo editing software. This was crucial as many photo editing software leave almost no trace of evidence of it being edited.

Using a DCT Quantization-based Image Authentication System they were able to identify whether a photo was fake or not by using a predefined prediction system.

Implementation in Real World

A real world case study was done in Taiwan where the government imposed a new law stating that all drivers should possess some sort of a recording device such as a camera or a chalk to record the event. If anyone gets hurt or killed in an accident and the vehicle still functions afterwards, the driver should mark the position of the vehicle and move it to the roadside quickly; if not, the vehicle will not only obstruct the traffic, but also the driver will be subject to a fine of NT$600 to NT$1800. In addition to traffic accidents, any events that involve personal rights and the interests, all these images which have recorded

Figure 9.

$$\overline{F(i)} = round(\frac{F(i)}{Q(i)}),$$

$$R(i) = F(i)\%Q(i) = F(i) - \overline{F(i)} \cdot Q(i)$$

the evidence of events. However, with the development of digital techniques and the prevalence of digital image devices, the data format of the image almost becomes digital form. When there is a controversy unable to be compromised and needed to be solved according to the law, these digital images provided to the court as the evidence will play a very decisive role consequently. The judiciary should also have the ability to reach a verdict rightly and objectively from these digital evidences.

Therefore, it is urgent and necessary to establish a secure and reliable image authentication system which can prove the truth of the digital evidence, and prevent the maliciously manipulating digital evidence from impairing the judgment. For the particular scenario they had proposed a particular method for implementing this.

The device manufacturer needs to register the serial number of each product to the authentication center in the producing procedure, and then the authentication center will provide the corresponding keys of each product. The device manufacturer puts the keys into the product in a secure place in which the keys are unable to read out. These keys will be used in the authentication process hereafter. The products, such as camera and video camera, in which the authentication keys have been inserted can be sold to the consumers. The establishment of the surveillance system or the system for a traffic offense and the capture of the important data or accident are some of the applications of the product.

Since the product having the built-in image authentication(Ye, Zhou, Sun, & Tian,1998) model and the keys issued by the authentication center, it will initiate the authentication procedure at the same time when taking the photo with this product and will produce the authenticator to verify the digital image. The authenticator will then be appended to the image as the tag or be embedded into the image as the watermark on the basis of the image authentication (Lin 2000) model used in the product. This authenticator should have the ability to prove the truth of the corresponding image and be kept secure enough.

Later to improve the Image Authentication schemes they had used a method proposed by Qubin Sun et al based on Integrating error correction code, watermarking and cryptographic hash. It corrects the distortion of acceptable manipulations by using the correction code to produce the invariable quantization value as the content feature.

They denote a DCT coefficient before quantization as F(i), the quantization step size specified in the quantization table as Q(i), and the output of quantizer as quotient F(i) and remainder R(i) respectively. The important equations of this scheme are (Figure 9).

In the JPEG lossy compression, the R(i) will be discarded and the F(i) will be losslessly compressed through entire manipulations is supposed as a noise model; the maximum absolute magnitude of noise is denoted as N. R(i) is recorded as the correction code and used to push the corrupted F(i) to the correct value after the image(Ng & Chang, 2004) has been distorted through acceptable manipulations copy coding. The incidental distortion introduced by acceptable

Database Available for Real World Implementation

With the use of UCID (Uncompressed Colour Image Database), which is available from http://vision. doc.ntu.ac.uk/datasets/UCID/ucid.html, for following experiments. The UCID dataset currently consists of 1338 uncompressed images and each image is full-color with 512x384 pixels. Hence, about four million blocks of Y components and one million blocks of each Cb and Cr components will be tested in our experiments. The images of UCID not only have sufficient quantity but also have common contents which are much similar to the snapshots taken by people or any surveillance system. Therefore, the UCID dataset is selected for the following experiments.

The study of learning in adversarial environments is an emerging discipline at the juncture between machine learning and computer security, that raises new questions within both fields.

Security and System Design

The interest in learning-based methods for security and system design applications comes from the high degree of complexity of phenomena underlying the security and reliability of computer systems. As it becomes increasingly difficult to reach the desired properties by design alone, learning methods are being used to obtain a better understanding of various data collected from these complex systems. However, learning approaches can be co-opted or evaded by adversaries, who change to counter them. To-date, there has been limited research into learning techniques that are resilient to attacks with provable robustness guarantees making the task of designing secure learning-based systems a lucrative open research area with many challenges.

The Perspectives Workshop, "Machine Learning Methods for Computer Security" was convened to bring together interested researchers from both the computer security and machine learning communities to discuss techniques, challenges, and future research directions for secure learning and learning-based security applications. This workshop featured twenty-two invited talks from leading researchers within the secure learning community covering topics in adversarial learning, game-theoretic learning, collective classification, privacy-preserving learning, security evaluation metrics, digital forensics, authorship identification, adversarial advertisement detection, learning for offensive security, and data sanitization. The workshop also featured workgroup sessions organized into three topics: machine learning for computer security, secure learning, and future applications of secure learning.

CONCLUSION AND FUTURE WORK

The information provided above contributes to digital forensics through the materials collected from various sources of digital forensics basics and how machine learning could be incorporated in the development of a novel machine learning methodology based on digital forensic strategy.

Our approach integrates feature weighting to refine existing Machine Learning algorithms and improve their classification performance based on real-life data. In this regard, the application of feature weighting using both AFW and MFW techniques has shown promise in improving classification performance with respect to other models in use today. Further, previous work has investigated the use of crime templates to solve specific crimes. In such work, the authors introduce the concept of crime-related templates which would help to identify relevant devices in a given category. In child pornography, for instance, a template would include the search for file names within a dictionary of commonly used words or by mathematical hash values compared with a repository of known terms and hash values related to the crime. Although representing a valid standpoint, such solutions lack generality as a crime template has to be chosen before the device is searched for evidence which implies that investigators should know what to search apriori.

Conversely, our model represents an evolution as we do make use of crime-related aspects (i.e. the features) but we extract as many data pertaining to a particular crime as possible and translate such data into features a-posteriori. This enables our approach to be more flexible as supported by Kent, et al.'s recommendation to develop methodologies due to the infeasibility of tailored solutions. Finally, even though we focused on specific crimes, the proposed methodology can easily be extended to support a variety of crimes.

It is hoped that the work achieved in this article acts as an inspiration to develop a practical tool for forensic triage investigations. As stated earlier, further validation of the proposed methodology and weighting techniques is required. Obtaining genuine, substantial corpora from law enforcement and corporate investigations would provide the ideal verification platform. If results supported the findings, the next logical step is to develop a practical tool. A fundamental part of a forensic (Palmer 2001) triage tools is its ability to obtain evidence quickly. Therefore, once the tool was established, further research into the speed of the automated and manual weighting tool would be worthwhile to test its practical viability as a triage tool for forensic investigators.

Finally, an initial research concept was to also include hypotheses which research the benefit of feature reduction. This would have included a performance comparison of feature weighting and feature reduction to determine the most effective method. Should feature reduction be beneficial, research could be carried out which combined both feature reduction and weighing to see if it improved classification performance. This would require experimentation with feature weighting and reduction techniques to find those which improve classification performance the most. Research of the best possible permutation of feature manipulation techniques would enable it to be utilized in a practical solution. The methodology would then incorporate the most effective feature manipulation techniques, as concluded from this and future research, to provide a practical forensic triage tool which has the leading classification performance.

Thus, we proposed some useful guidelines for the application of machine learning for digital forensics. Also, we provided a historical perspective for both computer security and forensics. Finally, we provided more formal comparisons of the two disciplines, in order to illustrate perspective according to which machine learning should be applied in computer forensics.

REFERENCES

Chen, Huang, Tian, & Qu. (2009). Feature selection for text classification with Naïve Bayes. *Expert Systems with Applications, 36,* 5432-5435.

Gomez. (2012). *Triage in-Lab: case backlog reduction with forensic digital profiling.* Academic Press.

Grillo, A., Lentini, A., Me, G., & Ottoni, M. (2009). Fast User Classifying to Establish Forensic Analysis Priorities. In *Proceedings of the 2009 Fifth International Conference on IT Security Incident Management and IT Forensics*. doi:10.1109/IMF.2009.16

Lin & Chang. (2000). *Semi-Fragile Watermarking for Authenticating JPEG Visual Content*. SPIE Security and Watermarking of Multimedia Content II, San Jose, CA.

Lin, C. Y. (2000). *Watermarking and Digital Signature Techniques for Multimedia Authentication and Copyright Protection*. (Ph.D. Thesis). Columbia University, New York, NY.

Lin, C. Y., & Chang, S. F. (2001, February). A Robust Image Authentication Method Distinguishing JPEG Compression from Malicious Manipulation. *IEEE Transactions on Circuits and Systems for Video Technology, 11*(2), 153–168. doi:10.1109/76.905982

Liu, S., & Jiang, H. (2012). School network security analysis and security countermeasures. In *IEEE International Conference on Cyber Technology in Automation, Control, and Intelligent Systems* (CYBER). IEEE.

Markman. (2000). *Performance Confirmation Data Aquisition System*. Academic Press.

Marturana, F., Bertè, R., Me, G., & Tacconi, S. (2011). Mobile forensics "triaging": new directions for methodology. In *Proceedings of VIII conference of the Italian chapter of the Association for Information Systems* (ITAIS). Academic Press.

Marturana, F., Me, G., Berte, R., & Tacconi, S. (2011). A Quantitative Approach to Triaging in Mobile Forensics. In *Trust, Security and Privacy in Computing and Communications (TrustCom),2011IEEE 10th International Conference on*. doi:10.1109/TrustCom.2011.75

Marturana, F., & Tacconi, S. (2013). A Machine Learning-based Triage methodology for automated categorization of digital media. *Digital Investigation, 10*(2), 193–204. doi:10.1016/j.diin.2013.01.001

Ng, T. T., & Chang, S. F. (2004). *A Model for Image Splicing*. IEEE International Conference on Image Processing, Singapore.

Palmer, G. (2001). *A Road Map for Digital Forensic Research*. Technical Report DTR-T0010-01, DFRWS. Report from the First Digital Forensic Research Workshop (DFRWS).

Rogers, M. K., Goldman, J., Mislan, R., Wedge, T., & Debrota, S. (2006). *Computer Forensics Field Triage Process Model*. Presented at the Conference on Digital Forensics, Security, and Law.

Sommer, P. (2005). *Directors and Corporate Advisors' Guide to Digital Investigations and Evidence*. Information Assurance Advisory Council.

Sommer, P. (1999). Intrusion Detection Systems as Evidence. *Computer Networks: The International Journal of Computer and Telecommunications Networking, 31*, 2477 – 2487.

Witten, I. H., Frank, E., & Hall, M. A. (2011). *Data Mining: Practical Machine Learning Tools and Techniques: Practical Machine Learning Tools and Techniques*. Morgan Kaufmann.

Ye, S., Zhou, Z., Sun, Q., & Tian, Q. (2003). A Quantization-based Image Authentication System. *Information, Communications and Signal Processing, 2003 and the Fourth Pacific Rim Conference on Multimedia.Proceedings of the 2003 Joint Conference of the Fourth International Conference*. Academic Press.

Chapter 10
Effective Recognition of Stereo Image Concealed Media of Interpolation Error with Difference Expansion

Hemalatha J.
Thiagarajar College of Engineering, India

Kavitha Devi M. K.
Thiagarajar College of Engineering India

ABSTRACT

In this chapter, a new data conceal technique is anticipated for digital images. The method computes the interpolation error of the image by using histogram shifting method and difference expansion. With the expectation of embedding high payload and less distortion, the undisclosed data has embedded in the interpolating error. Additionally for hiding the data, reversible data hiding technique is used. The histogram deviation is used as evidence for resulting the data conceal in the stereo images. To our best knowledge, by extracting the statistical feature from the image subsample works as steganalysis scheme. To enhance the revealing rate precision the well known support vector machine acts as classifier. In addition to that the experimental results show that the proposed steganalysis method has enhanced the detection exactness of the stego images.

INTRODUCTION

Steganography is the untimely knowledge of hidden statement. The communication can be takes place by together with the message endurance on the cover medium that no one is assume about the buried message. Steganography greatly recommends the concealment by shielding the confidential message when the undisclosed communication takes place. Hiding the data in the digital medium used several techniques; the digital medium is broadly specified as text, audio, video and an image. In different electrical device and application this steganography is largely used. However, like all the security tech-

DOI: 10.4018/978-1-5225-0193-0.ch010

niques this steganography has been propelled to grip the computational power, proliferation in security alertness and etc. On contrary the technique steganalysis which exploits the dissimilarity between the steganograme and cover image, to perceive the hidden messages.

The presence of image and video is primarily used by the website group of actors. The steganalysis endeavour is to recognize or presume the buried data without any awareness on the subject of steganography algorithm and parameter. Generally, covert data extraction might a tough exertion than simple revealing.

While hiding the payload, reversible data hiding method affords additional strength, robustness to the corresponding payload. Additionally it widens the variances among the pair of pixels followed by embeds single bit in relevant expanded difference. To our best knowledge, it is highly used in the digital signal processing community. It is the process of embedding data on the consequent host signal, hence recover the original signal once the embedded message extracted. In the related work, nearly all the algorithms are used to embed the concealed data on the image source. Optimistically wherever there is no need of changing the host signal permanently, the resulted RDH is the most excellent option.

The key shortcoming of reversible data hiding is that after data embedding, some pairs of pixels may be overflow or underflow, hence cannot be used for secret message embedding. The advantage is original image might be utterly restored after extracting the data. In the following section we will briefly see about the interpolation methods and reversible data hiding techniques.

INTERPOLATION AND REVERSIBLE DATA HIDING

Interpolation Methods

In digital images, interpolation ensues at some stage. The process of finding the function value at a particular position lies between the samples. It occurs owing to resizing an image, or maps an image from one pixel to other. Each and every time increasing or reducing the number of pixels and remapping arise on the scenarios such as image rotation, lens distortion correction. Whenever the interpolation is performing, there might be some quality loss in the resultant image, and it can be minimized. The fundamental thought of interpolation is by knowing the data and calculates the values at some unknown point. By putting on the low pass filter over the discrete signal, the bandwidth can be reduced for a particular. The image quality can be greatly achieved based on the interpolation technique used.

The interpolation technique can be broadly divided into two categories namely statistical and deterministic interpolation technique. In the deterministic techniques, among the sample point certain variation can be considered. While in statistical method, the signal can be approximated by reducing the estimation error. When comparing to deterministic methods the statistical method are computationally inefficient. Occasionally two dimension interpolation is problematic to define. In case of gridded data n dimension interpolation function can be termed as the multiplication of n 1-dimension interpolation functions.

In the deterministic method the subsequent methods are used namely nearest neighbor, spline, and linear interpolation techniques.

Nearest Neighbor Interpolation or Pixel Replication

In this technique the nearest sample point on the input image is assigned to the corresponding output pixel. The kernel is defined in the following Equation 1,

$$k(\mathcal{X}) = \begin{cases} 1 & 0 \le |\mathcal{X}| < 0.5 \\ 0 & 0.5 \le |\mathcal{X}| \end{cases} \tag{1}$$

where $k(\mathcal{X})$ denotes the kernel for nearest neighbor and $\mathcal{X}$ denotes the sample point. Whenever changes occur by large range, the nearest neighbor interpolation technique resulted in image with blockier effect.

Linear Interpolation Technique

This is a technique of passing a straight line of the input signal between two consecutive points based on first degree method. The sampled input that has been convolved with the kernel given in Equation 2 particularly specified on the spatial domain.

$$l(\mathcal{X}) = \begin{cases} 1 - |\mathcal{X}| & 0 \le |\mathcal{X}| < 1 \\ 0 & 1 \le |\mathcal{X}| \end{cases} \tag{2}$$

where $l(\mathcal{X})$ is the kernel used in linear interpolation and $\mathcal{X}$ is the input signal. This linear based method is most superior to the nearest neighbor interpolation method. In addition to that this linear based method gives image more smoothing. And also this delivers the better result at some reasonable cost. On the other hand for attaining the enhanced performance, further more algorithms are required.

B-Spline Interpolation Method

Cubic B-spline kernel is not considered as interpolator, once it does not satisfy the following constraints such as h [0] =1 and following to that h [1], h [2] =0. As an alternative, it behaves as an approximating function, crossing the points over that. Hence the resultant kernel is exactly positive. Once we are having the negative intensity completely meaningless then it should be to use positive interpolation kernel strictly for getting the positive interpolated image.

Reversible Data Hiding

Reversible data hiding method bury the message bits by altering the original signal, nevertheless after extraction of embedded data, enables the precise renovation of the original signal (Masoud Nosrati, Ronak Karimi, & Mehdi Hariri, 2012). There are many techniques proposed for Reversible data hiding as follows:

PWLC and DHTC Data Hiding

PWLC Pair-wise logical computation (Tsai, Fan, Chung & Chuang, 2004), this reversible data hiding technique uses XOR operations for hiding the payload in the cover image. For hiding the data first it chooses cover image and then scan it in some order, then the sequences '000000' and '111111' are always selected near to the boundaries for further hiding the payload. The main problem on PWLC is it may not correctly extract the concealed message, and also not clearly recover the original image. The hiding technique over the DHTC is it selects the low- visibility pixels for flipping and insertion. The benefit on the DHTC technique is that it is obviously having the excellent image visual quality.

Lossless Compression and Encryption of Bit-Planes

The algorithm starting from the 5th bit plane (Fridrich, Goljan, & Rui, 2001) of the image the reason for choosing the lowest bit plane is that it offers lossless compression. Generally in noisy image some bit-planes reveals strong correlation, and likewise easy to determine enough place for storing the hash. In this algorithm Fridrich et al. (2001) computes the redundancy by deducting the compressed data size form the total pixel numbers. The embedding algorithm starts from calculating the hash value for the given image, and then catches the proper bit-plane followed by add the hash value to the squashed bit plane data. Following on that, selected bit plane can be restored by the concatenated data. By adding security intention, the concatenated hash value can be encrypted by using some symmetric key encryption depends on the 2D chaotic map. No need of any padding for the encrypted message embedding, at the decoding phase the data can be decrypted by selecting the corresponding key and then separate the hash and compressed bit plane data. The original image can be found by replacing the bit plane by the decompressed data.

High payload and security are the two greater advantages, however could not provide enough space for hiding the bit planes, and not possible to embed large payloads are the major problems on this proposed method.

Wavelet Transform

The technique proposed by Fridrich (1998) is hiding large payloads based on the wavelet transform, hides the endorsement information in the middle plane part (high frequency) on the corresponding wavelet coefficients. When embedding the data, to avoid the overflow problem histogram modification was used. Finding that more number of 0's and 1's on the 2nd bit plane hence image distortion will occur, to overcome this author advised to hide the payloads on the middle frequency sub bands respectively. Hence resulted on the high PSNR value and image perception will be increased. While embedding a secret data is to be added with compressed data on the other side while extraction hash is to be extract for reconstructing the original image. The greater benefits of this technique is that high payload and security, on the opponent side the problem on this technique is that multiple bit planes are required and then need of gray scale mapping.

Difference Expansion

In digital images owing to the beneficial perspective of holding the high redundancy among the neighbourhood of the pixel, pixel difference techniques are used for message concealing. For entrenching the data and calculating the difference the following steps are used.

Step 1: For a given image find out the difference between the progress pixel and its corresponding neighbour pixels.
Step 2: Determine the changeable bit difference.
Step 3: Find the location map and its hash.
Step 4: Compress the changeable bit of the original.
Step 5: Concatenate the location map, hash and changeable bit.
Step 6: Output the watermarked pixel with exact pixel difference.

During the extraction calculate the differences of neighbour pixel, calculate the differences for changed bits, and then extract the changed bit with the help of pseudo random order while followed on the embedding procedure. Finally separate the compressed bit and hash value. The greater advantage of this technique is that no data loss, applicable to video, increased security.

BACKGROUND

Whenever going for high payload messages, reversible data hiding is the reasonable technique because of more robust. Likewise payload has been achieved when we go for this hiding method. The methodology used on the interpolation error based hiding is that (Luo, Chen, Chen, Zeng, & Xiong, 2010) secret data can be embed by the impact of interpolation error other than the prediction error and inter pixel error. This is can be highly achieved by combining the histogram shifting technique and difference expansion.

The technique suggested by Tian (2003) is the difference expansion achieved by addition rather than bit stream or bit shifting. The key difficulty of difference expansion is that after embedding the data, some pixel pairs may be overflow or else sometimes underflow. Hence it cannot be used for data embedding.

A distinct reversible technique offered (Xinpeng Zhang, 2013) for data hiding which afford the optimal rule of host pixel modification lower a payload distortion. Chia-Chen Lin and Pei-Feng Shiu (2009) showed in their work that the reversible data hiding based on DCT with very high embedding capacity. The optimal of picking transformation domain such as DCT, DWT, DFT for Steganography is that more robust rather than spatial domain. A data hiding method based on reversible manner in favour of stereo images was anticipated by Wen-Chao Yang and Lin-Hwei Chen (2014).

The HKC algorithm for resolving the distortion problem and resulted in Kuo attack was proposed by Chandramouli (2003). The idea is by using the histogram shifting method, produced the histogram with pair of empty bins followed by filled the neighbor bins via the embedding process.

The method proposed by Ni, Shi, Ansari and Su (2006) uses minimum point and or zero point histogram. In the histogram, find the peak which is lesser than the minimum point or the zero point, then the corresponding value of the pixel are to be increased by one. The entire image will be searched for embedding, on one occasion the peak pixel is encountered then message bit will be added to that. The algorithm decreases the pixel value once the peak is zero or minimum point, then if the embedding is 1 as a resultant the pixel values will be decreased by one. The pros of this techniques is that simple, provides peak signal to noise ratio values constantly as 48.0 dB, high payload.

Stereoscopy used to enhance the depth illusion in an image recognized as Stereoscopy 3D imaging. The work of Bai NY and Chiang (1998) discussed the technique of hiding process in stereo images by means of binocular fusion. Shrikalaa et al. (Shrikalla, Mathivanan, & Leena Jasmine, 2013) projected least significant based (LSB) replacement in a stereo pair.

PROPOSED STEGANALYSIS ALGORITHM

The proposed steganalysis scheme consists of stego revealing, parameter assessment. The SVM can be trained by GGD parameters of both cover and stego image. With the aid of SVM classifier the instructed image is distinguished as clean or stego image. Lastly estimate the parameter such as $L'M'$ and $R'M'$ for finding the inserted position and payload. The optimal features intended for separate the clean and stego are Generalized Gaussian Distribution, normal distribution, laplacian distribution. For the GGD feature maximum likelihood estimator is used as an estimator.

The SVM intention is to precisely categorize the clean or stego for the exacting stereo image. The objective of choosing stereo image is inserting additional payload than mono image. The dataset embrace of training, testing dataset. The outcome from the classifier is going beyond than the threshold then the consequent image is named as stego otherwise clear stereo image.

Data Hiding and Stego Revealing

Manipulating Interpolation Error

The interpolation error of stereo image is used to entrench the hush-hush message. It can be designed by finding the difference between the value of the pixel and its corresponding neighbour pixel value is known as interpolation value. In particular interpolation error is considered by means of Equation 3:

$$\bar{e} = p - p' \qquad (3)$$

where p referred as cover pixel and p' referred as interpolating value. In addition to that usual images $L'M' = 0$ and $R'M' = 1$, on one occasion the hush-hush data is entrenched with cover data then $L'M' = \{L'M', L'M' - 1\}$ and $R'M' = \{R'M', R'M' + 1\}$. In the above $L'M'$ and $R'M'$ are error values obtained from the most two highest bin of the consequent histogram error. If $\bar{e} < L'M'$ then the resultant error is known as left interpolating error $L'M'$, similarly on the other side if $\bar{e} > R'M'$ then it is called as right interpolating error $R'M'$.

Error Expansion and Extracting an Inserted Bit

The error expansion $\bar{E}$ is estimated by using Equation 4:

$$\bar{E} = \begin{cases} \left\{ \bar{e} \ sign\left(\bar{e}\right) \times b \right\} & where \ \bar{e} = L'M' \mid R'M' \\ \left\{ \bar{e} \ sign\left(\bar{e}\right) \times 1 \right\} & where \ \bar{e} = L'M' \cup R'M' \end{cases}$$ (4) where b is the embedding bit, $sign\left(\bar{e}\right)$ is the sign value. The embedded pixel is estimated as shown in Equation 5:

$$p'' = p' + \bar{E}$$ (5)

The inserted data can be extort by using the same embedding procedure, also the interpolating error can also trace out by using the same procedure given in the following Equation 6 and Equation 7:

$$b = \begin{cases} 0 & if \ \bar{e} = L'M' \mid R'M' \\ 1 & if \ \bar{e} = L'M' - 1 \mid R'M' - 1 \end{cases}$$ (6)

$$\bar{e} = \begin{cases} \left\{ \bar{E} \ sign\left(\bar{E}\right) \times b \right\} & where \ \bar{E} = L'M' - 1, L'M' \cup R'M', R'M' + 1 \\ \left\{ \bar{E} \ sign\left(\bar{E}\right) \times 1 \right\} & where \ \bar{E} = L'M' - 1, L'M' \cup R'M', R'M' + 1 \end{cases}$$ (7)

EXPERIMENTAL RESULTS

The proposed method is implemented using MATLAB. The stereo image is chosen from Middlebury stereo datasets and it is resized as 512x512. To ensure the correctness of proposed scheme, the PSNR value and image quality is considered. On behalf of the entire trial images extractions as well as detection were attained. Table 1 illustrates the image quality and the corresponding payload respectively. In addition to that the steganalysis technique meets the AUC probability is 0.94.

Table 1. PSNR value and payload

Method Type	Image Quality (PSNR)	Payload (Bits per Pixel)
Interpolation Error Method	34.3	0.45
	40.0	0.42
	28.4	0.28
	38.30	0.34
Lin's Method	32.72	0.40

CONCLUSION

In this chapter, data hiding with interpolation error on the stereo image has been anticipated. This ensures that attains greater embedding payload, less distortion, greater PSNR value. The experimental result ensures that it meets up the image quality. Furthermore with the advantage of reversible data hiding the exact image can be precisely recovered. Yet while further techniques are readily available subsequently however still methods necessitate to progress the performance of steganalysis.

In the future work, with the improvement of algorithm in the logic of image contrast, it can be applied to the satellite and medical appliances.

REFERENCES

Bai, N. Y., & Chiang, J. Y. (1998). Data hiding using binocular fusion of stereo pairs. In *Proceeding of eighth national conference in information security*, (pp. 245-254). Academic Press.

Chandramouli, R. (2003). A mathematical framework for active steganalysis. *Multimedia Systems*, *9*(3), 303–311. doi:10.1007/s00530-003-0101-8

Fridrich, J. (1998). Symmetric Ciphers Based on Two-Dimensional Chaotic Maps. *International Journal of Bifurcation and Chaos in Applied Sciences and Engineering*, *8*(6), 1259–1284. doi:10.1142/S021812749800098X

Fridrich, J., Goljan, M., & Rui, D. (2001). Invertible Authentication. In *Proceedings of SPIE Photonics West, Security and Watermarking of Multimedia Contents*, (vol. 3971, pp. 197-208). doi:10.1117/12.435400

Lin, C.-C., & Shiu, P.-F. (2009). DCT- based reversible data hiding scheme. In *Proceedings of 3rd International Conference on Ubiquitous Information Management and Communication*, (pp. 327-335). Academic Press.

Luo, Chen, Chen, Zeng, & Xiong. (2010). Reversible image watermarking using interpolation technique. *IEEE Transactions on Information Forensics and Security, 5*, 187-193.

Ni, , & Shi, , Ansari, & Su. (2006). Reversible Data Hiding. *IEEE Transactions on Circuits and Systems for Video Technology*, *16*(8), 354–362.

Nosrati, M., Karimi, R., & Hariri, M. (2012). Reversible Data Hiding: Principles, Techniques, and Recent Studies. *World Applied Programming*, *2*(5), 349–353.

Shrikalla, M., Mathivanan, P., & Leena Jasmine, J. S. (2013). *Conversion Of 2D Stego images into 3D stereo image using RANSAC*. Paper presented at IEEE Conference on Information and communication Technologies.

Tian, J. (2003). Reversible data embedding using a difference Expansion. *IEEE Transactions on Circuits and Systems for Video Technology*, *13*(8), 890–896. doi:10.1109/TCSVT.2003.815962

Tsai, C. L., Fan, K. C., Chung, C. D., & Chuang, T. C. (2004). Data Hiding of Binary Images Using Pair-wise Logical Computation Mechanism. In *Proceedings of IEEE International Conference on Multimedia and Expo, ICME*, (vol. 2, pp. 951-954). IEEE.

Yang, W.-C., & Chen, L.-H. (2014). *Reversible DCT- based data hiding in stereo images*. Springer Multimedia Tools and Applications.

Zhang, X. (2013). Reversible data hiding with optimal value transfer. *IEEE Transactions on Multimedia*, *15*(2), 316–325. doi:10.1109/TMM.2012.2229262

Chapter 11
Mobile Malware

Geogen G.
SRM University, India

Poovammal E.
SRM University, India

ABSTRACT

Why should everyone know about mobile malware? With the introduction of Internet of Things (IoT) and Cloud, you can't survive in a disconnected world. Thus from your home appliances to your window curtains, everything is connected to Internet which can be accessed through your hand held mobile device. Unlike Personal Computers, these devices give Hackers a greater attack landscape. Back in 2004, when the first mobile malware was introduced, we never thought that it would get such a big threat space, as we see today. So, we discuss the History of Mobile malwares and its categories with its motives. We also discuss few signs that indicate the presence of a mobile malware. To conclude we categorize the battle against malware into two namely prevention and response, which is forensically analysed using Static/Dynamic Methods/Tools.

INTRODUCTION

Smartphone usage is expected to reach 2082.7 million globally this year *(Number of smartphone users worldwide from 2014 to 2019 (in millions), Marlene Greenfield, Vice President, Hearst Magazines)* and mobile applications are going to become more and more important than ever. Companies are looking forward to create newer innovative apps to connect with suppliers, distributors and end users. Even though mobiles revolutionized the way in which data is exchanged, and delivery of services, it also created new security challenges. Compared to PC users, mobiles are always switched on and connected but large group of mobile users are tech illiterate which makes it difficult to update mobiles with security patches, once it is sold. Major share of worries related to mobile application security arise due to:

- No or Irregular vulnerability checking of mobile apps.
- Poor encryption and data leakage.
- Insecure data Storage, etc.

DOI: 10.4018/978-1-5225-0193-0.ch011

Malware in general covers all sorts of malicious software or codes written to harm you or your system. Let us introduce the terms one by one which are categorized as Malware:

- **Virus and Worms:** Virus is a malicious program/file which attaches itself to a genuine program mostly to an executable file and spreads from one system to another, leaving infections as it travels (Siciliano,2015). Virus uses stealthy techniques to remain hidden and unnoticed and the main purpose of virus is to reach protected networks. The major difference between virus and worm is the trigger by human or event. Virus needs a human/event trigger (like executing a file, clicking the icon etc) for propagating from system to system. Unlike Virus, Worm can replicate itself and spread from one system to all connected systems eating away system memory and network resources causing, web servers, network servers etc to stop responding.

- **Trojans and Backdoors:** Trojans are non-self-replicating malicious programs which can delete, block, modify, copy data without users authorization once allowed. But Trojans will be present as some useful email alert or new security path. When user allows the attachment or path, Trojans gain access to your system, in turn allowing hackers to gain remote access to your system. This remote hidden secondary access which bypasses all security measures is commonly referred as Backdoor.

- **Rootkits:** It is a combination of two words, Root and Kit. Root is UNIX/Linux term which is equivalent to Administrator in windows. Kit represents a group of programs which allow someone to obtain the root/admin privilege, without end users' knowledge. Rootkits are mainly deployed for two reasons: remote command/Control and Software Eavesdropping. They are non-self-propagating threats with three snippet codes in it. They are a dropper, a loader and a Rootkit. A dropper is a good looking link or attachment which prompt user to click on it. Once clicked, dropper launches the Loader Program and deletes itself. Loader program uses some exploits like buffer overflow and loads the Rootkit into memory. According to their function, Root kits are divided into User Mode Root kits, Kernel Mode Root kits, Hybrid Root kits, Firmware Root kits, Virtual Root kits, Generic Root kits etc(cooper,2016)

- **Logic Bombs:** They are programs designed to trigger when certain conditions are met like a particular time or log-off or after specific number of data base entries etc. Software Time Bomb is considered as a logic bomb because when the target time or date is reached, it executes. Until the time reaches, logic bomb will be in sleeping/dormant modes which make them hidden from antivirus.(Kelly,2015)

- **Key Loggers:** A highly specialized software or hardware tool designed to intercept and record every keystroke made on the machine, allowing the attacker to gain huge amount of sensitive information like username/password etc silently. Most of the sophisticated Key loggers can intercept virtual key strokes too.

- **Rouge Security Software:** Rogue AV (rogue antivirus) or rogue security software is a rogue (a form of Internet fraud using computer malware) that deceives or misleads users into paying money for fake. Rogue security software has become a growing and serious security threat in desktop/mobile computing in recent years (Bonadea, 2015)

- **Ransomware:** These are also known as Crypto Virus. It is a type of malware that attacks (mostly through email attachments) the system and prevents/limits users from accessing their system. It will take the control of the system and demands a ransom to undo it. Some Ransomware applications act like police or government agency, claiming that users' system is locked down for security reason and will send pop-up window asking users to pay a specific amount of money as fine to unlock the system.

- **Polymorphic Malware**: These are malwares that changes their signature constantly, making it difficult to detect with antivirus software. But the function of the malware remains the same. Changes can occur in a variety of ways such as filename changes, compression and encryption changes with variable keys etc. With Mutation Engine any malware can be converted to a Polymorphic Malware.
- **Armored Virus:** These are viruses designed with "armor" shields to break reverse engineering techniques, thus making it hard to analyze and design methods for defeating it. Mostly it contains large amount of misleading logic and false data making it difficult for computer experts to extract virus apart.
- **Browser Hijacking:** A method by which malwares installed in a system modifies browser settings and overrides the default functionality of the web browser without users knowledge and very hard to remove.
- **Spywares:** It is malicious software installed to your system. When you try to install freeware or cracked program or application, spyware will enable hackers to secretly monitor user's sensitive information like passwords, account numbers, browsing habits etc and send it to the remote hacker without your knowledge. Spyware and cookies are similar but spyware conducts infiltration until it is removed by specific anti-spyware tool.
- **Crime Ware:** It is a collection of programs designed specifically for online illegal activities. (e.g) Phishing. Kit is a tool which includes web development tools, sample codes, graphics etc. to create a phishing site. Harmful effects of crimeware include Private data theft, Copyright Fingerprinting, Financial Loss, loss of productivity, bandwidth saturation with unwanted spam, pop-up etc
- **Remote Access Trojan (RAT):** These are small programs normally attached to legitimate programs, games or email with a bad intention to take full control over victim's machine. For malicious activities, unlike virus and worm, RAT can exist in stealth mode, thus making it almost impossible for antivirus to detect them. Most popular RAT's in PCs are SubSeven and BlackOrifice. In Android, most popular RAT's are Zeus Botnet RAT and Andro RAT.
- **Bootkits:** It is a type of malware that affects the MBR, VBR or boot sector thus getting executed when operating system boots. Bootkits can't be detected using usual methods as it reside outside the OS File system. This advanced form of Rootkits can be detected using TDSS Killer utility

OWASP TOP 10 MOBILE RISKS OF 2015

Open Web Application Security Project is an online internet community dedicated to web application security (Curphey,2011). The OWASP community includes various corporations, educational organizations and individuals from around the world. This community works to create articles, methodologies, documentation, tools, and technologies for free for everyone. It is also a registered nonprofit organization in Europe since June 2011. One of the major projects from OWASP is the OWAP Top 10. According to OWASP, Top 10 Mobile Risks during 2014 are shown in Figure 1.

1. **Weak Server Controls:** Mobile apps which are basically thick clients, communicate with their backend server, and need strong server security controls. Even though the basic rule is "never trust a client", most often developers put too much trust in the client security controls and do not include similar server security controls. For example, Input Validation in the client trust that can be easily bypassed by using HTTP Proxies. This will bypass client apps security control, and having server –side control is the only way to ensure that validation and security checks

Figure 1. OWASP mobile top 10

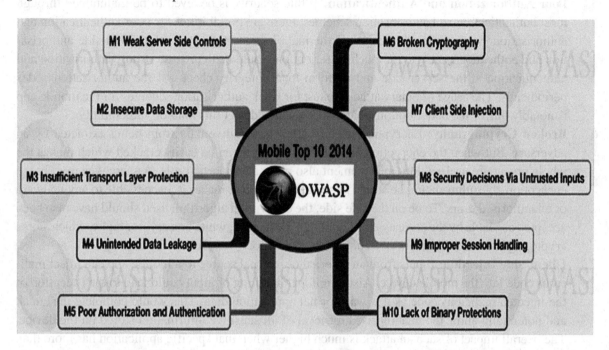

2. **Insecure Data Storage:** Storage on mobile devices is easily-accessible, convenient and readily available. However, there is a lack of privacy for most of the data stored on the device. Similarly, many of the mobile applications which are commonly used, store user credentials in an insecure manner. The primary reason that makes insecure storage is the incorrect assumption made by developers that the mobile file system cannot be easily compromised by malware or adversaries. The consequences of exposure to this vulnerability include loss of data, identity theft, and theft of user credentials among others. In addition to that, contrary to the popular myth that all encryption secures data, there are many special tools available which are used to extract information from weakly encrypted data. Therefore, storing personal credentials or any data of equal value within a mobile file system is not advisable. However, if it is highly necessary, then strong encryption methods can help to secure the data.

3. **Insufficient Transport Layer Protection:** Mobile data protection is required, not only for the data that are stored in the devices but also for the data transmitted through the network (which can be either public or internal). Mobile applications may use SSL/TLS for authentication purposes and still fail to protect network traffic. However, using SSL/TLS for data transmission through networks and also accepting only the certificates signed by trusted Certificate Authorities (CAs) is a better way to secure network traffic. Encryption of the network traffic is the best option to protect the traffic itself from a poor SSL setup.

4. **Unintended Data Leakage:** Malicious applications in mobile devices can access the data stored by other legitimate applications. So, any credential or sensitive data that is stored by an application as plain text can be leaked unintentionally. Developers should thus be careful while storing the user's sensitive data and also be privy to the way cache operations are done by the operating system. They should also identify the possible threats through threat modeling of the operating system and framework. They should also implement proper mitigation controls that will avoid unintended data leakage.

5. **Poor Authorization and Authentication:** While security is believed to be maintained through most authentication and authorisation schemes, there are possibilities for poor authentication and authorisation. Such weak schemes allow the malicious user to bypass the Client-side authorisation and authentication easily. A much better option would be to provide strong authorisation and authentication at the server side and perform local integrity checks of the authorisation codes periodically. The usage of binary attacks to test for weak authorisation schemes for the mobile app is notably one of the better options that can be used to detect this kind of vulnerability.

6. **Broken Cryptography:** Encryption usually protects sensitive data from being extracted by an adversary. But when the encryption algorithm is weak, it can be easily cracked which makes the whole procedure useless. Key management also plays an important role. A secret key used in the encryption algorithm should be stored in such a manner that makes it inaccessible to any malware or unauthorised users. To be on the safe side, the encryption algorithm used should have also been accepted as viable by the security community. In most cases, white box cryptography, which stores cryptographic assets in the most secured way, is the most preferred method.

7. **Client Side Injection:** Inputs from an external or internal source to a mobile app can inject malicious code into the mobile device. Also, improper handling of input could lead to the execution of the injected malicious code as if it was normal application data. This would complete the attack and potentially allow the unauthorised retrieval of all sensitive information stored on the device. The overall impact of such an attack is much higher when that specific application has more than one user. In such cases, proper validation of user inputs can help protecting mobile apps from this kind of vulnerability.

8. **Security Decisions via Untrusted Inputs:** Inter Process Communication (IPC) calls and system calls can be intercepted by an attacker through vulnerabilities such as hidden fields in a mobile app. Sometimes this can aid an attacker to escalate their privileges and get higher level permissions easily. This greatly increases the potential impact of the attack. In such cases, avoiding the usage of IOs pasteboards for IPC communication is advisable. The deprecated handle OpenURL method can protect a mobile app from this type of vulnerability. Also, validation of inputs before processing is a common and much better practice used to prevent security decisions being made by an un trusted party.

9. **Improper Session Handling:** An attacker can impersonate a legitimate user by hijacking the user's session and stealing the cookie values. In this way, sensitive information of the user can be accessed illegally. To add to that, failure to invalidate sessions, lack of proper timeouts, token creation without industrial standards and improper session management also help compromising the security easier for the attacker. To mitigate this, session creation, maintenance and destruction should be done in a proper and standard way by the backend server.

10. **Lack of Binary Protections:** A lack of binary protection tends to lead to a higher risk of reverse engineering and modification of code using malware. In special cases, even binary protection of code can also be bypassed and hence it is generally not a fully reliable security solution. To ensure strong binary protection, secure coding practices should be maintained and proper integrity checks of the code should be done during run time. In order to detect reverse engineering and modification of the app code, an appropriate notification can be set to pop up when a section of code has been subjected to change.

WIRELESS AND APPLICATION ATTACK TYPES

1. **Rogue Access Points:** Rogue Access point is a wireless Access point, that is created by an attacker, and it appears like legitimate access point, to fool victims and make them connect to their network (Snori,2015). By this, the attacker would sniff through all the communications the victim makes over the network and might steal all the confidential information. In public places like Airports, Railway stations, Colleges and in public places where free Wi-Fi is available, the attacker creates a Rogue Access points with a name, similar to the legitimate access point available in that area to confuse people. This way, Victims believe that the available Access points are genuine and immediately connect their devices to the Rogue Access points.

Airbase-NG, Airmon-NG, DNS Spoof and dhcpd3are the tools used to create Rogue Access points. The Social Engineering Toolkit (SET) could also be used to create Rogue Access point, we just need to enable the wireless attack vector in the SET.ARP Poisoning, DHCP attacks, STP attacks and DOS attacks are the common attacks that could be launched through Rogue Access Point. Detecting and preventing these kinds of attacks are the biggest challenge to the Organizations. Even the Firewalls and Anti-Virus could not detect the Rogue Access points because the firewalls works only at the traffic transfer point between the LAN and the internet, and the Anti-virus fails to detect since Rogue APs operate at a layer below the Anti-virus.Wireless IDS/IPS systems will detect and kill Rogue Access points. Nets tumbler is one another tool which could be used to detect the Rogue Access Points.

2. **Bluejacking and Bluesnarfing:** Bluejacking and Bluesnarfing are the two major Bluetooth attacks, which take advantage of the vulnerability present in the bluetooth devices. Bluejacking sends anonymous messages to the devices in discoverable mode and try to get response from people, and Bluesnarfing is an active attack in which the attacker connects to a phone wirelessly to download the confidential information without user's knowledge.

Bluejacking is the first attack that targets bluetooth to gain access to victim's device. Here the attacker scans for the devices in discoverable mode and sends a Business card in the form of anonymous message to the devices in discoverable mode, if the victim responds back then attacker tries social engineering to gain all the information.

Bluesnarfing is the process of hacking a mobile device wirelessly and gain access to the device to download contact details, photos and other confidential information. Tools like Bluesnafer or Bloover can be used to detect and hack the vulnerable mobile phones and steal data without victim's knowledge. RefFang is one program which follows brute-force technique and tries every possible combination of characters to get a response but this may be time-consuming.

3. **Wireless IV Attacks:** IV or the Initialization vector is used in the encryption of the wireless packets. This takes advantage of the security flaws in WEP. To avoid usage of same key for both encryption and decryption, IV is used which generates different key combinations every time and makes difficult for an attacker to trace the original key. IV uses the RC4 ciphering mechanism, The RC4 creates a keystream, which is a combination of plaintext and CRC XORed to create a cipher text. This was thought to be the most powerful method to protect the data passing over the network since it uses a different key streams every time, but in practice it didn't prove to be strong as accepted.

Since the generated Keystream is in plaintext, it takes minutes for the attacker to reverse the XOR to get the keystream in plaintext and reverses that to get the IV and WEP keys. The attackers build a decryption table and guess a possible set of keys that could be generated by an IV. WEP Cracker is the best tool that gives the WEP keys in seconds and there are so many attacks that target the IV in 802.11 WEP protocol, thus the WEP encryption lost its glory and organizations don't prefer WEP encryption.

4. **Near Field Communication:** NFC is a wireless technology that is primarily used for payment transaction or for sending information within a very short distance. The two devices in communication would be very closer to each other and the maximum distance between two devices doesn't exceed more than "4cms" and thus it becomes difficult for the attacker to sniff. A small NFC chip is embedded inside a smart phone and a virtual wallet, that stores the credit card information created. Now the users don't have to swipe their cards to make payment, it is just enough to wave his smart phone near the card reader to make payments. This is a boon to the attackers since the entire credit card information is stored inside the device, and the attacker could do anything to gain access to the device (Paganini,2013)

The most common attacks in NFC are Eavesdropping, Data modification, Relay attack, Data corruption, Spoofing, Man in the Middle attack, NFC protocol stack fuzzing and Android NFC Stack bug. NFC devices operate in three different modes: As card emulators, they use alternative storage for information, in Peer-to-peer mode allows different communication protocols to connect to the bluetooth or WiFi, in Card/tag reading and writing mode, the NFC can read and modify the information stored in the card. The high risk involved is losing the physical device, so it is always better to use a very strong password and once the device is lost, it is highly advised to remote wipe your mobile device. Anti-virus must be enabled and before downloading from internet, the content has to be scanned for any malicious programs.

5. **Reply and WEP Attack:** In Reply attack, the attacker copies the messages and retransmits at a different timestamp to the same party or many parties other than the intended parties to regain unauthorized access. It is a part of masquerade attack, which is performed by substituting malicious IP packets.To prevent these kind of attacks Session-keys, One-time passwords and Time stamping are being used. Google Reply attack is one of the attack that is being expected to happen in near future.

WEP attack takes the advantage of Initialization vectors. WEP uses RC4 ciphering method to ensure privacy and CRC-32 Checksum to ensure integrity of the data. The major WEP attacks are FMS attack (RSA Laboratories,2001), KoreK attack*(Beck & Tews 2008),* and Chopchop attack and these entire attacks target in gaining the IV keystream. The FMS attack targets the weakness in RC4, KoreaK targets the weakness in CRC32 and the fragmentation attack eavesdrops a packet, and guess the first few bytes of cleartext, by performing the reverse XOR operation, he could obtain the keystream for specific IV.

6. **WPA (Wi-Fi Protected Access) Attacks:** To overcome the security flaws in WEP, WPA was introduced which takes care of privacy and integrity of the data and this also avoids problems that aroused due to keystreams in WEP protocol. In WPA technology instead of Keystreams, passphrases are created by a function that generates a 256-bit key and a hash funtion that uses wireless access point's identification (SSID).To compromise WPA, an attack on the passphrase is executed, and it is time consuming since one needs to test large number of passphrases.

In this protocol, "Four-way handshake" is being performed, the attacker uses tools like airdump-ng to capture this four-way handshake. In this four-way handshake method, the Wi-Fi base station and the device connect with each other and exchange the passphrase and encryption information. If the attacker compromised the handshake he could get all the information he needs.

7. **WPS (Wi-Fi Protected System) Attacks:** WPS overcomes the problems with passphrase and uses 8-digit numerical PIN but this has become easier for the attacker to compromise the PIN. The PIN is checked in groups of two 4-digit and an attacker has to guess the first four digits and then guess the next four digits, this attack is performed more quickly. Reaver is the tool that is used to crack the WPS and it uses the mechanism similar to the Brute-force attack.

8. **Cross Site Scripting or XSS Attack:** XSS attack targets the application layer. It takes advantage of the vulnerabilities present in the web applications, the attacker embeds malicious Javascript, ActiveX or Flash in the code that creates dynamic page and when the victim visits that site the script gets executed on the machine and all the data are being gathered in the Attacker's machine. The malicious scripts might steal cookies or victim's confidential information on being executed. Web Vulnerability scanners like Acunetix are being used to crawl through the entire website and check for the XSS vulnerabilities. This tool gives us the report of all vulnerable URLs/Scripts, so that we could fix them easily.

9. **SQL Injection:** The database is one of the storage mechanisms where all the credentials are stored and the Structured Query Language (SQL) is a language to communicate with the database. All the information available in the database can be altered, modified, inserted, created or deleted using these SQL commands and thus these commands are used with malicious intention to gain unauthorized access to the database. This is a security exploit where the malicious SQL commands are given as a input into the HTML form.

10. **Zero Day Attack:** Zero day attacks are the attacks that target the vulnerabilities that don't have patches. These attacks are performed to cause maximum damage before a patch releases. The vulnerability window is a terminology in Zero-day attack which specifies the time frame within which the attack occurs. These attacks use malicious software/OS Vulnerability to exploit file types and steal valuable data.

11. **Cookie Manipulation and Session Hijacking:** The cookies are stored in a text file in the user's machine. They are transmitted via HTTP and are usually sent unencrypted, so it is very easy to get the cookies. Cookie Manipulation would be useful if only sensitive data are being stored in the cookie. This attack doesn't require any new methodologies or special programs. It just requires a text editor and the attacker should know where the cookies are stored.

Session Hijacking is the practice of taking control of the user session, it exploits the design flaws in TCP/IP protocol. Firesheep is a Firefox plugin that steels sessions over Unsecure Wi-Fi. This usually involves stealing a cookie from a user. The attacker uses a sniffer to capture Session ID to gain unauthorized access to the web server. Predictable session token, Session sniffing, Client Side Scripting and Man-in-the-middle attack are the most common ways to gain the session token (David Endler,2001)

12. **Locally Shared Objects and Flash Cookies:** Today most of the systems have flash players installed in their browsers to view any flash movies. Flash cookies are similar to normal web cookies but the normal cookies can be managed easily compared to the flash cookies. They remain in user's system

indefinitely since there is no time period set for expiry. Local shared object is a special feature of Adobe Flash Application, which the Flash cookies make use of. Flash cookies are unknown to users and even after the user clears the website cookies, these are not cleared and hence it is called a Zombie. These cookies help attackers to track user across the web.

BASIC FORENSIC PROCEDURE

1. **Order of Volatility:** Volatile memory is a type of memory which resides on RAM. This means data is retained in memory only until the device is powered on. If system power is interrupted or if system is shut down, the data in volatile memory is lost. The data loss may be immediate or it may happen gradually. In the event of an abnormal incident, tracing the event becomes an easy task using the data found in volatile memory. The volatile data in a system must be collected from most volatile to least volatile. The following order can be used:
   a. Current date/time.
   b. Data from CPU registers and cache.
   c. Data from routing table, ARP cache, process table, kernel statistics, memory.
   d. Data from temporary file system.
   e. Data from swap space on disk.
   f. Data from remote logs.
   g. Physical configuration of the system and its network topology.
   h. Data from archival media.
   i. Current date/time.

It is mandatory to start and end the volatile data collection by finding the system's current date/time. This is to ensure the correctness of the data collected and to establish a timeframe of the data collector's activity on the compromised system.

2. **Capturing System Image:** In digital forensics, a system image is a file that replicates the structure and contents of a storage device, regardless of the file system. Before capturing a system image, the investigator should determine the type of case he is handling. If the case would involve litigation or criminal proceedings, he should NOT take any system image and he should hand over the storage device to ISC Security. Otherwise the system image can be taken in two ways. The first option is to 'clone' the storage media. In this technique, a zero'ed drive is required. A zero'ed drive is one that has zeros written in all its sectors. The second option is to 'take an image' of the storage media. This method requires another hard drive with adequate capacity to store data collected from target media.

3. **Capturing Network Traffic And Logs:** Capturing network traffic allows the investigator to gain insight into the traffic that moves over a network. After collecting network traffic, it must be analyzed and interpreted to sense the occurrence of an abnormal incident. Network logs depict the complete sequence of activities that took place before, during and after the abnormal incident occurred. After analyzing the network traffic and logs, the investigator will be able to recreate the crime scene based on the timeframe in which the incident occurred. Few tools that may be used to capture network traffic are Wireshark, Snort, Kismet. Tools such as Arcsight Logger, LOGalyze, Splunk are used for analyzing log files. (Computer Software's Available from http://tools.kali.org/tools-listing)

4. **Capturing Video:** Capturing video for forensic analysis is scientifically examining, comparing and evaluating video for legal issues. Closed Circuit Television Surveillance (CCTV) is a technology that is implemented in almost all organizations to monitor the actions of employees visually, via video cameras. In spite of being aware that they are watched, some employees perform certain operations on systems, with malicious intentions. These actions usually leave visual evidence in video clippings that are recorded by the CCTV. It is possible to efficient monitor and retrieve evidence footage, when the timeframe of the abnormal incident is established. The video evidence is studied carefully by trained professionals to unearth information that would help to establish the identity of the user, who has compromised a system.

5. **Taking Hashes:** Hash is a value associated with a file that ensures the integrity of the file. It is a unique value that is generated based upon the contents of the file, using cryptographic algorithms like md5 or sha. Changes made to the contents of the file, reflects as a change in the hash value of the file. Any hash value should possess three main properties:
    a.   It must be easy to calculate.
    b.   It must be extremely difficult to reverse engineer the hash value.
    c.   It must be extremely unlikely for two different inputs, no matter how similar they are, to generate the same hash value.

A hash value behaves like a unique fingerprint for a file. It can help to identify if a file has been tampered with or not. Hash values help forensic analysts, to filter out ignorable files and alert files. 'Ignorable files' are mostly system files which have not been compromised yet. 'Alert files' are those files with inappropriate/malicious content whose hashes have been found and stored in a database. When a particular file has to be analyzed, its hash value is compared with known hash values found in the database. The tools that commonly used to generate the hash value for a file are md5, md5sum, sha256sum, sha512sum. The hash value of a file must be found only in the presence of a witness. This rule is known as 'Two-Man Integrity Rule'.

6. **Taking Snapshots:** A snapshot is a saved state of the system at a particular point of time. It is analogous to a digital photograph. A system's snapshot helps us to roll back to a previous state of the system in case of unexpected system crash or data loss. Details like system configuration, state of the disk, state of the files,etc . Details from snapshots are immediately available for the user to backtrack certain operations. Snapshots prove their value in the following ways (*Evans 2014*):
    a.   Zero-impact backup with no downtime.
    b.   Frequent backups to reduce recovery time.
    c.   Efficient backup for large volume of data.
    d.   Reduced exposure to data loss.
    e.   Instant recovery from snapshot.

7. **Investigating Witness/Client:** The process of investigating a witness/client must be done by a qualified professional who can interrogate the opponent gently. The interrogation should proceed in a way such that, the situation is favorable for the witness/client to be relaxed and verbalize all their observations accurately. The next step is for the investigator to make notes during the interrogation. Two options are available for the investigator. First, he may listen to the witness/client carefully for

their whole story and then make notes after the interrogation is over. Depending on those notes, the investigator may ask more relevant questions to the witness/client. Second, the investigator may take notes simultaneously when he is questioning the witness/client. However, this is not a very efficient practice because of two reasons- the investigator may lose his concentration on what the witness/client is speaking due to focusing on listening and writing at the same time, and the witness/client may get distracted watching the investigator write something without maintaining eye contact throughout the course of the investigation, which may result in the witness/client getting certain facts wrong. However, the process of investigating a witness/client purely depends on the skills of the investigator and the situation in which he is questioning the witness/client.

8. **Chain of Custody:** Chain of custody is a record that is used to trace the location of the evidence, from the time it was collected from the crime scene to the time it is presented in a court of law. This record makes sure that only authorized individuals have access to the collected evidence. It helps to keep the evidence in tamper-proof manner.

9. **Big Data Analytics:** With the vast growth of technology, digital forensics has been faced with a major challenge. Immense amount of data is available to be processed to enhance the digital investigation. This is a challenge as analyzing 'big data' has to be done in a short amount of time, while maintaining accuracy. The process of big data analytics proceeds in this way. The large amount of data is first collected, structured and organized based on various categories. This data are then stored in a database, on which forensic analysis is done to produce fast results. Usually dedicated systems are used to process data in the database. Three kinds of professionals are required to analyze big data:

    a. **A Database Expert:** Who writes database queries for quick and accurate data retrieval.
    b. **A Technical Expert:** Who is aware of the complete intended working of the system and is able to detect any unwanted behavior from big data results.
    c. **A Forensic Expert:** Who looks for signs of malicious activity.

SIGNS OF MALWARE

Main motives for designing malwares include Cybercrime, warfare, Hacktivism, Govt Monitoring etc. Over the years, malwares were extended as Cyber-weapons starting with Stuxnet and Flame. Apart from these, Duqu and many more complex agents are developed and are able to exploit non patched vulnerabilities including 0-day vulnerabilities. Experts at F-Secure, report a growth in increasing number of malware variants designed by hackers to evade antivirus protections by utilizing a greater number of signatures. The following are few signs that indicate the presence of Malware in your Mobile.

*   Excessive pop-up ads,
*   Significant decrease in Mobile OS speed,
*   Poor battery Life,
*   SMS/MMS to unknown numbers or to all contacts without users' consent,
*   Unexpected Device behavior (crashing or restarting frequently),
*   Data plan Spike.

The battle against these threads is mainly categorized as prevention and response. Prevention needs high level of awareness about the related risks. Second aspect can be restricted using better detection methods and stiff penalties. Malware analysis is the most challenging part. Static Analysis includes, Unpacking, Decompiling, analyzing decompiled code and detecting the malware. Dynamic Analysis includes executing an malicious app in a container (sandboxing) and analyzing the actions during the runtime.

Malware analysis are mostly conducted to assess the damage, number of systems affected and its severity, the vulnerability which was exploited and to identify the intruder. The easiest way to analyse an app for malware is using online sites like

- http://anubis.iseclab.org/
- http://dexter.dexlabs.org/
- https://www.virustotal.com/
- http://www.apk-analyzer.net/
- http://www.visualthreat.com/
- http://androidsandbox.net/reports.html
- https://hackapp.com/

MALWARE ANALYSIS

Malware analysis is the art of dissecting malware to understand how it works, how to identify it, and how to defeat or eliminate it. With millions of malicious programs in the wild, malware analysis is critical for anyone who responds to computer security incidents. In various levels malwares can be analyzed. They are: Basic Static Analysis, Basic Dynamic Analysis, Advanced Static Analysis, and Advanced Dynamic Analysis. Static Malware Analysis includes code analysis or manual analysis which includes File Finger printing, Virus Scanning, Decoding encrypted stored or transferred data, determining logic of the app and its capabilities, Disassembly etc. This method is time consuming and won't give accurate results. Reverse Engineering is a common methodology used in this stage. Commonly used tools are Mobile Sandbox, IDAPro, APKInspector, Dex2jar, JAD etc. Dynamic Malware Analysis includes behavioural analysis which includes detection of Hacker Server connection establishment, Zombie interaction etc. Here an app is installed and allowed to run in a sandbox. When the app runs, using tools we can detect data leakage, network interactions etc. Commonly used tools are DroidBox, AndroidSDK, Android AuditTools etc (Distler, 2007).

Basic Static Analysis

Static analysis describes the process of analyzing the code or structure of a program to determine its function (Mehta, 2016).

- **String:** The string in a program is a sequence of characters such as "the." A program contains strings if it prints a message and/or, connects to a URL, or copies a file to a specific location. Searching through the strings can be a simple way to get some hints about the functionality of a program. For example, if the program accesses a URL, then you will see the URL accessed stored as a string in the program. You can use the Strings program to search an executable for strings, which are typically stored in either ASCII or Unicode format.

- **PE Headers:** PE file headers can provide considerably more information than just imports. The PE file format contains a header followed by a series of sections. The header contains metadata about the file itself.
  - ◦ Using antivirus tools to confirm maliciousness. Upload sample to Virustotal.com and see results.
  - ◦ Using hashes to identify malware. Upload sample to Virustotal.com, malshare.com and see results.
  - ◦ Gleaning information from a file's strings, functions, and headers. Upload sample to malwr. com and see results.

Basic Dynamic Analysis

Dynamically analyzing the data lets you observe the malware's true functionality, because, for example, the existence of an action string in a binary does not mean the action will actually execute. Dynamic analysis is also an efficient way to identify malware functionality real time. During Dynamic Analysis, things we should monitor are, Registry Change, File System Interaction with malware, New Process created by malware, Network Connections made by malware. (Mehta, 2016).

- **Tools:** Cuckoo Sandboxing/malwr.com (Note: Malwr.com does both static and dynamic analysis to certain level of malware analysis).

Advanced Static Analysis

We take the malware binary as input and generate assembly language code as output, usually with a disassembler. IDA Pro will disassemble an entire program and perform tasks such as function discovery, stack analysis, local variable identification, and much more. IDA Pro includes extensive code signatures within its Fast Library Identification and Recognition Technology (FLIRT), which allows it to recognize and label a disassembled function, especially library code added by a compiler.

- **Tools:** IDAPro.

Advanced Dynamic Analysis

Debuggers provide information about a program that would be difficult, if not impossible, to get from a disassembler. Disassemblers offer a snapshot of what a program looks like immediately prior to execution of the first instruction. Debuggers provide a dynamic view of a program as it runs. For example, debuggers can show the values of memory addresses as they change throughout the execution of a program. (Lohit Mehta, 2016).

- **Tools:** OllyDbg/Immunity Debugger (32 bit) (Computer Software's Available from http://tools. kali.org/tools-listing).

Mobile Malware Analysis

Madware and malware are two types of Android security risks that have had a consistent presence over the past few years. They have been found in apps hosted both on Google Play Store and on third-party app stores. Madware refers to apps that use aggressive ad (advertisement) libraries. There are at least 65 known ad libraries and over 50 percent of them are classified as aggressive libraries. The percentage of madware on Google Play is steadily increasing, reaching over 23 percent in the first half of 2013. On average, apps were trending towards using two ad libraries, regardless of how aggressive the ad libraries are

The presence of malware in each app category varies on Google Play Store and on third-party app stores, as certain categories contain more compared to others. The growth of the number of known malicious samples is much higher than the linear growth of the number of malware families. Apps from the Personalization and Libraries & Demos categories contain the most madware. According to a recet study, most third-party app stores host more security risks than Google Play does. However, the level of security risks on 11 percent of known third-party app stores is lower than on Google Play.(Uscilowski,2013)

MITIGATION AND DETERRENT TECHNIQUES

The rise in the need for people to have access to their personal data from any remote location is one of the core reasons that have led to the widespread implementation of the policy of Bring Your Own Device (BYOD) implemented by many enterprises. However, this progressive policy is not without its faults. This is because whenever implementing any Information and Communications Technology (ICT) policies, a certain balance has to be met between convenience and security. Let us consider the use of mobile devices within a company's network. One improperly secured device can be the single point of failure in that enterprise's security model and it has the capability to compromise the whole company network. This is just one example of a scenario where proper knowledge if mitigation and deterrence techniques can help avert or reduce the impact of any attack on an enterprise.

Hence, it is necessary that general users and employees of companies that promote the BYOD policy to be well educated and trained in the mitigation and deterrent techniques to be used in handling threats on the mobile platform. The same knowledge can also be used by regular users of mobile devices interested in maintaining the privacy of data on their mobile devices and responding to any potential threats too.

Monitoring and Log Analysis

A great deal of data flows in and out of mobile devices each time we use them. A lot more data and signals are transmitted within the device itself in the same amount of time. Attackers are aware of this and will try as best as they can try and compromise the mobile device. They can try to intercept the sensitive traffic being transmitted to and from the device. In some cases, they can create their own malicious connection from the device and then siphon private information from it without the user's knowledge. One method the user can make use of is monitoring the device and then analyzing the generated logs periodically. Monitoring can be done from within the device itself through the use of inbuilt systems already available, the installation of a third party app to do the monitoring, or the use of a remote tool to monitor traffic coming in or leaving the device.

By default, within the app settings of most flavours of Android OS up to 5.0 Lollipop, there is a menu option where the user can see a list of all apps running on the device including those running in the background. On later versions, it also includes data on how many processes and services the app is running, how much memory it is using as well as how long the app has been running. Each process has a respective number of services it is running and an even deeper analysis can show the user what process initiated a service. This can be useful in cases where the device has suddenly become very slow due to the presence of a malicious app. The user can check to see which app is hogging the device memory and also take note of which specific service is causing the system to lag. If more investigation is required, dynamic malware analysis of the app in question may be undertaken by using a sandbox to run the app in a virtual environment and then analysis can be done.

Unlike desktop PCs, routers and other network devices, there are not many ports that need to be secured on most mobile devices. This is because most mobile devices simply possess a USB port (micro or mini) which is the main port that needs to be protected. With android devices, the best option is to disable USB debugging mode under the Developer Options menu in settings. This restricts an attacker from connecting the mobile device to a PC and using the Android Debug Bridge (adb) tool on it. This is a tool that allows the attacker to communicate with the mobile device and issue commands to it which include copying of sensitive data. If the device is rooted, the attacker can push and install malicious programs onto the device, copy browser databases containing saved browser history and possibly even saved credentials and then do a lot more nefarious activities. Therefore, the best method would be to avoid rooting or jail-breaking and Android or iOS device respectively.

Also, always setting a screen lock on the device (password, pin code or pattern) whenever the device is not in use is also advisable. This is because when a locked device running on the more recent flavors of Android is connected to a PC or laptop via USB cable, the USB cable will work as only a charging cable and not a data transmission cable. Only after the device is unlocked will data transmission facility be enabled. Another method is to configure the USB connection mode to disallow transfer of files not meeting a certain file type criteria. For example, if the user of the device needs to transfer only images to and from the device, then they should select the PTP (Picture Transfer Protocol) which only allows the transmission of images and no other file types. This means no malicious apps can be pushed onto the device via the USB connection since the .apk extension (the file extension for android apps) and file header is not recognized as an image format by PTP.

Security Related Awareness and Training

One of the main reasons why most devices are compromised is simply because the users and developers are not aware of the threats that may target their apps and devices. Most of them tend to believe the false assumption that mobile applications cannot be attacked by malware, which is simply not true. This is why security awareness and training is a requirement that should be met by both technical and non-technical parties who use of mobile devices. In other words, the training should accommodate both the regular users of the mobile devices as well as the developers of apps used on them. This is because threats can originate from malicious apps as well as weakly-secured apps within the device itself, or from another connected device. For the developers' side, GoatDroid, Damn Vulnerable iOS and iMAS (iOS Mobile Application Security project) are a few examples of open-source tools that can be used by developers to test the security of the apps they would have designed. Ideally, if developers are trained to use these tools and a variety of others not listed here to run penetration testing and vulnerability assessment of the apps they would have developed before uploading them online for the general public to use. Knowledge of the OWASP Top Ten Mobile Risks is also important so the developers know what threats are most likely to try and compromise their apps and implement systems that can help prevent exposure to these threats.

As for the general users, knowledge of the common ways to maintain security on their mobile devices such as physical security of the device itself (keeping it physically safe from potential adversaries) as well as protection from intangible threats such as malware through the use of antivirus software. This can be done through the undertaking of workshops and sharing helpful hints. It would also help if rules of thumb, basic hints and related crime statistics are shared as a supplement to the workshops so as to emphasize the gravity of the situation. In a nutshell, they should be taught to recognize threats, scams and ultimately understand the immense value of their information. Most people do not realize how important their private data is as well as how it can be misused and manipulated by adversaries.

They can also be trained in how to harden their mobile devices against threats such as sniffing and how to encrypt private data on the devices. Installing antiviruses and firewall software to monitor and manage data coming into and going out of their phones. Password security by ensuring that they do not share the passwords they have, they do not use "obvious" and uncomplicated passwords and also do not reuse the same password among many apps. This would mean that if one app is compromised, then all apps and accounts would be compromised as well.

They should also be wary of file sharing and copyright laws and avoid storing sensitive data from their place of employment on their mobile devices. It should be noted that most enterprises tend to make it a policy that employees are not to leave company premises with company documents/property but due to the growth of BOYD, that is becoming more difficult to manage.

Users should also avoid/limit banking on their smart phone and its always preferred to use a proxy or VPN when using public WiFi. In such cases, it would be more ideal to simply avoid sending sensitive data online while on a public WiFi connection. This will help bypassing hackers who use special tools that can strip SSL from HTTPS connections and leave them as HTTP in clear-text.

Also, it is strongly advised to avoid rooting android devices or jail-breaking iOS mobile devices unless the user knows what they are doing. This is because doing so gives a user root access (or pseudo-root access in iOS) to their device and allows them to access even more of its normally hidden functionalities. However, that also means the possible threats would increase as well, since doing so automatically increases the possible threat vectors with respect to the device.

To add to that, the user should always check the permissions required by the apps that they try to install. Some malicious apps tend to masquerade as simple and basic apps and the simplest way to notice them is to first check the permissions they request for upon installation. For example, if a torch app requires access to identity, contact and location information, then it would mean that the app most likely will perform malicious tasks beyond simply acting as a torch.

Furthermore, users should encrypt all private communication using secure apps such as TextSecure and Redphone so that the data being transmitted is not intercepted. They should also avoid installing pirated apps, which are the free versions of paid for apps/games which can be found around the internet. It is more than likely that these apps will collect your personal data without your knowledge.

It is advisable to encrypt the device itself, which is a facility that was introduced to Android in the 5.0 Lollipop version. This means that each time a user boots their phone, they have to enter the unlock password, pin code or pattern to decrypt the device and then proceed to continue the boot process. Without this login credential, an attacker would not be able to gain much data from the device. Installing antiviruses and firewall software to monitor and manage data coming into and going out of their phones is also a good practice.

REFERENCES

Bonadea. (2015). *Rogue security software*. Retrieved from wikipedia.com

Camilla-Cooper. (2016). *Introduction to Ethical Hacking Intro to Ethical Hacking*. Retrieved from docslide.us

Curphey. (2011). *OWASP*. Retrieved from owasp.org

Distler. (2007). *Malware Analysis- An Introduction*. Retrieved from sans.org

Endler, D. (2001). *Brute-Force Exploitation of Web Application Session ID's*. White paper from iDEFENSE.

Evans. (2014). *Backup vs replication, snapshots, CDP in data protection strategy*. Retrieved from computerweekly.com

Kelly. (2015). *Address Munging: Adware: Backdoor: Backscatter (also known as outscatter, misdirected bounces, blowback or collateral spam)*. Retrieved from docplayer.net

Mehta. (2016). *Malware Analysis basics, Part 1*. Retrieved from infosecinstitute.com

Paganini, P. (2013). *Near Field Communication Technology, Vulnerability and Principal Attack Schema*. Retrieved from resources.infosecinstitute.com

RSA Laboratories. (2001). *RSA Security Response to Weaknesses in Key Scheduling Algorithm of RC4*. Retrieved from cse.iitb.ac.in

Siciliano. (2015). *What is a virus?*. Retrieved from mcafee.com

Snori. (2015). *Rouge access point*. Retrieved from wikipedia.com

Uscilowski. (2013). *Mobile Adware and Malware analysis*. Retrieved from symantec.com

Chapter 12
Network Intrusion Detection and Prevention Systems on Flooding and Worm Attacks

P. Vetrivelan
VIT University, India

M. Jagannath
VIT University, India

T. S. Pradeep Kumar
VIT University, India

ABSTRACT

The Internet has transformed greatly the improved way of business, this vast network and its associated technologies have opened the doors to an increasing number of security threats which are dangerous to networks. The first part of this chapter presents a new dimension of denial of service attacks called TCP SYN Flood attack has been witnessed for severity of damage and second part on worms which is the major threat to the internet. The TCP SYN Flood attack by means of anomaly detection and traces back the real source of the attack using Modified Efficient Packet Marking algorithm (EPM). The mechanism for detecting the smart natured camouflaging worms which is sensed by means of a technique called Modified Controlled Packet Transmission (MCPT) technique. Finally the network which is affected by these types of worms are detected and recovered by means of Modified Centralized Worm Detector (MCWD) mechanism. The Network Intrusion Detection and Prevention Systems (NIDPS) on Flooding and Worm Attacks were analyzed and presented.

INTRODUCTION TO NETWORK ATTACKS

In today's world, it has become an almost every day situation where we hear about personal computer systems or the networks being attacked. In this age of technology, there are different types of computer attacks from which one has to protect their precious data, systems and even networks. While some of the attacks may simply corrupt the data on the computer, there are other attacks, where the data from the computer system may be stolen, and others where the entire network may be shut down.

DOI: 10.4018/978-1-5225-0193-0.ch012

Xiang, Y et al (2006) proposed the analytical model for DDoS attacks and defense. In December 2007, Cisco published its annual security report, which provided an overview of cybercrime trends drawn from significant amount of security information, gathered by the security intelligence in Cisco from January to October 2007. The Cisco security analysts identified numerous threats and vulnerability issues in the year 2007. The Cisco Security IntelliShield Alert Manager Service issued the most alerts for DoS, worms and arbitrary code execution threats. From the DDoS attacks that shut down the high-profile Web sites (for example, Yahoo, Amazon) in February 2000 to the above-mentioned incidents and studies in recent years, DDoS attacks and worms have demonstrated their prevalence, severe impact and consequences of the damage, and the importance and need for efficient detection and defense mechanisms.

CLASSIFICATION OF ATTACKS

To put it simply, there are two main types of attacks, passive attacks and active attacks. Passive attacks are the ones where the data transaction on the computer is monitored and later utilized for malicious interests, while active attacks are ones where either change is made to the data or the data is deleted or the network is destroyed completely. Figure 1 shows the common types of active as well as passive attacks that can affect the computers today.

Denial of Service (DoS) attacks is basically of two types namely flooding attacks and vulnerability attacks. A flooding attack sends a vast amount of seemingly legitimate packets whose processing consumes some key resource at the target. A vulnerability attack constructs a sequence of packets with cer-

Figure 1. Classification of attacks

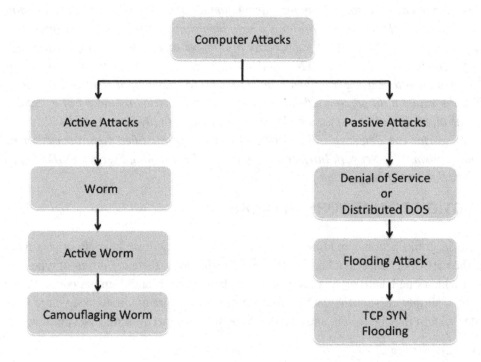

tain characteristics that cause a vulnerable system to crash, hang, or behave in unpredictable ways. TCP SYN Flood, UDP flooding, ICMP flooding are examples of the DoS flooding attacks. A new dimension of denial of service attacks called TCP SYN Flood attack has been witnessed which has amplified the severity of damage. Instead of aiming at a single organization, these attacks are now targeted towards the Internet backbone. As a result, millions of Internet users are denied access and all transactions come to a halt. Such shifting scenario necessitates a robust and resilient security approach, which effectively and efficiently identifies these attacks and reacts aptly.

The problem of detecting Denial of Service (DoS) attacks, and particularly TCP SYN Flood attacks, has received much attention in current literature. Any computer connected to the Internet has the possibility to be a victim at any time. Therefore, it is important for network administrators to develop means to comprehend the latest trend of DoS attacks. The work reported in this chapter has been motivated by these facts to develop efficient mechanisms to detect the source of TCP SYN Flood attacks. The malware includes computer viruses, computer worms, Trojan horses, most root kits, spyware, dishonest adware and other malicious or unwanted software, including true viruses. In the past, hackers were highly skilled programmers who understood the details of computer communications and how to exploit vulnerabilities. Today almost anyone can become a hacker by downloading tools from the Internet. These complicated attack tools and generally open networks have generated an increased need for network security and dynamic security policies.

Camouflaging worms belonging to a category of active worms has shown their predominance. An active worm refers to a malicious software program that propagates itself on the Internet to infect other hosts. The propagation of the worm is based on exploiting vulnerabilities of hosts on the Internet. Many real worms have posed much damage on the Internet. These worms include "Code-Red" worm, "Slammer" worm and "Witty"/"Sasser" worms. Since worms may infect a large number of hosts in a relatively short period of time. Detection of worms is one of the most important tasks in defense against them, which usually is based on the behavioral features of worms. Most existing detection schemes are based on a tacit assumption that each worm infected host keeps scanning the Internet and propagates itself at the highest possible speed. The work reported in this chapter is motivated by these facts which led to the proposal of new detection and recovery mechanisms of camouflaging worms.

TCP SYN Flood Attack

The following will explain about the TCP SYN Flood attack, its causes and its effects in detail.

A SYN flood attack is one in which an attacker sends a large number of TCP SYN packets to a victim. This causes the victim to use scarce resources (CPU time, bandwidth, and in the absence of SYN cookies, memory) to respond to the attacker's SYNs. If the attack rate is high enough, the server will begin to drop excess SYNs, and legitimate clients will be unable to connect, leading to a denial of service. The TCP SYN Flood happened when the three-way handshake had been exploited by the intruders without being realized by the server. A SYN flood is a form of denial-of-service attack in which an attacker sends a succession of SYN requests to a target's system in an attempt to consume enough server resources to make the system unresponsive to legitimate traffic.

The steps are as below:

1. An intruder uses spoofed address to send a SYN packet to victim server.
2. A victim server sends back a request SYN and ACK packet to the client or spoofed address and wait for confirmation or timeout expiration of SYN packets.
3. If the client does not send back the final ACK packet, the server's resources can be easily exhausted.
4. At this time the SYN flood attack occurs because too many SYN packet request from other clients.

Antonatos et al (2005) says that the camouflaging worms belonging to a category of active worms has shown their predominance. An active worm refers to a malicious software program that propagates itself on the Internet to infect other hosts. The propagation of the worm is based on exploiting vulnerabilities of hosts on the Internet. Many real worms have posed much damage on the Internet. These worms include "Code-Red" worm, "Slammer" worm and "Witty"/"Sasser" worms. Since worms may infect a large number of hosts in a relatively short period of time. Detection of worms is one of the most important tasks in defense against them, which usually is based on the behavioral features of worms. Most existing detection schemes are based on a tacit assumption that each worm infected host keeps scanning the Internet and propagates itself at the highest possible speed. The work reported in this chapter is motivated by these facts which led to the proposal of new detection and recovery mechanisms of camouflaging worms.

Figure 2 shows that the attacker sends several packets but does not send the "ACK" back to the server. The connections are hence half-opened and consuming server resources. Alice, a legitimate user, tries to connect but the server refuses to open a connection resulting in a denial of service. The main challenge in SYN flooding mitigation is to accurately identify attack packets and filter them without causing collateral damage to legitimate traffic designated to the victim.

Figure 2. SYN flood attack

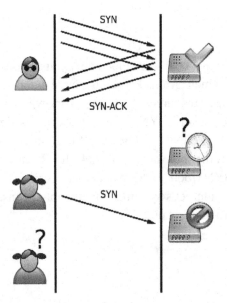

Effects of TCP SYN Flood Attack

- Systems providing TCP-based services to the Internet community may be unable to provide those services and may exhaust memory, crash, or be rendered otherwise inoperative.
- Some systems may also malfunction badly or even crash if other operating system functions are starved of resources in this way.

Camouflaging Worm (C-Worm)

A new class of active worms, referred to as Camouflaging Worm (C-Worm in short) has amplified the severity of damage. The C-Worm has a self-propagating behavior similar to traditional worms, i.e., it intends to rapidly infect as many vulnerable hosts as possible. However, the C-Worm is quite different from traditional worms in a way that it camouflages any noticeable trends in the number of infected hosts over time. The Characteristics of C-Worm is as follows:

- Camouflage is a method of concealment of object by blending with its environment.
- Packet of C-Worm is anomalous to normal data packets.
- C-Worm is a type of smart worm which switches from normal to sleeping mode when suspected under detection.
- C-Worm rapidly infects as many vulnerable computers as possible by changing the scan traffic volume frequently.

The C-Worm camouflages its propagation by controlling its scan traffic volume during its propagation. The simplest way to manipulate scan traffic volume is to randomly change the number of worm instances conducting port scans. However, this method may not be able to elude detection. The reason is that the overall C-Worm scan traffic volume still shows an increasing trend with the progress of worm propagation and as more and more hosts are being infected, they in turn take part in scanning other hosts.

OBJECTIVES OF DETECTION MECHANISMS FOR NETWORK SECURITY

The objective of this research is to develop new detection mechanisms for the flooding and worm attacks with a focus on:

1. To detect TCP SYN flood attack by allowing the victim to trace back the appropriate origin of source IP address.
2. To propose a finest solution to trace back the real source of attack in case of IP spoofing and trace back failure.
3. To detect the smart natured active worm called Camouflaging worms which naturally tend to conceal its presence and transmit the packets which will be similar to a normal packet.
4. To recover the network affected by camouflaging worms.

RELATED WORKS AND LITERATURE SURVEY

There are two main causes of SYN flood attacks. The first is the inherent asymmetry feature in TCP three-way handshake protocol, which enables an attacker to consume substantial resources at the server, while sparing its own resources. The other is that the server cannot control the packets it receives; especially the SYN packets can easily reach the server without its approval. Li, P (2008) described that the consequence of the SYN flooding attack is that a service can be brought down by flooding the server with a few tens of SYN requests per second. Many algorithms have been proposed in the past, to catch and stop the spread of camouflaging worms. Most research papers discuss efforts that are related to their proposed work.

TCP SYN Flood Attack Detection Techniques

Haris (2010) had proposed a mechanism for detecting threats in IP headers by taking into consideration the IP and TCP header and checked the packet using anomaly detection. TCP SYN Flood attacks and other attacks could be detected through the traffic monitoring tools and anomalies are alerted to the administrator. In this paper, rate-based detection is used for anomaly detection. Anomaly detection has three types of detection in network analysis behavior. Even though this approach detects the anomalies in the IP header, the source of the attack could not be traced back. In the experiment, the main threats like SYN Flood attack had been traced in a small amount. It is because the Linux operating system is stable and it is very hard to attack by the hackers.

Sandeep A.Thorat (2008) proposed Payload Content based Network Anomaly Detection (PCNAD) which takes into consideration the entire payload for profile calculation and effectively for anomaly detection. This detection mechanism analyzes normal payload for a particular service on a host and makes a set of payload profiles. In PCNAD, the system has two components Packet Profiler and PCNAD Anomaly Detector. The Packet Profiler deals with normal packet profiling and creates the reduced profile model. In PCNAD Anomaly Detector, incoming packet is compared with stored profiles and alerts are generated if incoming packet is significantly different from stored profiles. The drawback of this approach is that the system is showing poor results at ports like 22, 23, 25 and the complexity is very high.

Wang et al (2002) used the Flood Detection System (FDS), which in turn used Cumulative Sum (CUSUM) that detect the SYN flooding attacks at leaf routers which connect end hosts to the Internet, instead of monitoring the ongoing traffic at the front end (like firewall or proxy) or a victim server itself. The detection utilizes the SYN-FIN pairs' behavior and distinguish features make it immune to SYN flooding attacks. If the packets of the same TCP session go through different leaf routers, we need a loose synchronization mechanism between the FDSs in these leaf routers; this detection scheme does not work. If the spoofed source address is in the same stub network as a flooding source, it cannot detect the ongoing flooding attack.

Camouflaging Worm Detection

Wei Yu et al (2011), "Modeling and Detection of Camouflaging Worm", proposed a mechanism for detecting C-Worms based on analyzing the propagation traffic generated by worms. Active worms pose major security threats to the Internet. This is due to the ability of active worms to propagate in an automated fashion as they continuously compromise computers on the Internet. Active worms evolve during their propagation, and thus, pose great challenges to defend against them. In this paper, they investigated a new class of active worms, referred to as Camouflaging Worm (C-Worm). The C-Worm is different from traditional worms because of its ability to intelligently manipulate its scan traffic volume over time. Thereby, the C-Worm camouflages its propagation from existing worm detection systems based on analyzing the propagation traffic generated by worms. Their scheme uses the Power Spectral Density (PSD) distribution of the scan traffic volume and its corresponding Spectral Flatness Measure (SFM) to distinguish the C-Worm traffic from background traffic. Furthermore, they have shown the generality of the spectrum-based scheme in effectively detecting not only the C-Worm, but traditional worms as well.

Jiang Wu et al (2004), "An Effective Architecture and Algorithm for Detecting Worms with Various Scan Techniques" analyzes various scan techniques and proposed a generic worm detection architecture that monitors malicious activities. They evaluated an algorithm to detect the spread of worms using real time traces and simulations. They presented an analysis on potential scan techniques that worms can employ to scan vulnerable machines. They proposed a detection algorithm called victim number based algorithm, which relies solely on the increase of source addresses of scan traffic and evaluated its effectiveness. Their solution can detect worm activities when only 4% of the vulnerable machines are infected. The number of false alarms increases in the case of a DDoS attack or in the case of a hot website visit.

Venkataraman et al (2005), "New Streaming Algorithms for Fast Detection of Super spreaders" considered the problem of detecting super spreaders, which are sources that connect to a large number of distinct destinations. They proposed new streaming algorithms for detecting super spreaders and prove guarantees on their accuracy and memory requirements. They also showed experimental results on real network traces. One level filtering algorithm has several difficulties. It needs a certain minimum sampling rate in order to distinguish between sources.

Wei Yu et al (2006), "Effective detection of active worms with varying scan rate", modeled a new form of active worms called Varying Scan Rate worm (the VSR worm). In this paper, they contributed in Worm Modeling and Effective Detection Scheme. They modeled the above new form of worms as Varying Scan Rate worm (the VSR worm). The VSR worm is generic and simple to launch. Evaluation results demonstrated that DEC detection scheme has superior performance in terms of speed and accuracy in detecting not only VSR worms but also traditional PRS worms. They found that packets originating from one of the host machines in their network showed behavior typical of the slapper worm (attempting to infect other hosts). Zou, C et al (2003) have proposed a monitoring scheme and early warning for internet worms.

Ohsita, Y et al (2004) have identified the DoS attacks analyzing the TCP SYN packets. The existing state-of-the-art to detect the TCP SYN Flood attacks and Camouflaging worms are discussed with their drawbacks. To overcome all these issues in detecting the attacks and worms, the forthcoming sections propose advanced detection models.

DETECTING THE SOURCE OF TCP SYN FLOOD ATTACK

Computers connected to networks are exposed to potentially damaging access by unauthorized "hackers". Denial-of-service (DoS) attacks throw up an uprising threat to today's internet. Gavaskar, S et al (2010) described that the TCP SYN Flood attack is the most serious form of Dos attack in which the attackers easily exploit the TCP three-way handshake by exhausting the resources of the server and making it unavailable for the legitimate client.

TCP-based flooding attacks results in maltreatment of network resources and can bring about serious threats to the Internet. TCP SYN floods send large amount of TCP SYN packets. These SYN packets identify the initiation of a connection, and the receiving side of the connection must then acknowledge and wait for confirmation message from the initiator before the connection is half opened. One problem in detecting SYN flood is that server nodes or firewalls cannot distinguish between the SYN flood packets and the normal TCP packet.

The goal of this research is to detect TCP SYN Flood attack that occurs in TCP protocol. TCP SYN Flood is hard to detect and anomaly detection, which is a type of network intrusion detection system, is used because it is the most frequently suggested approach to detect attack variants, which look for abnormal behavior. Our proposed system is a simple and an efficient method.

Attack Methods

The scenario pictured in Figure 3 is a simplification of how SYN flooding attacks are carried out in the real world, and is intended to give an understanding of the basic idea behind these types of attacks. Figure 4 presents some variations that have been observed on the Internet.

Direct Attack

If attackers rapidly send SYN segments without spoofing their IP source address, it is called as direct attack. This method of attack is very easy to perform because it does not involve directly injecting or spoofing packets below the user level of the attacker's operating system. It can be performed by simply using many TCP connect () calls, for instance. To be effective, however, attackers must prevent

Figure 3. Attack demonstration

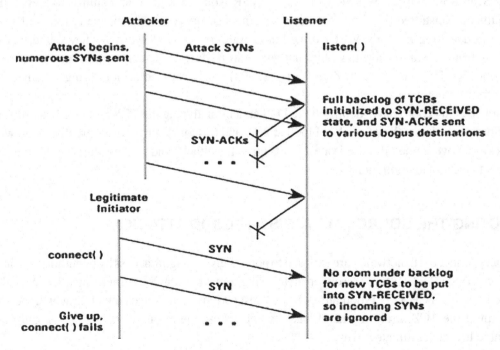

Figure 4. Some variants of the basic attack

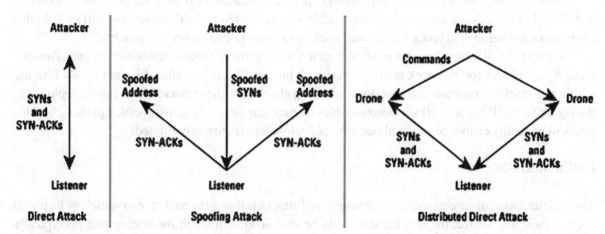

their operating system from responding to the SYN-ACKs in any way, because any ACKs, RSTs, or Internet Control Message Protocol (ICMP) messages will allow the listener to move the TCB out of SYN-RECEIVED. This scenario can be accomplished through firewall rules that either filter outgoing packets to the listener (allowing only SYNs out), or filter incoming packets so that any SYN-ACKs are discarded before reaching the local TCP processing code. When detected, this type of attack is very easy to defend against, because a simple firewall rule to block packets with the attacker's source IP address is all that is needed. This defense behavior can be automated, and such functions are available in off-the-shelf reactive firewalls.

Spoofing-Based Attacks

Another form of SYN flooding attacks uses IP address spoofing, which might be considered more complex than the method used in a direct attack, in that instead of merely manipulating local firewall rules, the attacker also needs to be able to form and inject raw IP packets with valid IP and TCP headers. Today, popular libraries exist to aid with raw packet formation and injection, so attacks based on spoofing are actually fairly easy.

For spoofing attacks, a primary consideration is address selection. If the attack is to succeed, the machines at the spoofed source addresses must not respond to the SYN-ACKs that are sent to them in any way. A very simple attacker might spoof only a single source address that it knows will not respond to the SYN-ACKs, either because no machine physically exists at the address presently, or because of some other property of the address or network configuration. Another option is to spoof many different source addresses, under the assumption that some percentage of the spoofed addresses will be not responding to the SYN-ACKs. This option is accomplished either by cycling through a list of source addresses that are known to be desirable for the purpose, or by generating addresses inside a subnet with similar properties.

If only a single source address is repetitively spoofed, this address is easy for the listener to detect and filter. In most cases a larger list of source addresses is used to make defense more difficult. In this case, the best defense is to block the spoofed packets as close to their source as possible.

Assuming the attacker is based in a "stub" location in the network (rather than within a transit Autonomous System (AS), for instance), restrictive network ingress filtering by stub ISPs and egress filtering within the attacker's network will shut down spoofing attacks—if these mechanisms can be deployed in the right places. IP Security (IPsec) also provides an excellent defense against spoofed packets, but this protocol generally cannot be required because its deployment is currently limited.

Distributed Attacks

The real limitation of single-attacker spoofing-based attacks is that if the packets can somehow be traced back to their true source, the attacker can easily be shut down. Although the tracing process typically involves some amount of time and coordination between ISPs, it is not impossible. Currently, distributed attacks are feasible because there are several "botnets" or "drone armies" of thousands of compromised machines that are used by criminals for DoS attacks. Because drone machines are constantly added or removed from the armies and can change their IP addresses or connectivity, it is quite challenging to block these attacks. From the above discussion, the different types of TCP SYN flood attack methods are reviewed.

ISSUES IN EXISTING TECHNIQUES

Various techniques have been proposed to detect the TCP SYN Flood attack. Table 1 illustrates the limitations of the existing works.

Table 1. Limitations of existing detection techniques

Existing Techniques	Limitations
Packet Marking Techniques - Al-Duwairi et al (2006)	• Fast detection of attacks is not possible • Complex and time consuming. • Lacks efficient and effective trace back • PPM incurs high computational work, especially when there are many sources. • Deterministic Packet Marking (DPM) needs enough packets to be collected for successful trace back • FDPM packet processing consumes resources such as memory and computing capacity of a participating router.
Other Trace back Techniques - Katiravan, J et al (2011)	• Packets from legitimate user will be lost • Cannot detect attack with lower rate • Cannot detect malicious attacker • Attackers could forge addresses from hundreds or thousands of hosts in ingress filtering • Trace back may be slow or impossible to complete in case of input debugging. • Controlled flooding is itself a denial-of-service attack • Enormous resource requirements in case of logging

PROPOSED SOLUTION TO DETECT THE SOURCE OF TCP SYN FLOOD ATTACK

There are two types of network intrusion detection system which are signature based detection and anomaly based detection. Signature detection is a technique often used in the Intrusion Detection System (IDS) and many antimalware systems such as anti-virus and anti-spyware. In the signature detection process, network or system information is scanned against a known attack or malware signature database. If match found, an alert takes place for further actions. Anomaly based detection infers malicious activity in a network by detecting anomalous network traffic patterns. The proposed system concentrates on the detection of threats in a local area network and also successfully puts forward mechanism to trace back the IP address of the source using Efficient Packet Marking algorithm.

Anomaly Detection System

The Anomaly detection system as shown in Figure 5 and follows the steps as given as follows:

- The Anomaly detection is used in checking the IP Header and payload of TCP header.
- The Anomaly Detection Algorithm first checks the arriving IP header. If the length of the IP header is equal to 20 and if the Type of Service (TOS) is zero then it chooses the TCP Protocol.
- TCP header is analyzed since TCP SYN Flood is the major threat. At this stage, packets are divided into two groups namely infected packets and normal packets.
- Arrived packets are distinguished by analysis to confirm whether the packet truly comes from the attackers. Packet filtering flowchart is shown in Figure 7.

Figure 5. Packet filtering process

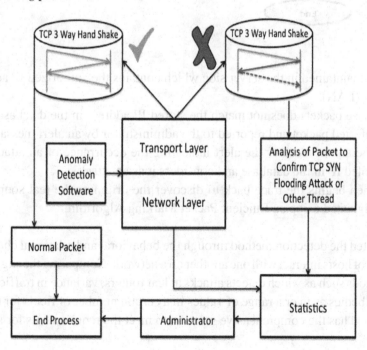

Figure 6. Anomaly detection for TCP SYN flood attack

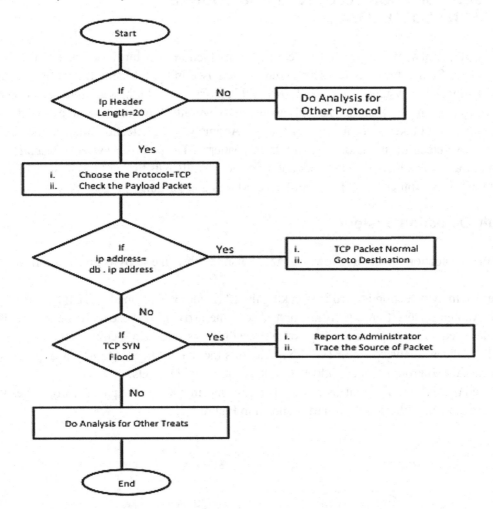

- A database is maintained in the server side which contains the authorized IP address of the Local Area Network (LAN).
- If the IP of those packets does not match the stored IP address in the database then the packet is reported as infected packet and reported to the administrator by an alert message.
- Once when the admin receives the alert indicating the occurrence of an attack, it automatically saves the spoofed IP in the database and considers it as an attack.
- The Server then begins the trace back to discover the origin or the real source from which the packet has originated using an Efficient Packet Marking Algorithm.

Figure 6 suggested the detection method through the behavioral and relational changes in which how individual or group of hosts interact with one another on a network. Comparing the suggested method with other existing methods such as which detects attacks at leaf routers, variance in traffic rate as in detectors generation and antibodies as in or a range of values in a certain number of fields for different protocols, the suggested method has the comprehensive solution to meet the requirements for such type of attack.

Advantages of Anomaly Detections

Anomaly detection systems offer several benefits such as:

- They can detect insider attacks or account theft very easily. If a real user or someone using a stolen account starts performing actions that are outside the normal user-profile, it generates an alarm.
- Probably the largest benefit, however, is that intrusive activity is not based on specific traffic that represents known intrusive activity (as in signature-based IDS).
- TCP flags such as SYN, ACK, RST, FIN, PSH, and URG are divided into each group to check whether the three way handshake is complete or not.
- IP address is valid and not a spoofed address, unrecognized IP address is considered an attack.
- An anomaly detection system can potentially detect an attack the first time it is used.
- Another benefit of this approach is that learning to describe normal activity can be automated.

Efficient Packet Marking

Gong, C et al (2008) says that tracing the paths of IP packets back to their origin, known as IP trace back, is an important step in defending against DOS attacks employing IP spoofing. The main idea behind packet marking is to record network path information in packets. Malliga, S et al (2008) says that the mark based IP trace back, routers write their identification information (e.g., IP addresses) into a header field of forwarded packets. The destination node then retrieves the marking information from the received packets and determines the network path. Due to the limited space of the marking field, routers probabilistically decide to mark packets so that each marked packet carries only partial path information. The network path can be constructed by combining the marking information collected from a number of received packets. This approach is also known as probabilistic packet marking (PPM). PPM incurs little overhead at routers. However, it requires a flow of marked packets to construct the network path towards their origin. The proposed method for IP trace back is Efficient Packet Marking Algorithm (EPM).

Design of EPM Procedure

- The server will trace back the source using the three fields which are stored in two reserved static address – Start (Ingress router ID), End (Egress router ID) and the hop count distance d.
- Hop Count is a count of the number of routers an IP packet has to pass through in order to reach its destination.
- Initially, when the packet enters the ingress node it is marked with the router ID of the ingress node.
- EPM store edges instead of router. Each edge is marked with start and end addresses and distance from edge to destination node.
- When the packet travels through the path, hop count is incremented for each hop and the mark is maintained till it reaches the egress router (TTL=1).
- When the packet reaches the egress router then the egress router ID is marked and sent to the server.
- All arrived packets in the server are checked for anomaly detection.

- If attack is identified then using the marked fields in the packet the server trace back the origin of attack.

Advantages of EPM Marking

- EPM is a fast, efficient simple reaction based trace back technique.
- EPM stores only the partial path information, so the network overhead is reduced.
- EPM can also be used to trace back the spoofing attacker node. Even though attacker node changes its IP address but it can't change the router ID exchanged between ingress router and itself.
- The marking overhead is low.
- EPM does not incur any storage overhead at routers.
- It can trace both flooding and software exploit DoS attacks.
- Effective means of improving the reliability.

Efficient Packet Marking scheme does not have address implementation in IPv6, the proposed successor of IPv4 which does not have an identification field. Some number of packets sent by the attack are unmarked by the intervening routers. The victim cannot differentiate between these packets and genuinely marked packets.

COMPARISON WITH EXISTING TECHNIQUES

The comparison of the efficient marking technique is carried out based on the following metrics:

- **No. of Packets Required for Trace Back:** It refers to minimum number of packets needed for attack paths reconstruction, reconstruction time; etc .The number of packets depends on the marking probability q at routers and the length of the attack path.
- **Marking Overhead:** IP protocol header does not have a field provisioned for storing packet marking information. It is widely accepted in PPM approaches to overload the 16-bit IP identification field, with the price of backward incompatibility with fragmented IP traffic. Although the 13-bit fragment offset field becomes meaningless when the IP identification field is overloaded, it is a challenging task to overload the fragment offset field. Since receivers regard the IP packets with non-zero fragment offset values as IP fragments, overloading the fragment offset field will collide with all the IP traffic in the Internet both non-fragmented and fragmented. Additional mechanisms must be in place when the fragment offset field is reused for packet marking.
- **Routing Overhead:** IP trace back schemes introduce processing overhead onto the routers in two phases:
  - While creating audit trails on network traffic and
  - While conducting trace back to find out an attack path.

Few other parameters such as time required for trace back, storage, type of marking technique used and the attacking source misuse of trace back techniques were also discussed.

Efficient packet marking algorithm proposed in this research has better performance over the other existing packet marking techniques in terms of number of packets required for trace back, marking and router overhead, etc. The proposed scheme thus enjoys many of the features. Efficient Packet Marking scheme adopts a novel packet marking scheme for IP trace-back which can reconstruct the attack path with less marked packets rapidly. This technique has very low network and router overhead and supports incremental deployment. In contrast to previous work, Efficient Packet Marking techniques have significantly higher precision (lower false positive rate) and lower computation overhead for the victim to reconstruct the attack paths under large scale distributed denial-of service attacks.

The approach of IP trace back is based on Efficient Packet Marking Algorithm and detects the real cause of TCP SYN Flood Attack using Anomaly Detection Algorithm. The imminent threats imposed by DoS attacks call for efficient and fast trace back schemes. Some of the desirable features of a good attack trace back scheme are providing accurate information about routers near the attack source rather than those near the victim. Avoiding the use of large amount of attack packet to construct the attack path or attack tree low processing and storage overhead at intermediate routers.

NETWORK INTRUSION PREVENTIVE STRATEGIES: FLOODING ATTACKS

Chen, S et al (2005), despite the differences in the mechanism, the purpose of the distributed denial of service (DDoS) attack is the same to deplete the resources on the victim's network. DDoS can be broadly divided into two types: bandwidth depletion and resource depletion. Nagaratna, M et al (2009) proposed scheme for protecting DDoS attacks. This section aims to give you a broad over of the various types of DDoS and their prevention techniques.

- **Direct Flood Attack (UDP Flood and Ping Flood):** This type of attack target layer 3 and layer 4 of the OSI model. The primary focus of direct flood attack is to overwhelm the target network with malicious traffic so as legitimate users cannot access the network. For example, if you network can withstand with 20GB of traffic and if the attacker sends you 21GB of traffic, your network will not be able to hand that much traffic. Flooding attacks can utilize UDP and ICMP packets to direct towards that target machine...
  - **Prevention:** To prevent UDP or ICMP flood attack you can Increase your bandwidth. Use load balancers. Or reflect the attack, protection against IP spoofing. Alternatively, you can reroute the malicious traffic to a third party data center by subscribing to a DDoS protection service provider.
- **Reflection Attack:** The idea behind reflection attack is to spoof the source IP of the packet. The attackers spoof the source IP so that it appears to come from a victim machine. When the attackers send spoofed IP to a number of machines, they reply to the spoofed address (the IP of the victim machine). If the victim's network and servers does not have enough resource to cope with the reply packet, it becomes inaccessible to the users.
  - **Prevention:** Implement ant spoofing technique in your network to detect and discard spoofed source IP address.
- **Smurf and Fraggle Attack:** Both types of attack exploit the router's broadcast address. In smurf attacks, a large number of spoofed ICMP traffic is sent to the target router's broadcast address, whereas a fraggle attack sends spoofed UDP traffic to a router's broadcast IP address. The goals of both the attacks are same-to make the network inoperable.

- ◦ **Prevention:** Configure your router and other network devices properly so as no can exploit the IP broadcasting facility of your router.
- **(TCP) SYN Flood Attack:** TCP SYN attack takes advantage of TCP three-way handshake process where a client sends a request (SYN or synchronize packet) to a server and the server responds with a SYN-ACK packet to the clients. Next, the client sends an ACK packet to start the connection. In this type of attack, client do not send ACK packet to the server. If the server does not receive any ACK, it waits for some time, causing the server resources engaged for listening to the ACK messages. When all of the server's resource gets exhausted, it cannot receive any more new connection request, making the server unavailable to the users.

Sometime, the attackers send spoofed IP addresses to server, making the server sends respond to such a client that never send a SYN request to that server. Since the spoofed IP never sends any SYN request to the server, it never responds to the server's SYN-ACK message.

You can implement a number of method to fight SYN flood attack such as filtering, increasing backlog, reducing SYN-RECEIVED Timer, recycling half-opened TCP connection, SYN caching, SYN cookies, firewalls etc.

- **HTTP Flood (Web Spidering):** This type of attacks use web spider to crawl websites in order to exhaust server's resources.
    - ◦ **Prevention:** Make sure your allow only a well-known bots such as Google bots or Bing bots to crawl your website.
- **PUSH and ACK Attack:** This type of attacks is similar to SYN flood attack. The only difference between a PUSH and ACK attack and a SYN Flood attack is that the former one sends TCP packets by setting PUSH and ACK bit to a value of one, which makes the target machine to load data into its buffer and sends back an Acknowledge packet. When the number of TCP packets with PUSH and ACK bit on exceeds the capacity of the buffer of the victim's machine, it overloads the target machine and causes it to crash.
- **Land Attack:** In this type of attack an IP packet is created where the source address and source port number remains the same as the destination address and destination port number.Land attack makes the target machine to reply to its own packets, making the system to crash eventually.
- **DNS Amplification Attacks:** The attacker send as DNS queries using spoofed IP address(IP address of the victim's machine) to a number of open DNS resolvers. The DNS resolvers respond to all the requests to that spoofed IP, which is the victim's IP. As you know the packet size of DNS response is normally 50 times greater than that of the requests, the client machine get overwhelmed with responses when a large number of resolvers start sending responses.

To prevent DNS reflection attack, use anti-spoofing technique, load balancers or spread the attack traffic to your other server with the help of anycast IP address.

- **Layer 7 Attacks:** This is also known as application level DDoS attack, where specific functions of a web application are targeted. For example, web servers keep opening new thread for each connection request and each new connection consume server's capacity to handle more traffic. At some point, server becomes unable to receive new connection; denying new visitors want to visit to webpages. This kind of situation can also occur when you site get popular or receive huge number of sudden traffic from social media.

The way to protect your server against resource exhausting attack or situation is to increase more capacity or buy on-demand cloud computing solution, optimize your web server's performance.

- **Multi-Vector Attacks:** It is not a specific type of attack; rather it is a technique that utilizes various types of DDoS at the same time. Instead of attacking a server using only SYN flood attack, the attacker can use DNS reflection attacks, UDP and ICMP flooding attacks as well. You need to remember that multi-vector attacks are more concerted and difficult to mitigate.

CENTRALIZED WORM DETECTOR (CWD) TECHNIQUE

The explosive growth of the new worms' number and severity of their destructive impact has attracted growing interest and resulted in a big number of articles dedicated to their behavior, control, and recovery. Modern worms are capable of gaining control over a substantial portion of the Internet hosts within several minutes. No human mediated response is possible to stop an attack that is so rapid.

Detecting worms is important, but it is just as important to stop them from spreading. If a worm can be found ahead of infection, say if the system detects the worm by its signature at the border gateway, the system can try to block the worm and prevent any machine from being infected. But this is not the case most of the time. System administrators and users do not realize there is a worm attack until a victim is having some abnormal behavior and the damage has already been caused. Reacting quickly and minimizing the damage after infection is as important as preventing and detecting worms. At this point, the worm is found to exist. Those characteristics used for detection no longer matter. Containment systems are needed to eliminate worms.

Controlled Packet Transmission (CPT) technique effectively detects the presence of C-Worms. The next aim is to detect the C-Worm node and recover the network which is affected by the C-Worms. Since C-Worm slows down the entire network, it is necessary to develop a mechanism to ensure the network from further attack or worm propagation. Hence to accomplish this idea, a secure and an effective algorithm based on the method of digital signature called Centralized Worm Detector (CWD) has been proposed. CWD enables the authentication of nodes on packet transmission. Using CWD algorithm, nodes are recovered from the C-Worms. A new detection technique called Centralized Worm Detector (CWD) technique using digital signatures has been proposed to eliminate and to recover the network affected by camouflaging worms. Finally this chapter also proves the efficiency of the proposed architecture by comparison with the existing techniques in terms of detection rate, time and maximal infection ratio.

Digital Signature

Applications such as secure e-mail and credit card transactions over the Internet use digital signature. Since a digital signature is just a sequence of zeroes and ones, it is desirable for it to have the following properties: the signature must be a bit pattern that depends on the message being signed. The signature must use some information that is unique to the sender to prevent both forgery and denial; it must be relatively easy to produce; it must be relatively easy to recognize and verify the authenticity of digital signature; it must be computationally infeasible to forge a digital signature either by constructing a new message for an existing digital signature or constructing a fraudulent digital signature for a given message; and it must be practical to get copies of the digital signatures in storage for arbitrating possible disputes later.

To verify that the received document is indeed from the claimed sender and that the contents have not been altered, several procedures, called authentication techniques, have been developed. However, message authentication techniques cannot be directly used as digital signatures due to inadequacies of authentication techniques. For example, although message authentication protects the two parties exchanging messages from a third party, it does not protect the two parties against each other. In addition, elementary authentication schemes produce signatures that are as long as the message themselves.

Creating a Digital Signature

In the symmetric key system, a secret key known only to the sender and the legitimate receiver is used. However, there must be a unique key between any two pairs of users. Thus, as the number of user pair increases, it becomes extremely difficult to generate, distribute, and keep track of the secret keys. A public key cryptosystem, on the other hand, uses a pair of keys: a private key, known only to its owner, and a public key, known to everyone who wishes to communicate with the owner. For confidentiality of the message to be sent to the owner, it would be encrypted with the owner's public key, which now could only be decrypted by the owner, the person with the corresponding private key. For purposes of authentication, a message would be encrypted with the private key of the originator or sender, who we will refer to as A. This message could be decrypted by anyone using the public key of A. If this yields the proper message, then it is evident that the message was indeed encrypted by the private key of A, and thus only A could have sent it. The general digital signature creation is shown in Figure 7.

Verifying Digital Signature

A hash function is applied to the message that yields a fixed-size message digest. The signature function uses the message digest and the sender's private key to generate the digital signature. A very simple form of the digital signature is obtained by encrypting the message digest using the sender's private key. The message and the signature can now be sent to the recipient. The message is unencrypted and

Figure 7. Digital signature creation

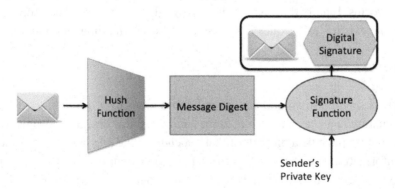

can be read by anyone. However, the signature ensures authenticity of the sender. At the receiver, the inverse signature function is applied to the digital signature to recover the original message digest. The received message is subjected to the same hash function to which the original message was subjected. The resulting message digest is compared with the one recovered from the signature. If they match, then it ensures that the message has indeed been sent by the (claimed) sender and that it has not been altered. The verification scheme of digital signature is shown in Figure 8.

Digital Signatures in Real Applications

Applications such as banking, stock trading, and the sale and purchase of merchandise are increasingly emphasizing electronic transactions to minimize operational costs and provide enhanced services. This has led to phenomenal increases in the amounts of electronic documents that are generated, processed, and stored in computers and transmitted over networks. This electronic information handled in these applications is valuable and sensitive and must be protected against tampering by malicious third parties (who are neither the senders nor the recipients of the information). Sometimes, there is a need to prevent the information or items related to it (such as date/time it was created, sent, and received) from being tampered with by the sender (originator) and/or the recipient.

Increasingly, digital signatures are being used in secure e-mail and credit card transactions over the Internet. The two most common secure e-mail systems using digital signatures are Pretty Good Privacy and Secure/ Multipurpose Internet Mail Extension. Both of these systems support the RSA as well as the DSS-based signatures. The most widely used system for the credit card transactions over the Internet is Secure Electronic Transaction (SET). It consists of a set of security protocols and formats to enable prior existing credit card payment infrastructure to work on the Internet. The digital signature scheme used in SET is similar to the RSA scheme.

Figure 8. Verification of digital signature

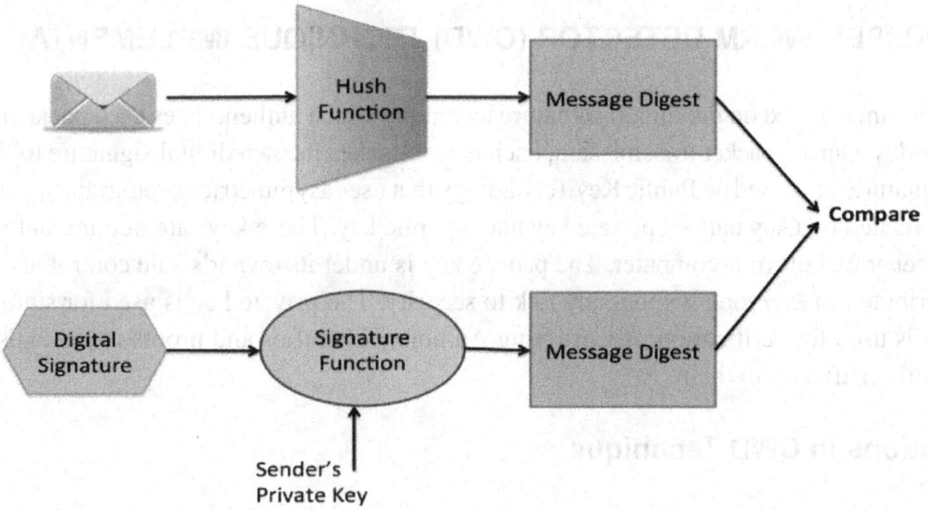

Table 2. Comparison with the existing techniques

Criteria	Existing Techniques			Proposed Techniques	
	VAR (Variance Based)	**TREND (Trend Based)**	**MEAN (Volume Mean Based)**	**MCPT (Modified Controlled Packet Transmission)**	**MCWD (Modified Centralized Worm Detector)**
Detection rate	Medium	NULL	Very Low	High	Very High
Maximal infection ratio	Low	FULL	Low	Low	Low
Detection time(minutes) for 500 worm	High	Infinite	Medium	Medium	Low
Detection time(minutes) for one worm	High	Infinite	Medium	Medium	Low

TWO FISH ALGORITHM

The algorithm used for encryption and decryption in digital signatures is similar to the two fish algorithm. Two fish is a block cipher by Counterpane Labs. It was one of the five Advanced Encryption Standard (AES) finalists. Two fish is unpatented, and the source code is uncopyrighted and license-free; it is free for all uses. Table 2 describes the performance of two fish algorithm.

Two fish is a 128-bit block cipher that accepts a variable-length key up to 256 bits. The cipher is a 16-round Feistel network with a *F* function made up of four key-dependent 8-by-8-bit S-boxes, a fixed 4-by-4 maximum distance separable matrix over $GF(2^8)$, a pseudo-Hadamard transform, bitwise rotations, and a carefully designed key schedule. A fully optimized implementation of Two fish encrypts on a Pentium Pro at 17.8 clock cycles per byte, and an 8-bit smart card implementation encrypts at 1660 clock cycles per byte. Two fish can be implemented in hardware in 14000 gates. The design of both the round function and the key schedule permits a wide variety of tradeoffs between speed, software size, key setup time, gate count, and memory.

CENTRALISED WORM DETECTOR (CWD) TECHNIQUE IMPLEMENTATION

CWD algorithm is based on the digital signature technique which authenticates each packet transmitted between nodes. During packet transmission, each node attaches its own digital signature to the packets. Digital Signatures are based on Public Key Technology that uses asymmetric cryptography. Each person's identity is related to a key pair - a private key and a public key. These keys are nothing but mathematical codes generated on your computer. The private key is under its owner's sole control and the public key is distributed to everyone without any risk to security. The private key is used for signing and the public key is used for verification. A Certifying Authority identifies and proofs individuals before issuing digital certificates to them.

Assumptions in CWD Technique

The assumption which is used to develop CWD algorithm is that digital signatures will be in encrypted hexadecimal format. Each node in the network has its own signature and they are tamper resistant so that it cannot be duplicated by any other node. Nodes which transmit the packet will attach its digital signature with the transmitted packet. At the receiver, the node uses the public key to decrypt the encrypted signature. This assumption works only if the sender is a normal node. In case of C-Worms, the sender C-Worm node will generate the signature. But at the receiver it cannot be decrypted with the public key. The reason is that C-Worm cannot tamper the digital signature of the legitimate sender node. So the C-Worm node generates digital signature of its own.

Architecture of Modified Centralized Worm Detector (CWD) Technique

Developing a solution for authenticating each node, the Centralized Worm Detector (CWD) algorithm has been introduced. In this technique, a master node which is a centralized node is maintained.

Figure 9 depicts the architecture of Modified Centralized Worm Detector technique which ensures the authentication of nodes in the network by monitoring the packet transmissions in the network. Master Node is intended to maintain the digital signatures of all the legitimate nodes in the network. Whenever the packet is sent by a sender node, it is been stamped with the signature of the sender. The receiver tries to decrypt this signature using the public key in common. If it can decrypt, the receiver node will accept the packet. Else, it will send the digital signature to the master node. The master node will check for the signature. If it is present, then it intimates the node which raised the request to allow the packet in the network. If the signature is not present, then it will block the packet and discard the node from which the packet has been received.

A Centralized master node is maintained in the network. This master node does not involve in the transmission of packet in the network. It is used to monitor the entire network as a watchdog of the packet

Figure 9. Modified Centralized Worm Detector (MCWD) architecture

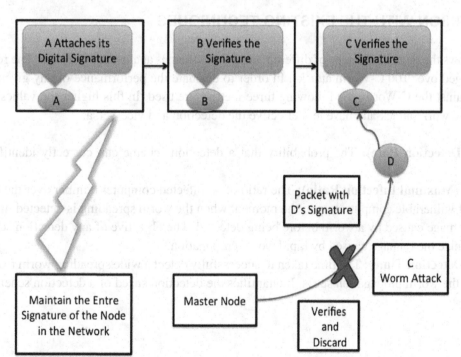

transmission. Also, the master node maintains the signature of each node in the network. When Node A starts sending the packets it attaches its digital signature and forwards to Node B. Node B can receive the packet only when it can decrypt the encrypted packet with the key of its own, since a normal node can decrypt by using the key common to the legitimate node in the network. Worms other than the normal node also generate signatures of hexadecimal values. But they cannot decrypt the normal node packet as it has a digital signature attached to it. When a normal node receives a packet it first tries to decrypt the packet with the public key of it. If it can decrypt, it will accept the packet. But when it cannot decrypt the packet, it automatically reports to the master node.

Master node will go to this unknown node and ask for the signature of the node. If the signature given by the unknown node matches the signature maintained in the network then it intimates the node to accept the packet which reported to check for anomaly. Else the unknown node is taken as a malicious one and it is discarded from the network by the master node. This technique is used not only to detect and recover C-Worm but it can also recover any type of worm in the network.

Advantages of Modified Centralized Worm Detector

- Modified Centralized Worm Detector technique can be used for any type of worm detection and recovery of the affected network.
- All the nodes are authenticated and Digital signatures are tamper proof such that the malicious node cannot duplicate it.
- Two fish algorithm which is used for encryption and decryption of digital signatures are extensively crypt analyzed, unpatented, uncopyrighted and license free.
- Digital signatures are used to detect the known attacks reliability.

COMPARISON WITH THE EXISTING TECHNIQUES

Table 2 shows the detection results of different detection schemes against the C-Worm. The results have been averaged over 100 C-Worm attacks. In order to evaluate the performance of any given detection scheme against the C-Worm, the following three metrics are used. In this higher the values, the more effective the worm attack and have less effective the detection and vice-versa.

- **DR (Detection Rate):** The probability that a detection scheme can correctly identify a worm attack.
- **MIR (Maximal Infection Ratio):** The ratio of an infected computer number over the total number of vulnerable computers up to the moment when the worm spreading is detected. It quantifies the damage caused by a worm before being detected. The objective of any detection scheme is to minimize the damage caused by rapid worm propagation.
- **DT (Detection Time):** The time taken to successfully detect a wide spreading worm from the moment the worm propagation starts. It quantifies the detection speed of a detection scheme.

The objective of any detection scheme is to minimize the damage caused by rapid worm propagation. Hence, MIR and DT can be used to quantify the effectiveness of any worm detection scheme. Modified Controlled Packet Transmission (MCPT) and Modified Centralized Worm Detector (MCWD) techniques achieve good DT performance in addition to the high detection rate values indicated above. In contrast, the detection time of existing detection schemes have relatively larger values. Since the detection rate values for the existing detection schemes are relatively small, obtaining low values of MIR for those schemes are not as significant as those for MCPT and MCWD.

Thus Modified Centralized Worm Detector technique is highly efficient than the Modified Controlled Packet Transmission technique in terms of its detection performance. Still MCPT technique is very much effective than the other existing schemes.

A novel approach for the recovery of the entire network from the C-Worm known as Modified Centralized Worm Detector (MCWD) mechanism has been developed. It is a centralized approach as the master node functions like a centralized node by maintaining the signatures of the node in the network. This is also known as Watch Dog Worm Detector mechanism because the master nodes act as a watch dog for the entire network and monitor the network. This MCWD technique uses the concept of digital signature in which the algorithm used for encryption and decryption is similar to the two fish algorithm used in many applications. Since Digital signatures are tamper proof the malicious node cannot duplicate it. Hence this technique is not only used to detect and recover the network from C-Worm but it is also used to recover from any type of worm.

NETWORK INTRUSION PREVENTION STRATEGIES: WORM ATTACKS

A worm is similar to a virus, apart from the fact that a worm manages to spread from computer to computer, without any user intervention. A worm is capable of replicating itself within a system and propagating undisturbed in multiple copies within the network infrastructure, infecting unsuspicious hosts in this way.

Worms may lead to system crashing due to their replication behavior which leads to excess memory consumption and eventually system crashing. Moreover, their ability to traverse network boundaries may lead to bandwidth exhaustion and service faulty operation. Recent worm attacks include opening backdoors for malicious users to remotely gain access to your system.

- **Network IPS:** Special hardware device is used which has many interfaces and is placed at the heart of the network in a place where there is traffic aggregation so that it could analyze and detect malicious packets. Its traffic analysis is based on stateful (keep-on going while session is active in bidirectional way) policies and firewall filtering rules. Attacks that exist at the low levels of the OSI model (layers 1 up to 3) can be identified and eliminated. Moreover, informative alerts can be triggered to inform the network manager for malicious traffic flows.
- **Host IPS:** Almost always, A HIP consists of specialized software that is installed on the host and its job is to monitor the activities of the specific host. The HIPS is able to monitor the operating system processes and protect system resources by using deep analysis methods and signature filters in conjunction with first class antivirus, application and network firewalls in one package

SUMMARY AND CONCLUSION

Denial of Service (DoS) attacks such as TCP SYN Flood attacks pose great security threat to the network. Trace back is an important step in defending against such DoS attacks. IP trace back facilitates holding attackers accountable and improving the efficacy of mitigation measures. Active worms such as Camouflaging worms wreak havoc by exploiting security loopholes and flaws in software design to propagate from one machine to another. Camouflaging worms (C-Worms) falls under the new category of active worms which conceals its presence by blending with the environment in such a way that it looks analogous to the normal data packet of the network. New detection techniques are thus proposed in this chapter to detect these kinds of threats. The newly developed techniques are simple, easy to launch, compatible and flexible with the current trends and also serve as an efficient mechanism even to recover the affected network. This chapter study proves that the proposed techniques eliminate the limitations of the existing works.

REFERENCES

Al-Duwairi, B., & Govindarasu, M. (2006). Novel hybrid schemes employing packet marking and logging for IP traceback. *IEEE Transactions on Parallel and Distributed Systems, 17*(5), 403–418. doi:10.1109/TPDS.2006.63

Antonatos, S., Akritidis, P., Markatos, E., & Anagnostakis, K. (2005). Defending against hitlist worms using network address space randomization. *Computer Networks*, 3471–3490.

Chen, S., & Song, Q. (2005). *Perimeter-based defense against high bandwidth DDoS attacks. IEEE Trans. Parallel Distrib. Syst.*

Gavaskar, S., Surendiran, R., & Ramaraj, E. (2010). Three Counter Defense Mechanism for TCP SYN Flooding Attacks. *International Journal of Computer Applications,* 12-15.

Gong, C., & Sarac, K. (2008). A More Practical Approach for Single-Packet IP Traceback using Packet Logging and Marking. *IEEE Transactions on Parallel and Distributed Systems, 19*(10), 1310–1324. doi:10.1109/TPDS.2007.70817

Haris, S., Ahmad, R., & Ghani, M. (2010). Detecting TCP SYN Flood Attack Based on Anomaly Detection.*2010 Second International Conference on Network Applications, Protocols and Services*, (pp. 240-244). doi:10.1109/NETAPPS.2010.50

Katiravan, J., & Chellappan, C. (2011). Improved IP Trace Back Using Pre-Shared Key Authentication Mechanism. *Asian Journal of Information Technology,* 51-54.

Li, P., Salour, M., & Su, X. (2008). A survey of internet worm detection and containment. *IEEE Communications Surveys & Tutorials,* 20-35.

Malliga, S., & Tamilarasi, A. (2008). A hybrid scheme using packet marking and logging for IP traceback. *International Journal of Internet Protocol Technology,* 81-81.

Nagaratna, M., Prasad, V., & Kumar, S. (2009). Detecting and Preventing IP-spoofed DDoS Attacks by Encrypted Marking Based Detection and Filtering (EMDAF).*2009 International Conference on Advances in Recent Technologies in Communication and Computing.* doi:10.1109/ARTCom.2009.167

Ohsita, Y., Ata, S., & Murata, M. (2004). Detecting distributed denial-of-service attacks by analyzing TCP SYN packets statistically. *IEEE Global Telecommunications Conference, 2004. GLOBECOM '04*, accessed on 3rd February 2016 doi:10.1109/GLOCOM.2004.1378371

Thorat, S. A., Khandelwal, A. K., Bruhadeshwar, B., & Kishore, K. (2008). Payload Content based Network Anomaly Detection. *2008 First International Conference on the Applications of Digital Information and Web Technologies (ICADIWT)*, 127-132. Doi: , accessed on 3rd February 2016 doi:10.1109/ICADIWT.2008.4664331

Wang, H., Zhang, D., & Shin, K. G. (2002). Detecting SYN flooding attacks. *Proceedings.Twenty-First Annual Joint Conference of the IEEE Computer and Communications Societies*, 1530-1539. , accessed on 3rd February 2016 doi:10.1109/INFCOM.2002.1019404

Yu, W., Wang, X., Calyam, P., Xuan, D., & Zhao, W. (2011). Modeling and Detection of Camouflaging Worm. *IEEE Transactions on Dependable and Secure Computing IEEE Trans. Dependable and Secure Comput.*, *8*(3), 377–390. accessed on 3rd February 2016. doi:10.1109/tdsc.2010.13

Yu, W., Wang, X., Xuan, D., & Lee, D. (2006). Effective Detection of Active Worms with Varying Scan Rate. *2006 Securecomm and Workshops*, 1-10, doi: , accessed on 3rd February 2016 Xiang, Y., & Li, Z. (2006). An Analytical Model for DDoS Attacks and Defense. *International Multi-Conference on Computing in the Global Information Technology - (ICCGI'06)*, accessed on 3rd February 201610.1109/seccomw.2006.359549

Zou, C., Gao, L., Gong, W., & Towsley, D. (2003). Monitoring and early warning for internet worms. *Proceedings of the 10th ACM Conference on Computer and Communication Security - CCS '03*, accessed on 3rd February 2016 doi:10.1145/948109.948136

Section 4
Visual Information Security

Chapter 13
A Systematic Mapping of Security Mechanisms

Gayathri RajaKumaran
VIT University, India

NeelaNarayanan Venkataraman
VIT University, India

ABSTRACT

In the Internet Era, millions of computer systems are connected to the Internet and the number is increasing infinitely. Maintaining proper Control and configuration for all such networked systems has proved to be impossible. This loophole makes the Internet systems vulnerable to various type of attacks. The objective of this research is to systematically identify a wide list of attacks in transport, session and application layers (Host layers). 148 effective controls are identified for the security attacks in addition to the 113 standard controls. The identified controls are analyzed in order to map and categorize them to the corresponding security layers wise.

INTRODUCTION

Internet is a dynamic environment in terms of both topology and emerging technology. Internet contains millions of connected computer networks that are accessible through the set of communication protocols; one among them is the Transmission Control Protocol / Internet Protocol (TCP/IP). Diverse categories of end users scattered throughout the globe are accessing Internet services for electronic mail, personal interaction, entrepreneurial ventures, e-commerce, and e-business and so on. However, along with its advantages and immense benefits, the internet is facing security risks. The key design feature of the internet makes it vulnerable to various kinds of attacks. Attack is an attempt to destroy, expose, alter, disable, steal or gain unauthorized access to or make unauthorized use of an asset. This is done by exploiting vulnerabilities in a computer system. The person who is involved in launching such attacks are categorized as attacker, hacker or cracker based on their motive. The need for attacking the computer system has changed over the years. Few years back, attacks are launched "by hand" as there are no sophisticated tools. But in recent years, more automatic attack generation tools are introduced

DOI: 10.4018/978-1-5225-0193-0.ch013

which makes the attack easy to launch. Intruders are Utilizing the automated tools to coordinate large scale distributed attacks by targeting hundreds of hosts. Hence all such drawbacks makes the Internet open to severe security attacks like eavesdropping, sniffing, IP spoofing, ARP poisoning and Distributed Denial Of Service (DDoS) attack. Security professionals are involved in developing an effective countermeasure to nullify the attacks. But the solutions are proven to be efficient only for known or identified attacks. The drawback in implementing the solution is, most of the Internet users are unaware that their system is under attack. Hence categorization of attacks and key points for attack identification plays a vital role. This motivation drives us to carry out a comprehensive study aimed at systematically identifying, analyzing and classifying the security attacks in the host layer.

A mapping study provides systematic and objective procedure for identifying the nature and extent of the empirical study data that is available to a specific research domain. The mapping process consists of the activities searching for relevant publications, definition of a classification scheme and mapping of publications.

INTERNET INFRASTRUCTURE ATTACKS

Attacks on the Internet infrastructure can lead to more destruction because different components have implicit relationship with each other. To provide solution for these attacks, Internet infrastructure attacks are broadly classified into the below four categories (Gayathri & Neelanarayanan, 2013):

- DNS Hacking,
- Route table poisoning,
- Packet mistreatment,
- Denial of Service.

The attacks are classified according to the above major category. Few of the attacks are listed below:

- Interruption,
- Modification,
- Fabrication,
- Replication,
- Link state,
- Distance vector,
- Interruption.

The impact caused only by the major attacks and general solution measures are tabulated. In this survey, all possible solutions are not provided related to the real time scenario. The attacks considered are restricted to types of DDoS, packet mistreating and link state attacks. The vulnerabilities caused by each attacks and its corresponding impact are not considered.

Present data security (Chakrabarthi & Manimaran, 2002) measures ensure confidentiality and integrity of data. Various solutions and drawbacks are identified in this survey specific to the transport and network layers. Major components in this analysis process are:

- Authentication measure,
- Authorization process,
- Storage mechanism,
- Trust,
- Identity,
- Anonymity,
- Privacy.

Distributed Denial of Service (Khan, Alghathbar, Sher & Rashid, 2010) is a rapid growing problem in the current Internet Infrastructure. More surveys are conducted each year specific to the DDoS attacks (Mirkovic & Reiher,2004; Peng, Leckie & Ramamohanarao, 2007; Xie & Yu, 2009) aiming to provide prevention measures and feasible solution to mitigate from the attack. Each of these performs attack classification criteria uniquely in the way of perpetrating DDoS attack, attack motives, vulnerabilities and analysis of existing defense mechanisms.

ATTACK MOTIVATIONS

With the development of large open networks, security threats have increased significantly. More security attacks are happening every day because today anyone can become a hacker by downloading tools from the internet. Hackers have discovered more network vulnerabilities as the hacking tools require no hacking knowledge for launching an attack. This made the internet open to severe threats like virus, worms, Trojan horse and other malicious threats. Motivation for such security threat or attack could be:

- Profit,
- Protest,
- Challenge,
- Personal gain,
- Revenge,
- Vandalism,
- Fame,
- Economic gain,
- Espionage.

ATTACK CLASSIFICATION

The authors have analyzed broad categories of security attack in the host layers. Each attack falls into the basic attack classification namely active and passive. An active attack (side channel attack) (Yaar, Perrig & Song, 2003) attempts to alter the system resources or affects the usual operation. A passive attack (fault attack) attempts learn or make use of the information from the system. The attacks in the host layers alone are focused. The below Figure 1 depicts general categories of attacks Specific to the host layers.

Figure 1. Distributed denial of service attack
Trinoo (Douligeris & Mitrokotsa, 2004; Criscuolo, 2000; Criscuilo & Rathbun,1999) is a first DDoS attack tool which is of widespread use. It is a bandwidth depletion attack tool.

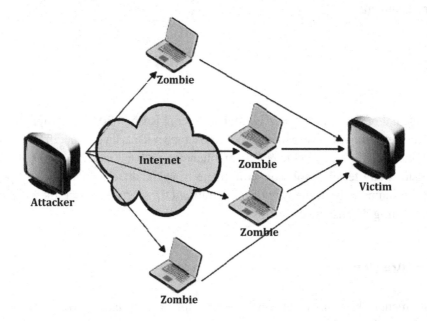

Numerous attacks are happening everyday by exploiting the vulnerabilities introduced during the design of Internet components. Out of which, some common attacks (Lin, 2011) are identified in wired network systems and the attacks are analyzed in order to map them to the corresponding layers. Each of the identified attacks are listed and explained below

- **Distributed Denial of Service Attack (DDoS):** A DDoS attack is one in which an attacker intentionally tries to deny access to a specific victim or target. It is done by sending large volume of useless packets from different locations on the internet. This attack disrupts the communication of the legitimate client with the web server and consumes network bandwidth by posing bogus packets. The first DDoS attack (Adeyinka, 2008) is reported in large web sites (Garber, 2000) such as Yahoo, Amazon, Buy.com, eBay, CNN.com. Usually, Large scale DDoS attacks (Yu, 2013; Gengler, 2001; Moore, Shannon, Brown, Voelker & Savage, 2006) will target the top rated Internet sites. DDoS is relatively simple but a very powerful attack to disrupt the Internet resources. The goal of this attack (Wurzinger, Platzer, Ludl, Kirda & Kruegel, 2009) is to overwhelm one or more server resources so that the legitimate clients may experience high delays or lower throughputs thereby eliminating the intended client's server capacity. It can be detected by constant monitoring of two-way traffic flows between the communicating parties. Refer Figure 1 to understand the DDoS attack scenario. The steps in DDoS are illustrated as below:
  - Identify vulnerable hosts,
  - Build network of computers for denying service,
  - Gaining access to the vulnerable systems,

- ◦ Install attack tools on the compromised hosts of the network. The compromised hosts of the attack network are termed as Zombies. The vulnerable design of the internet system provides opportunities for the attackers to launch different attack categories. Below are the few security issues:
  - ▪ Internet security is highly interdependent,
  - ▪ Internet resources are limited,
  - ▪ Intelligence and resources are not collocated,
  - ▪ No accountability,
  - ▪ Distributed resources.

- **Cross Site Scripting Attack (XSS):** XSS is a type of injection in which malicious scripts are injected into web application. These attacks occur when an attacker uses a web application to send malicious code in the form of a browser side script to a different user. Flaws that allow these attacks are quite widespread. XSS enables the construction of phishing attack. Refer Figure 2 for XSS attack. Using XSS attacks (Tiwari & Padhye, 2011), the below attacks can be launched:
  - ◦ Session hijacking,
  - ◦ Phishing attack.

- **Stored Attack:** Stored attack happens through embedding of malicious Java script in web server whereas the reflected attack is launched via sending email messages to the targeted user. If the user clicks on the fake link, the code which is injected in that link moves to the web application and will get reflected back to the targeted user's browser.
  - ◦ Reflected attack.

Figure 2. XSS attack

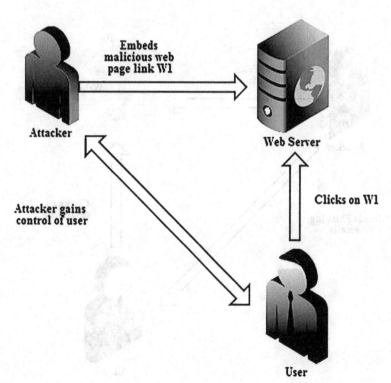

- **Phishing:** Phishing is a technique used to acquire personal information for the purpose of identity theft and fraudulent email messages. The main targets for the phishing attack are credit card numbers, account numbers and passwords, and social security number. It uses email messages that appear to be come from the legitimate source and it looks authentic and official. Once the link is clicked, it will result in financial losses or other fraudulent activity. Many users (Kirda, Kruegel, Vigna & Jovonovic, 2006) lack the knowledge of the working of Operating System, applications, email and web page. Refer Figure 3 for Phishing attack. The first Phishing attack (Shema, 2012) using the vulnerabilities in Internet Explorer was reported on December 18, 2003. Till 2003, 7.8% of various Phishing attacks have been reported. Phishing is successful because of the below listed drawbacks
  - Lack of computer system knowledge,
  - Lack of knowledge of security and security indicators,
  - Lack of attention on security mechanisms,
  - No proper checking of security controls,
  - Unclear text information.
- **Brute Force Attack:** Brute force attack is a trial and error method to gain information from the user such as password or personal identification number. To launch this attack, usually automated software is used to make desired number of guesses based on all possible combinations. It is targeted to any specific victim to crack the encrypted data or positively it can be used by the security professionals to test the organization's level of network perimeter security. This attack is also termed as dictionary attack. Brute force attacks are launched to targeting the encryption mechanisms, block ciphers, RC4 ciphers and Data Encryption Standard (Mirkovic & Reiher, 2004).

Figure 3. Phishing

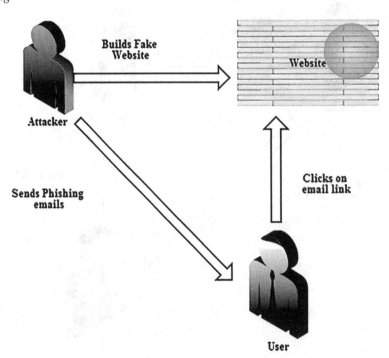

Figure 4. Masquerading

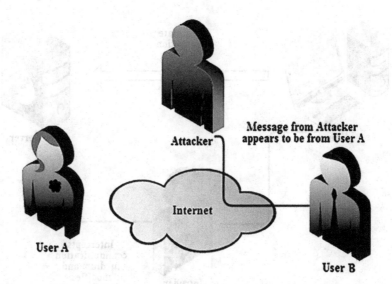

- **Spoofing:** Spoofing is an active security attack (Gupta & Kumaraguru, 2014; Tsudik, 1992) in which any one machine in the network masquerades as the different machine. In this attack, source IP address is forged by the attacker. Many protocols in the TCP/IP protocol suite do not provide any mechanism for authentication. Hence they are vulnerable to spoofing attacks because precautions are not taken by the applications to verify the identity of the sending or receiving host. Below are some of the spoofing categories.
  ◦ IP spoofing,
  ◦ Caller ID spoofing,
  ◦ Email address spoofing,
  ◦ GPS spoofing,
  ◦ Referrer spoofing.
- **Masquerading:** Masquerade attack uses fake identity to gain unauthorized access to personal computer information. These attacks are targeted to acquire stolen passwords and logos. Attacks can be triggered either by someone inside the organization or by an outsider by exploiting vulnerabilities in the authorization process. Once the intruder gains the valid password of the legitimate user, he can pretend to the outside world that he is a legitimate user. Unauthorized password is the most common category of electronic masquerading. If an outsider is able to steal or guess a password of legitimate user, there is no built-in mechanism available in the computer system to identify which person is performing login using the valid credentials. A person who is involved in launching these attacks is termed as the Masquerader. A Masquerader may get access to legitimate user account (Howard & Longstaff, 1998) either by stealing credentials or through break in and installation of rootkit which is depicted in Figure 4.
- **Man in the Middle Attack (MIM):** Man in the middle attack is an exploit in which the intruder intercepts the communication between the end user and website. Attacker uses the intercepted information to perform identity theft. It is a form of active eavesdropping in which the attacker

Figure 5. MIM

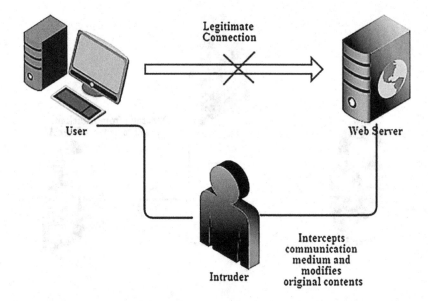

makes independent connections with the end user and relays messages between them. These attacks can utilize the readily available tools like airsnarf (Salem & Stolfo, 2011). Figure 5 depicts the MIM attack. Some of the MIM attack tools are listed below.

- PacketCreator,
- Ettercap,
- Dsniff,
- Cain and Abel.

- **Statistics Hacking:** Statistics hacking is a technique in which an attacker modifies the system usage statistics. This attack refers to the situation that a resource is available to the user for acceptable usage but the user modifies the restricted system resources which is not permitted even to a legitimate user. It is different from other forms of hacking as its target is only the system usage. The attacker termed as the malicious user gains unauthorized control and access to the host system resources and modification is done manually. Below are names of some of the leading news websites affected by this hacking type.

- BBC,
- CNN,
- MSNBC,
- BusinessWeek,
- ABC News.

- **Smishing:** This attack is also termed as SMS Phishing. It is type of criminal activity carried out using social engineering techniques. SMS phishing uses cell phone text messages to deliver the bait to induce users to divulge their personal information. Website URL is used to capture the personal information from user. The phishing messages usually contain messages that demands immediate attention by the user. Smishing is a technique that makes use of text messages to initiate a scam. Refer Figure 6 for Smishing attack.

Figure 6. Smishing attack

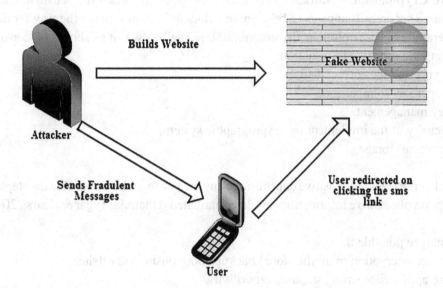

- **Data Diddling:** Data Diddling is the process of altering the data contents before or after entry in the computer system. This attack is launched to collapse the integrity of the stored information. Main aim is to steal the stored record details specific to the application which is depicted in Figure 7.

Figure 7. Data diddling attack

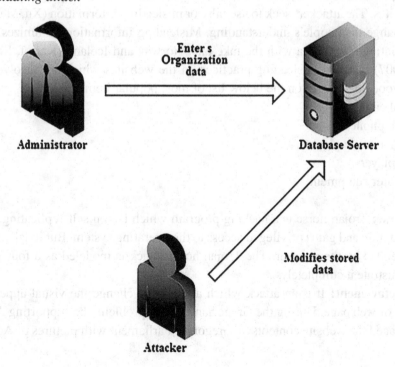

- **Insecure Cryptographic Storage**: This vulnerability occurs when the sensitive encrypted data is not stored securely. It appears to be a single vulnerability but it paves the way for the collection of vulnerabilities (Brustoloni & Brustoloni, 2005). The below things should be considered while encrypting the sensitive information:
  - Encrypting the correct data,
  - Proper key storage,
  - Key management,
  - Security of the implementing cryptographic system,
  - Database storage.

If the attacker retrieves the sensitive data through any means, to make it unusable the steps in performing the encryption of sensitive information should be hardened (Dhamija, Tygar & Hearst, 2006) as below

  - Analyze possible threats,
  - Ensure encryption of all the stored backups both onsite and offsite,
  - Use appropriate strong standard algorithms,
  - Strong keys,
  - Ensure all keys and passwords are protected from unauthorized access.
- **DNS Hijacking:** DNS Hijacking is the process of redirecting the resolution of Domain Name System (DNS) queries. China has the complex censorship system which includes DNS Hijacking (Pape, 2014). In this attack, the attacker steals the victims' information by acquiring domain name of the website and redirects that website traffic to his own forged web site by making the victims to click on the fake links. Dynamic pharming (Jellal, 2002) is a new attack which hijacks the DNS by designing a javascript to monitor the user interactions with trusted web site.
- **Misleading Information on Websites:** This attack focuses on modifying the displayed contents on the websites. The attackers seek to use false or misleading information (Xu, Mao & Halderman, 2011) to change the people's understanding. Misleading information minimizes the opportunity of differentiating actual data with the fake one. Norway and Iceland (Karlof, Shankar, Tygar & Wagner, 2007) revealed misleading practices on the websites which are involved in selling the electronic goods. It focuses on the below list of most popular items.
  - Digital camera,
  - Mobile phones,
  - Personal music players,
  - DVD players,
  - Computer equipment,
  - Games.
- **Trojan Horse:** Trojan horse is a hacking program which is non self-replicating appears as a legitimate program and gains privileged access to the operating system. But it delivers the malicious content intended by the attacker. The Trojan horse attack is modeled as a four-photon quantum signal to illustrate it completely.
- **Website Defacement:** It is an attack which attempts to change the visual appearance of either the website or web page. During the Gregorian conflict problem, the supporting Activist group of Russia replaced the website contents of Gregorian Parliament with pictures of Adolf Hitler.

- **Email Bomb:** Email bomb is a form of net abuse consisting of sending huge volumes of email to a targeted address in an attempt to overflow the mailbox or overwhelm the server where the email address is hosted. Such huge amount of mail may simply fill the targeted person's disk space on the server which in turn results in server crash. The email bombs can be launched in different attack scenarios which can easily shut down SMTP servers. Sendmail-based SMTP mail relays are used to distributing the flooding emails. The below techniques are used to create powerful email bombs in the Internet.
  - Chain bombs,
  - Error message bombs,
  - Covert distribution,
  - Mail exploder exploitation.
  - **Email Bomb:** Email bomb is one of the most common crimes in the cyberspace. The global and flexible networking infrastructure is used as a basis for attack. These attacks are launched by
    - Disgruntled employees,
    - Terrorists,
    - Industrial competitors.
- **Email Virus:** Email-virus is a computer code that is sent to any of the targeted system as an email-attachment. The link gets activated by clicking and causes unexpected harmful effect. Few effects of such virus type is given below.
  - Destroying certain files on hard disk,
  - Attachment re-emailed to everyone in the target's address book

Many detection mechanisms are available to analyze the spreading behavior of email virus with the intent of providing solutions. But, the topology of email network plays an important role in determining the behavior of such virus spreading. The email virus propagation is compared based on three topologies as listed below.

- Power law,
- Small world,
- Random graph.
- **Worm:** A computer worm is a standalone malware computer program that replicates itself in order to spread to the other computers. Unlike virus, it does not need any human intervention for replication. The effect of worms on targeted computer systems are listed below.
  - Consumes network bandwidth,
  - Increases network traffic.

The motivation for such worm attacks varies depending on the nature of the threat. Some common motivations are

- Experimental curiosity,
- Pride and power,
- Commercial advantage,
- Extortion,

- ○ Criminal gain,
- ○ Random protect,
- ○ Political protest,
- ○ Terrorism,
- ○ Cyber warfare.
- **Botnet:** A botnet is a collection of Internet connected programs communicating with similar programs to perform some task. By breaching the security mechanism implemented in the target computer system, botnet compromises computers and the entire system is under the control of the attacker. Each such compromised system is termed as a bot. The uses of botnets (Deng, Li, Zhou & Zhang, 2005) are listed below.
  - ○ Sending spam emails,
  - ○ Distributed Denial of Service attack,
  - ○ Trojan,
  - ○ Phishing email,
  - ○ Illegally distributing pirated media,
  - ○ Serving phishing sites,
  - ○ Performing click fraud,
  - ○ Stealing personal information.
- **Content Spoofing:** Content spoofing is a type of exploit used by an attacker to present fake or modified website to the victims proving to be a legitimate one. This attack is done to misrepresent the organization or an individual. This attack can be developed by exploiting vulnerabilities in code. This is also referred to as content injection or virtual defacement. Sequence of attack requests for content spoofing is illustrated as below.
  - ○ Attacker transmits login information to the system,
  - ○ System receives and process login information,
  - ○ Attacker requests some content,
  - ○ System retrieves and transfers the content,
  - ○ Attacker alters the content,
  - ○ System receives new content,
  - ○ Attacker requests replacing old content with the new content,
  - ○ System replaces content with new version.
- **Packet Sniffing:** Packet sniffing is the process of monitoring the packets traversing across the network. Packet sniffer tools facilitate the capturing and visualization of network traffic. Some of the tools (Mittal, Shrivastava & Manoria, 2011) are listed below.
  - ○ Ethereal,
  - ○ K sniffer,
  - ○ Snort,
  - ○ IpGrab,
  - ○ IpLog,
  - ○ Wireshark,
  - ○ Cain and abel,
  - ○ Tcpdump,
  - ○ Kismet,
  - ○ Ettercap,

- ◦ NetStumbler,
- ◦ Dsniff,
- ◦ Ntop,
- ◦ Ngrep,
- ◦ EtherApe,
- ◦ NetworkMiner,
- ◦ KisMAC.

- **IP Spoofing:** IP address spoofing or IP spoofing is the creation of Internet Protocol (IP) packets with a forged source IP address to impersonate the sender or any other computing system. IP spoofing is most frequently used in Denial of Service attacks (DoS). DoS attacks that use spoofing randomly choose addresses from the entire IP address space. IP spoofing can also be used by network intruders to defeat the authentication based on IP address. There are many variations on the attack types which employs IP spoofing.
  - ◦ Non blind spoofing,
  - ◦ Blind spoofing,
  - ◦ Man in the Middle attack,
  - ◦ Denial of Service attack.

- **DNS Spoofing:** DNS spoofing or DNS cache poisoning is a computer hacking attack in which data is introduced in DNS name server's cache database to make the name server to return incorrect IP address. It results in diverting traffic to another computer. Once the attacker poisons the DNS traffic, there are number of ways they can subvert protocols that rely on DNS. Some of the methods are
  - ◦ Redirecting network traffic,
  - ◦ Man in the Middle attack.

- **ARP Poisoning:** Address Resolution Protocol (ARP) cache poisoning is a MAC layer attack carried out by an attacker connected to the same local network. Its effectiveness is limited only to network connected with switches, hubs and bridges. The design of wireless access points and network architecture are vulnerable to such type of attacks. Attack scenario is illustrated below
  - ◦ Host C sends ARP reply to B stating that A's IP maps to C's MAC address,
  - ◦ Host C sends ARP reply to A stating that B's IP address maps to C's MAC address,
  - ◦ Hosts A and B updates ARP caches with new information.

- **Port Scanning:** Port scanning is an attack which targets to explore the open ports through probes. Port scanner is a software application designed for this purpose. This is used by administrators to verify the network security policies. The portsweep (Bass, Freyre, Gruber & Watt, 1998) is used to scan multiple hosts for a specific listening port. Attackers frequently conduct host scan and port scan as precursors for their attack. Few Port scanning categories are
  - ◦ TCP scanning,
  - ◦ SYN scanning,
  - ◦ UDP scanning,
  - ◦ ACK scanning,
  - ◦ Window scanning,
  - ◦ FIN scanning.

- **Ping of Death:** Ping of death is a type of attack that involves in sending malicious ping to a target computer system. A ping is normally 56 bytes in size. Sending a ping of larger size may crash the computer system.
- **SYN Flooding:** SYN flood is a category of Denial of Service attack in which an attacker sends successive number of SYN requests to a target system. All the server resources will be consumed by the SYN requests which make the system unresponsive to legitimate connections. The process of TCP 3 way handshake is illustrated below to understand this attack scenario.
  - A client requests connection by sending SYN message to server,
  - Server acknowledges client request by sending back SYN-ACK,
  - Client responds with ACK,
  - Connection is established between client and server .

In case of SYN flood attack, client will respond to the server with ACK. The server will be continuously waiting for the acknowledgement which results in network congestion.

- **Cross Site Request Forgery (CSRF):** In this attack, a system is exploited by tricking it to use its authoritative information on behalf of the attacker. The targeted system is allowed to respond to client requests but it behaves in a way intended by the attacker. The possibilities of CSRF attacks are related to the below situations.
  - Buying a book online,
  - Changing passwords,
  - Transferring funds.
- **Cyberstalking:** Cyberstalking (Zou, Gong & Towsley, 2002) is the use of Internet or other electronic means to harass an individual or an organization. Some forms of this attack are listed below.
  - Making false accusations,
  - Monitoring,
  - Making threats,
  - Identity theft,
  - Damage to data,
  - Sending unwanted abusive emails,
  - Sending computer virus,
  - Sending junk emails,
  - Fraudulent spams,
  - Solicitation of minors,
  - Gathering information,
  - Impersonation,
  - Obscene from one person to another.
- **Email Spoofing:** Email spoofing is the creation of emails with forged sender address. Fraudulent emails which comes under this category are:
  - Spam,
  - Phishing emails.

- **Broken Authentication:** Broken authentication is termed as the process of compromising the system to gain access to one's account or stealing secret credentials. This process usually exploits the vulnerability in the existing authentication mechanism. The risks that are faced due to this problem are:
  - Privacy violation,
  - Identity theft,
  - Loss of trust.
- **Insecure Direct Object References:** Applications that doesn't verify the proper authorization of user, results in insecure direct object references flaw. Such flaws can compromise all the data that can be referenced by the parameter. Hence an attacker compromises the system and changes the parameter value that directly refers to a system object to another object. The below are some of the measures to prevent such flaws.
  - Code analysis,
  - Per user object,
  - Session indirect object reference,
  - Access verification.
- **Security Misconfiguration:** Security misconfiguration attacks seek to exploit vulnerabilities in the underlying software components in a web page or application. Target for such attacks are:
  - Web servers,
  - Application platforms,
  - Database,
  - Networks,
  - Frameworks.
- **Failure to Restrict URL Access:** Failure to restrict URL access is integrity based common vulnerability found in most of the web applications. Through this vulnerability, attacker can gain access to protected web pages just by entering the respective URL in the browser's address bar. The website should verify the identity of the user before granting access to the protected pages or confidential information. This type of failure weakness allows the attacker even to retrieve the URL's by guessing the address and perform illegal operations on the data.
- **Invalidated Redirects and Forwards:** Invalidated redirects and forwards happen when a web application accepts untrusted input that may cause the web application to be redirected to untrusted URL. This can also be used to maliciously craft URL that would grant the application's access control to the attacker. If a web application have not implemented proper validation, this attack is quite easy. The feasible way to prevent this is to avoid invalidated redirects and forwards.
- **Credential or Session Prediction:** Credential or session prediction is a method of obtaining data about an authorized user to a website. The session ID is normally stored as a cookie or URL. Session ID enables users to track on a website. Using the session ID the attacker can perform the following:
  - Automatic authentication,
  - Session hijacking,
  - Session replay.

- **Known Vulnerability:** The attacker scans the list of target system to exploit the common vulnerabilities. Vulnerabilities are nothing but weakness in the computer system, identifying such things paves the way for malicious persons to launch attack on that system. Vulnerabilities may exist in:
  - Hardware,
  - Software component,
  - System programs,
  - User programs,
  - Web application,
  - Database.
- **Planting of Malware:** Planting of malware is done in a targeted system or group of system mainly for data destruction. Once a malware is planted, it will go out of control and commits lot of destruction. Malware is software used to disrupt computer operation, gather confidential data or gaining access to unauthorized systems. Few malware types are
  - Computer virus,
  - Worms,
  - Trojan horse,
  - Ransomware,
  - Rootkits,
  - Keyloggers,
  - Dialers,
  - Spyware,
  - Adware,
  - Rogue security software.
- **Remote File Inclusion (RFI):** RFI is a type of vulnerability that allows an attacker to include a remote file on the web server. This leads to outputting contents of confidential information. Few other effects are:
  - Code execution on the web server,
  - XSS,
  - DoS,
  - Data theft,
  - Manipulation.
- **Insider Attack:** Any malicious attacks on a corporate system or network where the intruder has authorized access to the network and also have knowledge on network architecture. The malicious insiders are categorized into two classes namely traitors and masqueraders. A traitor is a legitimate user of the organization who grants access to systems, but his actions violate the access policy rules. Masquerader is a person who steals credentials of a legitimate user and later impersonates him to gather confidential information.
- **Chosen Message Attack:** This is an attack model for cryptanalysis which assumes that the attacker has the capability to choose either plaintext or ciphertext and obtains the corresponding messages. The goal is to gain some information to reduce the security of the encryption scheme.
- **Sensitive Data Exposure:** The computer systems usually save the user's personal information, credit card numbers, passwords, house address and so on in a database. If a system is not protected from unauthorized access, attacker can steal access to the resources by exploiting that vulnerability. The vulnerability which induces such attack is termed as sensitive data exposure.

- **Malicious File Execution:** Malicious file execution attack allows an attacker to execute the intended operation remotely by installing a rootkit program. These results in compromise of the entire system, which paves way for the attackers to steal any secret data from the targeted system.

Security Ontology

Ontology is a specification of a conceptualization. It represents the gathered knowledge in a formal and structured form as well as provides a better communication, reusability and organization of knowledge and a better computational inference. Various security attacks are identified based on the below security ontology and the attacks are mapped to the corresponding host layers. The use of ontologies for representing knowledge in a formal and structured form that helps in clear understanding, better communication, reusability, organization of knowledge and better computational inference. The main objective of ontologies is to decrease the ambiguities in languages. The below classification is done for the various types of attacks in the host layers and control measures are suggested for each of these attacks. Based on the ontology concept, the below listed security attacks are identified in the host layers of the OSI model. We have considered the below parameters to have a detailed attack analysis.

1. **Attack Name:** To have a clear separation between various attack categories.
2. **Threat:** The source or origin which paved way for the attacker to launch attack.
3. **Vulnerability:** Weakness in the Computer system, network infrastructure or applications used by the Internet users which is perpetrated by the attackers.
4. **Asset:** Attacker's target.
5. **Control:** Protection measure against the attack.

The aim of this study is to discover more number of effective control measures in each of the identified attacks. Based on the collected data, analysis will be done in each and every protection mechanism for the selected attacks. The attacks can be selected on a random basis and the performance of each control measure will be proved experimentally.

The Table 1 covers solutions specific to each attacks. In general, the countermeasures for any security attack will come under the below mentioned category:

- Cryptography,
- IDS,
- Firewall,
- Antivirus,
- Filtering techniques,
- Monitoring tools,
- VPN,
- SSL.

Cryptography is the technique to secure the communication medium and transmitted data to prevent the unauthorized access, modification, fabrication and disruption of data. Cryptographic classification is done based on the nature of keys used for encryption and decryption. If both encryption and decryption

Table 1.

Sl. No.	Attack Name	Threat	Vulnerability	Asset	Control Measures
1.	DDoS	Server Crash	Failure to performs User verification process	Payment gateway	Ingres filter, EgresFilters, Referrer Mechanism,overlays
2.	XSS	Stealing of cookies, session tokens	Improper Anti-automation	Secret credentials	SWAP, XSS Guard, BEEP, Noxes, Web Application Testing, firewall
3.	Phishing	Secret data theft	Unverified IP's	User data	Check Sum Verification, Hash Technique, Web wallet
4.	Brute force attack	Signature forgery	Weak selection of encryption keys	Credit card information/ any other secret information	Digital Signature, Honey pots
5.	Spoofing	Social Engineering	Failure to verify the identity of sending or receiving host	Illegitimate access to user related data	TINGUIN,WT99 Security Filter,SSL,TLS
6.	Masquerading	Unauthorized access	Weak authentication mechanism	User login credentials	Examining MAC sequence number, Anomaly detection
7.	MIM	Eavesdropping	Weak key Agreement techniques, Failure to perform End-to-End encryption`	Secret credentials	Noise Cipher, Diffie Hellman key exchange technique, SSL, PKI, Carry Forward Verification, Second Channel Verification, Hash function
8.	Hacking	Content Modification	Failure to verify the sending host	Mail box/ other secret credentials	Probabilistic Packet Marking scheme, Pretty Good Privacy, S/MIME, Spam Filtering Technique
9.	Smishing	Social Engineering	Improper user authentication	Stealing user's finance related information	k-NN spam filtering
10.	Data diddling	Content Modification	Improper access controls	Forging/ counterfeiting documents	Virtual Private Network, Encryption, Auditing, Separation of duties
11.	Insecure cryptographic storage	Insider attack	Improper encryption of sensitive information, insecure use of strong algorithms, continued use of proven weak algorithms, hard coding keys and storing keys in unprotected stores	Abuse of Sensitive data	ADODB Performanc e monitor, code level protection
12.	DNS Hijacking	Phishing	No proper authentication mechanisms in place	Abuse of sensitive data	Logistic egression,CART,BART,SVM, RF,Nnet, anti Spam Filtering,authentication
13.	Misleading information in websites	Content modification	Failutre to verify the sending host	Website content	RSA,DES,AES, check sum verification, Hash technique
14.	Trojan horse	Eavesdropping	Outdated Antivirus	Secret credentials	Quantum Key Distribution, Antivirus, Firewall, IDS

continued on following page

Table 1. Continued

Sl. No.	Attack Name	Threat	Vulnerability	Asset	Control Measures
15.	Website defacement	SQL injection	Improper server security	Secret credentials	Anomaly based Intrusion Prevention System, SCIT Web Server, Markov Model, Vulnerability scanner
16.	Email bomb	Email account crash	Improper verification of sending host	Email account	Flow based intrusion prevention
17.	Virus	File corruption	Opening the links or files of Illegitimate persons, Browsing websites which violates the Internet policies	Sending emails to Address book recipients, crashing files	Antivirus, Throttling
18.	Worm	Consumes network Bandwidth, File corruption/ Modification	Software homogenity	User files	Content Shifting, Worm Signature, IDS, Honeypots
19.	Botnet	Consumes network bandwidth, File corruption/ Modification	Software homogeneity	User files, system resource	Content shifting, IDS
20.	Content spoofing	Social engineering	Poor coding, Improper Handling of user Supplied Data	Login credentials	TINGUIN,WT99,Security filters,SSL,TLS
21.	IP spoofing	Inaccurate data	Unverified IP's	Email	Ingress filters, egress filters, IDS,StackPi,interdomain packet filters
22.	Packet sniffing	Wiretapping, hacking	Absence of filtering techniques	Theft of private data	Filters, IDS
23.	DNS spoofing	Clogging	Buffer overflow errors, Unverified sending host Identities	Websites	LOT,HTTPS, digital certificates, cryptographically secure random number generators
24.	ARP poisoning	Sniffing, DoS	Unverified MAC and IP address	Information transmitted over the network	Snort,ARP Gurard,Ebtables, Anticap,DHCP,S-ARP,Dynamic ARP,SARP, port security,filtering
25.	Port scanning	Admin access	Buffer overflow errors, race condition/ deadlock`	Available services in the network	NADIR,IDES,NSM,GrIDS,IDS
26.	Ping of death	Sniffing	Unverified IP's	Available services in the network	Ingress filer, egress filter
27.	SYN flooding	DoS	Unverified IP's	Server resources	CUSUM algorithm, adaptive threshold detection, synkill mechanism, pushback, trace back, DARB, Berkley cookie, Linux cookies, random drop
28.	Cross site request forgery	Add or remove users in sms, send email	Improper authentication mechanism	Organization data, financial report, customer id, files	User authentication, SSL certificate, ADODB performance monitor

continued on following page

Table 1. Continued

Sl. No.	Attack Name	Threat	Vulnerability	Asset	Control Measures
29.	Cyberstalking	Identity theft	Unverified identity of users	User Identification details	Privacy protection act
30.	Email spoofing	Phishing, spam	Unverified sender's ID	Email account	Flow based intrusion prevention
31.	Broken authentication	Forgery, Tampering of information	Improper authentication mechanism	Organization's data	SSL
32.	Insecure direct object references	Access to sensitive data	Improper authentication mechanism	Financial reports	Reference map
33.	Security misconfiguration	Unauthorized access	Insufficient process validation	Files, directories	Code igniter, Request rodeo
34.	Failure to restrict URL access	Insider attack	Abuse of functionality	Sensitive data	ADODB Monitor
35.	Unvalidated redirects and forwards	Phishing	Unverified file permissions	Sensitive data	Burpsuite, fiddler, testing
36.	Credential or session prediction	Spoofing, session hijacking	Improper authorization checks	Session Identifier	RFC1750, HTTP digest authentication, URL encoding, session cookies, Single sign on
37.	Known vulnerability	DoS	Poor design	User and organization credentials	FIRST,CVSS,SVM, feature inspection
38.	Planting of malware	DDoS, Phishing	Outdated anti virus	User files, system resource	WebALPS, MAAWG, proxylock
39.	Remote File Inclusion	Unauthorized Modification	Outdated Anti Virus	User files	CRC,DIT MAC
40.	Insider attack	Theft of access rights and password	No proper authentication	Password	Lamport scheme, chien et al scheme, SSL
41.	Chosen message attack	Signature forgery	Modulus function, signature algorithm	Digitally signed document	Trapdoor signature, RSA, Merkle hellman,SHA,MD5
42.	Sensitive data exposure	Unauthorized access	No encryption, database flaw	Credit card information, id number	Taint Tracer, cryptography
43.	Malicious file execution	Keystroke logging, spyware installation, DoS, phishing	No pattern analysis	Secret credentials	WIPS, deperimeterised model, SAML, TestShibTwo

involves the same pair of keys, then it is termed as Symmetric cryptography or Public-key cryptography. Examples of Symmetric cryptography are Data Encryption Standard (DES), Advanced Encryption Standard (AES). If both encryption and decryption involves the different pair of keys, then it is termed as Asymmetric cryptography. Examples of Asymmetric cryptography are RSA, Diffie-Hellman key exchange protocol, ElGamal Encryption and elliptic curve techniques.

Intrusion Detection System (IDS) is a device which monitors the system activities in a network to identify any suspicious activity or policy violations and produces a report. The IDS categories are Network based IDS (NIDS) and Host based IDS (HIDS). The Intrusion Prevention Systems (IPS) helps in identifying the incidents and related log information about the reported incidents. IDS system is effective in identifying the possible network related security attacks but it fails to process the encrypted requests from the users.

Firewall is network security software which is involved in the process of monitoring and controlling all the inbound and outbound network traffic based on predetermined rule set. A request can be allowed inside a network. Firewalls are used to prevent unauthorized Internet users from accessing the private networks. The firewall examines each and every incoming request and allows it only, if it satisfies the criterial which is defined in the rule set. Firewall can be either hardware or software and it can be used to protect home as well as organizational networks. There are various categories of firewalls available to prevent unauthorized network access. They are Packet filter, Application gateway, Circuit-level gateway and Proxy server.

The various filtering techniques and monitoring tools like packet marking, Ingress filter, Egress filter, ADODB monitor and Honeypots proved to be effective in differentiating the benign traffic flow from the malicious one and raise the alarm signal to notify the System Administrators. The Virtual Private Network (VPN) allows the users to send and receive data across the shared networks while utilizing the security benefits of the private network. A VPN can be created by established a virtual point-to-point connection through the use of virtual tunneling protocols. VPN allows employees of the organization to securely access the intranet while in home or outside office. The VPN ensures the confidentiality, integrity and availability of the stored data. Secure Socket Layer (SSL) ensures secure connection between the Internet user's and websites to transmit the private data in a secure manner.

CONCLUSION

This paper summarizes various security attacks in the wired environment and the possible control measures available for mitigation. It provides an overview of existing mechanisms which are mandatory to carry out the control measures in a day-to-day scenario. This study is just a preliminary assessment step to understand the various attack categories and its controls. The next step is to study the existing attacks and implement the attack scenario in real time to understand its impact in the Internet environment. Further studies will be based on selecting a tool or platform to simulate an attack and provide solution for the same. The recent work focuses on selecting an appropriate tool to simulate the DDoS attack in a cloud computing environment. The simulation is executed in a single system to monitor the number of packets simulated by the DDoS tool HOIC (High Orbit Ion Cannon) and its effectiveness is verified by periodically probing the XAMPP server. Further research can be done by creating a testbed of 5 systems out of which 1 system act as a server. The flooding rate of a tool and solution can be analyzed by repeating the same process in the other available DDoS tools.

REFERENCES

Adeyinka, O. (2008). Internet Attack Methods and Internet Security Technology.*2008 Second Asia International Conference on Modelling & Simulation* (AMS). doi:10.1109/SECPRI.2003.1199330

Bass, T., Freyre, A., Gruber, D., & Watt, G. (1998). E-mail bombs and countermeasures: Cyber attacks on availability and brand integrity. *IEEE Network*, *12*(2), 10–17. doi:10.1109/65.681925

Brustoloni, X., & Brustoloni, J. C. (2005). Hardening Web browsers against man-in-the-middle and eavesdropping attacks. *Proceedings of the 14th International Conference on World Wide Web - WWW '05*. doi:10.1145/1060745.1060817

Chakrabarti, A., & Manimaran, G. (2002). Internet infrastructure security: A taxonomy. *IEEE Network*, *16*(6), 13–21. doi:10.1109/MNET.2002.1081761

Criscuolo, P. (2000). *Distributed Denial of Service Tools, Trin00, Tribe Flood Network, Tribe Flood Network 2000 and Stacheldraht*. Academic Press.

Criscuolo, P., & Rathbun, T. (1999). *Distributed System Intruder Tools*. Trinoo and Tribe Flood Network. doi:10.2172/792254

Deng, F., Li, X., Zhou, H., & Zhang, Z. (2005). Improving the security of multiparty quantum secret sharing against Trojan horse attack. *Phys. Rev. A Physical Review A*.

Dhamija, R., Tygar, J. D., & Hearst, M. (2006). Why phishing works. *Proceedings of the SIGCHI conference on Human Factors in Computing Systems - CHI '06*. doi:10.1145/1124772.1124861

Douligeris, C., & Mitrokotsa, A. (2004). DDoS attacks and defense mechanisms: Classification and state-of-the-art. *Computer Networks*, *44*(5), 643–666. doi:10.1016/j.comnet.2003.10.003

Garber, L. (2000). Denial-of-service attacks rip the internet. *Computer*, *33*(4), 12–17. doi:10.1109/MC.2000.839316

Gayathri, E., & Neelanarayanan, V. (2013). *A Mapping of Security controls to Host layer Security attacks.International Conference on Mathematical Computer Engineering*.

Gengler, B. (2001). CERT Victim of Three Day Denial-of-service Attack. *Network Security*, (7): 5.

Gupta, S., & Kumaraguru, P. (2014). Emerging phishing trends and effectiveness of the anti-phishing landing page. *2014 APWG Symposium on Electronic Crime Research* (eCrime).

Howard, J., & Longstaff, T. (1998). *A common language for computer security incidents*. Academic Press.

Jellal, M. (2002). Insecure old-age security. *Oxford Economic Papers*, *54*(4), 636–648. doi:10.1093/oep/54.4.636

Karlof, C., Shankar, U., Tygar, J. D., & Wagner, D. (2007). Dynamic pharming attacks and locked same-origin policies for web browsers. *Proceedings of the 14th ACM Conference on Computer and Communications Security - CCS '07*. doi:10.1145/1315245.1315254

Khan, Z. S., Alghathbar, K., Sher, M., & Rashid, K. (2010). Issues of Security and Network Load in Presence – A Survey. *Communications in Computer and Information Science Security Technology, Disaster Recovery and Business Continuity*, (pp. 224-230). Academic Press.

Kirda, E., Kruegel, C., Vigna, G., & Jovanovic, N. (2006). Noxes. *Proceedings of the 2006 ACM Symposium on Applied Computing - SAC '06*.

Lin, M. (2011). *Introduction to Information and Network Security*. McGraw Hilll.

Mirkovic, J., & Reiher, P. (2004). A taxonomy of DDoS attack and DDoS defense mechanisms. ACM SIGCOMM Computer Communication Review SIGCOMM. *Computer Communication Review, 34*(2), 39. doi:10.1145/997150.997156

Mirkovic, J., & Reiher, P. (2004). A taxonomy of DDoS attack and DDoS defense mechanisms. ACM SIGCOMM Computer Communication Review SIGCOMM. *Computer Communication Review, 34*(2), 39–39. doi:10.1145/997150.997156

Mittal, A., Shrivastava, A., & Manoria, M. (2011). A Review of DDOS Attack and its Countermeasures in TCP Based Networks. *International Journal of Computer Science & Engineering Survey*, 177-187.

Moore, D., Shannon, C., Brown, D., Voelker, G., & Savage, S. (2006). Inferring Internet denial-of-service activity. *ACM Transactions on Computer Systems*, 115-139.

Pape, S. (2014). *Authentication in Insecure Environments*. Academic Press.

Peng, T., Leckie, C., & Ramamohanarao, K. (2007). Survey of network-based defense mechanisms countering the DoS and DDoS problems. *ACM Computing Surveys*.

Salem, M. B., & Stolfo, S. J. (2011). Modeling User Search Behavior for Masquerade Detection. *Lecture Notes in Computer Science Recent Advances in Intrusion Detection*, 181-200.

Shema, M. (2012). HTML Injection & Cross-Site Scripting (XSS). *Hacking Web Apps*, 23-78.

Tiwari, N., & Padhye, S. (2011). *New proxy signature scheme with message recovery using verifiable self-certified public keys*. 2011 2nd International Conference on Computer and Communication Technology (ICCCT-2011).

Tsudik, G. (1992). Message authentication with one-way hash functions. *Computer Communication Review, 22*(5), 29–38. doi:10.1145/141809.141812

Wurzinger, P., Platzer, C., Ludl, C., Kirda, E., & Kruegel, C. (2009). SWAP: Mitigating XSS attacks using a reverse proxy.*2009 ICSE Workshop on Software Engineering for Secure Systems*. doi:10.1109/IWSESS.2009.5068456

Xie, Y., & Yu, S. (2009). Monitoring the Application-Layer DDoS Attacks for Popular Websites. *IEEE/ACM Trans. Networking, 17*(1), 15–25. doi:10.1109/TNET.2008.925628

Xu, X., Mao, Z. M., & Halderman, J. A. (2011). Internet Censorship in China: Where Does the Filtering Occur? Passive and Active Measurement Lecture Notes in Computer Science, 133-142.

Yaar, A., Perrig, A., & Song, D. (2003). Pi: A path identification mechanism to defend against DDoS attacks. *Proceedings 19th International Conference on Data Engineering* (Cat. No.03CH37405). Academic Press.

Yu, S. (2013). DDoS Attack Detection. Distributed Denial of Service Attack and Defense. *Springer Briefs in Computer Science*, 31-53.

Zou, C. C., Gong, W., & Towsley, D. (2002). Code red worm propagation modeling and analysis. *Proceedings of the 9th ACM Conference on Computer and Communications Security - CCS '02.* doi:10.1145/586110.586130

Chapter 14
Understanding Anti-Forensics Techniques for Combating Digital Security Breaches and Criminal Activity

Ricardo Marques
Pontifícia Universidade Católica de Campinas, Brazil

Alexandre Mota
Pontifícia Universidade Católica de Campinas, Brazil

Lia Mota
Pontifícia Universidade Católica de Campinas, Brazil

ABSTRACT

This chapter deals with the understanding of techniques that are used to create damage to the expert in an investigative process. The name used for these techniques is called anti-forensics, whose mission is to conceal, remove, alter evidence, or make inaccessible a cybercrime. These techniques aim to make the work of the slower expert or difficult to reach a conclusion; however, this chapter will explore some techniques used as measures to subvert digital evidence through anti-forensic measures.

INTRODUCTION

The computer forensics research appears in order to ensure that the evidence of crimes involving computers and network, preserved for presentation in court, constituting convincing aspect in the materiality of an offense. The difficulty in maintaining the integrity of digital evidence emerges as challenge, because they depend on a number of appropriate technical knowledge and use of specific tools for analysis and verification of all traces possibly left by the criminal in devices and networks.

Even as challenges ahead to enable the understanding of new research fronts in digital forensics field, it is also relate, the fields for the study of anti-forensic techniques, consisting of hiding evidence

DOI: 10.4018/978-1-5225-0193-0.ch014

and artifacts; purpose to further restrict access to devices with use of encryption, highlighting progress through techniques of steganography, which become reality as a matter of anti-forensic disciplines. Obviously, to speak of anti-forensic measures this article also address the principles of computer forensics.

Whereas the principles of Forensic Sciences also apply for Computer and Network Engineering, which features some basic processes, such as preservation, preparation, collection, examination, analysis and presentation of all traces and evidence at crime scenes, anti-forensic techniques can appear in any of these steps:

The techniques most used in anti-forensic concept are:

1. Working in networks, VPN's, the botnet or transparent proxy. The tools involved and discussed in this context are public VPN's and open proxy systems.
2. Acting on hard drives, data encryption. The involved and tools discussed in this context are Microsoft Bitlocker and Truecrypt.
3. Acting on hard drives, data wipe techniques in hard drives. Some tools will exhibited in this topic.
4. Acting on hard drives using the physical destruction of hard drives.
5. Acting images, steganography. Some tools will exhibited in this topic.

For techniques that work in networks, fraudsters use is the use of VPN's (Virtual Private Network), use of botnet networks or transparent proxy, so that they are not identified by IP address, because these network resources, create a mechanism to mask network connection outlet for criminal actions.

For data encryption techniques, the expert is faced with an environment where the files to be analyzed have encryption often is not possible to describe or interpret the information. This encryption can see through individual files, batch files, called containers and encrypted entire disks.

For cases involving wipe data on hard drives, the expert has involved a scenario where the hard drive in the investigation undergone several wipe techniques, eliminating the expert's work possibilities will be demonstrate some forms and mechanisms. Cases involving the unallocated disk space, it is an underdeveloped technique, which involves using tools to blind data through disk space slack where the fraudster uses is a dedicated hard disk space by operating systems, which for example in Microsoft systems are defined but not used.

- For cases involving hard drives using the physical destruction of hard drives, where this considered the safest in the fraudster's vision, where recovery becomes virtually impossible in the aspect of recovery of information stored there used in this aspect, drills holes in hard drives, among others.
- For cases involving steganography, the fraudster can hide any file type or codes in pictures, so that it is very hard to see if any kind of information or inserted file. Despite steganography, techniques used to create digital signatures on documents the objectives studied here focused on the use of steganography in order to hide evidence or data.
- For cases involving operating systems, the fraudster can use techniques and tools such as rootkits able to hide or camouflage the traces and remnants so that there are no conditions to investigate the source or origin of a particular fraud or attack, usually makes use of access administrative on the computer for installation.

Table 1. VPN and proxy service providers

Provider	Service	Protocols	Servers Regions
http://www.ipvanish.com	VPN	OPENVPN, PPTP, L2TP, PPTP, SSTP, IPSEC	Europe, North America, Asia
http://www.express-vpn.com	VPN	OPENVPN, PPTP, L2TP, PPTP, SSTP, IPSEC	Europe, North and South America, Asia
http://www.purevpn.com	VPN	OPENVPN, PPTP, L2TP, PPTP, SSTP, IPSEC	Europe, North and South America, Asia
http://www.sharedproxies.com	Proxy	HTTP, HTTPS, FTP, SOCKS5	Europe, North and South America, Asia
http://www.torguard.net	VPN and Proxy	OPENVPN, PPTP, L2TP, PPTP, SSTP, IPSEC, HTTP, HTTPS, FTP, SOCKS5	Europe, North and South America, Asia

- For cases of overwriting techniques in operating systems, the fraudster overrides files with plain text information, eliminating the real as was the file contents, where the purpose is to confuse or distract the forensic process.

At each step mentioned above, the expert has the means and tooling to address these actions and these will exploited by categories and usage examples. There are ways to manipulate the evidence, so that it can identify anti-forensic engineering it should be note, that although there are many tools and mechanisms to support the expert. It needs concrete evidence that the fraudster may have made use of a tooling for anti-forensics, otherwise the difficulty level and time for this forensic analysis can be incalculable in this sense (Garfinkel, 2015).

As the anti-based forensic disciplines, message encryption, so that persons cannot read, are used both for military and governmental purposes as the same group communication companies in different locations. The following topics should address ways to use anti-forensic mechanisms and demonstrate in each scenario reported as a person with criminal, can use the technology in favor of crime.

NETWORK ANTI-FORENSICS

The characterization of anti-forensics in computer networks, is responsible for concealment of information that travels on a network, this concealment is part of data encryption where information visualization possibilities that travel on networks with encryption, make the expert's work be impracticable in most cases skill.

The relevant data for forensic analysis in networks categorized by what the individual accessed, when accessed, frequency of access, the records that generated by the internet service provider and the information stored with the records of the supply source access the internet connection.

To elucidate the anti-forensic work, it is necessary to use services widely available, these days on the internet; many of these are commercial and involve monthly subscription costs, the Table 1 shows a list of services that can to be acquired traffic masking function.

Both services depend on applications that installed in the person that purchased equipment, as well as user passwords and private to ensure confidentiality in the hiring of the service.

Figure 1. Process for encryption data connections (VPN and proxy)

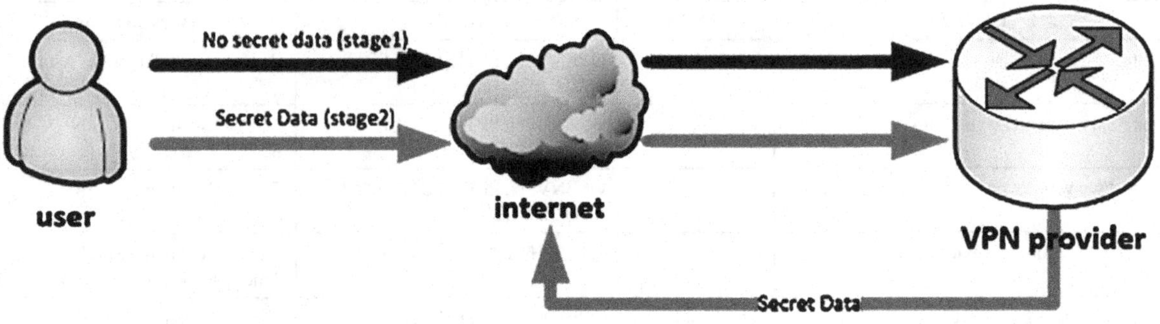

Whereas a person to hide network traffic, the example in Figure 1, show how is the communication networks in the first initial stage, characterized by the transfer of data without encryption and in a second stage, with encrypted access and camouflaged by the VPN service provider or proxy servers.

It should note that the initial stage, considered "the secret data" in Figure 1, is responsible for establishing communication with the service provider, not recommended any internet access, failing which access records captured by the providers services. At this stage, although it is suggested that the "user" check for applications that try to access network service information, such as Skype, Google Drive, among other services, it is recommended closing these accesses to not compromise proposal for anti-forensic .

HARD DISK ANTI-FORENSICS

The encryption hard drives, makes access information encapsulated in encryption is more access that is complex, may require in addition to passwords for access to the volume of data, certificates and tokens to when the owner meet the authentication rules implemented at the time the design of the volume of data it will have access to data stored on disk.

There are a number of tools that enable encryption the information disc, each using different algorithms and encryption keys with different lengths that can range from 40 bits to 2048 bits (Garfinkel, 2015);

This chapter is focused on anti-forensics, suggests the use of Truecrypt (TrueCrypt, 2015) and Microsoft Bitlocker tools, the first it is an open-source tool for encrypting volumes in file systems and even hard drives and the second, exclusive for proprietary operating systems in the case of Microsoft Company.

The Figure 2, denote how to enable encryption on the hard disk with Microsoft Bitlocker systems and Figure 3, shows the encryption options that can be used at the time of volume creation and the time for data to be encrypted. It is suggested the use of Truecrypt tool, mainly because it has support for encryption over an algorithm and therefore and compatibility options with different platforms that Microsoft Bitlocker does not support.

In both cases, the disk encryption makes can make the work of the expert impossible if you do not have the keys, information about the type of encryption used, and the digital certificates that may be involved in encryption hard drives.

Figure 2. Turn on Bitlocker on Microsoft Windows systems

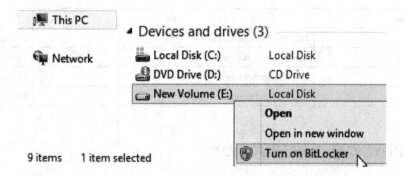

HARD DISKS WIPE

Ensure that the data are removed from hard drives is conceptually called "hard disk wipe", it is written functions overlap and removing information that is stored on hard drives. Ensure that there is no possibility of carrying out forensic expertise in hard drives since the proper use of tools "hard disk wipe" occur in a bulk data deletion process.

When the expert analysis of a hard disk, the expert has in his posture copy of all *inodes*, elements and slack spaces; that where data is stored, if these data are overlaid by other information or even struggling through sequences of deletion. Can said that the data stored on disk may not be recoverable, it can said that this record received deletions anti forensic data type.

A group of tools can considered when the scope of work is facing the hard disk wipe among which we can mention the items present in Table 2.

Figure 3. Turn on Truecrypt on Microsoft Windows systems or Mac OSX

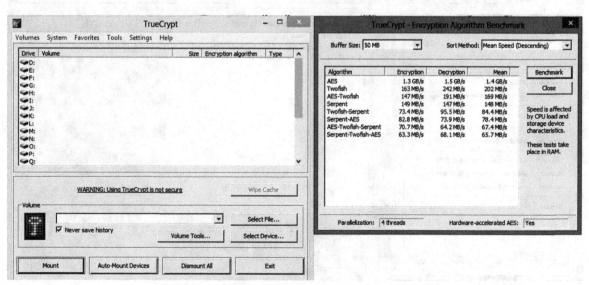

Table 2. Tools for wipe hard disk

Name	Site	License
ActiveKillDisk	http://www.killdisk.com	Commercial
Diskwipe	http://www.diskwipe.org	Freeware
Eraser	http://eraser.heidi.ie	Freeware
HDDlowLevel Format	http://hddguru.com	Freeware

HARD DISK PHYSICAL DESTRUCTION

For a hard disk becomes inaccessible or physically unusable, so that an expert cannot reconstruct the information, there are some ways in which this destruction occurs, informing that it is independent of the forms mentioned below it is essential that it is done in the logical destruction data through mechanisms of hard disk wipe, cited in the previous topic.

Figure 4. Preparation of steganography

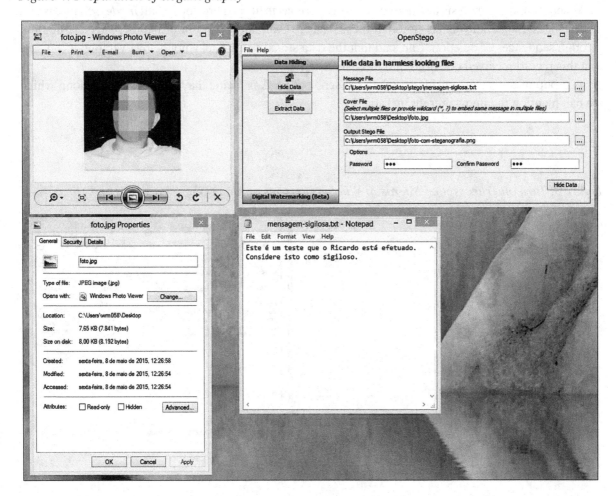

Figure 5. Comparative after application of steganography

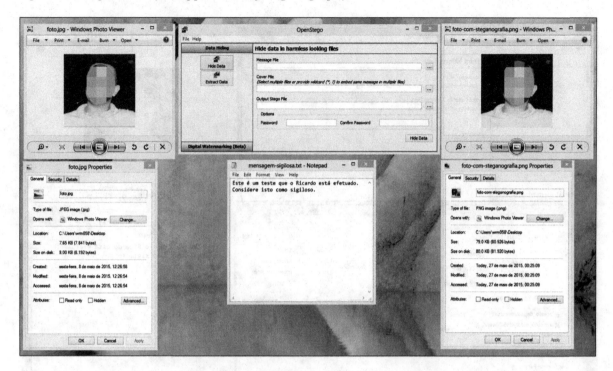

Notably, a widely used mechanism, but not effective is the removal of all electronic components and the destruction of the plates and disk magnetic structures. The low efficiency of this format will occur, the possibility of reconstitution of memory components that can reconstructed through a same configuration equipment.

The second mechanism can see through the actions mentioned above, including the possibility of crushing drilling with hard disk, or burning, or demagnetization with acid and to shredder plate industrial computers.

Regardless of medium physical destruction mechanism chosen, mechanisms, equipment and chemicals informed should handle with caution as they may bring harm to health when not handled with safety.

Although this topic inform these forms of physical removal of the device, it is worth informing that the evolution of recovery mechanisms and technologies to the expert in recent years, can create forms of recovery, especially when the discs do not use technologies with dishes but with chips non-volatile memory if the disks with SSD technology (Bell, 2010).

STEGANOGRAPHY

This section includes the understanding and examination of practices and possibilities involving steganography. It is a technique of hiding a message within another, while encryption encodes content, steganography conceals the message inside another (Eleutério & Machado 2011).

Given the scenario and context steganography technique, it is important to mention that for a person to have access to the camouflaged text, it will need the same tools used in camouflage to decipher the

Figure 6. Vision of receiver, extracting the message

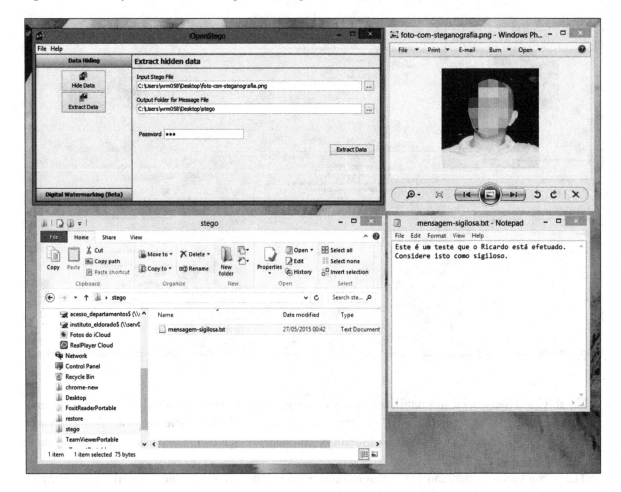

message. Thus, even if it is possible to intercept the data over the network, the masked information is encrypted and encapsulated within an image.

The Figure 4 illustrates the (OpenStego, 2015), and its installation on a machine with Microsoft Windows operating system. Understanding the mechanism steganography is through the implementation of OpenStego application, by placing a file with the message where you want to apply steganography. In this case, by way of experimentation, it decided to demonstrate by choosing a picture and a password. It is worth mentioning here that the image has a size of 7,841 bytes, before applying steganography.

The Figure 5 illustrates the comparison of the images and their properties. It may be noted that they have not changed in their qualities and resolutions, where the image on the left is the original and the one on the right is the image with steganography applied with a message inserted in the right image through the message-confidential file. txt. The differences between the images are in sizes where it is seen that before steganography the original image is 7,841 bytes, whereas the technique applied after inserting the secret message (the message destination), has changed the image size to 80,926 bytes.

The Figure 6 illustrates the OpenStego tool, operating in figure receptor function and extracting the encapsulated message.

The focus of this section is to allow a glimpse of the possibilities that can presented to an expert. Although, for steganography work occurs, the expert needs to have similar steganography tools use of evidence in the investigation equipment, for without it; you can set up a very time consuming and practically infeasible analysis. It should note that each steganography system operates with specific encryption algorithms and these messaging engines are a challenge for the computer forensics.

REFERENCES

Bell, G. B. (2010). Solid State Drives: The Beginning of the End for Current Practice in Digital Forensic Recovery? *Journal of Digital Forensics, Security and Law*, 5(3), 1–20.

Brito, A. (2013). *Direito penal informático*. Sao Paulo: Editora Saraiva.

Eleutério, P. M., & Machado, M. P. (2011). *Desvendando a computação forense*. São Paulo: Novatec Editora Ltda.

Garfinkel, S. (2015). *DTIC*. Fonte: DTIC. Retrieved from http://www.dtic.mil/dtic/tr/fulltext/u2/a576161.pdf

OpenStego. (2015). *OpenStego free steganography solution*. Retrieved from http://openstego.source-forge.net/

TrueCrypt. (2015). *Truecrypt.com*. Retrieved from http://www.truecrypt.com

Chapter 15
Visual Cryptography for Securing Images in Cloud

Punithavathi P
VIT University, Chennai Campus, India

Geetha Subbiah
VIT University- Chennai Campus, India

ABSTRACT

Images are becoming an inevitable part of knowledge in the modern day society. As data is growing at a rapid rate, costs involved in storing and maintaining data is also raising rapidly. The best alternate solution to reduce the storage cost is outsourcing all the data to the cloud. To ensure confidentiality and integrity of the data, a security technique has to be provided to the data even before it is stored on the cloud using cryptography. An attempt is made to explore the possibility of usage of visual cryptography for providing robust security to the secret image. Visual cryptography proves to be more efficient than other cryptography techniques because it is simple and does not require any key management technique.

INTRODUCTION

Images are becoming an inevitable part of knowledge in the modern day society. As the world changes, the technology is also changing rapidly. Various confidential data such as medical images, biometric images, space and geographical images taken from satellite and commercial important document are transmitted over the Internet and stored in remote locations for future access. The day-to-day needs for computing resources are increasing. As data is growing at a rapid rate, costs involved in storing and maintaining data is also raising rapidly. The best alternate solution to reduce the storage cost is outsourcing all the data to the cloud.

Cloud computing is an emerging technology which provides facilities for storage, computations, database-driven services for various industrial, financial, healthcare, educational and governmental sectors. Cloud model utilizes the computing resources with the capabilities of increasing the resources, providing pay-per-user privilege with a little or no up-front investment costs on the IT infrastructure.

DOI: 10.4018/978-1-5225-0193-0.ch015

This promising model moves the databases to the large data centers. However, the management of the data may not be reliable and the enterprises may not have any control over the data, since the data centers are remote. The common security concerns are:

- Securing data both during transmission and during storage,
- Securing software interfaces,
- User access control, and
- Data separation.

Since, the data in the cloud computing is placed in the hands of trusted third parties, ensuring the data security both during storage and during transmission is of great importance. The data integrity and confidentiality is maintained in the cloud by providing security to the data. This is an important quality of service in cloud computing.

Security of data in cloud is a challenge and is significant as many concerns and faults are yet to be categorized. As data is stored in the cloud, the user is unaware of where it is being stored and who are privileged to access the data. Eventually, the data owners are bothered about the confidentiality and integrity of the data. To ensure this, a security technique has to be provided to the data even before it is stored on the cloud. Such technique should be simple and user-friendly and at the same time should be less complex.

Data encryption techniques can be utilized on a great scale for successfully providing security to the data both during transmission and storage. Cryptography encodes a plain text to a cipher text and decodes the cipher text back to the plain text. There are two types of cryptography algorithms namely symmetric and asymmetric algorithm. The symmetric algorithm uses a single secret key while the asymmetric uses two different keys for encryption and decryption. But both these cases require heavy computation and as well as key management techniques. Moreover, user is required to have some knowledge of cryptography. Hence there is a serious requirement of a simple and less-complex cryptography technique which will be more feasible if there is no encryption/decryption key.

Visual cryptography (VC) is a paradigm in which a secret image is converted into two or more meaningless, non-identical shares, without using any encryption keys. The hidden secret can be revealed only when the shares are stacked together. The magnificence of VC lies in the facts that the hidden secret can never be recovered just by possessing one of the shares, and also that the secret can be revealed without any computer intervention. This allows VC to be used by anyone without any deep understanding of cryptography, and without any hard computations.

VC is different from the usual cryptographic secret sharing. In cryptographic secret sharing technique, each participant is allowed to keep a portion of the secret which could be revealed easily. But this discomfort is overcome by the VC as it uses the idea of hiding secrets into multiple shares which never reveal the secret until stacked together. The secret recovery is as simple as superimposing transparencies containing the shares, which allows the secret to be reconstructed. VC is a desirable scheme as it embodies both the scheme of perfect secrecy and a very simple mechanism for recovering the secret. While considering popular cryptographic schemes which are conditionally secure, VC provides robust security to the secret image. This makes VC suitable for highly sensitive applications like biometric authentication (Ross & Othman, 2010), secure electronic ballots (Chaum, 2004), safe online banking (Roy & Venkateswaran, 2014), digital watermarking (Tai & Chang, 2004), security against DoS attacks in WiMax authentication system (Altaf, Sirhindi, & Ahmed, 2008), etc.

The shares are also images which can be easily transmitted through fax and mails. The advantages of VC are listed as:

- Keyless encryption technique,
- Simple implementation,
- No decryption algorithm,
- Lower computational cost,
- Shares can be transmitted through FAX or EMAIL.

Various VC schemes have been discussed along with examples. An analysis report is also presented pertaining to each VC scheme is also added. The VC schemes have been analysed based on the criteria such as pixel expansion, security level and contrast loss. The pixel expansion describes the increase in the size of the recovered image when compared to the original image. The security level indicates the extent of the security provided by the VC algorithm. This describes whether the shares are strong enough to carry the secret. Contrast loss indicates the difference in the level of contrast between the recovered image and the original image.

VISUAL CRYPTOGRAPHY

The traditional VC, pioneered by Naor and Shamir in 1995, assumed that a secret image is a collection of pixels (black and white in color). The basic model is extended into a visual variant of k out of n i.e., (k, n) secret sharing problem. Given the secret image, n shares are generated so that the secret image is visible only if any k number of shares are stacked together (where k is less than or equal to n). The image cannot be reconstructed if fewer than k shares are stacked together. The shares are collections of m black and white pixels. The resultant structure is described as a $n{\times}m$ Boolean matrix, 'S'.

The structure of 'S' can be described as

$S=(S_{ij})_{m{\times}n}$ where $S_{ij}{=}1$ or $0{\leftrightarrow}$ the jth sub-pixel of the ith share is black or white, respectively.

The algorithm for the VC has been proposed as:

Input: Binary image (BI) of size $w{\times}h$.
Output: Share images (S1,S2).

The important considerations in the model (shown in Algorithm 1) are:

m: Number of pixels in the shares, and is equal to $m{=}2^{(k-1)}$. The value of m is responsible for resolution loss from the original secret image to the recovered one. Hence the value of m is kept as small as possible.

α: Simply the loss in contrast or relative difference in the weight between the stacked/superimposed shares. The value of α is equal to.

Algorithm 1. VC_Algorithm

```
Calculate m=2^(k-1) where n is the required number of shares
Calculate α=1/m
```
Generate Basis matrices B0 (for white pixel represented by '0') and B1
 (for black pixel represented by '1') of size n×m, such that the following
 conditions are satisfied:
 - Each row in B0 and B1 has equal number of 0's and 1's
 - B0 has identical rows and B1 has complementary rows
 - The "or" vector(V) of n rows in B0 satisfies $H(V) \leq d - \alpha m$, and the "or"
   vector (V) of n rows in B1 satisfies $H(V) \geq d$. (where d is a threshold
   such that $1 \leq d \leq m$)

Generate Collection of matrices C0 and C1 (of size m!) by permuting columns
of B0 and B1, respectively for each pixel (p) in BI, Construct S1 and S2 as
follows
```
        if p=0
          Randomly select a matrix from C0
        else if p=1
          Randomly select a matrix from C1
```

γ: The size of the collections – *C0* and *C1. C0* refers to the collection of basis matrices (*M0*) corresponding to the sub-pixel patterns representing a white pixel in the secret image, within the shares. *C1*
   refers to the collection of basis matrices (*M1*) corresponding to the sub-pixel patterns, representing
   a black pixel in the secret image, within the shares. The size of *C0* and *C1* is *n×m* always.

   The rows and columns of *M0* and *M1* are comprised of equal number of 1's (black pixels) and 0's to
maintain the gray level throughout the shares, irrespective of whether the pixel in secret image is black
or white. Accordingly, *M0* is comprised of even number of 1's in each column, and *M1* is comprised
of odd number of 1's in each column. Furthermore no two rows in *M1* should be identical vice versa of
identical rows in *M0*. Each row of the basis matrices *M0* and *M1* represent a separate share.

   The black subpixels in the combined shares are represented by Boolean 'OR' of the rows $i_1, i_2, i_3, \ldots$
i_r in S, when the transparencies $i_1, i_2, i_3, \ldots i_r$ are stacked together (in a proper way which neatly aligns the
subpixels). The gray level of the combined share is always proportional to the Hamming weight H(V)
of the ORed m-vector V.

   The Hamming weight *H(V)* is interpreted by the visual system as follows:

- A black pixel is interpreted if $H(V) \geq d$, and
- A white pixel is interpreted if $H(V) \leq d - \alpha m$ for some predetermined threshold $1 \leq d \leq m$ and a relative difference $\alpha > 0$.

   The construction of the shares can be clearly illustrated by a (2,2) VC scheme. The value of n is 2
and k is 2. The value of m becomes 2. Accordingly, each pixel in the secret image has to be represented
by 2 subpixels in each share. But in practice, this leads to the distortion of the aspect ratio of the secret
image. So it is recommended to use 4 subpixels arranged in a 2×2 array as shown in Figure 1.

Figure 1. Subpixel pattern and corresponding basis matrix

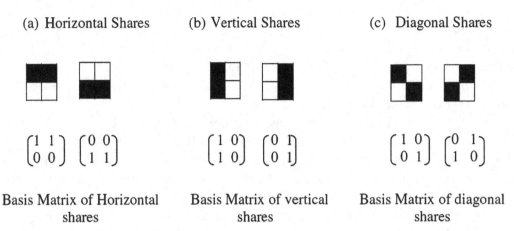

(a) Horizontal Shares   (b) Vertical Shares   (c) Diagonal Shares

$$\begin{bmatrix} 1 & 1 \\ 0 & 0 \end{bmatrix} \begin{bmatrix} 0 & 0 \\ 1 & 1 \end{bmatrix} \qquad \begin{bmatrix} 1 & 0 \\ 1 & 0 \end{bmatrix} \begin{bmatrix} 0 & 1 \\ 0 & 1 \end{bmatrix} \qquad \begin{bmatrix} 1 & 0 \\ 0 & 1 \end{bmatrix} \begin{bmatrix} 0 & 1 \\ 1 & 0 \end{bmatrix}$$

Basis Matrix of Horizontal shares   Basis Matrix of vertical shares   Basis Matrix of diagonal shares

The collections of 2×4 matrices *C0* and *C1* can be defined as:

C0 = {all the matrices obtained by permuting the columns of *M0*}
C1 = {all the matrices obtained by permuting the columns of *M1*}

The shares are generated in the following manner:

- If a pixel in the secret image is white, then same pattern of sub-pixels (from Figure 1) is selected for both shares. (This implies that to share a white pixel, one of the matrices is selected randomly from *C0* for each share).
- If a pixel in the secret image is black, then complementary pair of patterns of sub-pixels (from Figure 1) is selected for both shares.(This implies that to share a black pixel, one of the matrices is selected randomly from *C1* for each share).

It is clear from Table 1 that any single share is a random choice of two white and two black subpixels with respect to a particular pixel in secret image. This gives the impression of being medium gray. When the shares are stacked together, the result is either medium gray (representing white) or completely black (representing black).

Table 1. Subpixel pattern for (2,2) visual cryptography

	White	Black
Share 1		
Share 2		
Stacking result		

The ORed 'm' vector, V_0 corresponding to *C0* is (1,0) or (0,1) because of the process of selection of the same subpixel pattern. The ORed 'm' vector V_1 corresponding to *C1* is always (1,1) because of the process of selection of the complementary subpixel patterns. The Hamming weight of any two shares of a white pixel is 1 and the Hamming weight of any two shares of a black pixel is 2. Let us assume that the value of a predetermined threshold, '*d*' to be 1 (since the value of *d* must be $1 \leq d \leq m$). This implies that the pixels with Hamming weight of 1 is interpreted as white and 2 is interpreted as black, by the human visual system.

Analysis

- **Security Level:** Each share is comprised of several subpixel patterns which are built up of two white and two black pixels. The individual shares give no clue of the color of a specific pixel in the secret image. Hence it is impractical to decrypt the share even by applying enormous computation.
- **Pixel Expansion:** Each pixel in the secret image is represented using a subpixel pattern which is comprised of four pixels. Hence the size of the shares and revealed secret is four times greater than that of the secret image, which is evident from Figure 2.
- **Contrast Loss:** Contrast becomes an essential feature within VC because it determines the clarity of the recovered secret by clearly distinguishing the black and white regions in an image. Since the white pixels in secret image become 50% black and 50% white during the selection of subpixel pattern, the contrast of the recovered image becomes poor. An attempt has been made by Naor & Shamir in 1997 to achieve better contrast.

Figure 2. Results of traditional VC

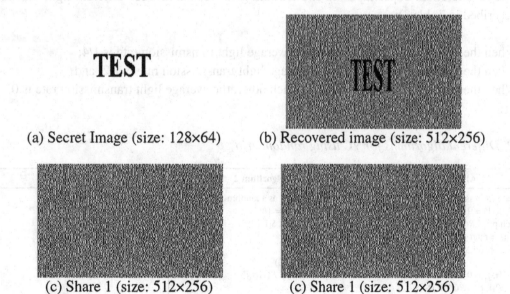

(a) Secret Image (size: 128×64)   (b) Recovered image (size: 512×256)

(c) Share 1 (size: 512×256)   (c) Share 1 (size: 512×256)

RANDOM GRID BASED VISUAL CRYPTOGRAPHY

Kafri and Keren in 1987 proposed a bit-based approach to encrypt binary images. They defined a random grid (RG) as a transparency comprised of a two-dimensional array of pixels which may be black or white, and the choice between them is made by a coinflip procedure. There is no association between the values of the pixels in the array. The transparent/white pixels permit the light to pass through while the opaque/black pixels prevent it. The average light transmission of a random grid is always 1/2 or 0.5 because the number of the white pixels is probabilistically equal to that of the opaque pixels in a random grid. That is, if RG is a random grid, then it has an average light transmission as $T(RG) = 0.5$.

There were totally three methods to encrypt a binary image, as suggested by Kafri and Keren. Given a secret binary image S, two random grids $RG1$ and $RG2$ are produced such that no information of S is leaked by the random grids individually, yet they reveal S when stacked.

Encryption of a Binary Image by Random Grids

Input: A binary image S of size $w \times h$ where $S[i, j] \in \{0,1\}$ (white or black), $1 \leq i \leq w$, $1 \leq j \leq h$
Output: Two random grids $RG1$ and $RG2$ which reveal S' when superimposed where $RGk[i,j] \in \{0,1\}$ (white or black), $1 \leq i \leq w$, $1 \leq j \leq h$ and $k \in \{1.2\}$

The algorithms 1, 2 and 3 for VC using random grid are listed in Table 2.

The value 1 (0) represents a black (white) pixel in the secret binary image or in the share. Note that the rand_pixel(0, 1) is a function which returns either 0 or 1 to represent a white or black pixel, respectively, by a coinflip procedure. denotes the inverse of $RG1[i, j]$.

The secret is revealed by superimposing the shares on each other. This operation is equivalent to logical 'OR' operation. Superimposing two random grids results in three different light transmission rates(described in Table 3):

- When the two RGs are independent, the average light transmission rate is 1/4;
- When the two RGs are identical, the average light transmission rate is 1/2; and
- When the two RGs are complementary each other, the average light transmission rate is 0.

Table 2. Different algorithms for VC using random grid

Algorithm 1	Algorithm 2	Algorithm 3

1.Generate $RG1$ as a random grid, $T(RG1) = 1/2$
//for (each pixel $RG1[i,j]$) do
//$RG1[i, j]$ = rand_pixel(0, 1)
2. for (each pixel $S[i, j]$) do
  {
    if ($S[i, j] = 0$)
    $RG2[i, j] = RG1[i, j]$
    else
    $RG2[i, j] = RG1[i, j]'$
  }
3. output ($RG1$, $RG2$)
	1.Generate $RG1$ as a random grid, $T(RG1) = 1/2$
	2.for (each pixel $S[i, j]$) do
	  {
	    if ($S[i,j] = 0$)
	    $RG2[i,j] = RG1[i,j]$
	    else
	    $RG2[i,j] =$
	      rand_pixel(0, 1)
	  }
	3. output ($RG1$,$RG2$)
		1.Generate $RG1$ as a random grid, $T(RG1) = 1/2$
		2.for (each pixel $S[i, j]$) do
		  {
		    if ($S[i,j] = 0$)
		    $RG2[i,j] =$
		      rand_pixel(0, 1)
		    else
		    $RG2[i,j] = RG1[i,j]'$
		  }
		3. output ($RG1$,$RG2$)

Table 3. Results of S'=RG1(OR)RG2 using different algorithms

Algorithm	Pixel in Secret Image	Probability	RG1	RG2	S'=RG1(OR)RG2	T(S')
Algorithm 1	□	1/2	□	□	□	1/2
		1/2	■	■	■	
	■	1/2	□	■	■	0
		1/2	■	□	■	
Algorithm 2	□	1/2	□	□	□	1/4
		1/2	■	■	■	
	■	1/4	■	□	■	1/4
		1/4	■	□	■	
		1/4	□	□	□	
		1/4	■	■	■	
Algorithm 3	■	1/2	□	■	■	0
		1/2	■	□	■	
	□	1/4	■	□	■	¼
		1/4	■	□	■	
		1/4	□	□	□	
		1/4	■	■	■	

The value of contrast of the superimposed binary image S' corresponding to the original secret image S is measured by using (1):

$$\delta = \frac{T\left(S'\left[S(0)\right]\right) - T\left(S'\left[S(1)\right]\right)}{1 + T\left(S'\left[S(1)\right]\right)} \tag{1}$$

The value of 'δ' can be as big as possible. In other words, the larger the value 'δ', the superimposed secret is more recognizable. Since Algorithm 1 achieves highest contrast, the image achieved as a result of superimposing shares of Algorithm 1 is easy to be perceived by the human eyes than other two algorithms.

Analysis

- **Security Level:** Let $RG1[S(b)]$ denote the area of pixels in $RG1$ that corresponds to $S(b)$ for b = 0 or 1. Note that $RG1 = RG1[S(0) \cup RG1[S(1)]$ where $RG1 = RG1[S(0) \cap RG1[S(1)] = \phi$. For example, consider Step 1in the Algorithm 1. It assumes $RG1$ as a random grid with T($RG1$)=1/2, then this implies that $T(RG1) = T(RG1[S(0)]) = T(RG1[(S1)]) = 1/2$. When $S[i, j] = 0$, then this implies that $RG2[i, j] = RG1[i, j]$. This proves $T(RG1[S(0)]) = RG2[(S0)]) = 1/2$. Moreover, when $S[i, j] = 1$, $RG2[i, j] = RG1[i, j]$. $T(RG2[B(1)]) = T(RG1[(B1)]) = 1 - 1/2 = 1/2$. Due to these facts that it is inferred that T($RG2$)=1/2 by the principle of combination. Therefore both $RG1$ and $RG2$ are merely random grids and none of them leak any information about S, individually.

Figure 3. Results of RG-based VC

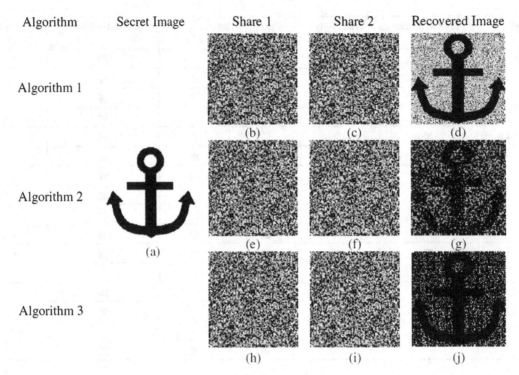

- **Pixel Expansion:** The size of the random grid is same as that of the size of the secret image. Hence there is pixel expansion.
- **Contrast Loss:** The contrasts achieved by the Algorithms 1, 2 and 3 are recorded as, 1/2, 1/4, and 1/4 respectively. Hence, the reconstructed image obtained by Algorithm 1 having the largest contrast among the three, can be recognized easily by human visual system than those by the other two algorithms. This can be understood from the results in Figure 3.

SEGMENT-BASED VISUAL CRYPTOGRAPHY

The segment-based VC (Borchert, 2007) is segment-based unlike pixel-based traditional VC. It is used to hide messages comprising numbers represented by seven- segment display. The advantage of the segment-based VC is that it may be uncomplicated to adjust the secret images and that the symbols are potentially easier to recognize for the human eye. The seven-segment display is comprised of seven bars (three horizontal and four vertical) which are arranged like a digit '8'. Every digit from 0,..., 9 can be represented just by highlighting the selective segments. The seven-segment display is comprised of seven bars (three horizontal and four vertical) which are arranged like a digit '8'. Every digit from 0,..., 9 can be represented just by highlighting the selective segments.

The principle of pixel-based VC is applied to the segment-based visual cryptography. Assume that every segment Sn (' = ' or ' ‖ ') in the seven segment display model, is comprised of two parallel segments $Sn1$ and $Sn2$.

Figure 4 Illustration of segment selection

('—' or 'l'), which are very close to each other but do not intersect each other. The digit '8' has been illustrated using this logic, in the Figure 4.

Generation of First Share

Let each segment in a seven-segment display model be represented as Sn (where n=0–6). Assume that a certain digit has to be revealed in white color on a black background. Consider a subset (C) of segments, among the segments $S0$-$S6$ that have to be highlighted in a seven-segment display such that the required digit can be shown.

Similar to the pixel-based visual cryptography (Figure 5), the first share is generated randomly. This means that one of the parallel segments, $Sn1$ or $Sn2$, is selected randomly for every segment Sn irrespective of whether the segment belongs to C or not. The selected segment (say $Sn1$) is kept white (or transparent), while the parallel segment (say $Sn2$) is left black (equal to the color of the background of the share). Such a random selection is illustrated with digit '8' in the Figure 4.

Figure 5. Comparison of segment-based VC with traditional VC

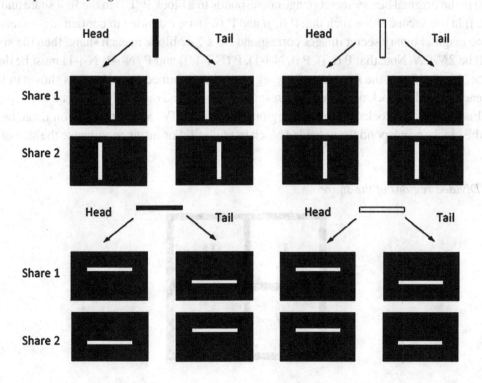

Generation of Second Share

If a segment Sn_1 or Sn_2 of $Sn \in C$ is kept white in first share, then in the second share the same selection of Sn_1 or Sn_2 is made and it is kept white. At the same time, the other parallel segment is turned black. (It is due to this selection that the white segment is shown off while overlaying the shares.)

On the other hand, if Sn does not belong to the subset C, then in the second share, the segment (Sn_1 or Sn_2) chosen on the random share (share 1), is turned black. This has the effect that while overlaying the shares, this segment is not highlighted.

In total, exactly the segments belonging to the subset C is showed off, when the shares are overlaid. Therefore, after overlaying, the required digit is displayed to the user which is illustrated in the Figure 4.

Analysis

Each share is comprised of a segment Sn_1 or Sn_2 with an equal probability of , for each $Sn \in C$. The individual shares give no clue of the hidden digit. Hence it is impractical to recover the secret even by applying hard computation.

MULTIPLE IMAGE VISUAL CRYPTOGRAPHY (MIVC)

The MIVC is a type of VC which can hide more than one secret. Wu and Chen (Wu and Chen, 1998), proposed a MIVC technique which can hide two different secrets within two shares, using the basic concept of traditional pixel-based approach. The idea behind MIVC is share rotation to embed two sets of secrets into two shares. Assume any two binary secret images of the size $N \times N$. While encoding, each pixel $S(i, j)$ in the original binary secret image corresponds to a block $P_a(i, j)$ in the first share and another block $P_b(i, j)$ in the second share such that $P_a(i, j)$ and $P_b(i, j)$ are extended to contain $n \times n$ pixels. If each pixel of two original binary secret images corresponds to a 2×2 block in each share, then the size of the shares will be $2N \times 2N$. Note that $P_a(i, j)$, $P_a(j, N\text{-}i\text{-}1)$, $P_a(N\text{-}j\text{-}1, i)$ and $P_a(N\text{-}i\text{-}1, N\text{-}j\text{-}1)$ must be defined to be same 2×2 blocks. Thus, the first share S_A is segmented into four equal regions, as shown in Figure 6.

Then, each extended block of the region I in share S_A is selected randomly from one of the patterns in Figure 7. Each extended blocks in the other regions (II, III, and IV) apart from region I, can be defined such that the blocks correspond the extended block in region I. For instance, suppose the size of a secret

Figure 6. Divided regions of the share

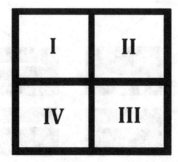

Figure 7. Patterns of the 2×2 extended blocks

image is 8×8, and if the extended block at the position (1, 1) of the region I is a pattern as shown in line 3 column 2 of Table 4, the extended blocks at (1, 6) of the region II, (6, 1) of the third region and (6, 6) of the fourth region must all be defined by the same pattern. According to this rule, share S_A is generated as shown in Figure 8. The extended block of S_B must be defined according to the distribution of the extended block of S_A by one of the lines from column 4 lines 2 to 17 in Table 4.

The share S_B is a pattern as in line 4 column 1 in Table 4. When two shares are superimposed, the extended block in S_A has only one white pixel and three black pixels, it means the superimposed block is white in color. Suppose, if all the four pixels in the superimposed block are black, then it means that the 2×2 stacked block is black in color. Therefore, after the two shares S_A and S_B are superimposed, black color is shown off. This means that, the pixel value of the corresponding position in the first secret

Figure 8. Results of MIVC

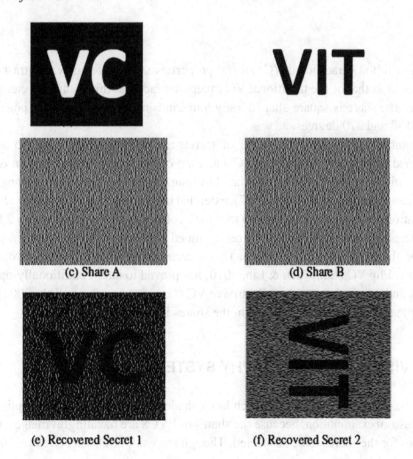

(c) Share A (d) Share B

(e) Recovered Secret 1 (f) Recovered Secret 2

Table 4. Implementation of Wu and Chen's MIVC

Pixel of the First Secret Image	W	W	B	B	W	W	B	B	W	W	B	B	W	W	B	B
Pixel of the Second Secret Image	W	B	B	W	W	B	B	W	W	B	B	W	W	B	B	W
2×2 Block of Share S_A																
2×2 Block of Share S_B																
Stacked Block																

image is black. Next, rotate S_A in anti-clockwise direction, and then, stack it with the share S_B as shown in Figure 8. It means that this stacked extended block appears to be white. That is, the pixel value of the corresponding position in the second secret image is white. Although the above method solves the problem, only one secret image can be hidden in traditional visual cryptography, it still has some limits. That is, during the secret image embedding process, the share generation is limited because the rotating angle can only be 0, 90, 180 and 270 degrees.

Analysis

Since the method follows traditional VC, all the properties such as security, contrast loss and pixel expansion are same as that of the traditional VC except the fact that this technique can hide more than one secret. Since the share is square-shaped, only four kinds of angle degrees are possible during the rotation: 0, 90, 180 and 270 degrees.

Hence the rotation angles and the number of secrets are limited. MIVC can also be implemented using random grid technique (Shyu, 2007), (Chen, Tsao & Wei, 2008) and (Lin, Lin & Chen, 2014). The problems of pixel expansion can be alleviated by using this technique. Shyu, Huang, Lee, Wang & Chen, (Shyu, Huang, Lee, Wang & Chen, 2007), extended the multi-secret VC scheme of Wu and Chang from single rotation to numerous rotations so that they could encode 'n' images into 2 transparencies. An attempt was made to adapt the circular-shares to embed two sets of confidential messages into different angles of the shares (Wu & Chang, 2005). This overcomes the limited choice of rotating angle and increases security. Flip VC (Lin, Chen & Lin, 2010) has proved to have conditionally-optimal contrast, perfect security and no pixel expansion. Recursive VC (Gnanaguruparan & Kak, 2002) was designed such that multiple secrets can be hidden within the shares in an efficient manner.

EXTENDED VISUAL CRYPTOGRAPHY SYSTEM (EVCS)

EVCS can also be treated as a technique which has a shade of steganography. An application of EVCS is to avoid the custom examination, because the shares of EVCS are meaningful images, hence there are only few chances for the shares to be suspected. Though the work of Droste, (Droste, 2001), pioneered

EVCS, the work of Ateniese, Blundo, Santis & Stinson, (Ateniese, Blundo, Santis & Stinson, 2001), is remarkable. Each pixel of the original image will be encoded into n pixels, each of which consists of m sub-pixels as per traditional VC.

Assume that $P=\{i_1,i_2,i_3,\ldots,i_n\}$ is a group of 'n' participants, and 2^P denotes the power set of P. T_{qual} denotes a set of subsets of from which the secret can be recreated; thus T_{qual} belongs to P, . Each set in T_{qual} is said to be a qualified set, while each set not in T_{qual} is called a forbidden set (denoted as T_{forb}). Noticeably, $T_{qual} \cup T_{forb} = 2^P$. When the shares associated with the participants in any set, S, which belongs to T_{qual}, are stacked together, the secret image can be created. But any S from T_{forb} has no information related to the secret image.

Assume T_0 consists of all the minimal qualified sets, then

$$T_0 = \left\{ A \in T_{qual} : A' \notin T_{qual}, \forall A' \subset A \right\} \tag{2}$$

In traditional secret sharing schemes, T_{qual} is found to be increasing monotonously and T_{forb} is decreasing monotonously. Hence the access structure is said to be very strong.

In such a strong access structure,

$$T_{qual} = \left\{ X \subseteq P : Y \subseteq X, \forall Y \in T_0 \right\} \tag{3}$$

and we say that T_{qual} is the closure of T_0. For example, if there are 4 users sharing a secret image (i.e., $P=\{ i_1, i_2, i_3, i_4 \}$) and $T_{qual}=\{\{ i_1,i_3, i_4 \}$ and $\{ i_1,i_2, i_4 \}\}$, superimposing any set of the subsets, $\{ i_1,i_3, i_4 \}$ and $\{ i_1,i_2, i_4 \}$, or $\{ i_1,i_2, i_3, i_4 \}$ can only reveal the secret, otherwise, no information is displayed.

The EVCS takes a secret image and original share images as inputs, and outputs shares (as in Figure 9) that satisfy the following conditions:

- Any share belonging to the qualified subset can be used to reveal the secret.
- Any share belonging to the forbidden subset cannot obtain any aspect of the secret except the size.
- All shares must be meaningful.

The first condition is related with the image contrast, and states that when a qualified set of users superimpose their shares they can reconstruct the secret correctly. The contrast should be as large as possible.

The second condition is related to the security-level, since it implies that, even after examining all their shares, a forbidden set of users cannot get any details regarding the color of the shared pixel.

Example: In this case there are three users – User 1, User 2 and User 3. $T_{Qual} =\{(1,2), (2,3), (1,2,3)\}$, $T_{Forb}=\{(1,3)\}$

Figure 9. Results of EVCS

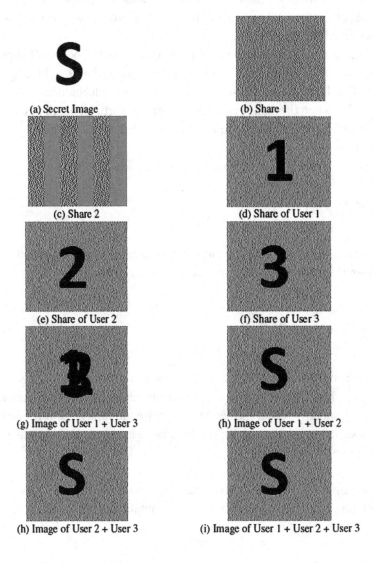

Analysis

Since the approach uses the basic principle of Naor and Shamir's VC technique, the problem of pixel expansion is evident. Liu, Wu & Lin, in 2009, proposed a step construction to construct EVCS for General Access Structures by applying (2,2)-VCS recursively such that the participants can take multiple share images for sharing one secret image. An EVCS approach was proposed by Lee & Chiu, in 2011 which avoids pixel expansion.

VISUAL CRYPTOGRAPHY FOR GRAYSCALE AND COLOR IMAGES USING HALFTONING TECHNIQUES

The VC techniques discussed so far are applicable to binary images only. In order to extend these methods to be applicable to grayscale and color images, a pre-processing technique is required. This pre-processing technique is called halftoning technique. Halftoning is a reprographic technique that simulates continuous tone imagery through the use of dots, varying either in size or in spacing, thus generating a gradient-like effect. The continuous tone imagery contains an infinite range of colors and grays. The halftone process reduces visual reproductions to an image that is turned out with only one color of ink, in dots of differing size or spacing. These tiny halftone dots are blended into smooth tones by the human visual system. The grayscale or color images are first halftoned, and then subjected to VC either under traditional system or under random grids. Several halftoning techniques described in (Ulichney, 1987) have been tabulated in Figure 10.

Several approaches for implementing VC on halftoned images has been proposed succeeding the work of (Hou, 2003) in (Hou & Tu, 2005), (Shyu, 2006), (Zhou, Arce & Di Crescenzo, 2006), (Wang, Arce& Di Crescenzo, 2009), (Cimato, Prsico & Santis, 2011), (Askari, Heys & Moloney, 2012), (Askari, Heys & Moloney, 2013), (Askari, Heys & Moloney, 2014), and (Ou, Ye & Sun, 2015). However halftoning itself is a reduction process. Hence the halftoned images subjected to VC will be affected by contrast loss surely.

Apart from halftoning, Moire's pattern (Desmedt & Van Le, 2000), chaotic mapping (Huynh, Bharanitharan & Chang, 2015) and gray-level relative difference (Blundo, De Santis & Naor, 2000) can be used for applying VC on grayscale images. Similarly, image hatching technique (Weir, Yan & Kankanhalli, 2012) can be used to apply VC on color images.

Figure 10. Types of halftoning techniques

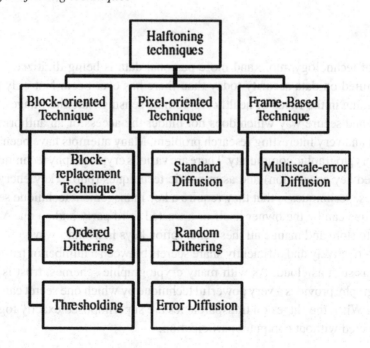

PROGRESSIVE VISUAL CRYPTOGRAPHY

The progressive VC is a simple technique to recover the secret image gradually by stackinging more and more shares. If a few pieces of shares are available, we could get only an outline of the secret; by increasing the number of shares and stacking them, the entire details of the secret information are exposed, progressively. Different techniques of progressive VC were proposed by Fang & Lin- (Fang & Lin, 2006), (Chen & Lin Chen & Lin, 2005), Fang (Fang, 2007) and Jin, Yan & Kankanhalli (Jin, Yan & Kankanhalli, 2005).

VISUAL CRYPTOGRAPHY USING CHAOTIC MAPPING

Apart from usual approach of processing the pixel values (based on algorithm) to generate shares, a new idea has been incorporated by Huynh, Bharanitharan & Chang in 2015. Along with the pixel values, the pixel positions are also employed to generate the shares using chaotic mapping. A Quadri-Directional Searching Algorithm has been employed to exploit the four-dimensional search strategy on Sudoku table while constructing the shares and while reconstructing secret image.

The approach is divided into two sub-processes: the share construction phase, and the secret image recovering and cover reconstructing phase. The pixels in secret image are at first converted into a base-9 numerical system to obtain a group of digits. While mapping this group of digits to the reference Sudoku table, there are four directions from the mapped value: North-West, North-East, South-East and South-West which contains all the pixels located in the upper-left corner, upper-right corner, bottom-right corner, and bottom-left corner, respectively. The main advantage of the method is that a grayscale secret image can be processed directly without any halftoning technique. Thereby the contrast loss due to halftoning technique has been cut-off. More over there is no room for pixel-expansion problem.

CONCLUSION

With the progress of technology, more and more personal data is being digitized, there is even more of an emphasis required on data security today than there has ever been. Not only personal data, the digitization is becoming in the fields of healthcare, remote sensing, satellite images, etc. Protecting all these data in a safe and secure way which does not hinder the access of an authorized authority is an immensely difficult and very interesting research problem. Many attempts have been made to solve this problem within the cryptographic community. There are various cryptography techniques in practice such as symmetric (shared key encryption) and asymmetric techniques (public key encryption). But major problem with all these techniques is that they require a key management technique separately. This key management technique can be the owner itself or a trusted third party and so on. A separate database has to be allocated to store and mange all these encryption keys in a smart way.

VC allows us to effectively and efficiently share secrets between a number of trusted parties or users and storage locations such as cloud. As with many cryptographic schemes, trust is the most difficult part. Visual cryptography provides a very powerful technique by which one secret can be distributed into two or more shares. When the shares on transparencies are superimposed exactly together, the original secret can be discovered without computer participation.

Many types of visual cryptography are examined that is from the very first type of traditional visual cryptography right up to the latest developments. Traditional VC specifically deals with sharing a single binary secret among a number of participants. The VC using random grids is an alternate to that of the traditional VC as it reduces the problem of pixel expansion. Segment-based VC is another approach which can be employed to encrypt numbers. Extended VC attempts to take this a step further by introducing shares that have significant visual meaning. This detracts from the suspicious looking encrypted shares that are generated using the traditional VC. MIVC allows encryption of more than one secret image. Progressive VC releases the secret progressively. Moire's cryptography and image hatching VC schemes are some of the other developments. Halftoning techniques have been briefed which makes VC to be employed on color and grayscale images. The grayscale and color images can also be an input to all the VC schemes. The VC using chaotic mapping is the latest model of VC which has been discussed.

The VC is simpler to be implemented since it needs an algorithm during encryption alone. There is troublesome decryption part. The secrets can be visualized by the human vision easily just by stacking the shares which is equivalent to logical OR operation. Another major contribution of VC will be that it is a keyless encryption technique. Obviously it does not need any external key management system. All these advantages of VC make it simpler than other cryptography techniques in practice. This can be a best alternative if explored. A small attempt has been made to explore the possibility of building a secure cloud storage using visual cryptography. Additionally, an overview of visual cryptography schemes from basic models to recent advanced schemes has been presented. This can be integrated in cloud environment to provide trustworthy image storage in future using visual cryptography.

REFERENCES

Altaf, A., Sirhindi, R., & Ahmed, A. (2008). A Novel Approach against DoS Attacks in WiMAX Authentication Using Visual Cryptography. *Second International Conference on Emerging Security Information, Systems and Technologies, 1*(1), 238-242. doi:10.1109/SECURWARE.2008.52

Askari, N., Heys, H. M., & Moloney, C. R. (2013). An extended visual cryptography scheme without pixel expansion for halftone images. *26th Annual IEEE Canadian Conference on Electrical and Computer Engineering*, 1-6. doi:10.1109/CCECE.2013.6567726

Askari, N., Heys, H. M., & Moloney, C. R. (2014). Novel visual cryptography schemes without pixel expansion for halftone images. *Canadian Journal of Electrical and Computer Engineering, 37*(3), 168–177. doi:10.1109/CJECE.2014.2333419

Askari, N., Moloney, C., & Heys, H. M. (2012). A novel visual secret sharing scheme without image size expansion. *25th IEEE Canadian Conference on Electrical & Computer Engineering*, 1-4. doi:10.1109/CCECE.2012.6334888

Ateniese, G., Blundo, C., Santis, A., & Stinson, D. (2001). Extended capabilities for visual cryptography. *Theoretical Computer Science, 250*(1-2), 143–161. doi:10.1016/S0304-3975(99)00127-9

Blundo, C., De Santis, A., & Naor, M. (2000). Visual cryptography for grey level images. *Information Processing Letters, 75*(6), 255–259. doi:10.1016/S0020-0190(00)00108-3

Borchert, B. (2007). *Segment-based visual cryptography*. Tübingen, Germany: University of Tübingen.

Chaum, D. (2004). Secret-ballot receipts: True voter-verifiable elections. *IEEE Security & Privacy Magazine*, 2(1), 38–47. doi:10.1109/MSECP.2004.1264852

Chen, S., & Lin, J. (2005). Fault-tolerant and progressive transmission of images. *Pattern Recognition*, 38(12), 2466–2471. doi:10.1016/j.patcog.2005.04.002

Chen, T., Tsao, K., & Wei, K. (2008). Multiple-Image Encryption by Rotating Random Grids.*Eighth International Conference on Intelligent Systems Design and Applications*, 3(1), 252-256. doi:10.1109/ISDA.2008.141

Cimato, S., Prsico, R. D., & Santis, A. D. (2011). Visual cryptography for color images. I Visual Cryptography and secret image sharing, (pp. 32-56). Boca Raton, FL: CRC Press.

Desmedt, Y., & Van Le, T. (2000). Moire cryptography.*Proceedings of the 7th ACM conference on Computer and communications security*, 116-124.doi:10.1145/352600.352618

Droste, S. (2001). New Results on Visual Cryptography. *Advances in Cryptology — CRYPTO '96. Lecture Notes in Computer Science*, 1109, 401–415. doi:10.1007/3-540-68697-5_30

Fang, W., & Lin, J. (2006). Progressive viewing and sharing of sensitive images. *Pattern Recognition and Image Analysis*, 16(4), 632–636. doi:10.1134/S1054661806040080

Fang, W. P. (2007). Multi-layer progressive secret image sharing.*Seventh WSEAS International Conference on Signal Processing, Computational Geometry & Artificial Vision*, 112-116.

Gnanaguruparan, M., & Kak, S. (2002). Recursive Hiding Of Secrets In Visual Cryptography. *Cryptologia*, 26(1), 68–76. doi:10.1080/0161-110291890768

Hou, Y. (2003). Visual cryptography for color images.*Pattern Recognition*,36(7),1619–1629.doi:10.1016/S0031-3203(02)00258-3

Hou, Y. C., & Tu, S. F. (2005). A visual cryptographic technique for chromatic images using multi-pixel encoding method. *Journal of Research and Practice in Information Technology*, 37(2), 179–192.

Huynh, N., Bharanitharan, K., & Chang, C. (2015). Quadri-directional searching algorithm for secret image sharing using meaningful shadows. *Journal of Visual Communication and Image Representation*, 28, 105–112. doi:10.1016/j.jvcir.2015.01.011

Jin, D., Yan, W. Q., & Kankanhalli, M. S. (2005). Progressive color visual cryptography. *Journal of Electronic Imaging*, 14(3), 033019–033019. doi:10.1117/1.1993625

Kafri, O., & Keren, E. (1987). Encryption of pictures and shapes by random grids. *Optics Letters*, 12(6), 377–377. doi:10.1364/OL.12.000377 PMID:19741737

Lee, K., & Chiu, P. (2011). An Extended Visual Cryptography Algorithm for General Access Structures. *IEEE Transactions on Information Forensics and Security*, 7(1), 219–229. doi:10.1109/TIFS.2011.2167611

Lin, K., Lin, C., & Chen, T. (2014). Distortionless visual multi-secret sharing based on random grid. *Information Sciences*, 288(1), 330–346. doi:10.1016/j.ins.2014.07.016

Lin, S., Chen, S., & Lin, J. (2010). Flip visual cryptography (FVC) with perfect security, conditionally-optimal contrast, and no expansion. *Journal of Visual Communication and Image Representation, 21*(8), 900–916. doi:10.1016/j.jvcir.2010.08.006

Liu, F., Wu, C., & Lin, X. (2009). Step Construction of Visual Cryptography Schemes. *IEEE Transactions on Information Forensics and Security, 5*(1), 27–38. doi:10.1109/TIFS.2009.2037660

Naor, M., & Shamir, A. (1995). Visual cryptography. *Advances in Cryptology — EUROCRYPT'94. Lecture Notes in Computer Science, 950*(1), 1–12. doi:10.1007/BFb0053419

Naor, M., & Shamir, A. (1997). Visual cryptography II: Improving the contrast via the cover base. Security Protocols Lecture Notes in Computer Science, 1189, 197-202. doi:10.1007/3-540-62494-5_18

Ou, D., Ye, L., & Sun, W. (2015). User-friendly secret image sharing scheme with verification ability based on block truncation coding and error diffusion. *Journal of Visual Communication and Image Representation, 29*, 46–60. doi:10.1016/j.jvcir.2015.01.017

Ross, A., & Othman, A. (2010). Visual Cryptography for Biometric Privacy. *IEEE Transactions on Information Forensics and Security, 6*(1), 70–81. doi:10.1109/TIFS.2010.2097252

Roy, S., & Venkateswaran, P. (2014). Online payment system using steganography and visual cryptography. *IEEE Students' Conference on Electrical, Electronics and Computer Science, 1*(1), 1-5. doi:10.1109/SCEECS.2014.6804449

Shyu, S. (2006). Efficient visual secret sharing scheme for color images. *Pattern Recognition, 36*(5), 866–880. doi:10.1016/j.patcog.2005.06.010

Shyu, S. (2007). Image encryption by random grids. *Pattern Recognition, 40*(3), 1014–1031. doi:10.1016/j.patcog.2006.02.025

Shyu, S., Huang, S., Lee, Y., Wang, R., & Chen, K. (2007). Sharing multiple secrets in visual cryptography. *Pattern Recognition, 40*(12), 3633–3651. doi:10.1016/j.patcog.2007.03.012

Tai, G., & Chang, L. (2004). Visual Cryptography for Digital Watermarking in Still Images. *Lecture Notes in Computer Science, 3332*(1), 50–57. doi:10.1007/978-3-540-30542-2_7

Ulichney, R. (1987). *Digital halftoning.* MIT Press.

Wang, Z., Arce, G. R., & Di Crescenzo, G. (2009). Halftone visual cryptography via error diffusion. *IEEE Transactions on Information Forensics and Security, 4*(3), 383–396. doi:10.1109/TIFS.2009.2024721

Weir, J., Yan, W., & Kankanhalli, M. S. (2012). Image hatching for visual cryptography. *ACM Transactions on Multimedia Computing, Communications, and Applications, 8*(2S), 32. doi:10.1145/2344436.2344438

Wu, C. C., & Chen, L. H. (1998). *A Study on visual cryptography.* (Master Thesis). Institute of Computer and information Science, National Chiao Tung University, Taiwan, China.

Wu, H., & Chang, C. (2005). Sharing visual multi-secrets using circle shares. *Computer Standards & Interfaces, 28*(1), 123–135. doi:10.1016/j.csi.2004.12.006

Zhou, Z., Arce, G. R., & Di Crescenzo, G. (2006). Halftone visual cryptography. *IEEE Transactions on Image Processing, 15*(8), 2441–2453. doi:10.1109/TIP.2006.875249 PMID:16900697

KEY TERMS AND DEFINITIONS

Extended Visual Cryptography: Extended Visual Cryptography can treated as a technique which has a shade of steganography. It outputs meaningful shares inorder to avoid the custom examination. That is the shares have a cover image.

Image Security: The process or technique of protecting the images stored in a database using encryption algorithm is called as image security. Mostly cryptography algorithms are used to secure the images in the database.

Multiple-Image Visual Cryptography: Multiple-image visual cryptography is used to hide more than one secret image within the shares.

Progressive Visual Cryptography: The progressive visual cryptography is a technique of visual cryptography which reveals the secret progressively with the increase in the number of shares being stacked.

Random Grid Based Visual Cryptography: Random grid based visual cryptography is a bit-based approach to encrypt binary images. A random grid is a transparency comprised of a two-dimensional array of pixels which may be black or white, and the choice between them is made by a coinflip procedure.

Segment-Based Visual Cryptography: Segment-based Visual Cryptography is a special type of visual cryptography which can encrypt numbers in seven-segment display format. The numbers 0 to 9 can be encrypted using this type of cryptography.

Visual Cryptography: Visual cryptography is a cryptographic technique in which a secret image is converted into two or more meaningless, non-identical shares, without using any encryption keys. The hidden secret can be revealed only when the shares are stacked together.

Chapter 16
Visual Sensor Networks:
Critical Infrastructure Protection

Suseela G
VIT University, India

Asnath Victy Phamila Y
VIT University, India

ABSTRACT

Visual Sensor Network (VSN) is a network of distributed battery-powered low-cost cameras and CMOS image sensors, each with the capability of capturing, processing, sending, and receiving images. VSN applications include remote monitoring, Security, elderly assistance, Visual Ubiquity, home monitoring, tracking. The highly sensitive nature of images makes security and privacy in VSNs even more important than in most other sensor and data networks. However, the direct use of security techniques developed for scalar WSN will not be suitable for VSN due to its resource constraint. Hence light weight security mechanisms need to be explored. In this chapter the challenging security issues at various layers in VSN are addressed. It also fosters discussion on privacy protection techniques like subjective privacy, Video masking techniques and identifies recent trends in VSN security and privacy. A discussion of open research issues concludes this chapter.

INTRODUCTION

The modern advancements in CMOS technology and micro electro mechanical systems, the traditional scalar Wireless Sensor Network (WSN) equipped with low cost digital cameras, fostered it to sense and transmit the visual data and conceived as Visual Sensor Network (VSN).The camera attached sensor nodes are called as VS node, and each such node has the ability to capture, manipulate and transmit image data to the base station or sink node using intermediate forwarding nodes in multi hop fashion.

DOI: 10.4018/978-1-5225-0193-0.ch016

Figure 1. Visual Sensor Network

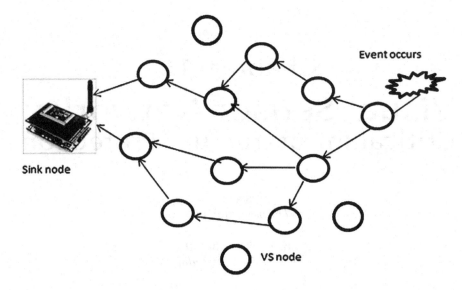

Figure 2. Sensor mote architecture

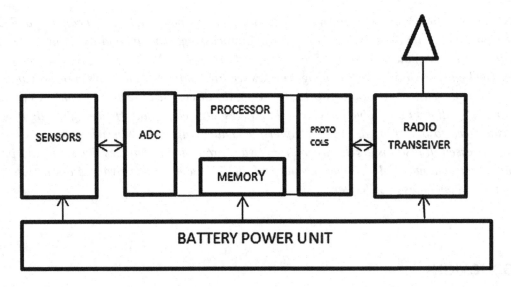

Usually the sink node will act as aggregator, it is more powerful and it will act as a gateway. The schematic architecture of VSN can be as shown in Figure 1. A sensor node defined as an embedded system with one or more sensors, micro controller, transceiver and a battery unit capable of sensing, processing and transmitting. Figure 2 shows the architecture of sensor node or mote.

The VSN differs from their predecessor scalar wireless sensor networks basically in two aspects. They are type and volume of pixel data being captured and transmitted. The inherent resource constraint nature of WSN in computation, memory, bandwidth and energy makes the visual sensor network designs more challenging for image transmission.

Figure 3. Visual Sensor Network applications

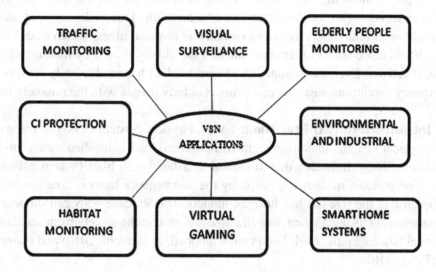

VSN APPLICATIONS

In Visual Sensor Network the VS nodes are arrayed in places where they can be used to monitor environmental conditions by cooperating and communicate with each other over the wireless communication channels.

Visual Sensor Networks will enrich the existing sensor network applications such as tracking, environmental monitoring, industrial control and smart home systems. Yet quite a lot of new commercial applications are emerging out (Hemant, Subhas, Xiang & Nagender (2015), (Bambang & Song, 2010). Figure 3 shows some of the applications of VSN. They are:

- **Visual Surveillance:** Low cost image sensors will be used to enhance and complement existing mission critical systems against criminality and terrorism like surveillance systems. The scalable visually equipped sensor network can extend the ability to support law prosecution activities to monitor zones, communal events, private stuffs, and hard to access areas like borders, high mountains.
- **Traffic Monitoring and Control:** The cheaper, easily organisable VSNs when deployed to monitor and regulate the vehicular traffic over the civilian structures such as highways, bridges. The image data or video streams along high level image processing system, the traffic COPS can enforce the rules and law of civilian bodies.
- **Environmental and Industrial:** Set of video sensors along with scalar sensors and efficient image processing systems are used by scientists to study the biological or physical phenomenon in the environment like sea, mines. Multimedia data such as image/video and scalar data temperature, pressure from the WSN can be used for time-critical industrial process control (Cristina, Pedro, Andres, Fulgencio, Juan & Roque, 2010).
- **Habitat Monitoring:** The video streams and still images, along with competent image processing techniques like back ground subtraction,video analytics, can be used to discover last person, trace the criminals or terrorists or even missing animals in the forest.

- **Elderly People Monitoring:** The quality living of elderly people has created a great demand for innovative technologies for the betterment of elderly life. Due to demography there is always high jeopardy of chronic illness including mental and physical illness which leads to many health problems. VSNs can be used to remotely nursing the elderly people by monitoring their day-to-day physical activity. Even the system can be enhanced with wearable body sensors and can decide emergency conditions, instantly can connect elderly people with the remotely located health centres.

- **Critical Infrastructure (CI) Protection:** Cyber Physical System (CPS) is the natural or engineered physical systems that are integrated monitored, and controlled by an intelligent computational core. The fulmination due to natural disasters bomb blast by terrorist are noticeably increased. The periodic manual inspection by the maintenance team is time consuming and expensive because of the size CIs like bridges, tunnels. The Scalable VSN can support in reporting the deterioration of CIs due to their long life time and protect the society from accidental let-down or intentional attacks(Frank, Neil, Ian, Peter, Campbell, & Kenichi, 2010) and (Levente, Dennis, Alban & Peter, 2010).

- **Smart Home System:** Revolutions in technology typically arise from the needs of human society (Hemant, Subhas, Xiang & Nagender (2015). Household automation and monitoring are the important tenders of VSNs, where a set of heterogeneous sensors including image sensors are deployed, to observe different conducts of occupants. Smart home system assimilated with IOTs (Internet of Things) has attained extra ordinary attention by the researchers.

The pervasive computing and distributed intelligence of the IOTs enabled with wireless sensing technology are going to be the most striking technology in ubiquitous monitoring and control systems. In an epoch of IOTs, more devices (even domestic appliances) are interconnected to the IP based network like internet. With this technology a person can control any of his household system like oven, Washing machine etc., by being remote.

- **Virtual Ubiquity and Gaming Systems:** Virtual ubiquity systems allow virtual appointments to some locations such as virtual shops, aqua life that are monitored by a group of camera equipped sensors. These systems deliver the viewer with the current view or shot from the viewing angle, and provide the feel of existing physically at a focused faraway location.

VSNs has wide spread applications in the area of VR (Virtual Reality) computer gaming (Taner, Alex, & Nazife, 2015). Along with camera equipped image sensors, the virtual effect and real feel of the players on the gaming will be greatly boosted. These sensors will record the player's activity and stream it to other side. Kinect sensor is the popular and commercial tool widely used in VR gaming.

Visual Sensor Network Security Requirement

As Visual sensor networks gain more civilian attention, security becomes a major design issue. The visual data are more sensitive than scalar data, such that if an image data is tampered they will explicitly reveal the information content of the captured image while tampering the scalar data will mean it is a number. The visual data are easily analysed by human, they will not conceal privacy content of the image and exploit the polished clues about when, what and where it was captured. The VSN is vulnerable and can be demoralized to compromise the network task or to obtain unconstitutional admission to relevant information. The major security requirements for Visual Sensor Networks are described as follows:

- **Confidentiality:** The security mechanism should well protect the sensed data, so that it is not over seen by third parties. Confidentiality is required is not only for the sensed data but for attached control information like location/position information, time stamps, cryptographic keys and it should extended to entire path from camera node till it travels to base station or sink node. Confidentiality is in the sense that the information from camera node may be interpreted to compromise the network. Besides, the harvested data, from the Intrusion Detection system /mission critical application of a nation may be highly confidential.
- **Data Integrity:** Data integrity will be concerned with modification of original data. The receiver desires to be sure that it is not altered during transmission either purposely or by fortune. To differentiate unmodified "true" information from modified bogus data, the initiator must be identifiable distinctively.
- **Authenticity:** The adversary can inject bogus additional packets into the network; hence there should be a way to authorize the packet's origins. In VSN or in any WSN it is essential for every node including the sink node to have the ability to assure that received data is from legitimate nodes and to differentiate legitimate packets from bogus illegitimate packets.
- **Freshness:** Control messages and the payload propagating in the network would only be effective in a definite span of time. Adversary can make replay attacks, as a preventing measure of such threats and maintain the freshness of image data they must be time stamped indicating *when* it was captured. Any manipulation on received data should be tightly coupled with the time stamps violating packets, will be discarded.
- **Localization:** Localization is the crucial function of any wireless networks, specifically when the communicating parties are dispersed extensively. In VSN the sensor nodes randomly deployed over the geographical area. Secure localization is that the sensor nodes must provide only accurate position information of its location for localization.
- **Controlled Access:** The confidential sensitive image data and attached control information's access should be granted and limited to a group of legitimate nodes/users. This access limits should be maintained over the hierarchy for ensuring security.
- **Privacy:** This is a subcategory of confidentiality. Privacy protection is that defending the sensitive information of image data from the legitimate users itself. Whereas confidentiality is, defending the captured image data all the way from originator (camera node) to sink node. The sensed and collected data may convey more information to interveners either implicitly or explicitly bothering the privacy of the individuals. The privacy protection is the key requirement in VSN.

VSN Security Issues and Challenges

As wireless sensor networks endure to grow, there is a need for effective security mechanism. The sensor networks are deployed for tracing the sensitive data and operate in hostile unattended environment. In general A VSN consists of cooperative collection of distributed sensors which are trust worthy. But new illegitimate nodes can be inserted by attackers as legitimate nodes. The network should be integrated with

Figure 4. Communication layered architecture

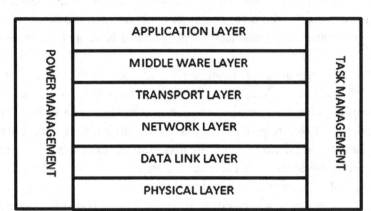

security mechanisms which authenticate the trust worthy members of the network. Also because of the undefended nature of wireless communication channel and untrusted transmission medium of wireless sensor networks, it becomes more vulnerable to many types of security attacks.

Due to inherent resource constraint nature and amount of pixel data produced by VSN, makes the traditional cryptographic algorithm inapplicable. Thus poses more challenges than any other wireless network or scalar WSN. It becomes mandate to have light weight security mechanisms to protect the image/video data.

Some of the common security threats or attacks are eavesdropping, masquerading, tampering attacks, wormhole, jamming attacks, black hole, Sybil attack, intruder nodes, collision attacks, Denial of service, compromised nodes, routing protocol attacks, and traffic analysis.

Vulnerabilities and Attacks in WSN: Layered Approach

The attacks and vulnerabilities are discriminated by their nature and by which layer they influence or target the protocol stack of the network architecture (Xiangqian, Kia, Kang, & Niki, 2009). Typical communication layered architecture of VSN is as depicted in Figure 4. Each layer is vulnerable to various attacks and some attacks can influence multiple layers. Also to have a light weight protocol stack, protocols designed for different task combined or cross coupled. Figure.4 is a typical depiction of Wireless Sensor Network layered architecture (Manel, Ruken, Barcelo, Kemal & Bulen, 2010). The attacks and threats in Visual Sensor Network are summarized in Table 1.

Physical Layer Attacks

Physical layer is responsible for choosing the physical medium for communication, in wireless network the medium is radio frequency band. Physical layer will be caring signal detection, modulation and demodulation of radio waves and carrier wave generation. The attacks at physical layer will aim at disrupting radio communication. They will be simply creating radio interference by broadcasting high frequency signal to jam the signal sent by the sensor node. This type of attack is called as jamming. This attack can be defended by using modulation schemes such as DSSS (Direct Sequence Spread Spectrum), frequency hopping techniques. Yet another way of mitigating jamming attack, on detection of the attacks the uncompromised legitimated node can adjust to low duty cycle intelligently. Because the attacker

Table 1. Types of attacks in VSN

Attacks	Description	Counter Measures
Eavesdropping	Unauthorized access of legitimate packets in network during its travel from originator to sink node.	Addition of artificial noise degrading only attacker's channel.
Traffic Analysis		
Homing Attack	Observing the network traffic pattern to detect the cluster head or Sink node where all data aggregated or adversary interested in knowing what event had happened, which had driven the communication.	Encryption of header data and by location privacy routing calls.
Intrusion		
Intruder Nodes and Compromised Nodes	The attacker aims in stealing the data by introducing illegitimate node or will obfuscate the legitimate node to work illegally.	By the use of node behaviour monitoring system like watch dog its trust worthiness can be measured and isolated (Youngho, Gang, & Yuanming, 2012).
Denial of Service Attacks		
Physical Attacks	Node capturing	Uncontrollable.
Tampering Attacks	Damaging the hardware of the sensor mote.	Uncontrollable.
Jamming Attacks	Distorting the radio communication at physical layer.	Use of Spread Spectrum, frequency hopping techniques and changing the duty cycle
MAC Protocol Attacks		
Collision	The intruder will make the receiver to overhear and discard packet by just by adding a byte into the original packet.T	Use of error correcting codes
Exhaustion	Compromising the system availability.	Random back off, TDMA slots
Unfairness	By non-priority MAC protocols, degrading the system performance.	Design of TDMA based MAC protocol with fair policy
Routing Protocol Attacks		
HELLO floods, bogus routing information, spoofing, Sybil attacks, sink hole, black hole and warm hole attack	False route advertisement, misdirection leading to loops or to malicious nodes.	Authentication, Encryption, multipath routing, identity verification, broadcasting authentication information to all sensor nodes and bidirectional link verification.
Transport Layer Attacks		
Flooding	The hacker will make excess number of connection request	Limiting the number of connections
Desynchronisation	Stealing sequence number and forging the bogus packets	Authentication of all the packets including control data.
Application Layer Attacks		
Overwhelm attack	By false sensor stimuli the sensor nodes will start sending more and more data to the sink node or base station.	Rate limitation, tuning sensors for desired event.
Deluge attack	By being remote the attackers will reprogram the nodes.	Authenticating the reprogramming process.

node is also with finite energy budget, its energy will be predepleted. Third way of mitigating jamming is identifying the jammed area and rerouting the packets around jammed area. Another physical layer attack is tampering. The attackers can physically tamper the sensor node, interrogate and compromise them. Tamper resistance hardware circuitry can be used for defending the attack. But the tamper resistance hardware itself often tampered (Karl & Willigs, 2005).

Data Link Layer Attacks

The data link layer is internally divided into Logical Link Control (LLC) layer and Medium Access Control (MAC) layer. The responsibility of this layer is framing, Flow Control, Error control and medium access control. The attacker can exhaust the communication channel by continuous channel access called as exhaustion. The counter measure is to use rate limiting MAC layer protocols, thus they will discard the excess channel request. Another way is to use TDMA (Time Division Multiple Access) slots. It is a channel access method based on reservation policy. Every node can access the channel only at their reserved time slot.

The other types of attacks in data link layer are collision, unfairness and Sybil attack. The attackers will attempt to send their frame simultaneously with the legitimate node. Thus the packets will colloid and original packets will be corrupted. The collided frames will be discarded at the receiver after error detection. The weaker form of denial of service attack is Unfairness. In non-priority MAC protocols the adversaries will not allow the legitimate nodes to transmit anything by over using the channel for long time. Being unfair will not degrade the entire network performance entirely but causes partial DoS attack which leads to minimal degradation of the system. This could be mitigated by use of small frame size so that a node can seize only for a short period of time. But this will increase framing overhead in VSN, because of the hugeness of the image data. Another way to defend this attack is use TDMA based priority MAC protocol with fair policy.

The prominent attack in link layer is Sybil attack. A single adversary node will hold multiple fake identities and provide false information to neighbouring genuine nodes. Thus single adversary acting as multiple Sybil nodes will make aggregated data at the cluster head as flawed or incorrect. This attack can also happen at network layer. Thwarting Link and MAC layer attacks are difficult but their effects are local.

Network Layer Attacks

Network layer is mainly responsible for routing. In WSN the sensor will send their data to the sink node in multihop fashion. The routing protocols for VSN have to be designed which are resilient to attacks. The attacks targeting the network will destruct the entire network operation. Black hole attack is prominent in network layer. The malicious will not forward and drop the incoming packets to its neighbour along the path to sink node. If all the packets are dropped it is defined to be Black hole attack. If certain packets alone dropped and remaining are forwarded it terms to be selective forwarding. Choice of random selection of path with multipath routing or implicit acknowledgement can be used to overcome this class of attack. In sink hole attack the compromised node will involve in routing decision and forged route advertisement will make all the packets to concentrate on its path. This attack can be prevented georouting protocols. The georouting protocols will establish the based on local position information. Another kind of attack is warm hole attack this is played by presence of two coordinated adversaries. One attacker node will record all the messages on its path and send it to the other attacker node. Then they will be replayed into network later on. This can be mitigated by shortest geographical to the base station with tight time synchronisation, which is rarely possible. Still more studies are needed handle worm hole and black hole attacks. Hello flood high powered adversary node will send hello packets to all the nodes in the network. The nodes will assume they are in the radio range of sender and causes more data to forwarded in the direction of these imaginary node. By use of proper authentication protocol this can be prevented.

The explicit attack in the routing protocol is targeting the routing information itself when it is being trafficked among the nodes. An adversary may modify, spoof, replay or reiterate the routing information to distract the traffic around the network. This can be counter measured by proper encryption and authentication systems. Homing is an attack in which the adversary targets to determine the physical position or geographic locations of the certain important node like sink node, cluster head by observing the traffic pattern. Once the position of the important nodes is known to the attacker he directs the other attacks to these for Denial of Service. Clearly the solution could be encryption of the location information.

Transport Layer Attacks

The transport layer is far most responsibility is establishing end to end reliable communication and session management of applications. This layer is mainly desired in WSN when the system needs to get gain access via IP based network like internet. Energy efficient transport layer protocols are proposed (e.g., CODA, GARUDA). The hacker will make excess number of connection request until the resources of the sensor node are exhausted; it is termed to be flooding attack. This attack can be prevented by limiting the number of connection request. Desynchronisation is continuously disturbing connection between the two end points by forging the sequence number which makes the end points to request for retransmission. The solution to this problem is authenticating all the packets including control data.

Application Layer Attacks

The attacks on this layer are overwhelming attack, deluge attack. The attacker tries to overwhelm the network by false sensor stimuli; the sensor nodes will start sending more and more data to the base station which lead to premature energy depletion of the sensor node. This attack could be countered by rate limitation and tuning the sensor node only for desired stimuli. By being remotely the adversary can reprogram the sensor node for his intension and control the network called as deluge attack. Authentication systems should be adapted for reprogramming process.

Security Vulnerability, Threats, and Attacks Classification Based on Goals

In general the attacks can be passive-illegitimate data access without disrupting the service of the VSN or active-Illegitimate access into network and glitch the service of the system for it was designed and deployed (Monika, Tushank, Sumit & Gunjan, 2014).

The attack can be internal or external. The internal attack is that, the legitimate node will act unintended fashion like compromised node. Whereas the external attack the attacker/hacker will stay exterior from the network and can make passive attack like eavesdropping or active attack like masquerading by overhearing the communication. The compromised nodes will reveal out all defence information to the adversary (Danilo, Gonçalves & Daniel, 2015). The uncompromised nodes will spend its energy in defending against the adversary's threats; the stressed node will get premature energy depletion and contract it life time. This will lead to attacks like service degradation, Denial of Service (DoS).If number of compromises increases, by executing malicious cryptographic tools uncompromised communication links will also compromised.

Further the attack can be node/mote level or laptop level. In node level attack sensors with equivalent capabilities of the legitimate nodes at the target network are engaged or the attacker can attain illegitimate control by reading the memory and make modifications in the software of which it was programmed and the second stated type of attack is called as node capturing, while laptop level attacks are based on devices with more processing and communication capabilities than the target node/mote.

The security threats are classified as following (Thomas,W., & Bernhard,R. 2014):

- User centric security,
- Data centric security,
- Network centric security, and
- Node centric security.

Data centric security, this type of security is based on nonrepudiation and secrecy for sensed image data. Data security can also be defined as security validity is guaranteed equivalent to the lifetime of the data.

Node centric security focuses all security aspects which are unswervingly influence the VSNs nodes, the node will be compromised on its software or even in hardware. Since the VSNs are deployed unattended hostile area physical capturing of the node or node destruction by attackers unpreventable. All defencing mechanisms done by a sensor node will entail additional energy. Stressing the node by attacks gives way to premature depletion and causing holes in the network. This is one specific type of a Denial-of-Service (DoS) attack.

Network centric security addresses peer to peer, broadcast and multicast communication. This kind of attack differs from data centric security. The network centric security assurances can hold true, only during that instance of the transmission.

User centric security defined to be making monitored society aware of VSNs and offering the opportunity to verify how society's personal data are privacy protected. From the perception of users, nonrepudiation and data confidentiality are greatly imperative. Need of privacy protection and privacy practices will be discussed in the following subsection.

Privacy Requirement and Protection Techniques

In context of scalar network, security means protecting the sensed and transmitted data from unauthorized access and modifications by the attacker. Privacy protection is that defending the information of image data from the legitimate users itself such that not admitting everyone in the network to access all transmitted data. Since the nature of image data is easily predictable even by exploring partial data. Images will reveal more information obviously like people's identity, location, time, behaviour, interactions, and many more.

Hence in VSN the data needs to be protected by privacy mechanism to have limited interactions within the network itself, The VSN is used prominently in visual monitoring and control systems and so Privacy in VSN seeks additional requirement as a feature of security. The privacy protection requirement makes the VSN to get its identity unique from other network applications.

But level of Privacy depends upon cultural attitudes of the individual who is monitored; also it depends on technological aspects of the system used. The task of incorporating Privacy promoting technologies with available technology resource constraint VSN system is a great technical challenge. Hence the level of privacy is usually stated through Privacy policies before designing the network.

Privacy Protection Techniques for Ensuring Security

Privacy means protecting the image data from the insiders of the network like network operators who have legitimate access. There are many techniques to ensure privacy. The simple and foremost is protecting the data by visual anonymisation. With complex image processing tools like computer vision system anonymisation is achieved in two steps. First the identity portion of the image data is detected example face of human or license plates of vehicles. Then in second step the detected identity information is obfuscated. The outcome of the anonymisation is that the identity portion of the image is protected while preserving the behavioural information. Another popular method called as abstraction, which is not allowing image data for transmission instead abstract of it is allowed to travel over the network. This gives good privacy protection but for the system operators it makes the processing impossible. On the other side allowing raw image data gives ease of processing by system operators and offers zero privacy protection. Because of these extremes the design space for privacy promoting techniques spans from no image data to raw image data yielding various classes of privacy protecting techniques as shown in Figure 5.

The privacy protection technique can be Global protection or Object Based protection. The Global protection, the privacy protection algorithm is uniformly applied for the entire visual frame. They are like blurring, edge detection, mosaicking and down sampling and the global protection techniques didn't gain popularity in the literature. In object based privacy protection scheme the privacy sensitive identity portion of the image obfuscated rest of the image is kept unprocessed.

Object Based Privacy Protection Techniques

This category of privacy protection techniques work by applying two algorithms: Detection Algorithm and Obfuscation Algorithm. All the techniques under this category purely rely on the strength of the detection algorithm, which detects private sensitive region of the visual frame. Privacy will be at risk if detection algorithm is not good enough in detecting. The prominent object based privacy protection techniques are blanking, pixelation, abstraction and encryption.

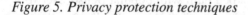

Figure 5. Privacy protection techniques

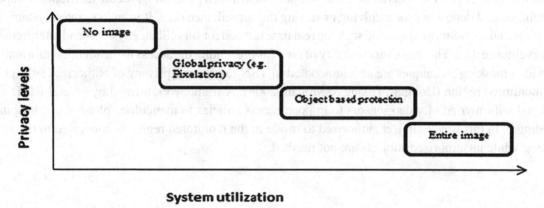

- **Blanking:** The identity region is completely removed from the image and left blank and behavioural information is also obfuscated implicitly. It will allow only existence and location the object sensed. This may not be suitable for systems for border surveillance because the system even cannot reveal about behaviour of the person monitored and it will not allow the system operators to identify the person.

- **Pixelation:** The general idea behind this category is to provide least detail of sensitive portion and behavioural information is preserved. The sensitive region is reconstructed with pixel blocks of various intensities. The obfuscation can also be achieved by mosaicking, blurring, scrambling, compression or fusion.

- **Abstraction:** In this method the sensitive image regions are replaced with bounding boxes, sticking figures, clipart's and even by cartooning. Alternate method of abstraction sending meta data about the image or video. The meta can be names of people, position and geometric elementary information. Depending upon the algorithm either or both identity and behavioural information is preserved.

- **Encryption:** Images are encrypted with cryptographic algorithm.The authourized users with decryption key alone will have the access to protected data.The encrption method preserves both identity and behavioural content of image data

One can make choice of selecting one of these methods or in combination based on stated privacy protection policy and system goals for which the network designated. Moreover multilevel privacy protection schemes can be employed. Based on the hierarchy of people or network operators different level of information can be observed by their priority.

Subjective Privacy

Beyond concentrating identity information, conveying behavioural information in visual surveillance is more trivial and that is called as subject privacy (Prabhu, Kumar, Mohankumar, 2014).The person or animal under surveillance is term as subject. In the sensor captured raw video, the identity information is removed and preserved behavioural information is conveyed to outside world with help of cryptography.

Douglas, Hoang & Mohan in 2004 had designed test bed architecture for measuring the subjective privacy called as NeST-Networked Sensor Tapestry. It is a test bed built with popular Sensor Network operating System TinyOS. This architecture supports distributed processing, secure distribution, capturing, and central depositary for archiving or storing the surveillance data. It is an integrated system core hardware and software, modular and scalable real time test bed for surveillance systems and interpretation of surveillance data. The major functionality of NeST is preventing the access to the identity information.

Video masking techniques are accommodated in VSN to preserve privacy of authorized subjects of the monitored region (Douglas, Hoang & Mohan, 2004). A frame work formed by several RFID sensors and with myriad of video sensors to impose access policies to meticulous places (e.g., hospitals, buildings). In this way, a subject authorized to reside in the monitored region is concealed in the video frames, while unauthorized subjects are not masked.

Image Cryptography

In general secure data transmission is assured with cryptography algorithms. The paradigm of securing visual data is called as visual cryptography. This is further categorized into symmetric and asymmetric based cryptographic key shared among the communicating parties.

Symmetric cryptography in this sub paradigm is a single key is used for both encryption at the source and decryption at the sink. This makes system simpler but key distribution in secured manner is the biggest challenge. Some of the classical symmetric cryptographic algorithms are AES-Advanced Encryption Standard, DES-Data Encryption Standard, IDEA -International Data Encryption Algorithm and modern algorithms designed using hash function are MD-5, SHA-1.

Asymmetric cryptography algorithm is also known as Public Key Cryptography (PKC).These algorithms use two different keys one for encryption at source and another for decrypting at the other end of the communication. All the nodes will use same key for encryption called as public key. Each node has their own private key for decryption. But PKC imposes more computational overhead which makes it is not feasible for resource constraint VSN. But over the years the cryptanalyst have proven the adaptability and feasibility of PKC in VSN. Some of the prominently used asymmetric cryptographic algorithms in communication networks are Rabin's scheme, Rivest, Shamir and Adelman (RSA), Elliptic curve cryptography (ECC). Rabin's scheme is based on factorization problem. In this encryption is faster than the decryption process than RSA for the same factors. RSA is based on classical number theory. This was employed to provide support for digital signature. Elliptic curve cryptography this is a combination for multiple key exchange algorithms and their associated negotiation.

Many researchers have experienced non suitability of PKC in VSN due to resource constraint. Symmetric Cryptography is comparatively superior than asymmetric cryptography in terms of resource utilization and time. The key management task is extremely hard task to promise security. Yet Competent and efficient key management schemes will make symmetric cryptography for wide acceptance in the VSN.

Key Management

The core part of any symmetric cryptography algorithm is always key management and it is a complex task. The dynamic network structure, adhoc nature also because of easily comprisable node the complexity of the key management task increased. In VSN the key management is mainly dedicated for establishing secure and reliable exchange of keys among the nodes, between nodes and the base station. These must be light weight and have the capability to adapt new node or revocation of the nodes at times. The key establishment can happen by probability or by network structure.

The key management task based on network structure can be done by dedicated node as centralised or the task can be shared among the nodes in a distributed fashion. Further the key management schemes can be categorized based on the operating styles. They are deterministic approaches or probability approach. Some of the schemes associate one or two above said approaches (Figure 6).

The dedicated node in centralised system is responsible for key generation, regeneration, dispensing and revoking. As with any centralised system this system also suffers with bottle neck problem, single point failure and not scalable. A popular centralised scheme based protocol is Logical Key Hierarchy for WSN (LKHW). On the other side in distributed scheme the key management task is shared among the nodes, which allows good scalability and fault tolerance and well adopted by its nature.

Figure 6. Classification of key management protocols

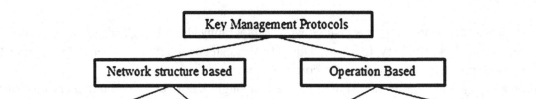

Moreover there are two other classifications based on the operation such as deterministic and probabilistic. In deterministic the keys are implanted in the node itself before deployment known as Pre-distribution. Localized Encryption and Authentication Protocol (LEAP) is based on pre-distribution scheme. In the following subsection will brief about pre-distribution schemes and probabilistic schemes. Probabilistic schemes are based on the likelihood or the probability of communication among nodes in their sensing region. A sensor node will share its key only if the neighbouring node is in its coverage area and makes communication. Random Key Pre-distribution (RKP) protocol is built with probabilistic scheme. Mostly the successful key management protocols are distributed and probabilistic in WSN.

Pre-Distribution Key Management System

Before deployment the sensors nodes stored with some initial keys. These initial keys are used by sensor nodes after deployment for secure communication and transmission. This is the simplest and easiest method of key management in terms of computation cost and energy. The keys are distributed in the nodes as distributed key management. Because of this property the number of communications between sensor node and sink node is lesser than the centralised approaches. Hence forth this method optimizes the resource utilization. There are several methods followed for pre distribution.

One simple method is to make all sensor nodes to hold a global master key. The interested nodes can communicate by sharing the master key. This method does not require additional memory requirement since single key is used, managed and stored by each node. The major challenge of this system is node compromization. If even a single node is compromised by attacker then entire sensor network will get compromised. Secure storage like tamper resistance hardware can be used to store master key. Equipping the cheap sensor node with this kind of tamper resistant hardware is impractical for this generation sensor mote.

Second method of pre-distribution key management is generating pairwise secret key for all the N nodes in the network and storing all N-1 pairwise key each sensor node. Each pairwise secret key is known only to the sensor and one of its associated pair among the N-1 nodes in the network. This could be mitigating the compromised nodes, if single node is compromised will not influence the network security. The size of pairwise key grows with number of nodes. It's impractical to store such a big set of pairwise key into the currently available sensor motes with memory in Kilobytes. Moreover addition of new node into the network will become labour some-for the newly added nodes the already existing nodes will have pairwise key. Yet another way to optimise the pairwise key list size is to use the probabilistic approach rather than deterministic. That is the shared key for a pair of nodes, is not certainly guaranteed and it is kept as probabilistic.

Probabilistic Key Management Scheme

The shared key for a pair of nodes is not certain and it is guaranteed by probability. A popular scheme of probability key distribution is Random Key Pre-distribution system, in short known as RKP. The sensor nodes are stored randomly with a subset of shared keys from a global set of keys prior to the node deployment. Another variant of key management scheme is probabilistic pre key distribution scheme. The ideology behind this scheme storing small set of shared key randomly from global set of keys into the sensor nodes will assure high probability of any two adjacent nodes have shared key for trusted communication with each of them. This scheme follows three steps for secure key distribution and communication. They are:

1. Pre-distribution of key before deployment,
2. Shared key detection among the nodes, and finally
3. Path-key establishment for secure connection establishment between the pair of nodes.

Deterministic Key Management Scheme

In deterministic the key is certainly shared among the nodes, thus key sharing is deterministic. Here a pair of intermediate nodes in the path from source node to destination node can share one or more pre-distributed secret key. These schemes require a small secure interval time after deployment. During this interval the nodes will start bootstrapping process and with small set of keys they start exchange of keys among the neighbouring nodes. The following are the deterministic based key management protocols, Peer Intermediaries for Key Establishment (PIKE), Localized Encryption and Authentication Protocol (LEAP).

1. **Peer Intermediaries for Key Establishment (PIKE):** This type of key management protocols will make key establishment between the neighbouring nodes by use of one or more trustworthy intermediate nodes. PIKE is deterministic hence guarantees the key establishment between any two node. The computational complexity and memory requirement of PIKE grows sub linearly with the size of the network. However the computational overhead in PIKE is more than Random Key Pre-distribution schemes (RKP).
2. **Localized Encryption and Authentication Protocol (LEAP):** In contrary with PIKE, LEAP will not allow intermediate nodes to expose the pairwise secret key. Like PIKE this also uses secure interval time for bootstrapping. LEAP defines four different types of key for each senor node suitable for all types of communication in the network. Such that:
   a. An individual key-Used for communicating with base station.
   b. A pairwise key-used for communicating with another sensor node.
   c. A cluster key-shared for communicating with neighbouring nodes within the cluster.
   d. A group key- shared for communicating with all the nodes in the network.

The security mechanisms employed for scalar wireless sensor networks can be applied for visual sensor networks, if the chaining of image data capturing, coding or processing and transmissions are appropriately deliberated.

Selective Image Encryption

The task of encryption and decryption is expensive and complex. Inherent nature of VSN may not afford such expense. Most of the contributions in WSN are in energy optimisation. Hence the security aspect is less desired or optimally sought even though it is highly necessitated. The volume of pixel data is large and difficulty of affording security mechanisms further increases for VSN. Generally data encryption is applied to the entire data but to exclude the computational overhead encryption is applied only to selective region of the image and that is the central idea behind selective image cryptography. Selective encryption provides reasonable secure data transmission while reducing the complexity. Many image transformations or coding algorithms will segregate the most significant portions of the image. To ensure the security it is enough to encrypt only most significant portion of the compressed image (Wickramasuriya, Datt, Mehrotra, & Venkatasubramanian,2004).

In VSN selective or partial image can be carried out by coding techniques or edge detection. These techniques will give the most significant portion of the image like face of human. The coding techniques will decompose the image and group the pixels by their significance. For selective image encryption quad-tree decomposition and Discrete Wavelet Transform (DWT) are well suited.

1. **Quadtree Based Image Decomposition:** Quadtree is a hierarchical data structure like binary tree. Each node in the tree has zero to four children. The nodes with children are internal nodes and nodes without next level are leaf nodes. The idea behind this coding technique number of bits needed to encode the image is proportional to the information content of that portion of the image. So the image is decomposed into variable sized blocks. The larger sized blocks are used to code the image portion with lesser information content at least number of bits and smaller sized blocks are used for coding image regions with significant information content at more number of bits.

   The Quadtree supports both lossy and lossless image compression. In lossless mode the algorithm, as a first step tests the image for homogeneity or for similarity. If the image is homogeneous, root node of the quadtree gets the grayscale information of the image. Then the grayscale image is decomposed into four quadrants as depicted in the Figure 7.

   The homogeneity test is done for each quadrant recursively. In lossless all the nodes are coded with same number of bits (same bit rate) and for lossless the leaf nodes are coded with different number of bits (variable bit rate). Unnecessary portions can be identified by quadtree and they can be removed for better compression. For selective encryption the significant regions are identified and they alone encrypted. Quadtree based selective encryption is simpler; also this approach uses constrained resources efficiently and hence adaptable for VSN.

2. **Discrete Wavelet Transform (DWT) Based Image Coding:** In this wavelets are used as filter coefficients. The DWT can be achieved with subband coding or with filter banks. The image is first applied one dimensional filtering by row wise, this gives two subband as L and H. Denoting Low pass filter and High pass filter respectively. Then these bands are again applied with one dimensional filtering by column wise, producing the resultant bands as LL, LH, HL, and HH. Figure 8 shows

Figure 7. Quadtree image decomposition

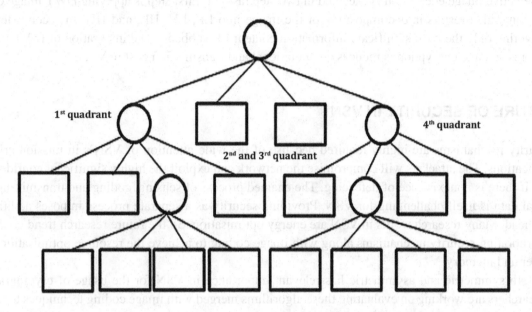

1st quadrant

2nd and 3rd quadrant

4th quadrant

encoding of two level decomposition of 256 x 256, image by DWT. This two dimensional wavelet filtering is called as first level decomposition. Iteratively the LL band is applied two dimensional filtering to second level decomposition. LL band represents the highly compressed small and smoothen version of the original image most significant regions of the image. LH band holds the row wise element, HL band holds the column wise elements and HH contains the diagonal elements of the original image.

Figure 8. DWT image transform

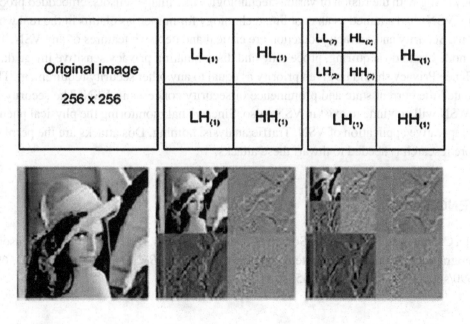

Selective image encryption is executed in two step fashion. First step is applying DWT image compression which results in decomposition of the image into LL, LH, HL, and HH. In second step by encrypting only the most significant information content LL subband. The integration of DWT image compression and encryption is reduces computational and transmission cost in VSN.

FUTURE OF SECURITY IN VSN

Security mechanisms are highly required because of the wide attention of VSN's in mission critical applications. The attackers will compromise the network and exploit the highly significant confidential data if there is nonexistence of defencing. The chained process of sensing, coding and transmitting the visual data is itself challenging for VSN. Providing security as a separate process imposes additional overhead. Many research works in VSN are energy optimisation. So the future research trend could be incorporating security mechanisms along with image coding to achieve the resource optimisation like power and memory.

Both symmetric and asymmetric has relevant importance in VSN for the usage of cryptography. Researchers are working on evaluating these algorithms merged with image coding techniques to make them feasible for VSN. Yet another trend is selective encryption with image coding.

The debate in any WSN is that the security and the expense of cryptographic algorithms. For such resource constraint environments providing security solution with fewer complexities is more required. The keyless visual encryption systems are emerging out to provide light weight security solutions for future pervasive computing systems.

CONCLUSION

VSNs have emerged due to the recent advancements in Micro electro Mechanical System (MEMS) Technology along with the fusion of various technologies like image sensors, embedded processing and computing. VSNs had attained as an enabling technology for numerous claims in the real world system applications. Security and privacy protection are critical and decisive features of any VSN. The camera equipped node has to do acquiring, processing and disseminating privacy sensitive image data or information. Hence Privacy should be given priority as equal to any other security requirement. This chapter has elucidated the current state and prominence of security concerns in VSN. The security challenges of scalar WSN will continue to exist in VSNs also. Since visual monitoring the physical phenomenon is the most imperative application of VSN, Traffic analysis, homing, Dos attacks are the perplexing areas where more research is needed to thwart these attacks.

REFERENCES

Albaladejo, C., Sanchez, P., Iborra, A., Soto, F., Lopez, J., & Torres, R. (2010). Wireless Sensor Networks for Oceanographic Monitoring: A Systematic Review. *Sensors (Basel, Switzerland)*, *1*(1), 6948–6968. doi:10.3390/s100706948 PMID:22163583

Buttyan, L., Gessner, D., Hessler, A., & Langendoerfer, P. (2010). Application of wireless sensor networks in critical infrastructure protection: Challenges and design options. IEEE Wireless Communications, 44-49.

Cevik, T., Gunagwera, A., & Cevik, N. (2015). A Survey of Multimedia Streaming in Wireless Sensor Networks: Progress, Issues and Design Challenges. *International Journal of Computer Networks & Communications, 7*(15), 95–114.

Chen, X., Makki, K., Yen, K., & Pissinou, N. (2009). Sensor network security: A survey. *IEEE Commun. Surv. Tutorials, 11*(2), 52–73. doi:10.1109/SURV.2009.090205

Cho, Y., Qu, G., & Wu, Y. (2012). Insider Threats against Trust Mechanism with Watchdog and Defending Approaches in Wireless Sensor Networks.*2012 IEEE Symposium on Security and Privacy Workshops, 1*(1). doi:10.1109/SPW.2012.32

Fidaleo, D., Nguyen, H., & Trivedi, M. (n.d.). The networked sensor tapestry (NeST).*Proceedings of the ACM 2nd International Workshop on Video Surveillance & Sensor Networks - VSSN '04, 1*(1), 934-939.

Ghayvat, H., Mukhopadhyay, S., Gui, X., & Suryadevara, N. (2015). WSN- and IOT-Based Smart Homes and Their Extension to Smart Buildings. *Sensors (Basel, Switzerland), 15*(5), 10350–10379. doi:10.3390/s150510350 PMID:25946630

Gonalves, D., & Costa, D. (2015). A Survey of Image Security in Wireless Sensor Networks. *Journal of Imaging*, 4-30.

Guerrero-Zapata, M., Zilan, R., Barcelo-Ordinas, J., Bicakci, K., & Tavli, B. (2009). The future of security in Wireless Multimedia Sensor Networks. *Telecommunication Systems Telecommun Syst, 1*(1), 77–91.

Harjito, B., & Han, S. (2010). Wireless Multimedia Sensor Networks Applications and Security Challenges.*2010 International Conference on Broadband, Wireless Computing, Communication and Applications, 1*(1), 842-846. doi:10.1109/BWCCA.2010.182

Monika, R., Tushank, B., Sumit, S., & Gunjan, B. (2014). Review of Threats in Wireless Sensor Networks. *International Journal of Computer Science and Information Technologies, 5*(1), 25–31.

Prabhu, T. N., Kumar, C. R., & Mohankumar, B. (2014). Energy-efficient and Secured Data Gathering in Wireless Multimedia Sensor Networks. *International Journal of Innovative Research in Computer and Communication Engineering., 2*(2), 3073–3079.

Stajano, F., Hoult, N., Wassell, I., Bennett, P., Middleton, C., & Soga, K. (2010). Smart bridges, smart tunnels: Transforming wireless sensor networks from research prototypes into robust engineering infrastructure. *Ad Hoc Networks, 8*(8), 872–888. doi:10.1016/j.adhoc.2010.04.002

Thomas, W., & Bernhard, R. (2014). Security and Privacy Protection in Visual Sensor Networks: A Survey. *ACM Computing Surveys, 47*(1), 2:1-2:47.

Wickramasuriya, J., Datt, M., Mehrotra, S., & Venkatasubramanian, N. (2012). Privacy protecting data collection in media spaces. *Proceedings of the 12th Annual ACM International Conference on Multimedia - MULTIMEDIA '04, 1*(1). doi:10.1145/1027527.1027537

ADDITIONAL READING

Costa, D. G., & Guedes, L. A. (2012). A Discrete Wavelet Transform (DWT)-based energy-efficient selective retransmission mechanism for wireless image sensor networks. *Journal of Sensor and Actuator Networks*, *1*(3), 3–35. doi:10.3390/jsan1010003

Eschenauer, L., & Gligor, V. D. (2002).A key-management scheme for distributed sensor networks. In *Proceedings of Conference on Computer Communications and Security*, (pp. 41–47). doi:10.1145/586110.586117

KEY TERMS AND DEFINITIONS

Asymmetric Cryptography: These algorithms use two different keys one for encryption at source and another for decrypting at the other end of the communication. All the nodes will use same key for encryption called as public key. Each node has its own private key for decryption.

Attacks: An attack is any unauthorized behaviour or attempt to access, copy and use or modify the data either by one or more entities in the network or by entities outside the network.

Confidentiality: Maintaining the secrecy of the information by security mechanisms which makes data or information, only accessible by authorized users and inaccessible by any other entity in the network.

Denial of Service (DoS): Rejection of an authorized user's access to the network by the system when its resource limits are exhausted. Usually the network resources will be intentionally exhausted by attacker to interrupt the service of the network.

Discrete Wavelet Transform (DWT): A popular widely accepted signal processing technique, which transforms signals from spatial to frequency domain. It preserves time information along with frequency information.

Image Cryptography: The paradigm of securing images or videos by applying cryptographic algorithms is known as visual cryptography or image cryptography.

Privacy: This is a subcategory of confidentiality. Privacy is shielding the sensitive information of image data from the legitimate users itself. Since images are self-descriptive, the sensed image data will convey more information to interveners either implicitly or explicitly bothering the privacy of the individuals. The privacy protection is the key requirement in VSN.

Quad Tree: It is tree type multidimensional or spatial data structure which has four branches as children. It is recursively subdivided to decompose the data stored.

Symmetric Cryptography: Single cryptographic key is used for both encryption at the source and decryption at the sink.

Compilation of References

10. th CSI/FBI Survey Shows "Dramatic Increase in Unauthorized Access". (2005). *IT Professional Magazine.*

Abate, A., Nappi, M., Riccio, D., & Sabatino, G. (2007). 2D and 3D face recognition: A survey. *Pattern Recognition Letters*, *28*(14), 1885–1906. doi:10.1016/j.patrec.2006.12.018

Abhishek Singh. (2010). *Demystifying Denial-Of-Service attacks*. Retrieved 02 November, 2010, from http://aka-community.symantec.com/connect/es/articles/demystifying-denial-service-attacks-part-one

Acuity. (2007). *Market intelligence, biometrics market development: Mega trends and meta drivers*. Retrieved January 2, 2016, from http://www.acuity-mi.com/hdfsjosg/euyotjtub/ Biometrics 2007 London.pdf

Adelsbach, A., Gajek, S., & Schwenk, J. (2005, January). Visual spoofing of SSL protected web sites and effective countermeasures. In ISPEC (Vol. 3439, pp. 204-216). doi:10.1007/978-3-540-31979-5_18

Adeyinka, O. (2008). Internet Attack Methods and Internet Security Technology. *2008 Second Asia International Conference on Modelling & Simulation* (AMS). doi:10.1109/SECPRI.2003.1199330

Agarwal, A., Gupta, M., Gupta, S., & Gupta, S. (2011). Systematic digital investigation model. *International Journal of Computer Science and Security, 5*(1).

Agrafioti, F., & Hatzinakos, D. (2008). ECG biometric analysis in cardiac irregularity conditions. *Signal. Image and Video Processing SIViP, 3*(4), 329–343. doi:10.1007/s11760-008-0073-4

Albaladejo, C., Sanchez, P., Iborra, A., Soto, F., Lopez, J., & Torres, R. (2010). Wireless Sensor Networks for Oceanographic Monitoring: A Systematic Review. *Sensors (Basel, Switzerland), 1*(1), 6948–6968. doi:10.3390/s100706948 PMID:22163583

Al-Duwairi, B., & Govindarasu, M. (2006). Novel hybrid schemes employing packet marking and logging for IP traceback. *IEEE Transactions on Parallel and Distributed Systems, 17*(5), 403–418. doi:10.1109/TPDS.2006.63

Al-Fedaghi, A., & Al-Babtain, B. (2012). Modeling the forensic process. *International Journal of Security and its Applications, 6*(4).

Altaf, A., Sirhindi, R., & Ahmed, A. (2008). A Novel Approach against DoS Attacks in WiMAX Authentication Using Visual Cryptography. *Second International Conference on Emerging Security Information, Systems and Technologies, 1*(1), 238-242. doi:10.1109/SECURWARE.2008.52

Altunbasak, H., Krasser, S., Owen, H., Sokol, J., Grimminger, J., & Huth, H. P. (2004, November). Addressing the weak link between layer 2 and layer 3 in the Internet architecture. In *Null* (pp. 417-418). IEEE.

Anomalous. (2012). *session-hijacking-explained*. Retrieved 15 July, 2012 http://hackingalert.blogspot.com/2011/05/session-hijacking-explained.html

Antic, B., Letic, D., Culibrk, D., & Crnojevic, V. (2009). K-means based segmentation for real-time zenithal people counting. *2009 16th IEEE International Conference on Image Processing (ICIP), 1*(1), 2565-2568. doi:10.1109/ICIP.2009.5414001

Antonatos, S., Akritidis, P., Markatos, E., & Anagnostakis, K. (2005). Defending against hitlist worms using network address space randomization. *Computer Networks*, 3471–3490.

Askari, N., Heys, H. M., & Moloney, C. R. (2013). An extended visual cryptography scheme without pixel expansion for halftone images.*26th Annual IEEE Canadian Conference on Electrical and Computer Engineering*, 1-6. doi:10.1109/CCECE.2013.6567726

Askari, N., Heys, H. M., & Moloney, C. R. (2014). Novel visual cryptography schemes without pixel expansion for halftone images. *Canadian Journal of Electrical and Computer Engineering, 37*(3), 168–177. doi:10.1109/CJECE.2014.2333419

Askari, N., Moloney, C., & Heys, H. M. (2012). A novel visual secret sharing scheme without image size expansion.*25th IEEE Canadian Conference on Electrical & Computer Engineering*, 1-4. doi:10.1109/CCECE.2012.6334888

Ateniese, G., Blundo, C., Santis, A., & Stinson, D. (2001). Extended capabilities for visual cryptography. *Theoretical Computer Science, 250*(1-2), 143–161. doi:10.1016/S0304-3975(99)00127-9

Bace, R. (1998). *An Introduction to Intrusion Detection and Assessment: for System and Network Security Management.* ICSA White Paper.

Badger, L., Bernstein, D., Bohn, R., Vaulx, F., Hogan, V., Mao, J., & Leaf, D. et al. (2011). *High priority requirements to further USG agency cloud computing adoption. In US Government Cloud Computing Roadmap* (Vol. I). NIST.

Badger, L., Bernstein, D., Bohn, R., Vaulx, F., Hogan, V., Mao, J., & Leaf, D. et al. (2011). *Useful Information for Cloud Adopters. In US Government Cloud Computing Roadmap* (Vol. 2). NIST.

Bai, N. Y., & Chiang, J. Y. (1998). Data hiding using binocular fusion of stereo pairs. In *Proceeding of eighth national conference in information security*, (pp. 245-254). Academic Press.

Barandiaran, J., Murguia, B., & Boto, F. (2008). Real-Time People Counting Using Multiple Lines.*2008 Ninth International Workshop on Image Analysis for Multimedia Interactive Services, 1*(1), 159-162. doi:10.1109/WIAMIS.2008.27

Barth, A., Jackson, C., & Mitchell, J. C. (2008, October). Robust defenses for cross-site request forgery. In *Proceedings of the 15th ACM conference on Computer and communications security* (pp. 75-88). ACM. doi:10.1145/1455770.1455782

Bass, T., Freyre, A., Gruber, D., & Watt, G. (1998). E-mail bombs and countermeasures: Cyber attacks on availability and brand integrity. *IEEE Network, 12*(2), 10–17. doi:10.1109/65.681925

BBC News. (2002) *Battling the net security threat.* Retrieved from http://news.bbc.co.uk/2/hi/technology/2386113.stm

BBC News. (2013). *Profile: Edward Snowden.* Retrieved from http://www.bbc.co.uk/news/world-us-canada-22837100

Bell, G. B. (2010). Solid State Drives: The Beginning of the End for Current Practice in Digital Forensic Recovery? *Journal of Digital Forensics, Security and Law, 5*(3), 1–20.

Bhandari, N. H. (2013). DDoS Attack Prevention In Cloud Computing Using Hop Count Based Packet Monitoring Approach. *International Journal of Advanced and Innovative Research, 2*(4), 954–956.

Bird, N., Masoud, O., Papanikolopoulos, N., & Isaacs, A. (2005). Detection of Loitering Individuals in Public Transportation Areas. *IEEE Transactions on Intelligent Transportation Systems, 6*(2), 167–177. doi:10.1109/TITS.2005.848370

Birk, D., & Wegener, C. (2011). Technical issues of forensic investigations in cloud computing environments. *Systematic Approaches to Digital Forensic Engineering,IEEE Sixth International Workshop.* doi:10.1109/SADFE.2011.17

Blundo, C., De Santis, A., & Naor, M. (2000). Visual cryptography for grey level images. *Information Processing Letters*, *75*(6), 255–259. doi:10.1016/S0020-0190(00)00108-3

Bonadea. (2015). *Rogue security software*. Retrieved from wikipedia.com

Borchert, B. (2007). *Segment-based visual cryptography*. Tübingen, Germany: University of Tübingen.

Brian. (2013). *Multi-vector DDoS Attacks Grow in Sophistication*. Retrieved 29January 2013 from: http://www.securityweek.com/multi-vector-ddos-attacks-grow

Brian. (2014). *2013-2014 DDoS Threat Landscape Report*. Retrieved 27 March 2014 from: http://threatpost.com/ntp-amplification-syn-floods-drive-up-ddos-attack-volumes

Brito, A. (2013). *Direito penal informático*. Sao Paulo: Editora Saraiva.

Brown, L. M., Senior, A. W., Tian, Y., Connell, J., Hampapur, A., Shu, C., & Lu, M. et al. (2005). Performance Evaluation of Surveillance Systems under Varying Conditions. In *Proc. IEEE PETS Workshop*, (pp. 1-8). IEEE.

Brustoloni, X., & Brustoloni, J. C. (2005). Hardening Web browsers against man-in-the-middle and eavesdropping attacks. *Proceedings of the 14th International Conference on World Wide Web - WWW '05*. doi:10.1145/1060745.1060817

Buttyan, L., Gessner, D., Hessler, A., & Langendoerfer, P. (2010). Application of wireless sensor networks in critical infrastructure protection: Challenges and design options. IEEE Wireless Communications, 44-49.

Camilla-Cooper. (2016). *Introduction to Ethical Hacking Intro to Ethical Hacking*. Retrieved from docslide.us

Canny, J. (1986). A Computational Approach to Edge Detection. *IEEE Transactions on Pattern Analysis and Machine Intelligence*, 679-698.

Carrier, B. (2003). *The Sleuth Kit Informer*. Retrieved from http://www.sleuthkit.org/informer/sleuthkit-informer-3.html

Carrier, B., & Spafford, E. (2003). Getting Physical with the Investigative Process. *International Journal of Digital Evidence*, *2*(2).

Casey, E. (2000). *Computer Evidence and Computer Crime: Forensic Science, Computers, and the Internet*. Cambridge, UK: Cambridge University Press.

Cevik, T., Gunagwera, A., & Cevik, N. (2015). A Survey of Multimedia Streaming in Wireless Sensor Networks: Progress, Issues and Design Challenges. *International Journal of Computer Networks & Communications*, *7*(15), 95–114.

Chakrabarti, A., & Manimaran, G. (2002). Internet infrastructure security: A taxonomy. *IEEE Network*, *16*(6), 13–21. doi:10.1109/MNET.2002.1081761

Chandramouli, R. (2003). A mathematical framework for active steganalysis. *Multimedia Systems*, *9*(3), 303–311. doi:10.1007/s00530-003-0101-8

Chaum, D. (2004). Secret-ballot receipts: True voter-verifiable elections. *IEEE Security & Privacy Magazine*, *2*(1), 38–47. doi:10.1109/MSECP.2004.1264852

Chen, Huang, Tian, & Qu. (2009). Feature selection for text classification with Naïve Bayes. *Expert Systems with Applications, 36*, 5432-5435.

Chen, S., & Lin, J. (2005). Fault-tolerant and progressive transmission of images. *Pattern Recognition, 38*(12), 2466–2471. doi:10.1016/j.patcog.2005.04.002

Chen, S., & Song, Q. (2005). *Perimeter-based defense against high bandwidth DDoS attacks. IEEE Trans. Parallel Distrib. Syst.*

Chen, T., Tsao, K., & Wei, K. (2008). Multiple-Image Encryption by Rotating Random Grids.*Eighth International Conference on Intelligent Systems Design and Applications, 3*(1), 252-256. doi:10.1109/ISDA.2008.141

Chen, X., Makki, K., Yen, K., & Pissinou, N. (2009). Sensor network security: A survey. *IEEE Commun. Surv. Tutorials, 11*(2), 52–73. doi:10.1109/SURV.2009.090205

Chothia, T., & Chatzikokolakis, K. (2005, January). A survey of anonymous peer-to-peer file-sharing. In Embedded and Ubiquitous Computing–EUC 2005 Workshops (pp. 744-755). Springer Berlin Heidelberg. doi:10.1007/11596042_77

Cho, Y., Qu, G., & Wu, Y. (2012). Insider Threats against Trust Mechanism with Watchdog and Defending Approaches in Wireless Sensor Networks.*2012 IEEE Symposium on Security and Privacy Workshops, 1*(1). doi:10.1109/SPW.2012.32

Cimato, S., Prsico, R. D., & Santis, A. D. (2011). Visual cryptography for color images. I Visual Cryptography and secret image sharing, (pp. 32-56). Boca Raton, FL: CRC Press.

Cisco. (2012). *What is Network security.* Retrieved 5 July 2012 from: http://www.cisco.com/cisco/web/solutions/small_business/resource_center/articles/secure_my_business/what_is_network_security/index.html

Clearswift. (2013). *The enemy within.* Retrieved from http://www.clearswift.com/sites/default/files/images/ blog/enemy-within.pdf

Cloud Computing Issues and Impact. (2011). Ernst & Young.

Condon, R. (2012). *Investigation reveals serious cloud computing data security flaws.* Retrieved on February 17, 2014 from http://www.computerweekly.com/news/2240148943/Investigation-reveals-serious-cloud-computing-data-security-flaws

Criscuolo, P. (2000). *Distributed Denial of Service Tools, Trin00, Tribe Flood Network, Tribe Flood Network 2000 and Stacheldraht.* Academic Press.

Criscuolo, P., & Rathbun, T. (1999). *Distributed System Intruder Tools.* Trinoo and Tribe Flood Network. doi:10.2172/792254

Curphey. (2011). *OWASP.* Retrieved from owasp.org

Cybercrime. (2015a). *Definition of Cybercrime.* Retrieved November 25, 2015 from https://www.techopedia.com/definition/2387/cybercrime

Cybercrime. (2015b). *Definition of Cybercrime.* Retrieved November 25, 2015 from http://techterms.com/definition/cybercrime

Cybercrime. (2015c). *Definition of Cybercrime.* Retrieved November 25, 2015 from http://www.britannica.com/topic/cybercrime

Daryabar, F., Deghantanha, A., Udzir, N. I., Sani, N. F., Shamsuddin, S., & Norouzizadeh, F. (2013). A survey about impacts of cloud computing on digital forensics. *International Journal of Cyber-Security and Digital Forensics, 2*(2), 77–94.

Decker, M. (2009, July). Prevention of Location-Spoofing-A Survey on Different Methods to Prevent the Manipulation of Locating-technologies. In ICE-B (pp. 109-114).

Delphinanto, A., Koonen, T., & den Hartog, F. (2011). Real-time probing of available bandwidth in home networks. *IEEE Communications Magazine, 49*(6), 134–140. doi:10.1109/MCOM.2011.5783998

Dempsey, K., Chah, N., Johnson, A., Johnston, R., Jones, A., Orebaugh, A., … Stine, K. (2011). *Information System Continuous monitoring for federal information Systems and Organizations.* NIST Special Publication 800-137.

Deng, F., Li, X., Zhou, H., & Zhang, Z. (2005). Improving the security of multiparty quantum secret sharing against Trojan horse attack. *Phys. Rev. A Physical Review A.*

Denning, D. E. (1987). An Intrusion Detection Model. *IEEE Transactions on Software Engineering, 13*(2), 222–232. doi:10.1109/TSE.1987.232894

Department of Justice. (2010). *Another pleads guilty in botnet hacking conspiracy.* Retrieved from http://www.cyber-crime.gov/smithPlea2.pdf

Desmedt, Y., & Van Le, T. (2000). Moire cryptography.*Proceedings of the 7th ACM conference on Computer and communications security,* 116-124.doi:10.1145/352600.352618

Dhamija, R., Tygar, J. D., & Hearst, M. (2006). Why phishing works. *Proceedings of the SIGCHI conference on Human Factors in Computing Systems - CHI '06.* doi:10.1145/1124772.1124861

Digital Evidence Standards and Principles. (April 2000). Forensic Science Communications. Retrieved from https://www.fbi.gov/about-us/lab/forensic-science-communications/fsc/april2000/swgde.htm/

Distler. (2007). *Malware Analysis- An Introduction.* Retrieved from sans.org

Douligeris, C., & Mitrokotsa, A. (2004). DDoS attacks and defense mechanisms: Classification and state-of-the-art. *Computer Networks, 44*(5), 643–666. doi:10.1016/j.comnet.2003.10.003

Droste, S. (2001). New Results on Visual Cryptography. *Advances in Cryptology — CRYPTO '96. Lecture Notes in Computer Science, 1109,* 401–415. doi:10.1007/3-540-68697-5_30

Duan, Z., Yuan, X., & Chandrashekar, J. (2008). Controlling IP spoofing through interdomain packet filters. *IEEE Transactions on Dependable and Secure Computing, 5*(1), 22–36. doi:10.1109/TDSC.2007.70224

Dustor, A., & Szwarc, P. (2010). Spoken language identification based on GMM models.*International Conference on Signals and Electronic Systems (ICSES),* (pp. 105–108).

Eddy, W. M. (2007). *TCP SYN flooding attacks and common mitigations.* Academic Press.

Ehrenkranz, T., & Li, J. (2009). On the state of IP spoofing defense. *ACM Transactions on Internet Technology, 9*(2), 6. doi:10.1145/1516539.1516541

Electronic CSI: A Guide for First Responders. (2008). Department of Justice, Office of Justice Programs, National Institute of Justice. Retrieved from http://www.nij.gov/pubs--sum/219941.htm

Eleutério, P. M., & Machado, M. P. (2011). *Desvendando a computação forense.* São Paulo: Novatec Editora Ltda.

Endler, D. (2001). *Brute-Force Exploitation of Web Application Session ID's.* White paper from iDEFENSE.

Endorf, C. F., Schultz, E., & Mellander, J. (2011). *Network Protocol Abuses.* Retrieved 12 May, 2011, from http://flylib.com/books/en/2.352.1.31/1/

Endorf, C., Schultz, E., & Melander, J. (2006). *Intrusion detection and Prevention.* Tata McGraw Hill.

Evans. (2014). *Backup vs replication, snapshots, CDP in data protection strategy.* Retrieved from computerweekly.com

Fang, W. P. (2007). Multi-layer progressive secret image sharing.*Seventh WSEAS International Conference on Signal Processing, Computational Geometry & Artificial Vision,* 112-116.

Fang, W., & Lin, J. (2006). Progressive viewing and sharing of sensitive images. *Pattern Recognition and Image Analysis, 16*(4), 632–636. doi:10.1134/S1054661806040080

Faundez-Zanuy, M. (2004). On the vulnerability of biometric security systems. *IEEE Aerosp. Electron. Syst. Mag.*, *19*(6), 3–8.

Feng, W. C., & Kaiser, E. (2011). *System and methods of determining computational puzzle difficulty for challenge-response authentication*. U.S. Patent Application 13/050,123.

Ferguson, P. (2000). *Network ingress filtering: Defeating denial of service attacks which employ IP source address spoofing*. RFC 2267.

Fidaleo, D., Nguyen, H., & Trivedi, M. (n.d.). The networked sensor tapestry (NeST).*Proceedings of the ACM 2nd International Workshop on Video Surveillance & Sensor Networks - VSSN '04, 1*(1), 934-939.

Ford, S. (2010, October). Managing Your Global Business with Cloud Technology. *Financial Executive*.

Fridrich, J., Goljan, M., & Rui, D. (2001). Invertible Authentication. In *Proceedings of SPIE Photonics West, Security and Watermarking of Multimedia Contents*, (vol. 3971, pp. 197-208). doi:10.1117/12.435400

Fridrich, J. (1998). Symmetric Ciphers Based on Two-Dimensional Chaotic Maps. *International Journal of Bifurcation and Chaos in Applied Sciences and Engineering*, *8*(6), 1259–1284. doi:10.1142/S021812749800098X

Gao, H., Hu, J., Huang, T., Wang, J., & Chen, Y. (2011). Security issues in online social networks. *IEEE Internet Computing*, *15*(4), 56–63. doi:10.1109/MIC.2011.50

Garber, L. (2000). Denial-of-service attacks rip the internet. *Computer*, *33*(4), 12–17. doi:10.1109/MC.2000.839316

Garfinkel, S. (2015). *DTIC*. Fonte: DTIC. Retrieved from http://www.dtic.mil/dtic/tr/fulltext/u2/a576161.pdf

Gavaskar, S., Surendiran, R., & Ramaraj, E. (2010). Three Counter Defense Mechanism for TCP SYN Flooding Attacks. *International Journal of Computer Applications*, 12-15.

Gayathri, E., & Neelanarayanan, V. (2013). *A Mapping of Security controls to Host layer Security attacks.International Conference on Mathematical Computer Engineering*.

Gengler, B. (2001). CERT Victim of Three Day Denial-of-service Attack. *Network Security*, (7): 5.

Ghayvat, H., Mukhopadhyay, S., Gui, X., & Suryadevara, N. (2015). WSN- and IOT-Based Smart Homes and Their Extension to Smart Buildings. *Sensors (Basel, Switzerland)*, *15*(5), 10350–10379. doi:10.3390/s150510350 PMID:25946630

Ghosh, A. K., Schwartzbard, A., & Schatz, M. (1999). Learning Program Behavior Profiles for Intrusion Detection. In *Proceedings of Workshop on Intrusion Detection and Network Monitoring*. Academic Press.

Gil, T. M., & Poletto, M. (2001). MULTOPS: a data-structure for bandwidth attack detection. *Proceeding 10th Usenix Security Symposium*.

Gnanaguruparan, M., & Kak, S. (2002). Recursive Hiding Of Secrets In Visual Cryptography. *Cryptologia*, *26*(1), 68–76. doi:10.1080/0161-110291890768

Gomez. (2012). *Triage in-Lab: case backlog reduction with forensic digital profiling*. Academic Press.

Gonalves, D., & Costa, D. (2015). A Survey of Image Security in Wireless Sensor Networks. *Journal of Imaging*, 4-30.

Gong, C., & Sarac, K. (2008). A More Practical Approach for Single-Packet IP Traceback using Packet Logging and Marking. *IEEE Transactions on Parallel and Distributed Systems*, *19*(10), 1310–1324. doi:10.1109/TPDS.2007.70817

Gonzalez, J. M., Anwar, M., & Joshi, J. B. (2011, July). A trust-based approach against IP-spoofing attacks. In *Privacy, Security and Trust (PST), 2011 Ninth Annual International Conference on* (pp. 63-70). IEEE.

Graevenitz, G. (2007). Biometric authentication in relation to payment systems and ATMs. *DuD Datenschutz Und Datensicherheit - DuD*, 681-683.

Grillo, A., Lentini, A., Me, G., & Ottoni, M. (2009). Fast User Classifying to Establish Forensic Analysis Priorities. In *Proceedings of the 2009 Fifth International Conference on IT Security Incident Management and IT Forensics*. doi:10.1109/IMF.2009.16

Grispos, G., Glisson, W. B., & Storer, T. (2013). *Calm before storm: the challenges of cloud computing in digital forensics*. Retrieved on March 27, 2014 from http://www.dcs.gla.ac.uk/~grisposg/Papers/calm.pdf

Grispos, G., Glisson, W. B., & Storer, T. (2013). *Cloud Security Challenges: Investigating Policies, Standards, and Guidelines in a Fortune 500 Organization*. Paper presented at 21st European Conference on Information Systems, Utrecht, The Netherlands

Grobauer, B., Walloschek, T., & Stocker, E. (n.d.). *Understanding clud computing vulnerabilities*. Retrieved on March 23, 2014 from http://www.infoq.com/articles/ieee-cloud-computing-vulnerabilities

Groß, T. (2003, December). Security analysis of the SAML single sign-on browser/artifact profile. In *Computer Security Applications Conference, 2003. Proceedings. 19th Annual* (pp. 298-307). IEEE.

Gubanov, Y. (2012). *Retrieving Digital Evidence: Methods, Techniques, and Issues: Part 1*. Retrieved from http://www.forensicmag.com/articles/2012/05/retrieving-digital-evidence-methods-techniques-and-issues-part-1

Guerrero-Zapata, M., Zilan, R., Barcelo-Ordinas, J., Bicakci, K., & Tavli, B. (2009). The future of security in Wireless Multimedia Sensor Networks. *Telecommunication Systems Telecommun Syst, 1*(1), 77–91.

Guilloteau, S., & Mauree, V. (2012). *Privacy in cloud computing*. ITU-T Technology Report.

Gupta, K. R. (2015). *An Overview Of Cyber Laws vs. Cyber Crimes: In Indian Perspective*. Retrieved November 25, 2015 from http://www.mondaq.com/india/x/257328/Data+Protection+Privacy/An+Overview+Of+Cyber+Laws+vs+Cyber+Crimes+In+Indian+Perspective

Gupta, S., & Kumaraguru, P. (2014). Emerging phishing trends and effectiveness of the anti-phishing landing page. *2014 APWG Symposium on Electronic Crime Research* (eCrime).

Hanley, S. (2000). *DNS overview with a discussion of DNS spoofing*. Academic Press.

Hare-Brown, N., & Douglas, J. (1995). *Digital Investigations in the Cloud*. Digital Forensics Laboratories. Retrieved on July 10, 2013 from www.qccis.com/

Haris, S., Ahmad, R., & Ghani, M. (2010). Detecting TCP SYN Flood Attack Based on Anomaly Detection. *2010 Second International Conference on Network Applications, Protocols and Services*, (pp. 240-244). doi:10.1109/NETAPPS.2010.50

Harjito, B., & Han, S. (2010). Wireless Multimedia Sensor Networks Applications and Security Challenges. *2010 International Conference on Broadband, Wireless Computing, Communication and Applications, 1*(1), 842-846. doi:10.1109/BWCCA.2010.182

Helland, P. (2013). Condos and cloud. *Communications of the ACM, 56*(1), 50. doi:10.1145/2398356.2398374

Hoekema, R., Uijen, G., & Oosterom, A. (2001). Geometrical aspects of the interindividual variability of multilead ECG recordings. *IEEE Trans. Biomedical Engineering, 48*, 551–559.

Hou, Y. (2003). Visual cryptography for color images. *Pattern Recognition, 36*(7), 1619–1629. doi:10.1016/S0031-3203(02)00258-3

Hou, Y. C., & Tu, S. F. (2005). A visual cryptographic technique for chromatic images using multi-pixel encoding method. *Journal of Research and Practice in Information Technology, 37*(2), 179–192.

Howard, J., & Longstaff, T. (1998). *A common language for computer security incidents.* Academic Press.

Huang, D., Jia, W., & Zhang, D. (2008). Palmprint verification based on principal lines. *Pattern Recognition, 41*(4), 1316–1328. doi:10.1016/j.patcog.2007.08.016

Huynh, N., Bharanitharan, K., & Chang, C. (2015). Quadri-directional searching algorithm for secret image sharing using meaningful shadows. *Journal of Visual Communication and Image Representation, 28*, 105–112. doi:10.1016/j.jvcir.2015.01.011

IBM. (2014). *X-Force Mid-year Trend and risk report.* Retrieved 5 July 2014 from: http://www-03.ibm.com/security/xforce

Information Technology Act (2000)

Israel, S., Irvine, J., Cheng, A., Wiederhold, M., & Wiederhold, B. (2005). ECG to identify individuals. *Pattern Recognition, 38*(1), 133–142. doi:10.1016/j.patcog.2004.05.014

Jagatic, T., Johnson, N., Jakobsson, M., & Menczer, F. (2005). Social phishing. *Communications of the ACM, 50*(10), 94–100. doi:10.1145/1290958.1290968

Jain, A., & Feng, J. (2011). Latent fingerprint matching. *IEEE Trans. Pattern Anal. Mach. Intell., 33*(1), 88–100. doi:10.1109/TPAMI.2010.59

Jain, A., Flynn, P., & Ross, A. (2008). *Handbook of biometrics.* New York: Springer. doi:10.1007/978-0-387-71041-9

Jain, A., & Kumar, A. (2012). Biometric recognition: An overview. *The International Library of Ethics, Law and Technology Second Generation Biometrics: The Ethical, Legal and Social Context, 11*, 49–79.

Jain, A., Ross, A., & Prabhakar, S. (2004). An introduction to biometric recognition. *IEEE Transactions on Circuits and Systems for Video Technology, 14*(1), 4–20. doi:10.1109/TCSVT.2003.818349

Jakobsson, M., & Stamm, S. (2006, May). Invasive browser sniffing and countermeasures. In *Proceedings of the 15th international conference on World Wide Web* (pp. 523-532). ACM. doi:10.1145/1135777.1135854

Jansen, W., & Grance, T. (2011). *Guidelines on Security and Privacy in Public Cloud Computing.* NIST Special Publication 800-144.

Jellal, M. (2002). Insecure old-age security. *Oxford Economic Papers, 54*(4), 636–648. doi:10.1093/oep/54.4.636

Jian, Z., Yong, & Jian, G. (2003). Intrusion Detection System based on Fuzzy Default Logic. In *Proceedings of IEEE International Conference on Fuzzy Systems* (*vol. 2*, pp. 1350-1356). IEEE.

Jin, D., Yan, W. Q., & Kankanhalli, M. S. (2005). Progressive color visual cryptography. *Journal of Electronic Imaging, 14*(3), 033019–033019. doi:10.1117/1.1993625

Joshua Wright, G. C. I. H., & Joshua, C. C. N. A. (2003). *Detecting Wireless LAN MAC Address Spoofing.* Cisco Certified Network Associate.

Joshua, J. I., Shosha, A. F., & Gladyshev, P. (2013). Digital Forensic Investigation and Cloud Computing. In K Raun (Ed.), Cybercrime and Cloud Forensics: Applications for Investigation Processes (pp 1-41). IGI Global. doi:10.4018/978-1-4666-2662-1.ch001

Juels, A., & Opera, A. (2013). New Approaches to Security and Availability for Cloud Data. *Communications of the ACM, 66*(2).

Kafri, O., & Keren, E. (1987). Encryption of pictures and shapes by random grids. *Optics Letters, 12*(6), 377–377. doi:10.1364/OL.12.000377 PMID:19741737

Karlof, C., Shankar, U., Tygar, J. D., & Wagner, D. (2007). Dynamic pharming attacks and locked same-origin policies for web browsers. *Proceedings of the 14th ACM Conference on Computer and Communications Security - CCS '07.* doi:10.1145/1315245.1315254

Kasperski. (2008). *Kaspersky Lab Detects New Worms Attacking MySpace and Facebook.* Retrieved from http://www. kaspersky.com/news?id=207575670

Katiravan, J., & Chellappan, C. (2011). Improved IP Trace Back Using Pre-Shared Key Authentication Mechanism. *Asian Journal of Information Technology,* 51-54.

Kavisankar, L., & Chellappan, C. (2011). *CNoA: Challenging Number Approach for uncovering TCP SYN flooding using SYN spoofing attack.* arXiv:1110.1753

Kavisankar, L., & Chellappan, C. (2011, June). A Mitigation model for TCP SYN flooding with IP Spoofing. In *Recent Trends in Information Technology (ICRTIT), 2011 International Conference on* (pp. 251-256). IEEE. doi:10.1109/ICRTIT.2011.5972435

Kayarkar, Ricchariya, & Motwani. (2014). Mining Frequent Sequences for Emails in Cyber Forensics Investigation. *International Journal of Computer Applications, 85*(17), 1-6.

Kelly. (2015). *Address Munging: Adware: Backdoor: Backscatter (also known as outscatter, misdirected bounces, blowback or collateral spam).* Retrieved from docplayer.net

Kent, K., Chevalier, S., Grance, T., & Dang, H. (n.d.). *Guide to Integrating Forensics into Incident Response.* Special Publication 800-86, Computer Security Division Information Technology Laboratory, NIST.

Keromytis, A. D., Misra, V., & Rubenstein, D. (2002). SOS: Secure overlay services. *Computer Communication Review, 32*(4), 61–72. doi:10.1145/964725.633032

Khan, Z. S., Alghathbar, K., Sher, M., & Rashid, K. (2010). Issues of Security and Network Load in Presence – A Survey. *Communications in Computer and Information Science Security Technology, Disaster Recovery and Business Continuity,* (pp. 224-230). Academic Press.

Khor, S. H., & Nakao, A. (2009). sPoW: On-Demand Cloud-based eDDoS mitigation mechanism. *Proceeding of HotDep (Fifth Workshop on Hot Topics in System Dependability),* (pp. 1-6).

Kirda, E., Kruegel, C., Vigna, G., & Jovanovic, N. (2006). Noxes. *Proceedings of the 2006 ACM Symposium on Applied Computing - SAC '06.*

Knorr, E., & Gruman, G. (2008). *What cloud computing really means.* Retrieved on July 31, 2010 from http://www. infoworld.com/d/cloudcomputing/what-cloud-computing-really-means-031

Kobrin, S. (2001). Territoriality and the governance of cyberspace. *Journal of International Business Studies, 32*(4), 687–704. doi:10.1057/palgrave.jibs.8490990

Kong, Z., & Jiang, X. Z. (2010). DNS Spoofing Principle and Its Defense Scheme. *Computer Engineering, 3,* 43.

Kong, A., Zhang, D., & Kamel, M. (2009). A survey of palm print recognition. *Pattern Recognition, 42*(7), 1408–1418. doi:10.1016/j.patcog.2009.01.018

Koops, B. J., Leenes, R., Hert, P., & Olislaegers, S. (2012). *Crime and criminal investigation in the clouds; threats and opportunities of cloud computing for Dutch criminal investigation.* Retrieved on March 23, 2014 from http://english.wodc.nl/onderzoeksdatabase/cloud-computing.aspx?cp=45&cs=6796

Kost & Kanter. (2006). *Spoofing Oracle session Information.* Integrigy Corporation.

KrishnaKumar, B., Kumar, P.K., & Sukanesh, R. (2010). Hop Count Based Packet Processing Approach to Counter DDoS Attacks. *International Conference on Recent Trends in Information, Telecommunication and Computing,* (pp. 271- 273).

Kruck, G. P., & Kruck, S. E. (2006). Spoofing-a look at an evolving threat. *Journal of Computer Information Systems, 47*(1), 95.

Kumar, Sofat, Agarwal, & Jain. (2012). Identification of User Ownership in Digital Forensic using Data Mining Technique. *International Journal of Computer Applications, 50*(4), 1-5.

Kumar, S., & Jagannath, M. (2015). Analysis of phonocardiogram signal for biometric identification system.*International Conference on Pervasive Computing (ICPC),* (pp. 154-157).

Kurose, J. F., & Ross, K. W. (2002). *Computer Networking, A Top Down Approach* (6th ed.). Pearson Education.

Kyoso, M., & Uchiyama, A. (n.d.). Development of an ECG identification system. In *2001Conference Proceedings of the 23rd Annual International Conference of the IEEE Engineering in Medicine and Biology Society.* doi:10.1109/IEMBS.2001.1019645

Lane, L. (2011). Analyst finds thriving local markets in Asia Pacific. *Biometric Technology Today, 2011,* 2–2.

Lee, K., & Chiu, P. (2011). An Extended Visual Cryptography Algorithm for General Access Structures. *IEEE Transactions on Information Forensics and Security, 7*(1), 219–229. doi:10.1109/TIFS.2011.2167611

Lehto. (2015). Phenomena in the Cyber World. InCyber Security: Analytics, Technology and Automation. Academic Press.

Leopold, G. (2014). *Forecasts Call For Cloud Burst Through 2018.* Retrieved on March 22, 2015, from http://www.enterprisetech.com/2014/11/03/forecasts-call-cloud-burst-2018/

Li, P., Salour, M., & Su, X. (2008). A survey of internet worm detection and containment. *IEEE Communications Surveys & Tutorials,* 20-35.

Lin & Chang. (2000). *Semi-Fragile Watermarking for Authenticating JPEG Visual Content.* SPIE Security and Watermarking of Multimedia Content II, San Jose, CA.

Lin, C. Y. (2000). *Watermarking and Digital Signature Techniques for Multimedia Authentication and Copyright Protection.* (Ph.D. Thesis). Columbia University, New York, NY.

Lin, C.-C., & Shiu, P.-F. (2009). DCT- based reversible data hiding scheme. In *Proceedings of 3rd International Conference on Ubiquitous Information Management and Communication,* (pp. 327-335). Academic Press.

Lin, C. Y., & Chang, S. F. (2001, February). A Robust Image Authentication Method Distinguishing JPEG Compression from Malicious Manipulation. *IEEE Transactions on Circuits and Systems for Video Technology, 11*(2), 153–168. doi:10.1109/76.905982

Lin, K., Lin, C., & Chen, T. (2014). Distortionless visual multi-secret sharing based on random grid. *Information Sciences, 288*(1), 330–346. doi:10.1016/j.ins.2014.07.016

Lin, M. (2011). *Introduction to Information and Network Security.* McGraw Hilll.

Lin, S., Chen, S., & Lin, J. (2010). Flip visual cryptography (FVC) with perfect security, conditionally-optimal contrast, and no expansion. *Journal of Visual Communication and Image Representation, 21*(8), 900–916. doi:10.1016/j.jvcir.2010.08.006

Liu, S., & Jiang, H. (2012). School network security analysis and security countermeasures. In *IEEE International Conference on Cyber Technology in Automation, Control, and Intelligent Systems* (CYBER). IEEE.

Liu, F., Wu, C., & Lin, X. (2009). Step Construction of Visual Cryptography Schemes. *IEEE Transactions on Information Forensics and Security, 5*(1), 27–38. doi:10.1109/TIFS.2009.2037660

Liu, M. (2010). Fingerprint classification based on Adaboost learning from singularity features. *Pattern Recognition, 43*(3), 1062–1070. doi:10.1016/j.patcog.2009.08.011

Luo, Chen, Chen, Zeng, & Xiong. (2010). Reversible image watermarking using interpolation technique. *IEEE Transactions on Information Forensics and Security, 5*, 187-193.

Ma, M. (2005). Mitigating denial of service attacks with password puzzles. *International IEEE Conference on Information Technology: Coding and Computing*. doi:10.1109/ITCC.2005.200

Madrid Resolution, International Standards on the Protection of Personal Data and Privacy, International Conference of Data Protection and Privacy Commissioners. (2009, November 5). Retrieved on July 3, 2015 from www.privacyconference2009.org/dpas_space/space_reserved/documentos_adoptados/common/2009_Madrid/estandares_resolucion_madrid_en.pdf

Malliga, S., & Tamilarasi, A. (2008). A hybrid scheme using packet marking and logging for IP traceback. *International Journal of Internet Protocol Technology, 81*-81.

MANAnet's Reverse Firewall. (2012). *Reverse Firewall*. Retrieved 15 January 2012 from: http://www.cs3-inc.com/pubs/Reverse_FireWall.pdf

Manusankar, C., Karthik, S., & Rajendran, T. (2010, December). Intrusion Detection System with packet filtering for IP Spoofing. In *Communication and Computational Intelligence (INCOCCI), 2010 International Conference on* (pp. 563-567). IEEE.

Marinescu, D. (n.d.). *Cloud computing: cloud vulnerabilities*. Retrieved on February 17, 2014 from http://technet.microsoft.com/en-us/magazine/dn271884.aspx

Marinos. (2012). *ENISA threat landscape: Responding to the evolving threat environment*. ENISA.

Markman. (2000). *Performance Confirmation Data Aquisition System*. Academic Press.

Marsico, M., Nappi, M., & Riccio, D. (2012). Noisy iris recognition integrated scheme. *Pattern Recognition Letters, 33*(8), 1006–1011. doi:10.1016/j.patrec.2011.09.010

Marturana, F., Bertè, R., Me, G., & Tacconi, S. (2011). Mobile forensics "triaging": new directions for methodology. In *Proceedings of VIII conference of the Italian chapter of the Association for Information Systems* (ITAIS). Academic Press.

Marturana, F., Me, G., Berte, R., & Tacconi, S. (2011). A Quantitative Approach to Triaging in Mobile Forensics. In *Trust, Security and Privacy in Computing and Communications (TrustCom),2011IEEE 10th International Conference on*. doi:10.1109/TrustCom.2011.75

Marturana, F., & Tacconi, S. (2013). A Machine Learning-based Triage methodology for automated categorization of digital media. *Digital Investigation, 10*(2), 193–204. doi:10.1016/j.diin.2013.01.001

Mehta. (2016). *Malware Analysis basics, Part 1*. Retrieved from infosecinstitute.com

Mell, P., & Grance, T. (2011). *The NIST Definition of Cloud Computing.* NIST Special Publication, 800-145.

Mirkovic, J., Prier, G., & Reiher, P. (2003). Source-end DDoS defense. *Second IEEE International Symposium on Network Computing and Applications.* doi:10.1109/NCA.2003.1201153

Mirkovic, J., Prier, G., & Reiher, P. (2002). Attacking DDoS at the source. In *Proceedings 10th IEEE International Conference on Network Protocols,* (pp. 312-321). doi:10.1109/ICNP.2002.1181418

Mirkovic, J., & Reiher, P. (2004). A taxonomy of DDoS attack and DDoS defense mechanisms. *Computer Communication Review, 34*(2), 39–53. doi:10.1145/997150.997156

Mittal, A., Shrivastava, A., & Manoria, M. (2011). A Review of DDOS Attack and its Countermeasures in TCP Based Networks. *International Journal of Computer Science & Engineering Survey,* 177-187.

Monika, R., Tushank, B., Sumit, S., & Gunjan, B. (2014). Review of Threats in Wireless Sensor Networks. *International Journal of Computer Science and Information Technologies, 5*(1), 25–31.

Moore, D., Shannon, C., Brown, D., Voelker, G., & Savage, S. (2006). Inferring Internet denial-of-service activity. *ACM Transactions on Computer Systems,* 115-139.

Mukkamala, S., & Sung, A. H. (2005). Feature Selection for Intrusion Detection using Neural Networks and Support Vector Machines. In *Proceedings of Second International Symposium on Neural Networks.* Academic Press.

Mukkamala, S., Janoski, G., & Sung, A. H. (2002). Intrusion Detection Using Neural Networks and Support Vector Machines. In *Proceedings of IEEE International Joint Conference on Neural Networks* (pp.1702-1707). IEEE Computer Society Press. doi:10.1109/IJCNN.2002.1007774

Mukkamala, S., Sung, A. H., & Abraham, A. (2005). Intrusion Detection using an ensemble of Intelligent Paradigms. *Journal of Network and Computer Applications, 28*(2), 167–182. doi:10.1016/j.jnca.2004.01.003

Nagaratna, M., Prasad, V., & Kumar, S. (2009). Detecting and Preventing IP-spoofed DDoS Attacks by Encrypted Marking Based Detection and Filtering (EMDAF).*2009 International Conference on Advances in Recent Technologies in Communication and Computing.* doi:10.1109/ARTCom.2009.167

Naor, M., & Shamir, A. (1997). Visual cryptography II: Improving the contrast via the cover base. Security Protocols Lecture Notes in Computer Science, 1189, 197-202. doi:10.1007/3-540-62494-5_18

Naor, M., & Shamir, A. (1995). Visual cryptography. *Advances in Cryptology — EUROCRYPT'94. Lecture Notes in Computer Science, 950*(1), 1–12. doi:10.1007/BFb0053419

Ng, T. T., & Chang, S. F. (2004). *A Model for Image Splicing.* IEEE International Conference on Image Processing, Singapore.

Ni, , & Shi, , Ansari, & Su. (2006). Reversible Data Hiding. *IEEE Transactions on Circuits and Systems for Video Technology, 16*(8), 354–362.

Nosrati, M., Karimi, R., & Hariri, M. (2012). Reversible Data Hiding: Principles, Techniques, and Recent Studies. *World Applied Programming, 2*(5), 349–353.

Noureldien, N. A., & Hussein, M. O. (2012). Block Spoofed Packets at Source (BSPS): a method for detecting and preventing all types of spoofed source IP packets and SYN Flooding packets at source: a theoretical framework. *International Journal of Networks and Communications, 2*(3), 33–37. doi:10.5923/j.ijnc.20120203.03

O'gorman, L. (2003). Comparing passwords, tokens, and biometrics for user authentication. *Proceedings of the IEEE, 91*(12), 2021–2040. doi:10.1109/JPROC.2003.819611

Ohsita, Y., Ata, S., & Murata, M. (2004). Detecting distributed denial-of-service attacks by analyzing TCP SYN packets statistically. *IEEE Global Telecommunications Conference, 2004. GLOBECOM '04*, accessed on 3rd February 2016 doi:10.1109/GLOCOM.2004.1378371

Oliveira, A. M. (2013). Cloud forensics- best practice and challenges for process efficiency of investigations and digital forensics. In *Proceedings of The Eighth International Conference on Forensic Computer Science.*

OpenStego. (2015). *OpenStego free steganography solution.* Retrieved from http://openstego.sourceforge.net/

Oppliger, R., & Gajek, S. (2005, January). Effective protection against phishing and web spoofing. In *Communications and Multimedia Security* (pp. 32–41). Springer Berlin Heidelberg. doi:10.1007/11552055_4

Ornaghi, A., & Valleri, M. (2003). Man in the middle attacks. In Blackhat Conference Europe.

Ou, D., Ye, L., & Sun, W. (2015). User-friendly secret image sharing scheme with verification ability based on block truncation coding and error diffusion. *Journal of Visual Communication and Image Representation, 29*, 46–60. doi:10.1016/j.jvcir.2015.01.017

Paganini, P. (2013). *Near Field Communication Technology, Vulnerability and Principal Attack Schema.* Retrieved from resources.infosecinstitute.com

Pal, A., Gautam, A., & Singh, Y. (2015). Evaluation of bioelectric signals for human recognition. *Procedia Computer Science, 48*, 746–752. doi:10.1016/j.procs.2015.04.211

Palaniappan, R., & Raveendran, P. (2002). Individual identification technique using visual evoked potential signals. *Electron. Lett. Electronics Letters, 138*(25), 1634–1635. doi:10.1049/el:20021104

Palmer, G. (2001). *A Road Map for Digital Forensic Research.* Technical Report DTR-T0010-01, DFRWS. Report from the First Digital Forensic Research Workshop (DFRWS).

Pape, S. (2014). *Authentication in Insecure Environments.* Academic Press.

Peng, T., Leckie, C., & Ramamohanarao, K. (2007). Survey of network-based defense mechanisms countering the DoS and DDoS problems. *ACM Computing Surveys.*

Peter, P. (2003). Biometrics continue to evolve. *Biometric Technology Today, 11*(9), 1–7.

Phua, K., Chen, J., Dat, T., & Shue, L. (2008). Heart sound as a biometric. *Pattern Recognition, 41*(3), 906–919. doi:10.1016/j.patcog.2007.07.018

Piccardi, M. (2004). Background subtraction techniques: A review. *IEEE International Conference on Systems, Man and Cybernetics (IEEE Cat. No.04CH37583).*

Pinguelo & Muller. (2011). Virtual crimes, Real damages. *VJLT, 16*(1).

Prabhu, T. N., Kumar, C. R., & Mohankumar, B. (2014). Energy-efficient and Secured Data Gathering in Wireless Multimedia Sensor Networks. *International Journal of Innovative Research in Computer and Communication Engineering., 2*(2), 3073–3079.

Ramachandran, V., & Nandi, S. (2005). Detecting ARP spoofing: An active technique. In *Information Systems Security* (pp. 239–250). Springer Berlin Heidelberg. doi:10.1007/11593980_18

Reilly, D., Wren, C., & Berry, T. (2011). Cloud computing: pros and cons for computer forensic investigations. *International Journal Multimedia and Image Processing, 1*(1).

Reveron, D. S. (Ed.). (2012). *Cyberspace and national security: threats, opportunities, and power in a virtual world.* Georgetown University Press.

Rivest, R. (1992). *The MD5 Message Digest Algorithm, RFC 1321.* Retrieved from http://www.rfc-editor.org/rfc/rfc1321.txt

Roberts, C. (2007). Biometric attack vectors and defences. *Computers & Security, 26*(1), 14–25. doi:10.1016/j.cose.2006.12.008

Rogers, M. K., Goldman, J., Mislan, R., Wedge, T., & Debrota, S. (2006). *Computer Forensics Field Triage Process Model.* Presented at the Conference on Digital Forensics, Security, and Law.

Romero, J. (2012). *Fast start for world's biggest biometrics ID project.* Retrieved January 2, 2016, from http://spectrum. ieee.org/computing/it/fast-start-for-worlds-biggest-biometrics-id-project

Ronen. (2013). *An Inside Look at One of the Most Complex DDoS Attacks to Date.* Retrieved 22 October 2013 from: http://www.incapsula.com/blog/ funded-persistent-multi-vector-ddos-attack.html

Rood, E. P., & Hornak, L. A. (2003). Are you who you say you are? *World & I, 18*(8), 142.

Ross, A., & Othman, A. (2010). Visual Cryptography for Biometric Privacy. *IEEE Transactions on Information Forensics and Security, 6*(1), 70–81. doi:10.1109/TIFS.2010.2097252

Roy, S., & Venkateswaran, P. (2014). Online payment system using steganography and visual cryptography. *IEEE Students' Conference on Electrical, Electronics and Computer Science, 1*(1), 1-5. doi:10.1109/SCEECS.2014.6804449

RSA Laboratories. (2001). *RSA Security Response to Weaknesses in Key Scheduling Algorithm of RC4.* Retrieved from cse.iitb.ac.in

Ruan, K., Carthy, J., Kechadi, T., & Crosbie, M. (2011). Cloud Forensics: An overview. *Advances in Digital Forensic, 7.*

Rush, H., Smith, C., Kraemer-Mbula, E., & Tang, P. (2009). *Crime online: Cybercrime and illegal innovation.* Academic Press.

Salem, M. B., & Stolfo, S. J. (2011). Modeling User Search Behavior for Masquerade Detection. *Lecture Notes in Computer Science Recent Advances in Intrusion Detection*, 181-200.

Santos, G., & Hoyle, E. (2012). A fusion approach to unconstrained iris recognition. *Pattern Recognition Letters, 33*(8), 984–990. doi:10.1016/j.patrec.2011.08.017

Saxena, A., Shrivastava, G., & Sharma, K. (2012). Forensic investigation in ccoud Computing environment. *International Journal of Forensic Computer Science, 2*(2), 64–74. doi:10.5769/J201202005

Shema, M. (2012). HTML Injection & Cross-Site Scripting (XSS). *Hacking Web Apps*, 23-78.

Sheng, Y., Tan, K., Chen, G., Kotz, D., & Campbell, A. (2008, April). Detecting 802.11 MAC layer spoofing using received signal strength. In *INFOCOM 2008. The 27th Conference on Computer Communications.* IEEE.

Shrikalla, M., Mathivanan, P., & Leena Jasmine, J. S. (2013). *Conversion Of 2D Stego images into 3D stereo image using RANSAC.* Paper presented at IEEE Conference on Information and communication Technologies.

Shyu, S. (2006). Efficient visual secret sharing scheme for color images. *Pattern Recognition, 36*(5), 866–880. doi:10.1016/j.patcog.2005.06.010

Shyu, S. (2007). Image encryption by random grids. *Pattern Recognition, 40*(3), 1014–1031. doi:10.1016/j.patcog.2006.02.025

Shyu, S., Huang, S., Lee, Y., Wang, R., & Chen, K. (2007). Sharing multiple secrets in visual cryptography. *Pattern Recognition*, *40*(12), 3633–3651. doi:10.1016/j.patcog.2007.03.012

Siciliano. (2015). *What is a virus?*. Retrieved from mcafee.com

Simon, B., & Eswaran, C. (1997). An ECG classifier designed using modified decision based neural networks. *Computers and Biomedical Research, an International Journal*, *30*(4), 257–272. doi:10.1006/cbmr.1997.1446 PMID:9339321

Singh, N., & Rishi, A. (2015). Pyramid- A case study of cyber security in India. *South Asian Journal of Business and Management Cases*, *4*(1), 135–142. doi:10.1177/2277977915574046

Singh, Y., Singh, S., & Gupta, P. (2012). Fusion of electrocardiogram with unobtrusive biometrics: An efficient individual authentication system. *Pattern Recognition Letters*, *33*(14), 1932–1941. doi:10.1016/j.patrec.2012.03.010

Sivabalakrishnan, M., & Manjula, D. (2009). An Efficient Foreground Detection Algorithm for Visual Surveillance System. *International Journal of Computer Science and Network Security*, *9*(5), 221–227.

Sivabalakrishnan, M., & Manjula, D. (2010a). Adaptive Background subtraction in dynamic environments using fuzzy logic. *International Journal on Computer Science and Engineering*, *2*(2), 270–273.

Sivabalakrishnan, M., & Manjula, D. (2010b). Human Tracking Segmentation using color space conversion. *International Journal of Computer Science Issues*, *7*(5), 285–289.

Sivabalakrishnan, M., & Manjula, D. (2010c). RBF Approach to Background Modelling for Background subtraction in Video Objects. *International Journal of Computer Science and Research*, *1*(1), 35–42.

Sivabalakrishnan, M., & Manjula, D. (2010d). Fuzzy Rule-based Classification of Human Tracking and Segmentation using Color Space Conversion. *International Journal of Artificial Intelligence & Applications IJAIA*, *1*(4), 70–80. doi:10.5121/ijaia.2010.1406

Sivabalakrishnan, M., & Manjula, D. (2010e). Adaptive background subtraction using fuzzy logic. *IJMIS International Journal of Multimedia Intelligence and Security*, *1*(4), 392–401. doi:10.1504/IJMIS.2010.039239

Sivabalakrishnan, M., & Manjula, D. (2011a). Novel Segmentation Method using improved edge flow vectors for people tracking. *Journal of Information and Computational Science*, *8*(8), 1319–1332.

Sivabalakrishnan, M., & Manjula, D. (2011b). Background extraction using improved mode algorithm for visual surveillance applications. *IJCSE International Journal of Computational Science and Engineering*, *6*(4), 275–282. doi:10.1504/IJCSE.2011.043927

Sivabalakrishnan, M., & Manjula, D. (2012). Performance analysis of fuzzy logic-based background subtraction in dynamic environments. *The Imaging Science Journal*, *60*(1), 39–46. doi:10.1179/1743131X11Y.0000000008

Sleuth Kit. (2008). *The Sleuth Kit*. Retrieved from https://github.com/coriolis/vmxray/tree/master/src/tools/sleuthkit

Snori. (2015). *Rouge access point*. Retrieved from wikipedia.com

Sommer, P. (1999). Intrusion Detection Systems as Evidence. *Computer Networks: The International Journal of Computer and Telecommunications Networking*, *31*, 2477 – 2487.

Sommer, P. (2005). *Directors and Corporate Advisors' Guide to Digital Investigations and Evidence*. Information Assurance Advisory Council.

Sörnmo, L., & Laguna, P. (2005). EEG signal processing. *Bioelectrical Signal Processing in Cardiac and Neurological Applications,* (pp. 55-179).

Sqalli, M. H., Al-Haidari, F., & Salah, K. (2011). EDoS-Shield -a two-steps mitigation technique against EDoS attacks in cloud computing. *2011 Fourth IEEE International Conference on Utility and Cloud Computing (UCC)*, (pp. 49-56). doi:10.1109/UCC.2011.17

Stajano, F., Hoult, N., Wassell, I., Bennett, P., Middleton, C., & Soga, K. (2010). Smart bridges, smart tunnels: Transforming wireless sensor networks from research prototypes into robust engineering infrastructure. *Ad Hoc Networks*, *8*(8), 872–888. doi:10.1016/j.adhoc.2010.04.002

Stavrou, A., Cook, D.L., Morein, W.G., Keromytis, A.D., Misra, V., & Rubenstein, D. (2005). WebSOS: an overlay-based system for protecting web servers from denial of service attacks. *Computer Networks, 48*(5), 781-807.

Tai, G., & Chang, L. (2004). Visual Cryptography for Digital Watermarking in Still Images. *Lecture Notes in Computer Science*, *3332*(1), 50–57. doi:10.1007/978-3-540-30542-2_7

Takabi. H., Joshi, J., & JoonAhn, G. (2010, November-December). Security and privacy challenges in cloud computing environment. *IEEE Computer and Reliability Societie, 24-31.*

The Future of Privacy. (n.d.). Retrieved from http://ec.europa.eu/justice/policies/privacy/docs/wpdocs/2009/wp168_en.pdf

Thomas, W., & Bernhard, R. (2014). Security and Privacy Protection in Visual Sensor Networks: A Survey. *ACM Computing Surveys, 47*(1), 2:1-2:47.

Thorat, S. A., Khandelwal, A. K., Bruhadeshwar, B., & Kishore, K. (2008). Payload Content based Network Anomaly Detection. *2008 First International Conference on the Applications of Digital Information and Web Technologies (ICADIWT)*, 127-132. Doi: , accessed on 3rd February 2016 doi:10.1109/ICADIWT.2008.4664331

Tian, J. (2003). Reversible data embedding using a difference Expansion. *IEEE Transactions on Circuits and Systems for Video Technology*, *13*(8), 890–896. doi:10.1109/TCSVT.2003.815962

Tiwari, N., & Padhye, S. (2011). *New proxy signature scheme with message recovery using verifiable self-certified public keys.* 2011 2nd International Conference on Computer and Communication Technology (ICCCT-2011).

Toyama, K., Krumm, J., Brumitt, B., & Meyers, B. (1999). Wallflower: Principles and practice of background maintenance.*Proceedings of the Seventh IEEE International Conference on Computer Vision*, (pp. 255-261). doi:10.1109/ICCV.1999.791228

TrueCrypt. (2015). *Truecrypt.com*. Retrieved from http://www.truecrypt.com

Tsai, C. L., Fan, K. C., Chung, C. D., & Chuang, T. C. (2004). Data Hiding of Binary Images Using Pair-wise Logical Computation Mechanism. In *Proceedings of IEEE International Conference on Multimedia and Expo, ICME*, (vol. 2, pp. 951-954). IEEE.

Tsudik, G. (1992). Message authentication with one-way hash functions. *Computer Communication Review, 22*(5), 29–38. doi:10.1145/141809.141812

UK Essays. (2013). *The Information Technology Act Information Technology Essay*. Retrieved from http://www.ukessays.com/essays/information-technology/the-information-technology-act-information-technology-essay.php?cref=1

Ulichney, R. (1987). *Digital halftoning.* MIT Press.

Unar, J., Seng, W., & Abbasi, A. (2014). A review of biometric technology along with trends and prospects. *Pattern Recognition, 47*(8), 2673–2688. doi:10.1016/j.patcog.2014.01.016

Uscilowski. (2013). *Mobile Adware and Malware analysis*. Retrieved from symantec.com

Von Ahn, L., Blum, M., Hopper, N.J., & Langford, J. (2003). CAPTCHA: Using hard AI problems for security. In *Advances in Cryptology—EUROCRYPT 2003*. Springer Berlin Heidelberg.

Wagner, R. (2001). *Address resolution protocol spoofing and man-in-the-middle attacks*. The SANS Institute.

Wang, H., Jin, C., & Shin, K.G. (2007). Defense against spoofed IP traffic using hop-count filtering. *IEEE/ACM Transactions on Networking, 15*(1), 40-53.

Wang, H., Zhang, D., & Shin, K. G. (2002). Detecting SYN flooding attacks. *Proceedings INFOCOM 2002. Twenty-First Annual Joint Conference of the IEEE Computer and Communications Societies*. IEEE.

Wang, H., Zhang, D., & Shin, K. G. (2002). Detecting SYN flooding attacks. *Proceedings. Twenty-First Annual Joint Conference of the IEEE Computer and Communications Societies*, 1530-1539. , accessed on 3rd February 2016 doi:10.1109/INFCOM.2002.1019404

Wang, H., Zhang, D., & Shin, K. G. (2004). Change-point monitoring for the detection of DoS attacks. *IEEE Transactions on Dependable and Secure Computing, 1*(4), 193–208. doi:10.1109/TDSC.2004.34

Wang, Z., Arce, G. R., & Di Crescenzo, G. (2009). Halftone visual cryptography via error diffusion. *IEEE Transactions on Information Forensics and Security, 4*(3), 383–396. doi:10.1109/TIFS.2009.2024721

Webb-Hobson, E. (2013). *Digital Investigation in Cloud*. Retrieved on July 10, 2013 from http://www.gartner.com/newsroom/id/707508

Weir, J., Yan, W., & Kankanhalli, M. S. (2012). Image hatching for visual cryptography. *ACM Transactions on Multimedia Computing, Communications, and Applications, 8*(2S), 32. doi:10.1145/2344436.2344438

Wickramasuriya, J., Datt, M., Mehrotra, S., & Venkatasubramanian, N. (2012). Privacy protecting data collection in media spaces. *Proceedings of the 12th Annual ACM International Conference on Multimedia - MULTIMEDIA '04, 1*(1). doi:10.1145/1027527.1027537

Witkin, A. (1983). Scale-Space Filtering. In *Proceedings 8th International Joint Conference* (pp. 1019-1022). Academic Press.

Witten, I. H., Frank, E., & Hall, M. A. (2011). *Data Mining: Practical Machine Learning Tools and Techniques: Practical Machine Learning Tools and Techniques*. Morgan Kaufmann.

Woollaston, V. (2013, July 30). Revealed, what happens in just ONE minute on the internet. *Daily Mail Online*.

Wu, C. C., & Chen, L. H. (1998). *A Study on visual cryptography*. (Master Thesis). Institute of Computer and information Science, National Chiao Tung University, Taiwan, China.

Wu, H., & Chang, C. (2005). Sharing visual multi-secrets using circle shares. *Computer Standards & Interfaces, 28*(1), 123–135. doi:10.1016/j.csi.2004.12.006

Wurzinger, P., Platzer, C., Ludl, C., Kirda, E., & Kruegel, C. (2009). SWAP: Mitigating XSS attacks using a reverse proxy.*2009 ICSE Workshop on Software Engineering for Secure Systems.* doi:10.1109/IWSESS.2009.5068456

Xie, Y., & Yu, S. (2009). Monitoring the Application-Layer DDoS Attacks for Popular Websites. *IEEE/ACM Trans. Networking, 17*(1), 15–25. doi:10.1109/TNET.2008.925628

Xu, X., Mao, Z. M., & Halderman, J. A. (2011). Internet Censorship in China: Where Does the Filtering Occur? Passive and Active Measurement Lecture Notes in Computer Science, 133-142.

Yaar, A, Perrig, A, & Song, D. (2006). StackPi: New packet marking and filtering mechanisms for DDoS and IP spoofing defense. *IEEE Journal on Selected Areas in Communications, 24*(10), 1853-1863.

Yaar, A., Perrig, A., & Song, D. (2003). Pi: A path identification mechanism to defend against DDoS attacks. *Proceedings 19th International Conference on Data Engineering* (Cat. No.03CH37405). Academic Press.

Yang, C. C., Wang, R. C., & Liu, W. T. (2005). Secure authentication scheme for session initiation protocol. *Computers & Security, 24*(5), 381–386. doi:10.1016/j.cose.2004.10.007

Yang, W.-C., & Chen, L.-H. (2014). *Reversible DCT- based data hiding in stereo images.* Springer Multimedia Tools and Applications.

Ye, S., Zhou, Z., Sun, Q., & Tian, Q. (2003). A Quantization-based Image Authentication System. *Information, Communications and Signal Processing, 2003 and the Fourth Pacific Rim Conference on Multimedia.Proceedings of the 2003 Joint Conference of the Fourth International Conference.* Academic Press.

Yu, S. (2013). DDoS Attack Detection. Distributed Denial of Service Attack and Defense. *Springer Briefs in Computer Science*, 31-53.

Yu, W., Wang, X., Xuan, D., & Lee, D. (2006). Effective Detection of Active Worms with Varying Scan Rate. *2006 Securecomm and Workshops*, 1-10, doi: , accessed on 3rd February 2016 Xiang, Y., & Li, Z. (2006). An Analytical Model for DDoS Attacks and Defense. *International Multi-Conference on Computing in the Global Information Technology - (ICCGI'06)*, accessed on 3rd February 201610.1109/seccomw.2006.359549

Yu, W., Wang, X., Calyam, P., Xuan, D., & Zhao, W. (2011). Modeling and Detection of Camouflaging Worm. *IEEE Transactions on Dependable and Secure Computing IEEE Trans. Dependable and Secure Comput., 8*(3), 377–390. accessed on 3rd February 2016. doi:10.1109/tdsc.2010.13

Zeng, Y., Cao, J., Hong, J., Zhang, S., & Xie, L. (2013). Secure localization and location verification in wireless sensor networks: a survey. *Journal of Supercomputing, 64*(3), 685-701.

Zhang, Z., Li, J., Manikopoulos, C. N., Jorgenson, J., & Ucles, J. (2001). HIDE: A Hierarchical NIDS using statistical preprocessing and Neural Network classification. In *Proceedings of IEEE workshop on Information Assurance and Security*. Academic Press.

Zhang, X. (2013). Reversible data hiding with optimal value transfer. *IEEE Transactions on Multimedia, 15*(2), 316–325. doi:10.1109/TMM.2012.2229262

Zhang, X., & Gao, Y. (2009). Face recognition across pose: A review. *Pattern Recognition, 42*(11), 2876–2896. doi:10.1016/j.patcog.2009.04.017

Zhang, X., Zhou, L., Zhang, T., & Yang, J. (2014). A novel efficient method for abnormal face detection in ATM. *2014 International Conference on Audio, Language and Image Processing*. doi:10.1109/ICALIP.2014.7009884

Zhou, Z., Arce, G. R., & Di Crescenzo, G. (2006). Halftone visual cryptography. *IEEE Transactions on Image Processing, 15*(8), 2441–2453. doi:10.1109/TIP.2006.875249 PMID:16900697

Zota, R., & Fraatila, L. (2013). Cloud standardization: consistent business process and information. *Informatica Economică, 17*(3).

Zou, C. C., Gong, W., & Towsley, D. (2002). Code red worm propagation modeling and analysis. *Proceedings of the 9th ACM Conference on Computer and Communications Security - CCS '02*. doi:10.1145/586110.586130

Zou, C., Gao, L., Gong, W., & Towsley, D. (2003). Monitoring and early warning for internet worms. *Proceedings of the 10th ACM Conference on Computer and Communication Security - CCS '03*, accessed on 3rd February 2016 doi:10.1145/948109.948136

About the Contributors

S. Geetha received the B.E. from the Madurai Kamaraj University, M.E., and Ph.D. degrees in Computer Science and Engineering from Anna University, Chennai, in 2000, 2004 and 2011 respectively. She has 14+ years of teaching experience. Currently, she is a professor at School of Computing Science and Engineering at VIT-University, Chennai Campus. She has published more than 50 papers in reputed IEEE International Conferences and refereed Journals. She joins the review committee for IEEE Transactions on Information Forensics and Security and IEEE Transactions on Image Processing, Springer Multimedia Tools and Security, Elsevier – Information Sciences. She was an editor for the Indian Conference proceedings of ICCIIS 2007 and RISES-2013. Her research interests include multimedia security, intrusion detection systems, machine learning paradigms and information forensics. She is a recipient of University Rank and Academic Topper Award in B.E. and M.E. in 2000 and 2004 respectively. She is also a pride recipient of the "Best Academic Researcher Award 2013" of ASDF Global Awards.

Asnath Victy Phamila Y. holds M.E and Ph.D degree in Computer Science and Engineering from Anna University, India. Her research area includes Image Processing, Wireless Sensor Networks and Network Security. She has around 11 years of academic and 4 years of industry experience. She has around 20 research papers to her credit. She also serves as reviewer in reputed journals.

* * *

K. Adalarasu received the B.E. degree in Electronics and Instrumentation Engineering from University of Madras, Tamilnadu, India, in 1998 and the Ph.D. degree in driver fatigue measurements from Indian Institute of Technology Madras, India, in 2010. At present, he is a Professor in the Department of Electronics and Communication Engineering at PSNA College of Engineering and Technology, Dindigul, Tamilnadu, India. He has published his research work in number of national and international journals and conferences. His research interests include cognitive neuroscience, industrial human safety and ergonomics testing of vehicles.

C. Chellappan is currently the principal of GKM College of Engineering & Technology. He was a senior Professor of Anna University Chennai, which is one among the Top Technological Universities in the world and the Top Technological University in India. He was the coordinator for Rupees One crore collaborative directed basic research project on 'Smart and Secure Environment' sponsored by National Technology Research Organization, Govt. of India, New Delhi. He is also the project team member of Indo-Australian Joint Research Project on 'Protecting Critical Infrastructure from Denial of Service

Attacks: Tools, Technology and Policy' sponsored by Department of Science and Technology, Govt. of India. He is the unique person having more than 32 years of service with both strong technical, academic, managerial, industrial and research experience in implementation and management of IT systems. He has published 157 papers in reputed International Journals and Conferences. He is author of 3 books in the field of network security. His current research is on Computer networks and Network security.

M. K. Kavitha Devi received her Under Graduate and Graduate Degree in Computer Science and Engineering, and her Ph.D. Degree in Information and Communication Engineering in 1994, 2004 and 2011 respectively. Her research focuses on Recommender Systems, Information Security & Hiding, Cloud Computing, and Big data. She has received the Best Computer Science Faculty Award in 2014 from Association of Scientists, Developers and Faculties (ASDF). She has published more than 20 refereed Journal and International Conference papers in these areas.She is the reviewer in referred Journals including IEEE Intelligent Systems and Springer - Journal of The Institution of Engineers (India): Series B. She organized Faculty Development Programs, Workshops and Conference. Under her guidance, 10 Ph.Dscholars from Anna University, Chennai are working in her area. Currently, she is an Associate Professor at the Department of Computer Science and Engineering, Thiagarajar College of Engineering, Madurai, India.

Uma N. Dulhare received her Ph.D from Osmania University Hyderabad. She has more than 20 years of academic experience. Currently, she is working as a professor, Department of Information Technology, Muff Kham Jah College of Engineering & Technology, Hyderabad. She has published more than 20 research papers in reputed National & International Journals. Her research interests include Data Warehouse and Data Mining, Intrusion Detection systems, Information Retrieval System, Big Data Analytics. She is the member of various professional bodies like ISTE, IAENG UCAEE,CSTA, ISRD. She is also a pride recipient of the "Best Computer Science Faculty 2013 & Best Academic Researcher 2015" of ASDF Global Awards.

Suseela G. is a Ph.D Research scholar at School of Computing Science and Engineering, VIT University, Chennai, Tamilnadu, India. She holds B.E., and M.Tech degrees in Computer Science and Engineering. Prior to her full time research she was working as Assistant Professor at SRM University, Chennai, Tamilnadu, India. Her areas of research include Wireless Image Sensor Network, Image Processing and network security.

R. Gayathri received her B.Tech (CSE) from Rajiv Gandhi College of engineering and technology and M.Tech from Pondicherry Engineering College, Puducherry. She is currently employed at VIT University Chennai campus as Assistant Professor in the department of Computer science. Her research interests include cloud computing, information security and network security.

Geogen George is currently working as Assistant professor in the department of Information Technology, SRM University. He is the co-ordinator for the Post Graduate Programme Information and computer forensics of SRM University. He is a certified Malware expert. Mr. Geogen is a specialized person in Network Security, Security Policy Design, Troubleshooting, Infrastructure Design and Analysis, risk assessment procedures, authentication technologies, policy formation, and security attack pathologies. He is also an expert in Designing and implementing Various Cisco Networks. He holds an M.Tech degree in Information Security and Computer Forensics after completing B.Tech degree in Computer Science and Engineering. He has published many papers in national and international conferences related to Malware and information Security.

Hemalatha J. received the B.E. and M.E., degrees in Computer Science and Engineering in 2007 and 2011, respectively, from the Anna University of Chennai, India. In July 2013, she joined the Department of Computer Science and Engineering at P.S.R Engineering College, Sivakasi, India. Currently she is working towards the Ph.D degree from Anna University at Thiagarajar College of Engineering, Madurai, India. She has published more papers in reputed IEEE International Conferences and refereed Journals. Her research interests include Steganography, Steganalysis, Image Processing and Machine Learning paradigms.

M. Jagannath is an Associate Professor in the School of Electronics Engineering at VIT University, Chennai, India. Prior to joining VIT University, he was heading the Department of Biomedical Engineering at SMK Fomra Institute of Technology, Chennai, India. He obtained his Ph.D. from IIT Madras, Chennai in the year 2012. He has served the position of Senior Project Officer at Indian Institute of Technology Madras, Chennai, India. He has taught at Sri Sai Ram Engineering College, Chennai; Madras Medical Mission, Chennai; Vellore Institute of Technology, Vellore. He received IndiraGandhi Sadbhavna Gold Medal Award for Individual Achievement and Service to the Nation from Global Economic Progress and Research Association, India, 2014. He received Technical Icon of the Year 2012 from the Institution of Engineering and Technology, Young Professional Society (Chennai Network), UK. He has more than 50 research articles published in various reputed conferences and journals. His research interests are ergonomics, biomedical instrumentation systems, biomechanics, control systems, mechatronic systems and robotics.

S. Jeeva is currently working as Research Associate in the School of Computing Science and Engineering at VIT University. He has served in academics sector for more than four years.

L. Kavisankar is currently working as an Assistant Professor in SRM University. He was the Research Associate for Rupees One crore collaborative directed basic research project on 'Smart and Secure Environment' sponsored by National Technology Research Organization, Govt. of India, New Delhi. He received Public Servicing Awards - 2014" (Technology Category), from Working Journalists Union of Tamilnadu, 2014. He was also a Senior Research Fellow in the UGC-BSR Fellowship. His Ph.D research work is under the "Intrusion Detection & Prevention" and his title of research is "an efficient mitigation framework to detect and defend against multi-vector DDOS attacks". He has published 7 papers in reputed International Journals and Conferences. His current research is on NLP (Natural Language processing) and Network security.

T. S. Pradeep Kumar received B.E. degree from Madras University and M.E. degree from Anna University, Chennai. Currently pursuing Ph.D. degree from VIT University, Vellore. Currently he is a full time faculty in School of Computing sciences and Engineering at VIT University, Chennai. His research interests are Wireless Sensor Networks, Embedded Systems, Open Source Programming, etc.

R. Menaka completed her Masters in Applied Electronics from Anna University. She received her Doctoral degree from Anna University. She is currently working as an Associate Professor in the School of Electronics Engineering, VIT University, Chennai. She has published several papers in reputed Journals and Conferences. Her areas of interest are image processing, neural networks and fuzzy logic.

S. Muthuramalingam received his PhD degree under the faculty of Information & Communication Engineering from Anna University, Chennai.His research interests include Mobile Communications and Internet of Things. He is currently working as an Associate Professor, Department of Information Technology, Thiagarajar College of Engineering, Madurai.

E. Poovammal is currently working as a Professor in SRM University and she is the Head of the Department of Computer Science and Engineering. She has more than 20 years of academic experience and 4 years of Industry experience. She is a Certified Adjunct Faculty for the two bridge courses Computer Science for Practicing Engineers and Hardware for Software Engineers, by Institute of software Research, Carnegie Mellon University, Pittsburgh, USA. She is a recipient of Woman Engineer Award-2013, from IET-YP-CLN. She is a member of various professional bodies like IEEE, IET, ACM, etc. She has published more than 20 papers in reputed International Journals and Conferences. Her current research is on Security in Cloud and data mining.

P. Punithavathi received Bachelor of Eng. in Computer Science from Anna University, Chennai, and M. Tech in Computer Science from Bharath University, Chennai. She has achieved University Rank for M. Tech. She has served as Senior Editor in Scientific Publishing Services (Part of Springer Science + Business Media) for four years. She also has four years of teaching experience. She is pursuing Ph. D. at VIT University, Chennai, presently.

Shaik Rasool received the Master of Technology in Computer Science & Engineering from Jawaharlal Nehru Technological University in 2011. He is currently working as Assistant Professor in the Department of Information Technology at M.J.C.E.T., Hyderabad, India. He has published six research papers in the feild of Computer Science in various International Journals. His research interest includes Network Security, Biometrics, Data Mining and Information Security.

Nimisha Singh holds a degree of Bachelor in Applied Science from Delhi University and MCA from SNDT University, Mumbai. Currently she is pursuing FPM. Prior to joining BIMTECH, she worked at TCS as Software Programmer and WSI, USA as web developer later on moving to internet marketing. Nimisha's teaching and research interest are in the area of Software Project Management, ERP and Cyber Security. She has published and presented papers in national and international conferences. She has conducted training programs for information management and social media marketing.

M. Sivabalakrishnan is currently working as Associate Professor in the School of Computing Science and Engineering at VIT University. He has served in academics sector for more than ten years. He received his Doctoral degree in image processing from Anna University. He has presented and published over 25 research papers in various national and international journals & conferences. His areas of interest are image processing, video analytics, database, neural networks and fuzzy logic.

S. Sridhar received his B.Tech - Information Technology degree under the faculty of Information & Communication Engineering from Thiagarajar college of Engineering, Affiliated to Anna University, Chennai.His research interests include Cloud Security and Network Security. He is currently pursuing his M.E. Computer Sciennce and Information Security degree under the Department of Information Technology, Thiagarajar college of Engineering, Madurai.

M. Thangavel is a PhD candidate under the faculty of Information & Communication Engineering (Cloud Security) at Madras Institute of Technology, Anna University, Chennai. He holds an ME in Computer Science from J.J College of Engineering, Tiruchirappalli.He is currently working as an Assistant Professor in the Department of Information Technology, Thiagarajar College of Engineering, Madurai. His research interests include Cryptography Network security, Compiler Design and Data Structures.

P. Vetrivelan received the M.E. degree in Embedded System Technologies from College of Engineering Guindy, Anna University, Tamilnadu, India, in 2008 and the Ph.D. degree in Information and Communication Engineering from College of Engineering Guindy, Anna University, Tamilnadu, India, in 2014. At present, he is an Associate Professor in the School of Electronics Engineering Engineering at VIT University Chennai, Tamilnadu, India. He has published his research work in number of national and international journals and conferences. His research interests include wireless sensor networks, wireless communication and embedded systems.

Index

A

Access Control 7-8, 23, 32, 40, 43, 49-50, 85-86
Anti-forensics 235, 237-238
ARP spoofing 43-44, 49
Artificial Neural Networks 87
Asymmetric Cryptography 13, 20, 205
ATM Surveillance 95, 98, 110, 120
Authentication 2, 5, 8-9, 14-15, 22-25, 31-32, 35-36, 40, 77, 85-86, 145, 155-156, 202-203, 205, 238
Authentication Mechanism 85

B

Background Estimation 95, 99-101, 103, 110, 117, 120
Background Subtraction 95, 99, 101-103, 110, 112, 114-118, 120
base station 1, 8-9, 13, 176
Biometry 23, 34, 40

C

Centralized Worm Detector (CWD) 186, 202, 205, 207
chaotic mapping 16-18
chaotic scenarios 23
CIA Triad 85
cloud computing 1-2, 21, 70-73, 75-77, 79-82, 85, 201
cloud environment 18, 71-73, 75-79, 81-82
cloud security 70-71, 78-79, 82
Cloud Service Provider (CSP) 85
Computer Vision 11, 96, 99, 108, 110, 120
Computerized proof 1-2, 10
Confidentiality 1-2, 10, 20-21, 71-72, 77-78, 81-82, 85-86, 203, 237
Control measures 17, 21
Controlled Packet Transmission (CPT) 186, 202, 207
Countermeasures 1-3, 6, 17, 19-20
Crime 1-2, 18-20, 60, 66, 68, 70, 76-78, 82, 98, 144-145, 147, 153-155, 157-158, 184, 236-237

D

DARPA Intrusion 89
data hiding 161-166, 168
Defamation 59, 68
Denial of Service (DoS) 2-4, 21, 42-44, 51-54, 75, 187, 192, 200
Digital crime 70, 76
Digital Evidence 1-6, 10-11, 18-21, 76-77, 144-145, 147, 156, 235
Digital Forensic 76-77, 144-145, 147, 149-154, 157
Digital Forensics Triage 153
digital resources 1
Digital Sphere 1-4, 7, 9, 19-20, 93
Disaster Recovery Plan 85-86
Discrete Wavelet Transform (DWT) 16, 20
DNA 26, 31, 40
DNS spoofing 47
Domain Name 43, 53
DoS 2, 6, 8-10, 18, 20, 42-43, 51, 54, 88, 174, 187-188, 192, 195, 198-199, 208
dynamic analysis 180-181

Cross border 80-82
C-Worms 191, 202, 205, 208
Cyber Security 1, 87
Cybercrime 1, 60, 67-68, 70, 179, 187, 235

E

Efficient Packet Marking algorithm (EPM) 186, 198
Electrocardiogram 22, 34, 40
Electrocardiography 40
Encryption Techniques 2, 236
Extended Visual Cryptography 13, 21

F

Feature Weighting 154, 157-158

Printed in the United States
By Bookmasters

Printed in the United States
By Bookmasters